THE BROKEN
TABLE

THE BROKEN TABLE

The Detroit Newspaper
Strike and the State of
American Labor

Chris Rhomberg

Russell Sage Foundation
New York

The Russell Sage Foundation

The Russell Sage Foundation, one of the oldest of America's general purpose foundations, was established in 1907 by Mrs. Margaret Olivia Sage for "the improvement of social and living conditions in the United States." The Foundation seeks to fulfill this mandate by fostering the development and dissemination of knowledge about the country's political, social, and economic problems. While the Foundation endeavors to assure the accuracy and objectivity of each book it publishes, the conclusions and interpretations in Russell Sage Foundation publications are those of the authors and not of the Foundation, its Trustees, or its staff. Publication by Russell Sage, therefore, does not imply Foundation endorsement.

Library of Congress Cataloging-in-Publication Data

Rhomberg, Chris, 1959–
   The broken table : the Detroit Newspaper Strike and the state of American labor / Chris Rhomberg.
      p. cm.
   Includes bibliographical references and index.
   ISBN 978-0-87154-717-0 (pbk. : alk. paper) – ISBN 978-1-61044-775-1 (ebook)
   1. Newspaper Strike, Detroit, Mich., 1995–1997.   2. Strikes and lockouts-Newspapers-Michigan-Detroit.   3. Collective bargaining-Newspapers-Michigan-Detroit.   4. Newspaper employees-Labor unions-Michigan-Detroit.   5. Newspaper publishing-Michigan-Detroit.   6. Knight-Ridder (Firm)   7. Gannett Company.   I. Title.
   PN4899.D53R46 2012
   331.892'977434—dc23   2011053536

The paper used in this publication meets the minimum requirements of American National Standard for Information Sciences-Permanence of Paper for Printed Library Materials. ANSI Z39.48-1992.

Text design by Suzanne Nichols.

RUSSELL SAGE FOUNDATION
112 East 64th Street, New York, New York 10065
10 9 8 7 6 5 4 3 2 1

Contents

About the Author

CHRIS RHOMBERG is associate professor of sociology at Fordham University.

Acknowledgments

I COULD NOT HAVE PRODUCED THIS BOOK without the help of a great many people, more than I can name in this brief space here. Above all, I am deeply grateful to all of the persons who entrusted to me their knowledge, insights, and stories of their personal experiences in and related to the events of the strike. In addition, I received special help from a number of individuals. Barb and Bob Ingalls showed great enthusiasm, hospitality, and support for the project and helped me get started with the research. At Wayne State University, David Fasenfest and Heidi Gottfried also offered their friendship and hospitality, and Steve Babson shared his knowledge of Detroit. Ben Burns, director of the Wayne State Journalism Program, and Bill Cooke, former director of the Douglas A. Fraser Center for Workplace Issues, kindly volunteered their resources and assistance. At the Walter P. Reuther Library, director Mike Smith and all of the staff were extremely helpful and always gracious. I am also indebted to the members of the Region 7 office of the National Labor Relations Board in Detroit, especially regional director Stephen Glasser and FOIA officer Joe Barker.

Many people also generously shared materials with me from their own files, referred me to important sources, or patiently explained complex and technical matters. Among others, I thank Steve Anderson, Larry Bechard, Tom Bernick, Bill Brabenec, Tom and Janice Breyer, Tom Brown, Gilbert Cranberg, Alan Forsyth, Steve Jones, Randy Karpinen, Roger Kerson, Steve Lacy, Sam McKnight, Rob Penney, David Radtke, Jordan Rossen, Tom Schram, Ben Solomon, Jim St. Louis, Joe Uehlein, and Tom Walsh. Alan Lenhoff very kindly took me on tours of both the North Plant in Sterling Heights and the Riverfront Plant in Detroit. Julie Hurwitz and the Sugar Law Center provided valuable information on the civil rights cases involving the Sterling Heights police, as did Kevin Ernst. Thanks also to Scott Martelle for organizing the panel discussion on the strike at the 2010 North American Labor History Conference at Wayne State, and to Rob and Ann Musial, Ed Wendover, and Mike Whitty for their cordiality to an out-of-town visitor.

I am also greatly indebted to my academic colleagues for their criticism and encouragement over the long period of research and writing for this book. Special thanks go to Michael Schwartz, Ruth Milkman, Jeff Haydu, Larry Isaac, John Walton, Wolfgang Streeck, Ellen Dannin, Howard Kimeldorf, Dan Clawson, Jeff Goodwin, Mike Zweig, Ian Robinson, Barry Eidlin, Anthony Chen, Rod Benson, and Julia Adams. Several anonymous reviewers at the *American Journal of Sociology*, along with its editor, Andrew Abbott, offered important criticism that helped me sharpen my analysis.

Financial support for this research was provided by the A. Whitney Griswold Fund at Yale University and by the American Sociological Association's Fund for the Advancement of the Discipline Award, supported by the ASA and the National Science Foundation. I benefited greatly from a year as a visiting scholar at the Russell Sage Foundation and from the assistance of its staff members Galo Falchettore, Alexa Rosa, and Jeffrey Ruiz. I owe a special debt of gratitude to Suzanne Nichols, director of publications at Russell Sage, for her patient and steadfast faith in the project while I struggled to write the manuscript, and to Cindy Buck, copyeditor. The work of doing the research and analysis would also have been impossible without the valiant help of my research assistants Josh Howard, Joe Salamon, Patrick Inglis, Rachel Haut, Rachel Criswell, Bonnie Speck, Tim Wilson, and Jenny Hirsch.

The story of the Detroit newspaper strike is really many stories, of many different people brought together in many different ways. I was scarcely able to include everything in one book, but I have tried to do justice to the events as best as I know how. As always, along the road Maida Rosenstein has been an unfailing source of inspiration, commitment, and love. I look forward to where that road goes next.

Introduction | Labor Day in America

LABOR DAY, September 4, 1995, came and went much as it had in previous years in Sterling Heights, Michigan, a predominantly white, middle-class suburb in Macomb County, exactly six miles north of Detroit. Clouds billowed in from over the Great Lakes to fill the late summer sky, while the sun kept temperatures seasonably warm. Local residents took advantage of the long weekend to go fishing or sailing or just stay at home and watch sports on television. In quiet neighborhoods of orderly streets and cul-de-sacs, families and friends gathered around dinner tables or backyard barbecues. In the evening hours, as the holiday weekend wound down, people gradually prepared themselves for the return of the regular working week.

Across town, however, a very different scene was taking place. Along its commercial highways and boulevards, Sterling Heights was also home to several large industrial employers: the Ford Motor Company, Chrysler Corporation, and other big firms had major facilities within the town's borders. Near the intersection of Mound Road and 16 Mile Road (Metropolitan Parkway) stood the giant North Plant of the Detroit Newspaper Agency (DNA), a sprawling, forty-two-acre complex of integrated pressroom, mailroom, loading dock, warehouse, and truck maintenance facilities, with its own railroad spur to bring boxcar loads of newsprint directly into the plant. There, on the center island of Mound Road across from the plant's main south gate, more than one hundred police officers from Sterling Heights and other nearby towns stood ready in full riot gear, while squads of private, high-security guards patrolled inside the chain-link fence circling the property. In between, as many as three hundred striking newspaper workers and their supporters gathered in and around the driveway onto Mound Road. The strikers, members of the local Newspaper Guild, Teamsters, and printing craft unions, chanted slogans and carried signs on a picket line, joined by supporters from the United Auto

1

Workers (UAW) and other area unions as well as more radical splinter groups.

Since the start of the strike nearly eight weeks earlier, protesters and police had enacted a daily ritual. At designated times, police would stop traffic on Mound Road, line up in a V-formation, and march across the street toward the gate, parting the crowd to clear the driveway for vehicles entering and exiting the plant. On this night, however, the crowd refused to give way. Rows of helmeted police officers wielding shields, batons, and pepper spray drove into the picket line, only to be pushed back by the throng of picketers holding each other in linked arms, while others swung picket signs and hurled rocks, sticks, and other objects. The police fired canisters of pepper gas at the demonstrators, who defiantly picked them up and threw them back. Before long, a dense plume of gas hung in the air, choking protesters, police, and news reporters alike. The officers brought out large industrial fans to keep the fumes in front of the strikers, and amid the fog a lone picketer held an American flag aloft in the middle of the street. Mound Road quickly filled with debris, and at one point individuals in the crowd began throwing five-inch steel rods, lifted from the refuse of a nearby machine shop, at the police and at the guards inside the plant. The guards then threw them back over the fence into the crowd, and a CBS news camera operator was struck in the head. Again and again the two sides clashed, resulting in at least half a dozen injuries to police and an unknown number of injuries to strikers.

Surveying the scene, Sterling Heights police lieutenant Frank Mowinski did not like what he saw. A thirteen-year veteran of the Sterling Heights Police Department (SHPD), Mowinski was the official SHPD coordinator for the strike and had devised the department's plan for handling it. He had arrived at the North Plant late Monday afternoon and was the officer in charge at the Mound Road gate, during which time the crowd swelled from perhaps fifty marchers to more than two hundred. At approximately 9:40 PM, and again at 10:08 PM, Mowinski declared the picket line an unlawful assembly and ordered the strikers to disperse. But each time the officers failed to remove the crowd and were forced to pull back to the median. At 11:45 PM, after several hours of tense confrontation, Mowinski gave the order again. This time the police used tear gas, which quickly scattered the crowd and forced them northward along Mound Road. Within minutes, the area was emptied of picketers and more than fifty police officers, holding shields and facing outward, lined the north and south sides of the driveway.

One of the picketers that night was forty-year-old Ben Solomon, a mailroom worker and member of the International Brotherhood of Teamsters

(IBT), Local 2040. Married and the father of a two-year-old son, Solomon had worked for the Detroit papers for twenty-two years, starting right out of high school. As a mailer, he operated the machines that took newspapers from the presses, inserted advertisements, and bundled and sorted them before they were taken away for distribution across metropolitan Detroit. Solomon had arrived for picket duty at the North Plant around 7:00 that evening and was among those who had refused to leave when ordered to disperse. Shortly after 10:00 PM he was pepper-sprayed in the face, and he was then taken by fellow strikers to get treatment from paramedics working out of an ambulance parked on the Mound Road median.

Overcome and disoriented by the spray, he left the picket line and sat down on the grass below the south side of the driveway. Sometime after midnight, he returned and found the rows of police stationed in the driveway. For nearly two months, Solomon had seen the police use their authority and force to protect the company's ability to operate, unimpeded by the picket line. Now, frustrated and unarmed, he approached the officers on the south side, and from about ten feet away he pointed his finger at them and screamed, "You're a disgrace to the badge."

When Lieutenant Mowinski saw Solomon confronting his officers, he had had enough. He rushed over and grabbed Solomon by the hair, pulled him face down to the ground in the middle of the driveway, and ordered his arrest for interfering with police. Solomon was immediately surrounded by other officers and punched, kicked, and hit in the groin with a police baton. One officer held a baton at his throat while another knelt on his back, attempting to handcuff him. Solomon could not see who arrested him, since the officers wore helmets and had removed or taped over their ID badges. Within seconds, he could not see anything, as his eyes were pepper-sprayed from an inch away, the condensed mist dripping down the side of his face. At around 12:47 AM, he was led away and put in a police wagon, where he remained until around 3:00 AM, without medical attention. He was finally brought to the Sterling Heights police station, again was denied treatment, and was placed in a holding cell until 9:30 the next morning, when his wife Debbie secured his release and took him to a hospital.

Sterling Heights police records for that night include no report of the use of force in arresting Solomon; departmental rules mandating such reports had been suspended during the strike. Nor did Lieutenant Mowinski, the arresting officer, complete the required incident report for an arrest involving force. Solomon was not even identified in the police station until Tuesday morning, by another officer. At that time the charge was changed to unlawful assembly, a felony carrying a possible five-year prison sentence. Photographs taken later that day showed bruises on Solomon's legs and face and blood in his eyes; he also sustained injuries to the shoulder, knee, back, and neck. He would later undergo surgery on his shoulder and endure months of rehabilitation. Around a year and a half after the incident, Solomon received a letter from the City of Sterling Heights stating that the charges against him were dismissed.[1]

AN EXTRAORDINARY CASE: THE DETROIT
NEWSPAPER STRIKE, 1995 TO 2000

On July 13, 1995, unions representing some 2,500 workers went on strike against the morning *Detroit Free Press*, owned by Knight-Ridder, Inc.; the evening *Detroit News*, part of the Gannett media chain; and their joint operating agency, Detroit Newspapers, Inc. The strikers were members of six local unions, including journalists, printers, press operators, circulation workers, janitors, and truck drivers. They walked off their jobs after contract negotiations broke down, amid union charges of bad-faith bargaining and unlawful declaration of impasse by the employers. Taking a hard line, the newspapers hired permanent replacements for the strikers and effectively militarized their operations. Altogether, the companies spent an estimated $40 million on private security forces and paid more than $1 million to suburban municipalities to cover police overtime at their production and distribution sites.[2]

The conflict quickly turned violent and bitter, with hundreds of altercations, injuries, and arrests, particularly at the newspapers' giant printing plant in suburban Sterling Heights. The strikers rallied support from the Detroit-area community, organizing circulation and advertising boycotts, mounting civil disobedience and protest actions, and publishing their own alternative weekly strike paper, the *Detroit Sunday Journal*. In addition, the strike drew upon the organized culture of labor solidarity in southeastern Michigan: hundreds of rank-and-file members from other unions joined mass picket lines in mobile teams deployed out of local and regional offices of the UAW and other unions. Prominent area civic, political, and religious figures also stepped forward to condemn the use of permanent replacements and urge a settlement. By their own estimate, the two papers combined lost nearly $100 million in the first six months, while circulation dropped by as much as one-third. Yet the unions were unable to stop either production or distribution of the newspapers, and the strike stretched into its second year.

Meanwhile, the dispute generated an enormous body of litigation. The six unions, united as the Metropolitan Council of Newspaper Unions

(MCNU), formally struck over three principal unfair labor practice (ULP) complaints issued by the Detroit regional office of the National Labor Relations Board (NLRB). The first complaint charged the DNA with unfairly transferring work out of the printers' bargaining unit, in violation of a previous agreement to negotiate such changes with the union. The second accused the *Detroit News* management of unlawfully declaring a bargaining impasse in order to impose a merit pay plan on the Newspaper Guild. Third, the NLRB charged that the companies had reneged on a prior commitment to bargain jointly on economic issues with the MCNU.[3]

Once the strike began, the employers systematically fired strikers for alleged picket line misconduct, some of them several times, which led the NLRB to issue more complaints of illegal discharge.[4] The unions and several individual strikers (including Ben Solomon) filed federal civil rights cases against the employers, their security firms, and various local police and governmental authorities for conspiracy and police misconduct. In turn, the employers brought charges against the unions under the federal Racketeer Influenced and Corrupt Organizations (RICO) Act and later named the UAW as a codefendant in the suit. Finally, union protests and hand-billing of customers at merchants advertising in the papers led to legal maneuvers with the NLRB and local police over the strikers' freedom of speech.[5]

On February 14, 1997, after nineteen months on strike, the unions made unconditional offers to return to work. But the employers announced that they would take back only a fraction of the striking workers, as new vacancies allowed. On June 19, 1997, an NLRB administrative law judge (ALJ) found the newspapers guilty of unfair labor practices that had "caused" and "prolonged" the strike. The judge ordered the companies to reinstate the striking workers, displacing, if necessary, the replacement workers and making any strikers not reinstated eligible for back pay. Two days later, an estimated sixty thousand union members and supporters from across the country arrived in Detroit for a giant march and rally in a national show of solidarity led by the AFL-CIO.

The newspapers immediately appealed the ALJ's decision, while the NLRB petitioned for an interim injunction requiring that all strikers be returned immediately to their jobs. Despite an NLRB record of favorable rulings or settlements in around 90 percent of such cases, in August 1997 a U.S. district court judge refused to grant the injunction. In the spring of 1998, religious, civic, and union leaders across the Detroit metropolitan area convened a community summit to try to bring the parties together, again without success. In August 1998, the NLRB in Washington, D.C., unanimously agreed that the strike was caused by management's unfair labor practices. But the companies pursued the case to the U.S. Appeals Court, and the litigation continued. By the end of 1999, more than two hundred strikers had been fired and several hundred more remained locked out.

The strikers' fate was now tied to the unfair labor practice case. Already upheld by the regional and national NLRB, the charges in the Detroit case might have required the employers to pay out more than $100 million in back wages. On July 7, 2000, a federal Appeals Court overturned the NLRB decision, destroying the unions' hopes for a reinstatement order. Deprived of their legal leverage, the unions were forced to accept contracts on management's terms. The last of the six unions settled in December 2000, and more than five years after it began, the Detroit newspaper strike was over.

Ratification of the contracts, however, did not bring an end to the litigation. The agreements offered no amnesty provisions for fired strikers, including prominent writers and columnists who had participated in nonviolent civil disobedience. The newspapers refused to take those employees back, and the legal appeals went on for several more years. Finally, most of the individual civil rights suits were dismissed or settled out of court, but at least one case went all the way to trial and a verdict. On December 21, 2000, a federal jury found the newspapers, the City of Sterling Heights, and its police officials guilty of conspiracy to deprive Ben Solomon of his civil rights. A key piece of evidence at the trial was a series of memos from the city to the newspaper agency, from July 1995 to October 1996, itemizing weekly police overtime costs related to the strike. The memos were followed by checks from the company to the city that were made out for the exact amount, down to the penny, and ultimately totaled nearly $1 million.[6]

Although costly, the employers' victory nevertheless set a new standard in national labor relations and prefigured subsequent mass lockouts in the 2003 Southern California grocery and 2004 San Francisco hotel disputes.[7] In 2002, President George W. Bush politically affirmed the companies' stance by appointing Robert Battista, the lead counsel for the companies in the unfair labor practices trial, as chair of the NLRB. Meanwhile, in Detroit the strike permanently altered the newspapers' relationship to the local community. Circulation fell at eight times the rate for the industry as a whole between 1995 and 1999, and dozens of veteran journalists left the papers and the city, taking with them years of local knowledge and public memory.[8] Finally, in late 2004, top executives at the DNA quit to take over the struggling *San Francisco Chronicle*, and in 2005, after sixty-five years in Detroit, Knight-Ridder sold the *Free Press* to Gannett, which in turn sold the *News* to MediaNews Group, Inc., a national suburban newspaper chain.

THE DETROIT STRIKE AND LABOR
IN AMERICA

Violent clashes on the picket line, police and private security forces in riot gear, boycotts and mass firings, prolonged protest and civic conflict—for some readers, these images may appear odd or anachronistic, more like faded news photographs from the 1930s than reflections of the prosperous, high-tech economy of the 1990s. The era of industrial strife was supposed to have ended long before, relations between unions and management were now regulated by federal law, and strikes seemed almost a thing of the past. The city of Sterling Heights lay in the heart of Michigan's Macomb County, the home of the "Reagan Democrats" studied by political scientist and consultant Stanley Greenberg. Sixty-seven percent of county residents had voted for the Republican president in 1984, and the county had a median household income in 1985 that was $7,000 above the national average.[9] As partners with management in pursuit of economic growth, local workers seemed to have achieved the American Dream. Yet, here in 1995, apparently, class struggle had come to the suburbs.

How could such things occur, and what do they mean? As remarkable as it may have seemed, the Detroit newspaper strike was not an isolated event. The period of the 1980s and 1990s witnessed a series of hard, wrenching strikes in American industry, recorded in outstanding historical studies like Jonathan Rosenblum's *Copper Crucible*, on the 1983 Phelps Dodge strike in Arizona; Julius Getman's *The Betrayal of Local 14*, on the workers at the International Paper Company in Jay, Maine; and Stephen Franklin's *Three Strikes*, on the labor wars at Caterpillar, Bridgestone/Firestone, and the A. E. Staley food processing mills in Decatur, Illinois.[10] These studies and others have clearly traced the renewed corporate offensive against unions since around 1980, the erosion of collective bargaining, and the failure of traditional legal protections for workers. In a rare case of union victory, Tom Juravich and Kate Bronfenbrenner's *Ravenswood* shows how the United Steelworkers of America overcame such barriers in a 1990 strike of aluminum workers in rural West Virginia.[11]

For decades now, the hostile environment for labor has accelerated the decline of union density in the American economy; by 2004 the proportion of the private-sector labor force belonging to unions had fallen below 8 percent, a level not seen since before the New Deal.[12] Along with this has come an even more dramatic drop in the incidence of strikes. The strike itself has almost disappeared: during the 1970s, an average of 289 major work stoppages involving a thousand or more workers occurred annually in the United States. By the 1990s, that number had declined to about thirty-five per year, and in 2009 there were no more than five.[13] By com-

parison, the contentious struggles mentioned earlier seem more like mete-
oric explosions that stretch out across an empty night sky. The combination
of depressed national strike rates and intense, episodic conflicts suggests a
more far-reaching, historic change in the structural and institutional context for strikes and for the system of industrial relations as a whole.

Faced with these challenges, leaders in the American labor movement
have responded with a renewed commitment to organizing new members. Unions like the Service Employees International Union (SEIU),
among others, have developed a range of alternative approaches, including outreach to low-wage, often immigrant workers, alliances between
unions and other groups in the community, and new forms of protest and
collective action. In social science, a new generation of labor scholars has
analyzed these campaigns, drawing on sociological theories of social
movements. Much of this work adopts a "strategic" perspective, focusing
on the conditions that foster union revitalization, the most effective mobilizing tactics, and the organizational "best practices" that can serve as a
model for other unions.[14] As in the historical studies, researchers often
debate what various actors have done—or might have done differently—
to alter the outcome of the events.

Despite a wealth of empirical evidence, however, these new studies
have not yet sufficiently changed the way we think about labor relations,
and especially strikes, in our law and public policy, in the discourse of the
news media, and in social science. Perhaps not surprisingly, employers
and their representatives argue that nothing is wrong with the current
system and that serious reforms are unnecessary.[15] In the news media,
coverage of labor disputes often goes no further than the imagery of conflicting private special interests and the risk of inconvenience to consumers.[16] Among academics, many economists and legal scholars remain
doubtful about the prospect of significant labor movement revival.[17] Even
those observers who are sympathetic to unions often take the goals of revitalization for granted, without fully addressing why a nonspecialist audience should care. Beyond the strategic question of what makes the few
strikes that do occur succeed or fail are deeper, underlying problems: Why
do unionized workers confront such extraordinary conditions in the first
place? And what does the state of the labor movement mean for us as
members of a wider, democratic public?

In this book, my goal is to do something different. The standard ideas
about unions and collective bargaining often reflect traditional social science concepts that no longer correspond to current realities. For my point
of departure, then, I engage directly with traditional theories of strike behavior as a way of challenging the conventional wisdom. I propose an alternative framework that allows us to see the causes and meaning of con-

temporary strikes in a new way. The strike, I argue, has been transformed from an economic tactic and protected legal right to a more high-risk confrontation in which the issues at stake are not just the dollars and cents on the table but the continued existence of the collective bargaining relationship. At the same time, the disputes that emerge now spill over into other public arenas and raise questions about the role of workplace governance in the local community and in American society.

This theoretical argument is based on the well-established method of deviant case analysis in social science. By maximizing its differences from the norm, a deviant case offers the opportunity to observe and analyze previously unexamined causes and effects.[18] The goal is not to explain away unusual data, but to revise previous models and construct a broader, more encompassing explanation.[19] The case serves as a diagnostic device, highlighting the contours of normalized relations and providing a critical standpoint for generating new, more historically grounded insights.

By any objective measure, the Detroit strike was an extreme case. The strike covered a total of approximately 2,500 employees and lasted for 583 days, making it larger than 97 percent—and longer than 99 percent—of all private-sector strikes from 1984 to 2002. According to one estimate, fewer than 10 percent of such strikes from 1982 to 2001 involved multiple bargaining units striking against the same employer.[20] In Detroit, no fewer than six local unions, representing diverse occupational groups, including white-collar professionals, blue-collar laborers, and skilled craftspersons, struck in unison against the newspapers.

As a case study, the newspaper strike also offers a window onto several important historical changes. Its location in Detroit, literally the capital of twentieth-century industrial Fordism, placed it in the heart of what remains one of the most unionized regions in the country. At the same time, the strike displayed the impacts of growing corporate concentration, rapidly changing technology, and the rise of the information and media sectors. As such, it illustrated the problems for unions of reasserting solidarity in the "new" economy. Finally, the strike registered ongoing changes in the role of the state in industrial relations, underscoring the contrast between a declining New Deal system of protection for labor rights and the rise and consolidation of an ascendant anti-union regime. As an unfair labor practices strike lasting more than five years, the Detroit case provides a unique occasion for a close analysis of these conflicts.

The Detroit newspaper strike was "one of the most bitterly fought labor battles of the 1990s," historian Philip Yale Nicholson writes. "All of the elements of the currently hostile labor management environment were present in the five-and-a-half-year-long struggle."[21] The analysis of such a complex event cannot be reduced to the individual arrogance or ineptitude of a handful of leaders, though there was enough of that on both sides. Rather, the strike represented a distinct historical juncture of social forces. To understand this landmark case, I begin with previous models of strike activity. The historic context of the Detroit strike, however, calls for the development of a new approach.

EXPLAINING STRIKES: THE PROBLEM OF HISTORICAL CONTEXT

Studies of strikes have a long tradition in American social science. Conventional theories of strike behavior, however, have failed to keep pace with recent changes in American labor relations. A key problem, sociologist Jake Rosenfeld notes, is that research on aggregate strike activity in the United States "all but disappeared" following the 1982 decision by the federal Bureau of Labor Statistics to stop collecting data on strikes involving fewer than one thousand workers (the majority of all strikes).[22] Partly as a result, strike theory remains dominated by two primary traditions, the "economic" model and the "political-organizational" approach. The former typically asks *why* strikes occur, while the latter studies *how* workers mobilize for collective action.[23]

Traditional Strike Theory: The Economic Model

Economic theories of strikes begin with a market relationship in which employers and unions bargain the price of labor. Each party is assumed to enjoy organizational security, to be acting rationally, and to have calculated the costs and benefits of the decision to strike. Ideally, through negotiation both sides should be able to estimate each other's room for concessions and thereby reach agreement without enduring the actual costs of a strike. In this model, the central questions are, first, the sheer incidence of strikes (or why they should occur at all), and second, the strong correlation of strike frequency with short-term fluctuations in the business cycle (that is, strikes increase in a growing economy when labor markets are tight and wages lag behind inflation, and they decrease in downturns when unemployment is high). For the first question, the conventional answer suggests some form of error or failure in bargaining, due to imperfect or uncertain information or the behavioral psychology of one or both sides.[24] Indeed, many industry observers saw the Detroit strike as simply a colossal mistake, driven by irrational decisions on the part of the unions, or management, or both.[25]

Some economists have stressed the role of long-term bargaining relationships or coordination in reducing uncertainty. Others distinguish union leaders from the rank and file and attribute imperfect information to the latter: compelled to strike by restive members, leaders must equilibrate workers' wage demands with the economic needs of the firm.[26] This makes the bargaining relationship one-sided—employers are presumed to act with market efficiency, while only workers must change their concessions in order to come around to an acceptable compromise. The analysis of the actors' behavioral mechanisms, moreover, fits uneasily with long-term changes in strike patterns, and the question of why failures of information should vary systematically with external economic conditions remains a problem.[27]

A Critical Alternative? The Political-Organizational Approach

While economists operate within a market model, political scientists and sociologists have developed an alternative view that focuses on *how* strikes occur. In this approach, attention shifts to relations of conflict and power, and particularly how law and political institutions shape workers' capacity to mobilize. So, for example, in the pre–New Deal United States, or in France and Italy through much of the twentieth century, formal collective bargaining procedures were poorly established. Strikes challenged the general public order and balance of power among groups, and all too often government responded with police or federal troops. In this view, political conditions as much as economic ones affect the forms of strike activity, as legal or political realignments provide workers with greater or lesser opportunities for collective action.[28]

This approach historicizes the assumptions of the economic model. That is, organizational security and rational cost-benefit calculation depend on the historically contingent formation of strong institutions governing relations between business and labor.[29] Thus, the business cycle variables are most powerful in the United States in the post–World War II period—*after* the implementation of the National Labor Relations Act (NLRA). This period, often described as an era of labor "accord," both empowered workers and channeled their action toward specific means and ends.[30] Under the accord, the government intervened to regulate and protect workers' rights, and strikes became limited mainly to the bread-and-butter issues of wages and compensation that arose at moments of contract renewal.

The accord represented a historic shift in government policy, from repression to what sociologist Holly McCammon calls a legal regime of "integrative prevention."[31] With the rise of the social movements of the 1960s and 1970s, some critics argued that institutionalization had led to the co-optation of unions and the suppression of worker militancy. Yet such integration was also a condition for the economic incorporation into the suburban middle class of unionized workers, whose ambivalent status was reflected in the political volatility found among the voters in Macomb County.

Once the accord began to break down, however, neither of the traditional theories could explain contemporary changes in strike behavior. As economist Bruce Kaufman writes, "The level of strike activity in the 1980s plummeted to the lowest level of the post–World War II period and, furthermore, remained at this level even as the economic environment changed in ways that historically have led to increased strike rates."[32] Similarly, labor's integration into the postwar system turned out to be a temporary settlement, not a final stage of development. The assumption of stable class incorporation failed to anticipate the radical *deinstitutionalization* of unions that has occurred since around 1980.[33]

Strikes in Context: A Historical Framework

To explain the Detroit strike we need an approach that can better account for changes in the historical environment. Sociologist Bruce Western argues that market conditions generate structural conflicts between workers and employers, while institutions shape the ways in which societies manage those conflicts.[34] Building on this approach, I propose to modify traditional strike theory by distinguishing three analytic dimensions or arenas: the economy, the state, and the independent field of voluntary association that sociologists call "civil society."[35] Relations of civil society extend across the social environment and include workplace associations like unions as well as non-workplace affiliations such as churches, social and civic associations, neighborhood and ethnic clubs, and the like.[36] Together, these form the organizational nexus of cultural norms, collective identities, and social ties that makes up our everyday sense of "community."

This framework is represented in table I.1. No single dimension acts as the primary causal factor; the combination of all three determines why and how strikes occur in a given historical case.[37] The economic arena includes the pressures of competition and supply and demand in the labor market. Within the state, law and political institutions serve to regulate market forces, on the one hand, and to channel forms of worker militancy, on the other. In turn, civil society creates a field for collective action, an extension of the normal political and institutional means for organizing and making claims.

A growing scholarly literature has focused on "bringing civil society back in" to studies of American labor.[38] Much of this research, however, is

Table I.1   Causal Framework and Periodization: Strike Activity in the United States, 1890 to the Present

	Economy	State	Civil Society
Causal context	Responses to market pressures on employment relationship	Regulation of market, institutional channeling	Cultural norms, social ties, "community"
Pre-accord (1890 to 1937)	Craft union control (versus Fordist mass production)	Judicial repression of collective action	Boycotts, sympathy strikes, popular protest
Accord era (1937 to 1981)	Decentralized bargaining in manufacturing and trades (versus union avoidance)	NLRB procedures, industrial democracy, preventive integration (versus Taft-Hartley, right-to-work)	Relatively excluded
Post-accord (1981 to the present)	Ascendancy of corporate anti-unionism	Weakened NLRB, hostile federal courts (unfair labor practice strike)	"Metro-unionism," consumer appeals, social movement tactics

Source: Author's compilation.

concerned with union efforts to organize new members rather than with strikes per se.[39] By contrast, traditional strike theory includes the economic and political arenas but tends to isolate strikes from relationships in the community. In part, this reflects the historic reality of the postwar accord, in which private-sector labor disputes were largely confined within institutional channels. Bringing civil society back into strike theory thus historicizes both sides of the earlier debate, transforming the causal logic of the other two dimensions.[40]

In the economy, the emphasis shifts from the analysis of information or behavioral problems in bargaining to the larger strategic responses of corporate or collective actors to market pressures on the employment relationship. Most importantly, this includes whether the parties accept any mutual negotiating relationship in the first place. Similarly, the state's channeling of tensions under the accord is not a necessary outcome but one among several contending paths, subject to persistent conflict. Finally, separating mobilization from its formal regulation permits a closer analysis of the interaction among labor, community, and other cultural movements across civil society as a whole.[41]

This framework leads to the rough periodization of American labor relations summarized in table I.1. Throughout the pre–New Deal era, boycotts, sympathy strikes, and other forms of local communal action remained a vital part of workers' protest repertoire and the object of legal repression by the state.[42] During the accord, many of these practices were prohibited as forms of "secondary" collective action. In the post-accord period, as American unions have lost institutional standing and power, they have been forced to turn (or return) to organizing methods often labeled "social movement unionism."[43] This move has featured tactics like home visits and other non-workplace sites for member outreach, alliances with religious and community groups, corporate consumer campaigns, appeals to ethnic or gender identities, and alternative organizational forms from advocacy groups to immigrant worker centers to mutual benefit associations—in other words, mobilization in civil society.[44]

A Signal Juncture: Post-1981 Labor Relations in the United States

This more historically grounded framework allows us to see the Detroit conflict in a new light. Sociologists have long treated moments of intense conflict or disruption as occasions when conventional perceptions are peeled away, exposing the durable social structures that shape everyday life. "It is when hell breaks loose and all men [sic] do their worst and best that the powerful forces which organize and control human society are revealed," wrote W. Lloyd Warner and J .O. Low in their classic study of a Depression-era shoe workers' strike in Newburyport, Massachusetts.[45] Such episodes, however, can also be read more dynamically—as moments when underlying developmental paths "collide" and latent contradictions become intensified or burst into the open.[46] The newspaper strike embodied just such a collision, between the declining New Deal system of collective bargaining and an ascendant order of corporate anti-unionism.

In the United States, the institutions of the postwar accord were never entirely stable and from the start were accompanied by a constant undercurrent or opposing layer of "union avoidance."[47] The law limited the scope of collective bargaining, and gave employers privileged access to workers in order to campaign against unions in NLRB elections. "Right-to-work" provisions in the 1947 Taft-Hartley Act allowed companies to

Introduction   15

move away from unionized areas in the Northeast and Midwest to non-union areas in the southern states, long before the current era of globalization. Taft-Hartley also excluded managers and frontline supervisors from protection under the NLRA. Throughout the postwar period, firms aggressively resisted unionization in the growing white-collar and service sectors of the economy, leaving unions concentrated in an eventually declining blue-collar sector.

As a result, a rival anti-union path of development grew alongside and apart from the New Deal system. The two paths coexisted for years, and direct conflicts between them did not emerge all at once. The turning point for American labor came in the early 1980s, with the rise to dominance of the anti-union regime. In 1981, President Ronald Reagan fired the striking federal air traffic controllers, announcing a critical juncture in the government's attitude toward union rights.[48] Backed by Republican administrations and increasingly conservative federal courts, private corporations escalated from a strategy of avoidance to attempts to break established unions and deunionize altogether. Workers in the core manufacturing and transportation sectors fought back during the bitter strikes of the 1980s, but by then the institutional balance of power had shifted in favor of the employers.

In this sequence of events, the Detroit strike corresponds to what I call a "signal juncture," as distinguished from the better-known concept of a "critical juncture."[49] Social scientists define a critical juncture as a historic turning point when opposing forces collide and two or more alternative future paths are possible. A process of closure then occurs in which one road is taken, others are blocked off, and various "lock-in" mechanisms reproduce the chosen path in a new historical period or stable order.[50] The transition between periods, however, may include longer struggles in which concentrations of old and new institutional power persist in different organizational or geographic locales. Subsequent events may then mark the extent to which one path has gained (or retains) the advantage, and at the same time reveal internal "unlocking" mechanisms or sources of resistance. Such events may be described as signal junctures for the ways in which they signal ongoing, underlying conflicts within a dominant regime.

As a concept, the signal juncture applies the logic of deviant case analysis to the theory of institutional path dependency. Unlike a critical juncture, a signal juncture occurs not at the beginning or the end of a path, but in the middle. A critical juncture is a transformative case that remakes the rules between one period and another. A signal juncture is a deviant case that departs from the dominant pattern but thereby exposes persistent contradictions and countertendencies. The result suggests a more spatially and temporally uneven process of path consolidation, marked by episodes when opposing institutional logics continue to clash with one another, producing moments of exceptional conflict.

The newspaper strike offers a clear example of this process. Both sides invoked different and conflicting norms: the companies pursued a neoliberal agenda of corporate restructuring and management autonomy, while the unions mobilized to defend New Deal values of collective bargaining. In Detroit the collision of these larger institutional paths would produce the extreme levels of both extensive litigation and popular protest in the strike. Under the circumstances, a pragmatic or negotiated solution was nearly impossible, because the actors were effectively operating under different sets of rules. The specific issues on the table were not the most important object of dispute; rather, it was the relationship between the parties itself that was fundamentally at stake.

THE BROKEN TABLE: THE PROBLEM OF WORKPLACE GOVERNANCE

In the newspaper strike, the unions targeted the workplace in production and circulation, including the relations between the companies and their consumers and advertisers. Those actions carried the struggle deep into the social tissues and capillaries of the urban community—from the public streets and jurisdictions surrounding the printing plants and warehouses to the commercial areas of the businesses that continued to advertise in the papers, to the neighborhoods and doorsteps where the papers were delivered each day, to the foundations of the civic media sphere of which the *News* and the *Free Press* were vital parts.

In so doing, the strike brought to the surface larger questions not normally considered to be part of industrial relations. In service to its community, what does a newspaper, or any other business enterprise for that matter, exist *for*? What norms and goals is it obliged to respect, and to whom is it accountable? Who are the proper stakeholders, how are their interests articulated, and how should disputes be resolved? For the past few decades, mainstream economists have operated from an unequivocal and dogmatic assumption: like any other enterprise, a newspaper exists to augment shareholder value.[51] In stark contrast, the strike showed that the rules and institutions governing these matters are historically variable, subject to conflict with other norms and goals and at times strongly contested by other actors.

This perspective forms the central axis of the analysis in this book. I argue that the Detroit strike displayed the tensions arising from the collapse of the post–World War II accord in U.S. labor relations. As the formal institutions regulating labor conflict have declined, the boundaries of disputes have likewise become blurred, and workplace struggles have expanded into or reentered other arenas of the state and civil society. The system for negotiating the interests at work, the "table" where the parties might come together to determine their future, has broken down, and the consequences now extend far beyond the traditional dollars-and-cents of collective bargaining.

For many political theorists, modern mass democracy requires multiple institutional spaces for dialogue and decision-making among plural collective actors, including the actors in the workplace.[52] Decades of neoliberal restructuring have now radically altered the spaces for such dialogue—on the job, in the community, and in the public sphere. The result highlights a historic *de-democratization* of the institutional regulation of labor disputes in the United States, from the scope of collective bargaining in the workplace to the civic spaces for group mediation, to the protection for workers' and citizens' rights to protest under the law. Under the current regime, *all* strikes are now "exceptional," and to the extent that they escape their institutional constraints, all raise the same fundamental questions. The Detroit case powerfully displays the contours of this change and signals an important shift in American political development.

In the last several decades, economic inequality has risen sharply in the United States, as both academics and journalists have noted.[53] During the middle of the twentieth century, the distance between rich and poor steadily declined, but in the last quarter of the century the pattern was reversed: income inequality increased by 23 percent while inequality of wealth rose by 11 percent. In the private-sector labor market, wage inequality increased by 40 percent between 1973 and 2007, with declining unionization accounting for one-fifth to one-third of the increase.[54] For more than a generation, the benefits of economic growth have gone disproportionately to corporate profits and to the top fifth of households, while incomes for the middle and bottom fifths have remained stagnant and fallen behind. In the course of our lifetimes, as sociologist and demographer Douglas Massey writes, "class stratification [has] returned with a vengeance."[55]

While some may deplore such trends, the role of ordinary working people in challenging these conditions has been largely forgotten. What has become of the frontline institutions that once governed the workplace and gave voice to those employed there? What can be done to reestablish a degree of equity in the labor market, and how might workers empower themselves as agents of change? Can we now find ways to restore democratic governance of relations at work and in their intersection with the community?

The freedoms of association and collective bargaining in the workplace are basic human rights, recognized in global social conventions like those of the International Labor Organization (ILO), a specialized agency of the United Nations.[56] The right to strike is an essential element of these freedoms, but all of these rights are now poorly protected in American public policy. That is the product of our current institutional arrangements, however, not the result of any economic necessity or historical law. The institutions that we have may not change easily, but they do change, and they remain subject to our collective political choice. As a signal juncture, the Detroit newspaper strike is an indicator of how far we have come. The possibility remains that things could yet be another way.

THE ORGANIZATION OF THIS BOOK

In the narrative analysis that follows, I examine these issues in detail. The book is organized into four parts. Most books about strikes focus mainly on the events of mobilization, and the action begins more or less on the day the strike starts. Here, I beg the reader's patience while I take a different route. Part I, "Worlds of Work," begins with a discussion of the structural preconditions of the strike, the relations between the economy and the community, and the social embeddedness of the labor process. Chapter 1 examines the evolution of the newspaper business nationally, the organization of the market for news, and the relationship of the industry with the urban public sphere. For much of the twentieth century, that relationship was governed by the twin forces of "church" and "state": the professional ethics of newspaper journalists and the market power of the owner-publishers. By the end of the century, however, the balance between these two forces had undergone definitive change.

Chapter 2 paints a portrait of metropolitan Detroit, with its legacies of urban social and cultural development. I show how historic patterns of elite organization, working-class formation, and racial division defined the landscape of local civil society, thereby shaping the field of mobilization for the strike. Chapter 3 brings the camera lens down to the newspaper workplace, at the intersection between the economics of the industry and the social relations in the community. I describe the traditional process of daily newspaper production, the restructuring that overtook the industry in the 1980s and 1990s, and the everyday working lives of the employees at the *News* and the *Free Press*. Together, those workers' interconnected labors performed the "daily miracle" of producing and distributing two big-city American newspapers. Their experiences illuminate the question of who held a stake in the enterprise, how well the papers served the community, and the substantive relationships underlying the contract negotiations between the employers and the unions.

Part II, "The Institutional Regulation of Labor," resets the analysis to focus on the arena of the state and institutional change, tracing the reasons why the strike occurred when and where it did. The economic, technological, and social processes described in part I brought new pressures to bear on the employment relationship, in the newspaper business as in the larger economy. By themselves, however, these processes did not require that firms adopt an aggressive anti-union stance. Rather, as comparative studies of other industrialized nations have shown, the central variable was how societies chose to manage those pressures through the institutional regulation of the labor market.[57] Here, the dense complex of rules governing collective bargaining, contract language, and procedural appeals formed a crucial battleground, with decisive consequences for actors in the workplace and society.

Chapter 4 sketches the changing role of the federal government and labor law in the United States in the mid- to late twentieth century. The New Deal system of industrial relations established spaces for negotiation but also channeled the actors within certain boundaries. By the 1980s, the system was in rapid decline, challenged by a renewed anti-union corporate agenda. I review two key strikes of the period that marked important milestones in the struggle between the rival institutional paths: the strike at the Phelps Dodge Arizona copper mines in 1983 and the strike at the *New York Daily News* in 1990. Chapter 5 begins with the events that triggered the collision of those paths in Detroit. The entry of the Gannett corporation into the local news market and its creation of a joint operating agency with Knight-Ridder altered the relationships at the bargaining table, while the contract negotiations in 1989 and 1992 set the groundwork for the coming confrontation.

The context of restructuring helps make sense of the issues for management in the 1995 bargaining round and its extraordinary plans to operate during a strike, analyzed in chapter 6. Never before or since had the companies put such resources into strike preparations, including an unprecedented outreach to local law enforcement agencies well before the negotiations even began. Chapter 7 explains the 1995 contract talks in detail, including the principal unfair labor practice charges filed by the unions and their attempts to avoid a strike in the final hours. In the facts of the case one can almost hear the grinding of institutional gears as competing norms and values grate against one another and actors struggle to operate within a set of rules even as those rules are breaking down.

The chapters in part II address the question of why the strike happened and deal mainly with events that occurred before the walkout began on July 13, 1995. With the start of the strike, the analysis shifts again. Part III, "The Spaces of Conflict," takes up how the strike occurred and the forms of struggle that played out over the course of more than five years. Chapter 8 describes the initial mobilization by the unions on the picket line and in the community, the newspapers' determination to break the strike, and their decision to use permanent replacements. That decision especially highlights what might be called the failure of corporate paternalism, personified by the editorial management of the *Free Press*. Chapter 9 carries the story through to the end of 1995, detailing the newspapers' efforts to contain and control collective action, the polarization on the picket line, and its descent into violence.

These processes signaled how much the terrain of labor conflict had changed by the mid-1990s. By the beginning of 1996, the strike had become a long war of attrition whose trenches spread across the legal system and the Detroit-area community. Chapter 10 surveys the expansive litigation associated with the unfair labor practice charges. In addition, the unions and their allies attempted to open up spaces for public engagement with the employers through acts of ambulatory picketing, civil disobedience, protests at local merchants advertising in the papers, and the publication of an alternative weekly strike newspaper, the *Detroit Sunday Journal*.

Whether through technical procedures in court or moral appeals to the community, the two sides fought over both how the strike could be conducted and what it was centrally about. After nearly two years on the streets, the unions offered to return to work in February 1997. The papers' insistence on keeping the replacements, however, created a new set of hurdles. Chapter 11 examines the pivotal year of 1997, which featured the peak of national popular mobilization and decisive turns in the legal case. The process of litigation brought the conflict inside the institutional corridors of the state and led to a long denouement that would not see a contractual settlement of the dispute until the end of 2000.

The concluding part IV, "Governing the Workplace," offers a broad reassessment of the case as whole. Chapter 12 brings the facts of the strike back into a dialogue with strike theory in order to set a new baseline for how we can talk about strikes and labor relations in the United States. I present some conditional propositions on the causes and meaning of contemporary strike activity, and I compare the Detroit strike with other labor struggles of the 1990s, highlighting its role as a signal juncture. Finally, I consider the competing visions of workplace governance as a problem for institutional reform. Although intended in part to reduce industrial strife, the Wagner Act recognized the importance of the right to strike in promoting the voluntary exchange of labor through collective bargaining. The events of the strike show how much that system has been undermined, and what has been lost as a result.

The case study of the strike relies on data collected from approximately one hundred interviews with key informants drawn from four categories of respondents: strikers and union leaders; company executives and representatives; nonstriking employees; and local and national civic leaders and public officials. I also collected hundreds of news stories from the *Detroit News*, the *Detroit Free Press*, and the *Detroit Sunday Journal*, the weekly newspaper published by the strikers from 1995 to 1999, as well as reports from other major and local news, business, and professional media. Other archival sources included thousands of pages drawn from the trial transcript, exhibits, and decisions in the principal unfair labor practice complaints issued by the NLRB, along with testimony, depositions, and legal records arising from the civil rights cases and other litigation. Finally, I obtained copies of documents from organizational and individuals' personal files, such as collective bargaining agreements, internal communications, flyers and press releases, and videotape recorded by security forces and local television news media.

This book is not meant to be a post-hoc analysis of who should have done what during the strike, nor does it offer an easy guide for how one or the other side might win the next battle. Rather, it is addressed to all readers concerned about the future of workplace governance in the United States. The collapse of the relationship between business and labor represents a significant decline in the spaces for collective negotiation and decision-making in American economic and social life. For the country as a whole, declining unionization has contributed to rising economic inequality and a diminished working-class voice in the public sphere.[58] The economic future of millions of people has become ever more uncertain, subject to blind forces that seem far beyond their reach. How can we regain a capacity to govern our working relationships democratically and provide for a more just, cooperative, and secure system for all? This book aims to contribute to the search for an answer.

PART I | Worlds of Work:
Economy and
Civil Society

Chapter 1 | The Industry: Gannett and Knight-Ridder

FEW INDUSTRIES HAVE BEEN as romanticized in American popular culture as the newspaper business. Hollywood versions have ranged from classic films like *Citizen Kane*, *The Front Page*, and *All the President's Men* to fictional thrillers like *The Pelican Brief* and *State of Play*, the biographical drama *The Soloist*, and the Disney musical *Newsies*. The strength of the popular myth is well grounded: in 1991 media scholar Michael Schudson wrote that the American newspaper was "the most representative carrier and construer and creator of modern public consciousness."[1] For much of their history, local newspapers have served as a vital medium of civic communication and urban community, with the names of their home cities inscribed on their mastheads and their relations with local economic, political, and social actors more direct and intimate than any other mass media can claim.

Today, however, as newspapers face challenges to their very survival, it has become clear that their contribution to a democratic society rests on a *contingent* historical juncture of forces and ideas. As media scholar C. Edwin Baker writes: "Meaningful presentation [of the news] often requires intelligent decision making by skillful, independent, and financially backed media professionals—a difficult to find combination."[2] Over time, the industry has seen periodic transformations in the structure of its market, in the labor of newspaper workers, and in the relationship of the papers to their audience and community. In Detroit these historic changes formed the economic and cultural backdrop for the events leading to the 1995 strike.

The American newspaper business took off in the nineteenth century, giving rise to the major actors and forms of organization that defined its identity. By the twentieth century, the industry had entered a phase of economic consolidation, on the one hand, and journalistic professionaliza-

25

tion, on the other. Toward the end of the century, however, the uneasy truce between these two trends was breaking down, a tension symbolized by the two largest newspaper chains of the time, Gannett and Knight-Ridder. In the 1980s, these two corporate giants would come together in the joint operating agreement (JOA) between the *Detroit News* and the *Detroit Free Press*.

THE NEWSPAPER BUSINESS: INVENTING THE MARKET

Newspaper markets are not born but made. As historian Paul Starr has shown, politics and public policy have always been central to the development of American news media, beyond the protections of the First Amendment.[3] The 1792 Post Office Act gave newspapers special subsidies and privileges and reduced the cost of obtaining and distributing news across long distances, making it possible to reach subscribers deep in the country's interior. Publishers were freed from licenses, stamp duties, and taxes on paper, ink, and type, while government printing contracts, fees for legal notices, partisan sponsorship, and other patronage directly supported the nascent industry. More broadly, the extension of the franchise and the rise of the common school helped create an interested, literate reading public and a mass market for news.[4] With the rise of Andrew Jackson and the Second Party System, newspapers emerged as zealous advocates of competing political parties and leading promoters of a vigorous public sphere.

The early Federalist republic of letters, historian Mary Ryan writes, quickly became a democracy of print.[5] Nationally, the number of newspapers grew from 376 in 1810 to around 900 by 1832. A prime example was the *Detroit Free Press*: founded as a weekly in 1831, within four years the *Free Press* became the first daily paper published in the Michigan Territory. With only a few hundred subscribers and almost no paid advertising, the *Free Press* initially relied on party support, income from the publication of official notices, and printing contracts from city, territorial, and state governments. Fiercely Democratic, the *Free Press* backed Jackson for president, championed local movements for statehood, and railed against Republicans and abolitionists in the antebellum era.[6]

Across the nation, urbanization and reductions in the cost of printing and paper made possible another kind of journalism by the 1830s, the "penny press." The penny papers actively pursued commercial success and mass readership, using higher circulation rates to attract independent revenues from advertisers. Costing a fraction of traditional papers and hawked by newsboys on city streets, the penny press appealed to the growing market of urban, white working-class men. The content of news shifted to attract the new popular audience. Once produced by small printer-operators from partisan copy, papers hired reporters (a newly emerging occupation) and gathered their own stories of current local events, including crime, scandal, and the latest sensations.[7] The first major successful penny paper, the *New York Sun*, was founded in 1833 and within two years had achieved a circulation of 20,000, the largest in the nation.

These trends continued after the Civil War. Between 1870 and 1900, the number of daily newspapers rose from 574 to 2,226, and their average circulation grew from 2,600 to 15,000. Cheaper newsprint, the introduction of Linotype machines, and improved rotary presses further reduced the costs of printing, while advertising revenues, stimulated by the rise of national product markets and urban department stores, doubled during the 1870s and grew another 80 percent the following decade. Lower costs and higher revenues allowed newspapers to cut prices and extend their markets. In 1870 total daily circulation nationally stood at 34 papers per 100 households; by 1910 it had reached 121, an average of more than one paper per household.[8]

Much of the growth came from urban commuters purchasing afternoon papers from newsstands; by 1890 evening editions surpassed morning papers in circulation. Newspapers developed a new look and feel, with larger headlines, simpler language, more illustrations, and an eye-catching front page to attract street sales. New sections were added, including sports, comics, advice columns, and women's pages, to meet a more diverse audience. The news itself was transformed with the new practice of interviewing, almost unknown before 1860.[9] Such innovations contributed to developing notions about urban community and the public sphere. The nineteenth-century newspapers were themselves key instruments of urbanization, as Schudson observes: they "provid[ed] a community identity that held a city together when it was no longer a face-to-face community or even a 'walking city.'"[10]

Among the pioneers of these changes were Joseph Pulitzer and William Randolph Hearst, whose *New York World* and *New York Journal*, respectively, battled for readers at the turn of the century. In Detroit, entrepreneur James Scripps launched the *Evening News* in 1873, reaching an untapped working-class market with a cheap, tabloid paper written in a condensed, no-nonsense style. The *Evening News* was an immediate hit, and by 1876 its circulation exceeded that of all other Detroit dailies combined.[11]

With his brother Edward, James Scripps soon replicated the model in Buffalo, Cleveland, Cincinnati, and St. Louis, creating the prototype of the national newspaper chain.[12] Newspapers became large, industrial enterprises: by 1870 the major New York dailies each had at least one hundred employees. As the workplace expanded, production workers organized into local and then national unions. The first national printers union was established in 1852 and renamed the International Typographical Union (ITU) in 1869; among its founding "chapels" was the local from Detroit. Mechanization gave birth to even more specialized crafts, including unions of press operators (organized in 1889), photoengravers (1900), and stereotypers (1901).[13]

THE TWENTIETH CENTURY: CONSOLIDATION AND PROFESSIONALIZATION

In the twentieth century, newspapers reached the height of their influence: household penetration hit 130 percent in the early 1920s and remained near that level through the 1960s.[14] Long before then, however, competitive expansion had already begun to slow down. The number of dailies peaked at 2,609 in 1909, well in advance of the rise of commercial radio, and then rapidly declined, falling to 2,441 in 1919 and 1,911 in 1933. The industry consolidated as major chains bought and closed rival papers, and high start-up costs for mass production and distribution discouraged new entrants.[15] Newspapers became more dependent on advertising, which grew from 44 percent of revenue in 1879 to 60 percent in 1909. The shift reinforced trends toward monopoly; top-circulation papers achieved market centrality and economies of scale, while secondary papers faced increasing disadvantage in pursuit of advertising dollars. By 1933, 63 national and regional chains owned 361 dailies, mainly in urban centers, and nationwide they controlled 37 percent of daily and 46 percent of Sunday circulation.[16]

One such chain was the string of papers in upstate New York owned by Frank Gannett. A tall, dry, conservative Yankee, Gannett and his associates had bought a half-interest in the *Elmira Gazette* in 1906. The company acquired the *Ithaca Journal* in 1912 and in 1918 moved its offices to Rochester, New York, purchasing two papers and merging them into the *Rochester Times-Union*. Gannett gained full ownership of the firm in 1923 and then steadily acquired more properties, preferring to invest in smaller, lower-risk, single-paper markets. By 1936 the Gannett Company owned nineteen newspapers. The following year, facing competition from Hearst, Gannett closed its morning and afternoon papers in Albany, New York, and a short time later Hearst shut his papers in Rochester, leaving Gannett with a monopoly in its hometown.[17]

The changes in the industry altered both its standard business model and the structure of the public sphere. The need for wide circulation to attract advertising reduced incentives for political controversy, and with the decline of nineteenth-century popular rituals of voter mobilization, the last vestiges of partisan reporting fell away. Drawing on Progressive ideas of professionalism, objectivity, and public service, journalists created a new identity for themselves. As sociologist Richard Kaplan writes, newspapers "were to represent no particular political interests, but rather, the general public good; their remuneration would come only from the profits to be gained by general service to the reading public, not partial political communities."[18]

Alongside this mission came a more sharply defined separation of "church" (the newsroom) from "state" (the business side).[19] The former was led by an emerging body of professionals with their own occupational culture and autonomy. Training was formalized with the founding of journalism schools at the University of Missouri (1908), Columbia University (1912), and Northwestern University (1921). The Society of Professional Journalists was started as the Sigma Delta Chi fraternity in 1909, followed by independent associations of journalism educators, news editors, and managing editors. Finally, the notoriously underpaid reporters, copy editors, and newsroom workers organized themselves into the Newspaper Guild in 1933 and ultimately achieved collective bargaining rights covering terms and conditions of their employment.[20]

Leading the new style of journalism was the chain of newspapers owned by the Knight family. The brothers John S. "Jack" and James Knight had inherited the *Akron Beacon-Journal* when their father, Charles L. Knight, died in 1933. As head of the enterprise, Jack Knight reorganized the company into Knight Newspapers, Incorporated, buying big city dailies like the *Miami Herald* in 1937, the *Detroit Free Press* in 1940, and the *Chicago Daily News* in 1944. Aggressive in its business operations, Knight Newspapers became equally known for its commitment to news as a public service, and Jack Knight came to personify the image of the powerful, independent, and often irascible owner-publisher, confidant to presidents, and stern conscience of the community. Similarly, when newsprint was scarce during World War II, the *Miami Herald* under James Knight and editor Lee Hills stopped running display ads for the duration, to save space for wartime reporting. The move cost money, but earned reader loyalty for the paper, and after the war the *Herald* went on to become the dominant daily paper in Miami.[21]

The industry continued to flourish after World War II, despite a widening media environment and competition from television, radio, and magazines. Total revenues from advertising and circulation grew from $2.4 billion in 1950 to almost $6 billion in 1970.[22] Yet consolidation proceeded apace. Chain-owned papers outnumbered independents 879 to 869 by

1960. Direct competition practically disappeared: more than 90 percent of firms operated in single-paper cities by the early 1960s, and 95 percent of cities with daily newspapers had no local daily competition.[23] Single-market newspapers might enjoy profit rates of 15 percent or more, but as privately held firms they were not required to disclose financial data, and their profitability remained something of a secret. That situation would change with the next major transformation of the industry: the turn to publicly traded stock ownership.

Takeover Bid: Wall Street Gets the News

By the 1960s, many family-owned papers had reached the third generation and, with the death of their founders, often faced heavy tax liabilities and a multitude of heirs with a mixed taste and aptitude for publishing. On the other side, a handful of acquisitive chains were eager to expand their reach and needed large sources of capital to finance new purchases.[24] To do so, they turned to Wall Street, which discovered the lucrative returns available from investment in newspapers. The result was a rapid turnover of formerly independent papers as family owners, seeing the value of their holdings skyrocket, willingly sold their stocks or converted them into shares in the expanding chains. The 1990s witnessed another wave of mergers and acquisitions, this time of chains buying other chains, with some smaller papers changing hands two, three, or even four times. By the late 1990s, just 17 publicly traded companies owned more than 280 papers and accounted for 40 to 50 percent of total circulation nationwide.[25]

Gannett was one of the first to embrace the new business model, and it would come to define the paradigm of the publicly traded newspaper chain. On his death in 1957, Frank Gannett left a small conglomerate of twenty-three dailies and three television and four radio stations, mainly in his native upstate New York. He was succeeded as chief executive by Paul Miller, a patrician midwesterner and former manager for the Associated Press, who hired the thirty-nine-year-old Allen Neuharth in 1963. Four years later, Gannett became only the fourth newspaper company to go public. With a $10 million stake from the initial public offering, Miller and Neuharth began purchasing papers in small and medium-sized towns across the country. By 1973 the Gannett Company, Incorporated (GCI), was netting a profit of nearly $23.7 million on revenues of $288 million and owned more dailies than any other U.S. publisher.[26]

It was only the beginning. The ambitious and outspoken Neuharth took control from Miller in 1973 and soon built up a sprawling, diversified media empire. Leveraging stock instead of cash to avoid borrowing, by 1979 Gannett owned seventy-eight daily newspapers, a national news service, seven television and fourteen radio stations, and other media and research assets. With each round of acquisitions, Gannett pursued a typical management approach in its new papers, raising prices and advertising rates and cutting costs, including staff and less profitable circulation among lower-income groups. The formula allowed Gannett to post a record of eighteen consecutive years of quarterly earnings growth, from 1967 to 1985.[27] By then, Neuharth could brag that "sixteen percent operating margins are simply not acceptable at the Gannett Company."[28]

Knight Newspapers also prospered in the postwar era, and it went public in April 1969. By the early 1970s, the company owned sixteen papers, including metro dailies in Detroit, Philadelphia, Miami, and Charlotte, North Carolina. Within the Knight organization, however, local executives retained significant autonomy, and each paper reflected a distinct editorial identity and community character. In 1968, Knight Newspapers became the first publisher in history to win three Pulitzer Prizes in the same year, with awards going to the *Detroit Free Press* for its coverage of the 1967 riots, to the *Charlotte Observer* for editorial cartooning, and to Jack Knight himself for his editorial writing in opposition to the Vietnam War.[29]

In 1974, Knight Newspapers joined with another chain, Ridder Publications, Inc., in the largest newspaper merger up to that time. The Ridder papers traced their roots to the son of a poor Westphalian immigrant, Herman Ridder, who purchased the German-language daily *Staats-Zietung* in New York City in 1906. After Herman's death, his heirs bought *The Journal of Commerce*, a New York business paper, in 1926 and acquired a series of small to medium-sized papers in monopoly markets in the Midwest and West. Following this model, Ridder newspapers achieved a reputation for reliable business success, if not necessarily exceptional journalism. The company went public in 1969, and Bernard Ridder Jr., Herman's grandson, became president and CEO. By 1973, Ridder Publications, Inc., operated dailies in California, Minnesota, Colorado, and Kansas and was the fourth-largest newspaper corporation in the United States.[30]

Knight-Ridder, Incorporated (KRI), was born on November 30, 1974, and immediately became the largest American newspaper company in weekly circulation. The combined chain included thirty-five dailies in twenty-five cities, with 14,500 employees, total assets of $468 million, and operating revenue of $506 million.[31] The merger drew strengths from both sides, matching Knight's East-South geographic concentration with Ridder's base in the Midwest and West. The Knight papers also brought editorial quality and experience with large urban dailies, while Ridder offered steady returns from smaller, noncompetitive markets. Leadership of the organization alternated between top managers from both church and state: in 1976, Knight business executive Alvah Chapman was named CEO while journalist James Batten became president, and when Batten succeeded Chapman in 1989, his job was filled by Bernard Ridder's son, P. Anthony "Tony" Ridder.[32]

Managing the Newspaper Market

For a time, the delicate balance worked: Knight-Ridder produced both profits and outstanding journalism. By 1985 the corporation was worth $1.7 billion and annual profits had reached $133 million. Meanwhile, between 1977 and 1985 Knight-Ridder papers won fourteen Pulitzer Prizes, and in 1986 the chain took home an unprecedented seven Pulitzers in one year. But the company was not immune to the pressures sweeping the industry. Like its predecessor firms, it had gone public with a single class of stock, unlike other publishers who preserved family voting rights and control through two-tiered systems of ownership. At the time the founders kept a majority position, but within a few decades almost 90 percent of the shares would pass to institutional and outside investors.[33]

Knight-Ridder posted eight consecutive years of rising profits to 1985, with margins reaching 15 percent, but its return on equity lagged behind the industry as a whole.[34] The company had a relatively greater concentration of big-city papers in older, slower-growth markets, and its commitment to quality journalism frequently conflicted with pressures from investors. On the day when the company's seven Pulitzer Prizes were announced in 1986, the value of its stock actually dropped. As media scholar and former Knight-Ridder journalist Philip Meyer tells the story: "[KRI executive Frank] Hawkins called one of the [Wall Street] analysts and asked him why. 'Because,' he was told, 'you win too many Pulitzers.' The money spent on those projects, the analyst said, should be left to fall to the bottom line."[35]

Knight-Ridder's problems highlighted new stresses emerging within the newspaper business as publicly traded stock ownership once again altered the structure of the industry and the public sphere for news. Dependent on advertising, newspaper profits formerly followed the ups and downs of the retail market, although, for the chains, recessions in one part of the country might be balanced by prosperity elsewhere. With exposure to the stock market, publishers now faced demands for even higher margins and continuous profit growth, regardless of local economic conditions.[36] Acquisition costs rose as chains competed to buy papers, especially in single-ownership markets. Buyers often took on steep levels of debt, reinforcing the need for quick, high returns.[37]

Ironically, such problems were reinforced by public policy. In 1970, President Richard Nixon signed the Newspaper Preservation Act, legalizing the establishment of joint operating agreements between competing papers in the same market.[38] Informally in use for years, the practice involved merging the production, circulation, advertising, and business operations and pooling the profits of two separately owned papers, while leaving their newsrooms distinct and independent. The 1970 law protected such arrangements against antitrust claims and allowed "failing newspapers" to create new JOAs with the approval of the attorney general of the United States. While nominally intended to preserve a diversity of editorial voices, the law effectively sanctioned the overall monopoly organization of the newspaper market.[39]

Other government policies bolstered the trend toward mergers and consolidation. Antitrust law allowed papers to acquire a failing competitor outright if no other buyer was willing to purchase it. Federal tax laws, including accumulated earnings and tax carry-forward provisions, differential rates favoring capital gains over dividends, and tax-free stock exchanges, gave incentives to corporate chains to make even more acquisitions.[40] More broadly, postwar government support for development in the suburbs and in the Sun Belt created an imbalance between market potentials in different areas of the country. By simply purchasing papers in growing markets, chains increased profits more easily than they could by reinvesting in established operations in stagnant or declining cities.

The importance of monopoly increased as newspapers came to rely ever more on the growing advertising market. Papers used their market advantage to raise their ad rates by 253 percent between 1975 and 1990, nearly twice the 141 percent increase in consumer prices for the period. Across the industry, income from advertising went from $4.4 billion in 1965 to $43.9 billion in 1998, climbing an average of 5 to 6 percent a year and rising from 68 percent of total revenue in 1970 to 82 percent in 2000.[41]

At the same time, publishers cut costs. Statehouse, national, and foreign bureaus were closed, editorial focus shifted to cheaper local news, and newsroom staff and budgets were cut. Circulation departments targeted affluent, suburban consumers and abandoned less profitable, downmarket subscribers in the inner city or outer rural areas. New technologies permitted a radical downsizing of composing and pressroom staff, while chains used regional "clustering" of papers to share reporting and printing duties.[42]

These strategies were effective. According to one estimate, average newspaper operating margins almost doubled from 1991 to 2002, increasing from 14 to 27 percent. Industry profits as a whole grew by 207 percent during the period, while stock prices for the top-performing chains more than doubled between 1992 and 1997.[43] Although newspapers faced growing challenges from competitive media and fading circulation, the business kept pumping out increasing returns to investors. "The newspaper industry is sorely besieged," senior industry analyst John Morton wrote in 1996, "but not from a lack of profits."[44]

THE CRISIS OF CHURCH AND STATE: THE DETROIT JOA

Such trends underscored tensions in the industry between standards of market performance and values of public service. The conflict was illustrated in the 1985 petition for government approval of a joint operating agreement between the *Detroit News* and the *Detroit Free Press*. For years, the two papers had engaged in a classic newspaper war: locked in an intense competition for readers, each tried to drive the other out of business and capture a metropolitan market estimated to be worth $350 million in 1984. As Michigan's largest newspaper, the *News* came in slightly ahead in circulation and held a two-to-one command in the advertising market, an amazing feat for a private, family-controlled, afternoon newspaper. The *Free Press*, however, dominated in morning home delivery, and in 1984 Knight-Ridder committed $27 million to "Operation Tiger," a campaign of marketing promotion, improvements in news coverage, and investments in production facilities aimed at overtaking the lead in daily circulation.[45]

By 1985 the *News* had a Sunday circulation lead of 838,000 to 755,000 and received 62 percent of the total advertising linage and 72 percent of Sunday classified ad linage. But the contest was extremely close and costly for both firms. Both papers kept their street prices at fifteen to twenty cents, lower than 95 percent of daily papers nationally. Both offered deep discounts on circulation and advertising rates, losing valuable revenue. Finally, both were squeezed by rising newsprint costs and the recession that hit the auto industry and the Michigan economy especially hard in the early 1980s. Between 1980 and 1984, the *News* ran a deficit of $21 million. Counting Knight-Ridder's investments in Operation Tiger, the *Free Press* lost a total of $43.4 million from 1979 to 1985.[46]

The *News*, notwithstanding its competitive lead, was especially vulnerable. Owned by the Evening News Association (ENA), a small media conglomerate still led by the descendants of James Scripps, it could not match the deep financial pockets of Knight-Ridder. It might take years for the *News* to win a definitive victory, and in the stock market boom of the mid-1980s even family shareholders were becoming restless. On August 29, 1985, the ENA was sold to Gannett for $717 million, or $1,583 per share, more than six times the price its board had offered in a buyback scheme only nine and a half months earlier.[47]

At the time, Gannett's overall business strategy was still anchored in small and medium-sized papers in safe markets, but it expanded dramatically with the nationwide *USA Today*, introduced in 1982. Under the leadership of company chair Neuharth, Gannett invested heavily in *USA Today*, but the new paper lost millions of dollars at first and was widely criticized for its editorial quality. In an effort to win journalistic credibility, Neuharth in the mid-1980s purchased several respected regional dailies, including the *Des Moines Register,* the *Louisville Courier-Journal*, and, by far his largest acquisition, the *Detroit News*.[48]

Gannett's entry into Detroit might have opened up a competitive market showdown between the respective business models represented by Knight-Ridder and Gannett. Instead, three weeks before submitting a formal bid for the ENA, Neuharth telephoned Knight-Ridder CEO Alvah Chapman to inquire about a joint operating agreement between the *News* and the *Free Press*. Top executives from both chains met to discuss the proposal on September 25, 1985, and again on February 4, 1986. By the time Gannett closed on its purchase of the *News* two weeks later, the outlines of a deal were nearly complete.[49]

Neuharth and Chapman announced their plan at a press conference in Detroit on April 14, 1986. Despite its rising circulation and dominance in morning home delivery, Knight-Ridder agreed to designate the *Free Press* as the failing newspaper. On May 9, lawyers for the companies filed a petition with the U.S. Justice Department for an exemption from antitrust law under the Newspaper Preservation Act. The companies pushed for a quick approval to avoid further losses, and they anticipated a sympathetic response from Attorney General Edwin Meese III.[50]

The petition for the JOA, however, developed into a three-and-a-half-year-long legal and civic battle over the legitimate forms of market organization and the proper role of the news media. The announcement of the plan surprised and alarmed many local observers, and within a short time a range of civic and political elites, including former Michigan governor William Milliken, Detroit mayor Coleman Young, U.S. congresspersons John Dingell and William Ford, business and union leaders, suburban publishers, and current and former Detroit journalists, had written Meese to request a formal hearing on the JOA.[51]

Their concerns were not unfounded. The law was supposed to preserve diverse editorial voices when a competing newspaper was "failing." Yet, perversely, it also gave publishers the means to pursue monopoly control. Companies could willfully sacrifice short-term profits through predatory pricing with the fallback that, if that strategy failed to eliminate competition, the resulting losses could still be used to justify a petition for a JOA. In Detroit both papers ran huge deficits and were kept afloat by their parent corporations, but neither one was clearly failing. The *News* held its slim lead only through artificially low prices; even a small increase, matched by the *Free Press*, might have restored both papers to profitability. That outcome, however, paled beside the potential profits from a JOA, which Gannett might now need to recoup its $717 million purchase of the *News*. "It was absolutely clear that there were tons of red ink being spilled on those two newspapers' books," said Rick Rule, a Justice Department official working on the case, "but it looked awfully voluntary. It looked like it was a conscious, rational decision, because they were investing in this billion-dollar pot of gold."[52]

For more than eight months, Attorney General Meese delayed making any decision, before finally ordering a public hearing on February 25, 1987. Several more months would pass before the hearing convened in a federal courtroom in Detroit on August 3. For sixteen days, administrative law judge Morton Needelman heard witness testimony and arguments from lawyers for the newspapers, the Justice Department's Anti-Trust Division, and the six principal local unions recognized as intervenors in the case. On the fourth day, Knight-Ridder chief Chapman testified under oath and for the first time stated openly that if the JOA was not approved, he would move to close the *Free Press*.[53]

The judge, however, was not persuaded. In a 129-page opinion released on December 29, Needelman found no proof that the Detroit market could not sustain two papers, if they were priced appropriately. The *News* was not clearly the dominant paper, and the *Free Press* was not in the classic downward spiral of a failing paper. As for Chapman's threat, Needelman wrote, "The record . . . contains no convincing evidence that he seriously considered closing the *Free Press* prior to his witness stand bolt out of the blue." Needelman recommended that Meese deny the JOA.[54]

For nearly two years, the companies had acted as if the JOA was a purely internal business decision, virtually entitled to approval by the Justice Department. Now Knight-Ridder risked losing both the JOA and the *Free Press*. In response, Chapman quickly took a more aggressive political approach. He asked influential Washington attorney and Knight-Ridder board member Clark Clifford to take charge of the legal case. Together, Chapman and Clifford enlisted top Michigan business and political leaders, including former president Gerald Ford, to write amici letters to Meese, and they got the Knight-Ridder board to commit to a plan to shut down the *Free Press* if the merger was not approved. *Free Press* publisher David Lawrence wrote a front-page editorial asking for public support for the JOA, while the paper's editors and columnists echoed the drumbeat. In one controversial incident, *Free Press* editors tried to suppress several editorial cartoons critical of Meese, only to see their actions reported in the *Washington Post*.[55]

On August 8, 1988, in his last official act as attorney general, Meese finally approved the JOA. Chapman's campaign was evidently a success, but it disturbed many in the newspaper industry and in the Detroit community. The publishers had openly sought favor from powerful corporate and political interests they routinely covered in their papers. They had arguably crossed legal and ethical boundaries in order to influence the attorney general after the close of the public hearing. The *Free Press* had used its own pages to promote its economic self-interests, further eroding the wall between business and editorial functions. As Bryan Gruley, former Washington correspondent for the *News* and historian of the Detroit JOA, wrote, "It carried, at the very least, the appearance of impropriety, the scent of political manipulation, the taint of greed."[56]

And it was not over yet. Eight days after Meese gave his approval, an ad hoc coalition called Michigan Citizens for an Independent Press filed suit in federal court in Washington, DC, and won a temporary restraining order blocking the start-up of the JOA. Led by Michigan state legislator John Kelly, suburban Detroit newspaper publisher Ed Wendover, and lawyers from Ralph Nader's nonprofit organization Public Citizen, the group pursued the case for another fifteen months, through the DC Circuit Court of Appeals to the U.S. Supreme Court. In a stunning end to more than three years of legal proceedings, the Supreme Court deadlocked 4–4 after Justice Byron White recused himself from the case. The Court's action cleared away the last legal challenges, and the JOA went into effect in November 1989.[57]

In the process of winning a legally sanctioned monopoly, the papers had initially ignored and then actively fought with Detroit-area civic and political leaders to achieve the JOA. Private economic interests seemed to overrule values of public responsibility, notwithstanding the alleged purpose of the Newspaper Preservation Act. The result highlighted a growing anxiety among journalists over their mission and identity in the industry. As *News* reporter Gruley reluctantly concluded, "[The goal of] 'editorial diversity' has almost nothing to do with decisions to close a paper or keep it alive. Journalists don't make those decisions; 'businesspersons' do. . . . The hardest lesson of the three long years of waiting for the JOA was that the journalists did not matter. At least not much."[58]

CONCLUSION: THE FINAL HARVEST?

At the end of the twentieth century, the American newspaper business was a deeply troubled industry. Total daily circulation had peaked in 1973 at 63.1 million; by 2000 it had fallen to 55.8 million, the lowest level since 1954. Household penetration, still around one-to-one in 1970, was down to 0.60 only twenty years later. Ad revenues rose by 60 percent during the 1990s, but competition from direct mail, the Internet, and other media reduced newspapers' share of the advertising market from 30 percent in 1970 to 20 percent in 2000.[59]

Repeated cost cuts further strained editorial management as newsrooms were forced to be more accountable to corporate goals. Some critics worried that stockholders had shifted to an endgame strategy of "harvesting market position," that is, exploiting the media's credibility and extracting maximum cash flow without investment in the long-term future of the product.[60] This was nowhere more evident than in the eventual fate of Knight-Ridder, which abandoned Detroit and sold the *Free Press* in 2005. The following year, CEO Tony Ridder was unable to defend the company against a hostile takeover bid from Bruce Sherman, a Florida-based hedge fund manager with no professional experience in the newspaper industry.

Sherman's Private Capital Management (PCM) fund had begun buying KRI stocks in 2000 and by 2005 owned about 19 percent of shares, by far the largest stake in the corporation. From 2000 to early 2004, the price of KRI stock increased from the low $50s to just under $80 a share, but then faltered and declined along with that of other newspapers. Accustomed to better than 20 percent returns, Sherman's own PCM fund became critically overextended, and by the third quarter of 2005 its performance dipped slightly below the market. Hoping to regain his ground, Sherman pushed aggressively for the sale of the entire Knight-Ridder chain.[61]

With Sherman in position to win up to seven seats on the company's ten-member board, Ridder and his management team gave in. In March 2006, Knight-Ridder—with 18,000 employees, 32 daily newspapers, and a combined circulation of 3.7 million—was sold for $4.5 billion to the much smaller McClatchy newspaper group. McClatchy immediately announced plans to unload nearly one-third of its new properties, including the *Philadelphia Inquirer*, the *Philadelphia Daily News*, and the *San Jose Mercury News*. Yet at the time it was put up for sale, Knight-Ridder had an operating margin of 16.4 percent, higher than many Fortune 500 firms, including global corporations like Exxon Mobil.[62]

Beset by financial pressures, newspapers as a whole have faced internal controversy and heightened uncertainty about their prospects as an industry and as a public service. The principal management response to the crisis, however, has been a strategy of relentless cost-cutting and downsizing of newsroom operations, or "survival by continuous amputation," in the words of one critic.[63] In the face of such cuts, newspaper journalists have been notably unable to defend their professional status, as the business of "state" has overwhelmed the ethics of "church." Writing in the *American Journalism Review* in 2006, industry analyst Morton said bluntly: "Public [stock] ownership of newspaper companies is not good for journalism. . . . [The] pursuit of a robust return to the exclusion of everything else can have evil effects on companies that provide services deemed essential to our democratic government."[64]

If journalists no longer sustained their former position, however, as economic enterprises the papers were still accountable to their local metropolitan markets and to their unionized employees. Over the course of two hundred years, American newspapers had undergone repeated transformation in their standard business model, their processes of production, and their relationship to their audience. Between them, the Gannett and Knight-Ridder chains encompassed the economic pressures, corporate identities, and competing journalistic philosophies in the industry at the end of the twentieth century. Similarly, the Detroit papers embodied the changing relationship of the press with the urban community. Over their long history, the *Free Press* and the *News* epitomized the grand traditions of the big-city daily newspaper. The next chapter looks more closely at the newspapers' interaction with the economic, political, and civic life of Detroit in the constitution of the local public sphere.

Chapter 2 | Detroit: Labor and Community

IN 1950, DETROIT, MICHIGAN, was without a doubt the Motor City, an industrial powerhouse with a population of 1.8 million and close to one-third of a million manufacturing jobs within the city limits. Less than half a century later, the population had fallen to just over 1 million, and only 62,000 manufacturing jobs remained. Unemployment in 1992 was 17 percent, and one-third of city residents lived in households with cash incomes below the poverty line. During that time, the number of African Americans in Detroit grew from around 300,000 in 1950 to 770,000, or 76 percent of the total in 1990. By contrast, the white population fell from 1,546,000 in 1950 to 222,000 in 1990, a decline of over 1.3 million persons, or more than the entire 2000 population of Dallas, Texas, or San Diego, California.[1]

This familiar picture of big-city economic stress and racial change, however, masks another, parallel phenomenon. From 1960 to 1990, Detroit's tri-county metropolitan area of Wayne, Oakland, and Macomb Counties *gained* a total of more than 850,000 jobs. In 1990, Detroit's suburbs counted nearly 2.9 million residents, only 5 percent of whom were black. This area outside the central city enjoyed enormous prosperity. Family incomes in the boom decade of the 1990s were 13 percent above the national average, higher even than in suburban New York or Los Angeles. "Metropolitan Detroit is not an impoverished place," one study observed at the time. "As the nation's major retailers know, Detroit's suburban ring is a good place to do business."[2]

Such extreme social and economic contrasts affect both the market for news and the urban public sphere. Newspapers traditionally have been important actors in what political scientist Marion Orr calls the local "ecology of civic engagement," by which he means "the terms by which major community and institutional sectors of a city relate to one another and their role in the structure and function of local political regimes." Accord-

40

ing to Orr, the possibilities for elite or popular action, and the civic spaces for collective dialogue, depend on the ways in which "the major stakeholders in a community align themselves to respond to broad cultural, social, economic, and political change, and how that alignment is shaped by the character and history of interaction among and between them."[3]

In this case, the conditions of Detroit's metropolitan civic ecology framed the decisions of both management and the unions in the events leading up to and during the strike. To understand how these conditions evolved, we can trace the historic processes of local city-making in Detroit in the twentieth century. In this history, three features stand out: (1) the relative absence of a close-knit business elite or urban "growth machine" focused on central-city development; (2) a legacy of industrial militancy, unionization, and labor solidarity among the working population; and (3) the deep-seated racial and political split between majority-black Detroit and the largely white suburbs.

This often troubled history shaped relations among the newspapers, the unions, and the broader community, producing the local social and political context for the events of the strike. The roots of Detroit's civic ecology begin in the rise of the industrial city from the first half of the twentieth century. That legacy would be transformed in the postwar era, with the economic decline of the central city and rapid suburban growth. As major civic actors, the *News* and the *Free Press* contributed to the formation of the local public sphere, and their internal disputes were likewise implicated in the alignment of groups and stakeholders in the community.

THE RISE OF THE INDUSTRIAL CITY, 1900 TO 1945

Detroit was already America's fifteenth-largest city and a busy manufacturing hub when the auto industry began to take shape in the early 1900s, enmeshing the city in a network of modern factories and rail lines. Yet, despite their economic dominance, from the start the big automakers kept their distance from the civic destiny of Detroit. Ford retreated first to the industrial enclave of Highland Park and then to Henry Ford's hometown of Dearborn, west of the city. Chrysler also located in Highland Park and in Hamtramck, and General Motors maintained production centers for Buick in Flint and for Oldsmobile in Lansing. Away from the factory corridors and the central city, Detroit remained a low-rise, low-density midwestern city of tree-lined streets and private homes.[4]

Nonetheless, the expansion of industry attracted a mass influx of population, and Detroit swelled from 286,000 residents in 1900 to 1.5 million in 1930.[5] The city pressed outward as native-born Protestants and Anglo-

Saxon descendants moved into neighborhoods on the West Side of Woodward Avenue and immigrant Polish, German, and Italian Catholics and East European Jews settled on the city's older East Side. In 1920 about one-third of white Detroiters had been born outside of the United States, and another one-third had at least one foreign-born parent.[6] As in other cities, the concentration of ethnic minorities prompted a cultural reaction among native-born whites. Leading industrialists promoted Americanization programs for their workers and backed a statewide dry law that took effect in 1918, two years before the start of national Prohibition. Similarly, Ford's famous five-dollar day was coupled with extensive surveillance of his employees' morals and with Ford's own strident anti-Semitism.[7]

Elite bias found its popular counterpart in the post–World War I rise of the Ku Klux Klan, which claimed 35,000 members in Detroit and nearly elected Charles Bowles, its write-in candidate, as mayor in 1925. Facing discrimination in the job market, many ethnic workers entered the underground economy, and during the 1920s rival Jewish and Italian gangs thrived on the illicit but ubiquitous booze trade with nearby Canada.[8] The most severe prejudice, however, fell on African Americans, who frequently obtained only the lowest-status jobs and the oldest, most crowded inner-city housing. As the population grew, white residents organized neighborhood protective associations and used restrictive covenants and physical violence to keep blacks concentrated in the inner-city Paradise Valley and Black Bottom districts.[9]

By the 1920s, just three major daily newspapers survived in Detroit: the *News*, the *Free Press*, and William Randolph Hearst's *Detroit Times*.[10] Growing amid a dynamic economy, the *News* and the *Free Press* announced their civic stature with impressive new buildings located within a few blocks of each other in the central business district. In 1917 the *News* moved into a five-story, faux-stone concrete building, with large window arches rising from street level, on Lafayette Boulevard at Second Avenue. Designed by architect Albert Kahn, whose reinforced-concrete methods had revolutionized factory construction, the massive structure seemed to mirror the industrial might of the city. In 1925 the *Free Press* erected its own new building, a fourteen-story tower, a few blocks away on Lafayette between Washington Boulevard and Cass Avenue. Also designed by Kahn, the limestone high-rise housed the paper's business and editorial offices, composing room, and mailroom, with the printing presses installed in the basement.[11]

Editorially, the *News* inherited James Scripps's independent Republicanism and urban reformism, while losing much of his economic populism. The Progressive-era *News* routinely attacked ethnic machine politicians and saloon keepers and their political alliances with the privately owned utility companies. In 1918 the advocacy of the *News* helped to pass a reform city charter replacing the ward system with nonpartisan, at-large mayoral and council elections, and in 1922 the paper backed a successful referendum authorizing municipal takeover of street transit.[12] By that time, the *News* had turned itself into the dominant, blue-blood, establishment newspaper, the "august voice of the business class, champion of Prohibition, good government, and Anglo-Saxon virtue," in the words of historian Kevin Boyle.[13]

In turn, the *Free Press* appealed to its working-class audience with a mix of homespun conservatism and folk racism, particularly in its humor columns, like C. B. Lewis's blackface "Lime Kiln Club" and the sentimental poems of Edgar Guest. Traditionally Democratic, the paper broke with William Jennings Bryan's 1896 free silver campaign and endorsed Republican William McKinley for president; it would not support another Democrat for that office for the next eighty years. The *Free Press* was more tolerant of ethnic and machine interests before and after World War I, opposing city ownership of the streetcars and favoring the wet Catholic John Smith against Bowles and the Klan in 1925. However, its quality remained lackluster, its circulation lagged, and it fell into third place behind the *News* and the *Times*.[14]

Economic Crisis and Civic Struggle

The bustling urban growth of the 1920s was abruptly halted by the economic crisis of the Great Depression, which led to a pivotal juncture in the pattern of class formation in the city. In 1932 auto production stood at one-third of the level of four years earlier; and nearly one of seven persons in Detroit was on relief.[15] The city devolved into an industrial war zone as the nascent United Auto Workers (UAW) union and Congress of Industrial Organizations (CIO) fought in the streets against fierce employer opposition and corrupt law enforcement. Among the militant unionists was a young James R. Hoffa, who led successful strikes for the International Brotherhood of Teamsters (IBT). As Hoffa later recalled, "The police would beat your brains in for even talking union. The cops harassed us every day. If you went on strike you got your head broken. [Winning] didn't take months, it took years."[16]

At Ford, the company's infamous Service Department employed hardened gangsters to intimidate union activists, while local police officials were often willing partners with the racketeers. The conflicts in the workplace circulated throughout the community, amplified by the news media. In 1937, *News* photographer James Kilpatrick captured the widely published images of the "Battle of the Overpass," when Ford's private thugs attacked and beat Walter Reuther and other UAW leaders near the massive River Rouge Plant southwest of Detroit.[17]

Against the combination of business and local government antagonism, Detroit's labor movement developed deep traditions of militant solidarity and combative toughness.[18] In the UAW, political scientist J. David Greenstone observed, "in order to overcome bitter management hostility the union had to quell racial and ethnic hostility within its own ranks, as well as conflicts between skilled and unskilled workers. UAW leaders therefore appealed for solidarity based on their common status as industrial workers."[19] By 1941 the UAW had won contracts with General Motors and Chrysler but had not even secured recognition at Ford, which employed 85,000 workers in Detroit area factories, 21 percent of them African American. In a decisive campaign that year, the union overcame Ford's resistance through a strategic alliance with black churches, community organizations, and the local NAACP, and the victory established an important precedent of black-white labor unity on the shop floor.[20]

As Detroit workers gravitated toward the Democratic Party of Franklin Roosevelt, the *News* joined the *Free Press* in opposing the New Deal and denouncing the radicalism of the UAW and CIO.[21] The newspapers' anti-unionism extended to their own house: in 1933 reporters and office workers from all three Detroit dailies met to organize a chapter of the Newspaper Guild. Campaigns at the *News* and the *Times* faltered, but employees at the *Free Press* pushed on, spurred by three successive pay cuts. Owner E. D. Stair threatened to "board up the front door" if the union won recognition, and editor Malcolm Bingay fought continually with the staff over wages and working conditions, but contract talks finally began in earnest in October 1939. A Guild contract was signed on April 30, 1940, the same day that Stair sold the *Free Press* to the Knight newspaper chain.[22]

The upsurge of the labor movement marked a turning point in the civic ecology of Detroit, altering its balance of economic power, local political organization, and collective cultural identity. By 1945, 60 percent of the city's adult population either belonged to a union or was related to someone who did.[23] With their grassroots infrastructure and ideological commitment, the UAW and CIO moved quickly into the political arena. Earlier government reforms had weakened the traditional urban patronage factions in Detroit, and in the absence of strong competitors the unions were able to dominate the state Democratic Party apparatus in the postwar era. Finally, the new generation of labor leaders built organizational ties and acquired civic legitimacy with other groups in urban civil society. The UAW under Walter Reuther developed long-standing relations with liberal civil rights organizations like the NAACP and its Detroit branch, the largest in the nation. Similarly, the United Way of Michigan was founded in 1947 through the joint efforts of Henry Ford II and leaders of the UAW and CIO.[24]

Yet powerful forces of division persisted. In the 1930s and 1940s, racist demagogues like the Detroit-based Father Charles Coughlin and the Rev. Gerald L. K. Smith spread ethnic hatred and a homegrown fascism over the modern medium of the radio.[25] During World War II, white workers conducted spontaneous "hate strikes" to prevent black entry or promotion in segregated plants, and white residents protested the 1942 opening of the Sojourner Truth public housing project for black war workers. The worst violence came in June 1943, when racial tensions ignited a riot, resulting in more than 1,800 arrests and 34 deaths, including 17 blacks killed by police. UAW and CIO leaders worked to suppress the hate strikes and supported black community efforts to defend the Sojourner Truth project. Local politics, however, continued to center on issues of race and property values, and UAW-endorsed candidates lost repeatedly to more conservative politicians in elections for city government.[26]

CENTRIFUGAL COMMUNITY: EXPANSION AND POLARIZATION, 1945 TO 1980

By the end of the war, the principles of both hard-won labor solidarity and enduring racial division had become powerfully ingrained in Detroit's civic culture. Nevertheless, within a few years it seemed as if the return of prosperity might at last permit a more liberal accommodation among groups. The unions had become established in manufacturing during World War II, and in the years afterward workers won economic gains from collectively bargained wage hikes based on increased productivity. In the city, the black population grew from 149,000 in 1940 to 300,000 in 1950, and despite prejudicial barriers, black Detroiters began to accumulate economic resources and the kind of cultural optimism that would later be heard in the sounds of Motown, one of the largest-selling and most successful styles of American modern popular music.[27]

Rather than becoming a more inclusive community, however, Detroit civil society suffered grievous fissures under the multiple pressures of deindustrialization, racial discrimination, and the dispersal of the white population. First, changing patterns of corporate investment led to divergent economic paths of growth in the suburbs and job loss in the city. In search of larger lots, cheaper land, and lower taxes, the big automakers built twenty-five new plants in the suburbs between 1947 and 1958, the majority of them more than fifteen miles from Detroit.[28] Similarly, technical advances in production or "automation" reduced needs for unskilled labor, eliminating jobs across the East Side and other older industrial zones.

As historian Thomas Sugrue notes, corporate managers frankly viewed automation as a means to take back control of the shop floor from the contractual work rules gained by unions.[29] But manufacturing was not the only sector to decentralize. Hudson's, the leading downtown department store, opened the Northland Shopping Center in suburban Southfield in 1953, and other retailers soon joined in the exodus from the city. In 1958 ten of the region's major shopping venues were located in Detroit; twenty years later only one—the downtown Hudson's—remained. When that store closed in 1982, a city of more than a million people was left with no major retail area within the city limits.[30]

These processes challenged the commercial and civic centrality of Detroit within the growing metropolitan area. At the same time, efforts at downtown urban renewal were deeply implicated in the politics of race. Mayor Albert Cobo (1950 to 1957) oversaw redevelopment plans and freeway construction that demolished inner-city black neighborhoods and displaced thousands of residents. In deference to white homeowners, Cobo canceled planned public housing units in outlying white areas and opposed any further projects; virtually no new public housing was built in Detroit from the mid-1950s until the 1970s.[31] Meanwhile, African Americans who sought private-market housing in white areas often faced discrimination, harassment, and organized violence. The boundaries of suburban apartheid were symbolized by Dearborn's Mayor Orville Hubbard (1943 to 1978), who gained national notoriety for his decades-long efforts to keep black residents out.[32]

As the urban black population increased, the combination of block-by-block white resistance and then rapid abandonment only reproduced existing patterns of segregation, continually enlarging the boundaries of the black ghetto. In the end, the majority of whites in Detroit simply left. East Side blue-collar whites fled north across Eight Mile Road to Macomb County, whose population more than tripled, from 184,961 in 1950 to 625,309 in 1970. In the same period, the adjacent, more white-collar Oakland County more than doubled in size, from 396,001 to 907,871.[33] Typical of the trend was the city of Sterling Heights, a municipality of around 60,000 in Macomb County, officially incorporated in 1968. At the time of its founding, no black homeowners lived within the city limits. More than two decades later, the population had nearly doubled to 117,810 residents, but the proportion of black residents was still less than 1 percent.[34]

Civil Rights and Black Power: The 1960s

With the growth of the black community came increasing demands for change. The rise of the local civil rights movement in the 1960s, however, was shaped by the prior impact of the labor movement on Detroit's civic ecology. Perhaps more so than in any other American city, in Detroit the unions offered an alternative vehicle for African American political mobilization in addition to the black church.[35] "It was in the framework of the trade union movement that Detroit's Black leadership got its start in politics," said George Crockett, a leading African American attorney and activist who served as a judge on the Wayne County Recorder's Court from 1966 to 1978. "They learned their political ropes in being elected or influencing the election of trade union leaders, and from that they went out to organize the community."[36]

The labor movement was not only a medium and an ally for black activists, but also a target. Dissatisfied with the slow rate of racial progress within the movement, black unionists like Horace Sheffield, Ernest Dillard, Nelson Jack Edwards, and Nadine Brown formed the Trade Union Leadership Council (TULC) in 1957. The TULC pressured the UAW to increase black representation on its staff and in its top leadership positions and to open up jobs for blacks in the skilled trades. In 1961, TULC leaders broke with the UAW and joined the NAACP and the black Interdenominational Ministerial Alliance to back liberal challenger Jerome Cavanagh for mayor of Detroit. With the support of black votes, Cavanagh won an upset victory over the incumbent Louis Miriani.[37]

Cavanagh embraced both the civil rights movement and the federal government's War on Poverty, but the scope of inequality far exceeded the limited local and national policy response. Throughout the postwar era, rates of black joblessness measured two to three times those for whites; in 1967 inner-city unemployment was estimated at 12 to 15 percent for black men and 30 percent or higher for those under age twenty-five.[38] Through the 1950s and 1960s, black residents reported a constant stream of abusive and sometimes fatal incidents at the hands of the local police. Yet, as African Americans approached 40 percent of the city population, they still made up only 5 percent of the Detroit Police Department.[39] The frustrations finally exploded in July 1967 in four days of violent civil disorder, centered on the African American neighborhood of Twelfth Street in the near West Side. Forty-three persons were killed in the insurrection, including thirty shot by police and National Guardsmen. Some 2,500 stores were looted or burned, 388 families lost their homes, and more than 7,200 persons were arrested, 88 percent of them black.[40]

Belatedly, local elites turned their attention to the central city, yet they were unable to generate a strong new urban coalition. In August 1967, Governor George Romney, Mayor Cavanagh, and downtown business-man Joseph Hudson created the "New Detroit" committee to promote so-cial and economic development. Major employers made commitments to hire thousands of black workers, and the UAW's Walter Reuther champi-oned the initiative before his untimely death in an airplane crash in 1970. Yet even as they provided nominal opportunities in Detroit, the big auto-makers, retailers, and real estate developers continued to move jobs and housing to the suburbs. As the Rev. Charles Butler, a leading black minis-ter and member of the New Detroit board of directors, remarked, "The same persons who exercised power, then came to the rescue, at least titu-larly, to fix the thing. The *fixes* came from the persons who we felt had caused the problems in the first place."[41]

Within the UAW, black activists had wrestled for years with the union's internal hierarchy, and the redevelopment program lacked support, espe-cially among younger blacks.[42] On the job, grievances accumulated over the harsh treatment, speed-ups, and hazardous working conditions, espe-cially at the aging Detroit plants of the Chrysler Corporation. Such ten-sions led to the rise of Revolutionary Union Movements (RUMs) at Chrys-ler's Dodge Main, Eldon Avenue Gear and Axle, and other Detroit-area factories. Loosely united as the League of Revolutionary Black Workers, the RUMs led wildcat strikes and challenged the official union leadership before receding after 1971. Yet their brief insurgency illustrates how much the black power movement in Detroit was interwoven with the industrial workplace and the labor movement, unlike other cities where the Black Panthers and other groups focused on the unemployed ghetto poor. "Be-cause of League pressure," historian Steve Babson writes, "Chrysler hired more black foremen, the UAW hired more black staff, and the whole tenor of internal-union politics was transformed in many locals."[43]

THE STRUCTURE OF THE PUBLIC SPHERE

During this time, Detroit's newspapers both mirrored and embodied the contradictions of the larger community. In 1960 the *News* bought and closed the fading *Detroit Times*, and by 1962 it claimed a sizable circulation lead of some 200,000 over the *Free Press*.[44] In the region, the *News* retained its reputation as the businesslike if somewhat gray paper of record, and it won national exposure for its economic reporting on the auto industry. A strong proponent of elite-led urban renewal, the *News* sponsored an influ-ential 1955 Urban Land Institute report recommending inner-city slum clearance and replacement with market-rate rather than lower-income or public housing. By the early 1960s, urban renewal and highway construction had demolished much of the old Black Bottom neighborhood.[45]

As racial tensions increased, the *News* alienated many African Americans by racially identifying black suspects in often inflammatory crime reports and blaming black neighborhoods for lawlessness. Community leaders felt that the *News* reinforced stereotypes of blacks as criminals, but despite protests and occasional boycotts, the paper maintained the practice, as well as its conservative editorial stress on law and order. Finally, after 1967, the *News* walled up the first-floor arched windows on its Lafayette Street building, and in 1973 it moved its pressroom and distribution facilities to a new $40 million plant in suburban Sterling Heights.[46]

Inside the downtown editorial offices of the *News*, the high ceilings and oak-paneled walls preserved an aura of established authority. By contrast, the cramped desks and fluorescent lighting at the *Free Press* evoked a more hectic, freewheeling scene.[47] In the 1950s, the *Free Press* had streamlined its morning delivery schedule, providing suburban readers with a dependable paper at home before their daily commute. Meanwhile, editor Lee Hills revamped its content, adding lifestyle features, expanding metro coverage, and adopting a more approachable style that earned the paper the nickname "Morning Friendly." With a smaller news hole than the *News* and limited staff, the *Free Press* remained a journalistic underdog, but it gradually became the more liberal counterpoint to its rival, and it was the first major Detroit paper to hire a black reporter, in 1953.[48]

As news media and as private enterprises, the Detroit papers struggled to reconcile conflicting trends in the community and in their own industry. In particular, disputes over employment restructuring led to ongoing contention between the newspaper unions and the employers, led by the *Free Press* and Jack Knight. The troubles came to a head in 1955 in a forty-seven-day strike affecting 4,500 employees at the *Free Press*, the *News*, and the *Times*. A generation of conflict followed: over the next twenty-five years, the Detroit papers would experience almost forty authorized and unauthorized strikes, including work stoppages of one week in 1957, 29 days in 1962, 134 days in 1964 and 1965, and nearly nine months from November 1967 to August 1968. The last stoppage came only three months after the events of July 1967, and in their aftermath it deprived the Detroit-area community of a central forum for information and public dialogue.[49]

In 1950 the *Free Press* hired a young copyboy named Neal Shine. Over the next four decades, his career would span the changing character of the paper and that of much of its audience. Born in 1930 to immigrant working-class parents on the East Side, Shine attended St. Rose Catholic High School and the University of Detroit, graduating in 1953. He landed a reporter's job at the *Free Press* in 1955, working the city desk, the police beat, and the eastern suburbs. Paralleling the postwar socioeconomic mobility of his ethnic contemporaries, Shine rose to city editor in 1965, became managing editor in 1971, and was named senior managing editor of the newspaper in 1981.

Described as a "ruddy-faced Irishman" and a combination of "chaplain, counselor, coach, and stand-up comedian," Shine became an iconic figure and beloved pater familias in the *Free Press* newsroom. As city editor, he helped direct the paper's Pulitzer Prize–winning coverage of the 1967 uprising, and during the crisis he persuaded a friend at Chrysler Corporation to loan him a military armored car to transport reporters in safety. In an often repeated story, Shine allegedly rode the vehicle down Lafayette Street to the rival *News* building after the dangers subsided and through a loudspeaker demanded that its editor be turned over as a hostage.[50] The story burnished the lore surrounding Shine's personality and passion for journalism, yet it also revealed the newspapers' professional insulation from the hazards that many Detroit residents continued to endure.

Managing Urban Crisis: Coleman Young and After

By the time Coleman Young became the city's first black mayor in 1974, the patterns of metropolitan economic and racial division were already well entrenched. Young, a veteran politician and former union militant and civil rights activist, brought significant changes to city government, implementing affirmative action policies and most critically reforming the police department. He also gained federal support for urban social programs and won influence in the national Democratic Party through his political alliance with the administration of President Jimmy Carter. At the same time, the mayor maintained the focus on downtown and industrial renewal, backing controversial projects like the 1981 demolition of the Poletown neighborhood for a new General Motors plant.[51]

Young's attempts to build a liberal pro-growth coalition, however, failed to stem the outflow of business and the white population. In November 1971, Henry Ford II announced plans for construction of the Renaissance Center, a thirty-three-acre riverfront complex featuring four office towers surrounding a seventy-three-story hotel. Ford assembled a consortium of fifty-one private investors, including dozens of auto industry suppliers and business partners, to finance the project's eventual $330 million cost. Designed by architect John Portman and completed in 1977, the enclosed, fortress-like skyscraper, with massive concrete berms fronting a busy, ten-lane traffic artery, stood notoriously aloof from the rest of the city. The Ren Cen, as it became known, lost $130 million in its first five years of operation and failed to spark additional office investment downtown.[52]

By 1980 a survey showed that 35 percent of downtown first- and second-floor retail space remained vacant and sales were only one-half their level in 1967.[53] The collapse of the city center was underlined by the 1982 closing of Hudson's flagship Woodward Avenue store; the mammoth thirty-three-story structure would remain vacant for seventeen years before it was razed in 1999. Local financial institutions, in turn, shunned the city's redevelopment schemes. A 1988 report found that banks from Cleveland and other cities funded more of Detroit's downtown reinvestment than did local lenders; of $580 million for new projects, Detroit banks put up only 11 percent.[54] Finally, the city lost political leverage and millions of dollars in federal aid after the election of Ronald Reagan as president in 1980. By that time, white residents made up only about one-third of Detroit's population of 1.2 million.[55]

In the neighborhoods, legacies of racial segregation and white flight created an invisible wall between Detroit and the suburbs. Repelled by white hostility and aversion, many black Detroiters turned their loyalties inward to the city, relying on philosophies of racial nationalism and economic self-help. In turn, some white suburbanites expressed pride in never having to go below the border of 8 Mile Road.[56] Whatever their personal attitudes, and however much blacks and whites across the region worked together, they typically went home to different areas, attended different churches, and sent their kids to different schools.

As the city's crime rate rose in the 1970s and 1980s, Detroit became a stereotype for civic breakdown, inspiring the violent dystopian imagery of Hollywood movies like *Robocop* (1987) and *New Jack City* (1991).[57] Yet ordinary Detroiters proved remarkably resilient, organizing in their neighborhoods to control crime, drugs, and arson and voting to tax themselves to relieve the municipal fiscal crisis. Frustrated by the regional abandonment of the city, Mayor Young voiced increasing antagonism toward the suburbs, which now accounted for much of the Detroit papers' circulation.[58] In his first term, Young claimed to have a copy of a *Detroit News* internal memo promoting sensational stories of inner-city depravity, particularly the "horrors that are discussed at suburban cocktail parties." Although the *News* ran a page-one disclaimer, columnists like Pete Waldmeir continued to find a steady readership by criticizing the mayor, who did not hesitate to respond in kind.[59]

After five terms and twenty years in office, Young retired in 1993. He was succeeded by another African American candidate, former Michigan

Supreme Court justice Dennis Archer. As mayor, Archer offered a more moderate and conciliatory tone, hoping to repair relations with business elites and suburban and state governments. Slowly, investment dollars came back to downtown. In 1996, General Motors purchased the Renaissance Center for $73 million and moved its headquarters there from the New Center area in midtown. After rejecting similar proposals four times over the previous two decades, in 1994 Detroit voters approved a ballot initiative allowing casino gambling in the city. Two years later, a statewide referendum authorized three land-based casinos near the riverfront. Finally, in the late 1990s, construction began on a new downtown baseball stadium and adjacent professional football field, the former with $135 million in city, county, and state financing and the latter with $85 million in city funds alone.[60]

Aided by a national economic recovery, unemployment in Detroit fell from 12.5 percent in 1994 to 9.6 percent at the end of 2000. Nevertheless, the city faced constant problems of population loss, decaying infrastructure, and severe budgetary constraints. Acres of vacant property, burned-out buildings, and overgrown lots covered Detroit's 140 square miles, and in some areas the industrial city reverted startlingly to nature: on warm spring days, the smell of tall grass and wildflowers drifted over the air, and pheasants and other wildlife found refuge in the underbrush. Meanwhile, new housing and economic development continued to absorb greenfield land on the urban fringe. "Edge cities" like Troy and Auburn Hills in Oakland County attracted businesses and residential growth, and by 1990 substantial numbers of middle-class blacks had begun to move into suburban enclaves like Southfield.[61]

CONCLUSION: THE CIVIC ECOLOGY OF DETROIT

Social scientist June Manning Thomas notes an apparent paradox of Detroit history: a city with a single dominant industry and a powerful union movement lacked a central, long-term urban development partnership or leadership coalition.[62] The anomaly, however, reflects the ecology of civic engagement that emerged in Detroit. The automakers generated enormous wealth, but rarely focused their attention on the city proper. Through decades of strife, Detroit workers built strong unions in the workplace, achieving some of the highest labor market density in the nation. Yet even after employers agreed to bargain, negotiations often remained adversarial, and as jobs moved outward the unions followed. No broad and powerful public or private institutions arose to plan economic development, coordinate elite decision-making, or mediate conflicts among groups.

Within the labor movement, workers inherited an unusually strong culture of labor solidarity. In the postwar era, political scientists J. David Greenstone and Paul Peterson write, "the 1930s depression-generated battle between labor and management in the automobile industry left a legacy of class identification and awareness in Detroit and Michigan politics almost comparable to class consciousness in western European countries."[63] For generations of Detroiters of all kinds, the collective memory persisted even decades later. "I grew up in a strong union household," *Free Press* executive Neal Shine recalled. "We didn't buy bread that was made by a company that wasn't unionized. We didn't go to the barbershops where you get a cut-rate haircut because the barbers weren't in the unions." "Detroit is a hugely strong labor town," Shine concluded. "It's a town that exists on organized labor."[64]

By the 1980s, suburbanized workers were no longer the dispossessed, hungry masses of the 1930s, but conflicts at work had hardly disappeared. The region was traumatized by the downturn in the auto industry at the start of the decade, and only a federal bailout narrowly averted bankruptcy at the Chrysler Corporation. By 1982, over 250,000 autoworkers in Michigan had lost their jobs, and in Wayne County alone, forty-two auto-related companies closed their factories between 1978 and 1981.[65] In the UAW, differences over concession bargaining led to the break-off of the Canadian Auto Workers union in 1985, and UAW membership fell from a peak of 1.5 million in the late 1970s to around 800,000 two decades later.[66]

The American automakers rebounded, however, during the economic boom of the 1990s. Sales in the United States reached around 15 million vehicles for an unprecedented six consecutive years from 1994 to 1999, led by the Big Three's success in producing and marketing light trucks, minivans, and sport utility vehicles (SUVs). In southeastern Michigan, high-wage manufacturing employment grew by 69,000 jobs from 1990 to 1998, and General Motors, Ford, and Chrysler re-centered their corporate design and technical facilities in the area. With the resurgence of the industry, the UAW took a more aggressive stance in contract negotiations, organizing short-term, strategic strikes to maintain unionized jobs and resist outsourcing to non-union suppliers.[67]

In Detroit a culture of solidarity endured, even across the boundaries of race. On the shop floor, as union organizer Roger Robinson said in 1991,

> even with the racism and the craziness, you go into most auto plants and the Black workers and the white workers generally look out for one another. . . . In a plant where the white tendency is Polish, you have a Black-Polish coalition. Where it's Italian, you have a Black-Italian coalition. Or a Black–southern white coalition. There's a political culture in the industrial

unions where coalitions are made based on real power. And they don't even necessarily *like* each other.[68]

The legacy extended beyond the auto factories. At the *Free Press*, newsroom secretary Jocelyn Faniel-Heard, an African American native of Detroit, got involved in the union almost from the day she started in 1976, serving as vice chair of the *Free Press* bargaining unit and as an officer in the local Newspaper Guild. Faniel-Heard's father had joined the International Brotherhood of Electrical Workers (IBEW) in the 1950s, and her cousins were members of the UAW and the Detroit Federation of Teachers (DFT). "I was raised in a union family," she said. "I believe in trade unionism to the depths of my being."[69]

At the *News*, editorial assistant Alesia Cooper-Cunningham was not active in the union when she started as a clerk at the paper in 1988. But her father had been on strike at Ford when she was a child, and "my mom was very supportive of it," she said. "I don't know if it's just, you know, because being African American, knowing what we went through, and then the unions, although bad and good, there was bad and good in that, but you know, if it wasn't for the union they wouldn't have gotten the wages they got." When the newspaper strike began, she recalled, "the only thing I kept thinking about was, you know, if I sit here and do nothing, my ancestors, they could have just sat there and did nothing, and I wouldn't be where I was."[70]

The tensions of race and class were likewise reflected in the newspapers' content and audience. The *News* held steady as the conservative Republican voice of the establishment, while the *Free Press* evolved into a liberal, Democratic alternative for the middle-class children and grandchildren of Neal Shine's Detroit. Both papers appealed to the growing suburban market, while relations with the inner-city black community were often ambivalent. Yet Faniel-Heard and Cooper-Cunningham each remembered the newspapers as an integral part of everyday life. Faniel-Heard's family had the *Free Press* delivered to their home in the north end of Detroit. Cooper-Cunningham, who lived on the southwestern edge of the city, recalled that in the 1960s and 1970s, "I would say [the *News* and *Free Press*] had a close relationship with the community. . . . I remember there wasn't a house probably on my block where I grew up that didn't get one of the papers, the *Free Press* or the *News*. It was just something you did at that time."[71]

With all of its contradictions, the Detroit area supported a thriving market and an intensely engaged public for news. "Race riots, urban blight, population loss, and the decline of the auto industry did nothing to slake Detroiters' thirst for news of their troubled home," wrote former *News* reporter Bryan Gruley. By the mid-1980s, the *News* and the *Free Press* were the ninth- and tenth-largest daily papers in the country, with a combined daily circulation of 1.2 million and more readers per capita than any other big daily in the country.[72] *Free Press* music writer Gary Graff, a native of Pittsburgh, recalled the vitality of the news culture that he found on moving to Detroit in 1982. "[The newspapers] were very strong in the community . . . people really read and consumed the papers. You got a sense that part of the daily routine of Detroit was consuming the newspaper in addition to all the other news media. You know, I think some of that was definitely helped by the competitiveness of it at that time, the great newspaper battle at that time."[73]

Reporter Joe Swickard, Graff's colleague at the *Free Press*, agreed. When he started in 1979, he recalled, "one of the things that really struck me was just the volume of phone calls coming in to the city desk from citizens, residents, city officials. I mean, I really felt I was a part of a major component of a big American city, that people were really connected with the newspaper. People called to complain about things, they called for solutions, they called with news tips. And I think they felt that their voice would be heard when they called, that there was a very personal connection with the paper. And I think that there was a sense that the *Free Press* really was, I don't want to sound like a commercial, but like a fabric, a part of the fabric of the community, really cared about what was going on. And that really impressed me, and I really wanted to be a part of that. It was something that really mattered in a city that I felt was important."[74]

In their competition with each other, the two papers depended on a high level of public trust, and their relations with the community permeated the entire labor of the enterprise. In the newspaper business, there was no easy divide between the workplace, on the one hand, and the community, on the other. The workplace was not confined to a single downtown newsroom or suburban printing plant; on the contrary, it extended throughout the metropolitan area, to every county news bureau and distribution warehouse, to every district manager's neighborhood station and every driver's route. The next chapter looks more closely at the process of producing and distributing a daily newspaper, the impact of technical and organizational change, and their effects on the participants in the process in Detroit.

Chapter 3 | A "Daily Miracle": The Life of the Workplace

IN 1979, THIRTY-THREE-YEAR-OLD Leo Jenkins Jr. left his factory job and hired on as a district manager for the *Detroit Free Press*, distributing newspapers to carriers, stores, newsstands, and coin-operated boxes, or "racks," near his home on the west side of Detroit. The husky, genial Detroit native already had three sons delivering papers. Now he supervised up to fifty boys, girls, and adult carriers in his district. Under the "buy-sell" system, Jenkins and his crew would collect money from subscribers and retailers, pay for the papers at wholesale, and keep the difference; together, they acted as small-business persons and neighborhood sales ambassadors for the newspapers. For Jenkins, a member of Teamsters Local 372, it was "like a family affair." "Every district manager had his own paper station which was in the area that he delivered. All the customers knew where the paper station was. They could come up to the station, see the district manager if they got complaints about their carrier or their service. It was very personified." That relationship, Jenkins believed, sustained the papers' circulation against competition from other media. "We had it so personalized that we had literally fooled people that there's only one way to get information and that's from the newspaper."[1]

Twenty-five years later, Jenkins was still working for the newspapers, but his job looked very different. Instead of a neighborhood station, he now worked out of the central printing plant in the suburbs, far from his home, servicing stores and racks in a territory three times the size of his old district. Handled in a separate department, home delivery employed only adult agents, who carried hundreds of papers by car or van on extensive routes. The newspaper agency billed subscribers directly, collecting money and valuable data on them along the way. Jenkins was paid straight salary and no longer dealt directly with the carriers, and new subscriptions were coordinated through a telemarketing program.

At first glance, the issues in the Detroit newspaper strike might seem to have been about purely business matters like wages and compensation, job classifications and layoffs, and other dollars-and-cents subjects. But these often dry, technical issues are also about what people do for a living, how they do it, and who will benefit. We cannot make sense of the strike without first understanding the contract negotiations that preceded it, and we cannot make sense of the contract negotiations without appreciating the work that people actually do. As an urban service sector, the newspaper "workplace" is spread out over literally hundreds of sites across a wide metropolitan area; it is located at the interstices between public space and private production and consumption. As a result, decisions about those workplace relationships touch the lives of businesses, workers, and residents throughout the community.

At a micro level, the labor process in the industry and the work that newspaper employees do lie at the intersection of the economic and civic development paths discussed in chapters 1 and 2. This chapter focuses on that labor and how it has changed. Starting from a baseline description of the traditional methods for producing a daily newspaper, I review the technological changes that swept through the industry from the 1960s on. In Detroit the effects of these changes began to take hold by the 1980s and can be seen in the experiences of the employees at the *News* and the *Free Press*. By the late 1980s, the sale of the *News* to Gannett and the formation of the joint operating agreement with Knight-Ridder promised even greater ruptures, foreshadowing the confrontation that emerged in the 1995 strike.

THE FRONT PAGE: NEWSPAPER
PRODUCTION IN THE TWENTIETH CENTURY

News is a perishable product, produced in constantly renewed batches or runs that cannot be stockpiled—yesterday's newspaper is, after all, yesterday's news. Producing a daily paper traditionally required the careful and intense coordination of several distinct labor processes, including writing and editing, typesetting and page composition, plate-making and press operation, and packing and distribution. These processes required much skilled, semiskilled, and often arduous physical labor, some of it performed under conditions once described as "a combination of a dungeon and a blacksmith shop, with the added discomforts of ink mists and loud noises."[2] Because of the pressure of deadlines, these integrated production activities—divided among areas known as the newsroom, the composing room, the pressroom, and the mailroom and docks—were often located in close proximity or in the same building.[3]

At a typical newspaper of the 1960s, reporters gathered information in the field or by telephone and then typed their stories in a central news-room or called them in to a rewrite desk; other copy came in by teletype from remote bureaus or wire services. Various news, sports, and features desk editors would assign and evaluate the stories, request changes, and decide their length and placement on the page. News photographers brought in their film to develop in the paper's darkroom, and pictures were selected for publication. Finally, a team of copy editors checked and trimmed the finished stories, wrote headlines, and captioned photos. In a separate department, advertising staff received classified ads, while account representatives managed larger clients' needs and design specialists prepared display ads and page layout.[4]

News and advertising copy came together in the composing room, the "biggest and busiest staging area in the newspaper production line."[5] In the old hot-metal era, dozens of typesetters entered text into rows of bulky Linotype machines, a few of which might run on prepunched perforated tape. The machines automatically justified the lines of type and cast them from heated liquid metal into thin slugs, which were assembled into galleys, proofread, and matched with headlines. Following a page dummy sketched by the editors, compositors set the ads first and then filled the remaining news hole with stories and pictures. Historically, typesetting was the most highly skilled, labor-intensive core of the entire newspaper production process. Even as mechanization caused other skills to branch off, the typographers kept the name of "printers," and workers in the composing room called their shop organizations "chapels," recalling the roots of the printing craft in the monasteries of early modern Europe.

By the twentieth century, a variety of other trades had emerged as part of the production process. Thus, as newspapers came to feature photographs in their pages, engravers used special cameras to convert film negatives into half-tone images to be etched onto metal plates. The completed typeset page, called a "chase," was locked in a frame and sent to skilled stereotypers, who pressed a papier-mâché mat onto it and used the impression to cast a curved metal printing plate. The curved printing plates, each weighing up to forty-seven pounds, were then sent to the pressroom and attached to the rotary press machines.

Conventional newspaper presses consisted of several components forming a "unit" that might occupy several floors. Underneath, large "reels" holding multiple, one-ton rolls of newsprint fed a continuous web of paper into the press, automatically pasting a new roll onto a nearly spent one while the press was running. Above, the web might pass through several press cylinders stacked on top of each other to print on both sides or in different colors. On letter presses, the inked printing plates applied type directly to the paper. The pressmen (who were nearly always men) prepared the machines for operation, fixed the plates, ink levels, and web tension, and checked quality during the run. The printed pages were mechanically cut into broadsheet or tabloid size, folded, and moved by conveyor to a large warehouse area called the mailroom.[6]

In the mailroom, workers inserted preprinted supplements like comics, feature magazines, and special advertisements. The papers were counted, stacked, bundled and tied, and taken to adjacent loading docks. There, strong-backed workers called "jumpers" loaded the bundles onto semi-tractor-trailers for shipment to distribution centers or onto smaller "bread trucks" for local delivery. The step-van drivers took the bundles from the printing plant or distribution center to area newsstands, retail outlets, and coin-operated racks for single-copy sales and to neighborhood stations for pickup by the young carriers who delivered papers to individual subscribers' homes.

Stop the Presses: Technological Change and Workplace Reorganization

With few modifications, this basic process remained stable from the early twentieth century until around the 1960s. Over the next generation, however, employers introduced a series of new technologies that transformed the entire system. Beginning in the composing room, "cold type" replaced hot metal with a photographic process that produced columns of type on sensitive paper, which were cut and pasted onto cardboard page dummies using razors and a waxlike glue. Similarly, half-tone images no longer required engraved metal plates but could be printed and pasted alongside the text. The completed pages were then photographed and projected onto thin, lightweight metal or polymer plates weighing just a few ounces. Compositors were still needed to operate the photo-typesetting machines and do layout, but cold type drastically reduced composing room labor and virtually eliminated the work of engravers and stereotypers.[7]

The adoption of cold type fostered backward and forward linkages that affected both the newsroom and the pressroom.[8] With the computerization of the newsroom, reporters and editors could write and manage copy electronically and have it printed out without re-typesetting. In time, digital cameras would eliminate the darkroom, desktop pagination would replace pasteup by hand, and a complete newspaper could be laid out on computer and transmitted directly to the pressroom. Page composition gradually shifted to the newsroom, and the composing room, once the core of the production process, was made largely redundant.

In the pressroom, the polymer plates could be fitted onto older letter presses but were especially compatible with newer offset presses. With offset, images from the plate cylinders were transferred first to a blanket cylinder and then onto the printing surface, through a chemical process using oil and water to separate inked from non-inked areas. Conversion from letter to offset machines called for a high initial investment but allowed for better quality, faster runs, and more sophisticated color separation using microprocessor controls. The changes both deskilled and reskilled pressroom labor: plate-handling and make-ready time were reduced, but more careful press maintenance and monitoring of water and ink levels was required. Finally, when electronic transmission permitted the physical separation of editorial and press functions, newspapers began to relocate their printing plants away from their downtown headquarters to remote suburban sites with better highway access.[9]

Automation came more slowly in the mailroom, but eventually machines would take over much of the work of counting, stacking, bundling, and tying papers. More importantly, the growing business in advertising inserts—which rose in volume nationally from 8 million to 27 million pieces during the 1970s—turned the mailroom from a cost center into a profit center. Advertising sales shifted emphasis from traditional run-of-press display ads to more lucrative zoned inserts targeting zip codes, made easier with digital tracking of subscribers. As circulation moved to the suburbs, home delivery replaced kids on bicycles with adults in automobiles hauling hundreds of papers over much larger territories.[10]

A New Order? Governing the Labor Process

Together, the new methods raised productivity and eliminated thousands of blue-collar jobs. One study of 493 U.S. dailies found that the number of composing room workers fell by more than half between 1970 and 1983. Wages declined along with employment: real hourly wages for newspaper production workers fell almost 26 percent between 1976 and 2000, from $18.58 to $13.81.[11] At the same time, job skills and responsibilities were radically redefined. In the newsroom, copy editors took on much of the work of layout and pagination, while reporters produced "content" for television and Internet outlets as well as the daily print edition. With corporate consolidation, and with their own compensation tied to financial performance, local publishers and editors lost discretionary freedom on issues from budgets to personnel to the size and shape of stories.[12] As marketing and production imperatives increasingly dominated the newsroom, "stress fractures appeared everywhere along the traditional wall between business and editorial," former Gannett executive editor Geneva Overholser observed.[13]

On the printing and distribution side, newspaper owners and unions fought a decades-long war over the number of jobs and the organization and governance of the workplace. Much of the controversy centered on union claims of "jurisdiction," management charges of "featherbedding," and related questions of shop-floor supervision. For managers, the concept of union jurisdiction—associated with excess staffing, anachronistic work rules, and the gratuitous obstruction of progress—was anathema. In their view, jurisdiction issues interfered with their right to manage, introduce new technology, assign job duties, and determine the most efficient organization of work. As an editor for the *News* declared, "Management owns the jobs," and management had the right to do with them as it saw fit.[14]

To the unions, however, jurisdiction meant nothing less than the employer's obligation to bargain with the workers who performed those jobs. The attorney for the Detroit printers' union explained it this way: "[The] composing room sometimes can be considered a physical place. To the union it's the [bargaining] unit, and the work we do, no matter where that work is done . . . it is this work which gives meaning and content to the concept of a bargaining unit."[15] The content of the work might change, activities might be added or dropped, and the boundaries of the workers' duties could be altered with the introduction of new machines. But jurisdiction required employers to negotiate those changes, not simply impose them, and to maintain the legitimately constituted bargaining relationship with the employees.

Ever since the invention of the Linotype in the late nineteenth century, the International Typographical Union had successfully embraced technological innovation, incorporating the skills needed for new machines into its apprenticeship and training programs. Similarly, installing and operating the expensive, complicated presses often required dozens of on-the-job custom adaptations and mechanical fixes by press operators steeped in the nuances and unique personalities of the machines and their local environment. These applications of jurisdiction gave craft unions a role in the direction as well as the execution of skilled labor, including the training and hiring of competent workers, the assignment of job duties, and the day-to-day supervision on the shop floor.[16] As new forms of work emerged, different unions might make competing claims of jurisdiction over jobs or the assignment of tasks, sometimes resulting in costly disputes and lengthy arbitrations or National Labor Relations Board proceedings. But the stakes in these contests were not trivial, because without a claim of jurisdiction, employers might have no accountability to any union.

Indeed, in the postwar era newspaper employers used technical change to try to abolish the craft governance of the labor process. Over the course of several bitter strikes during the 1940s and 1950s, the printers effectively lost their apprenticeship system and their capacity to supply reskilled labor for the new technologies. By the 1960s, it was clear that employers aimed not merely to modernize the composing room but to do away with it entirely. The typographers' strikes of the subsequent decade represented a last hurrah for the union as it gradually surrendered its jurisdiction, allowing management to reduce jobs in exchange for buyouts or lifetime employment guarantees for the existing workers.[17] Before long, managers began to see even the remaining union members as redundant and attempted to renege on their agreements, claiming that the "lifetime" guarantees lasted only for the life of the contract.[18] By then, companies like Gannett had already assumed a non-union standard in their small-town papers. At the big-city dailies, disputes over jurisdiction were reduced to the question of whether or not there would be any negotiating relationship at all.

Far from a simple question of technical progress, the reorganization of production changed the relationship of the newspaper enterprise to its workforce and its service community. In Detroit the changes took effect gradually and unevenly, their larger impact not always apparent at first. Altogether, however, they shifted the ground affecting the everyday experience of the workers employed at the two newspapers.

MAKING A NEWSPAPER AND A COMMUNITY: THE NEWS AND THE FREE PRESS

For aspiring young journalists, the city of Detroit in the 1970s and 1980s was an exciting regional magnet, with top-ranked metropolitan dailies offering big-league professional opportunities. Among the career-seekers was Nancy Dunn, who got a job at the *Free Press* in 1986 as a special sections editor, working in the features department on the fifth floor of the old Lafayette Street building. A fourth-generation "ink-stained wretch" from a family of newspaper workers in Port Huron, Dunn had attended Marygrove College in Detroit and worked first at several small-town papers in southeastern Michigan. "It was a plum job to come into the *Free Press* and start," she recalled. "As grueling as the job was, it was a wonderful job because it was just, you know, plunged right into the middle of the muck of putting out that paper and listening to all the politics and picking up on running with it, and it was wonderful."[19]

For those who worked there, the two papers' downtown offices embodied the image of newspaper journalism as both intrepid public service and a vital communications system for the civic community. Dunn later moved to the third-floor newsroom of the *Free Press*, covering Michigan political news and elections as state editor. She recalled the rows of desks jammed together in a long, shotgun-style room, with worn carpeting and computer wires hanging from the ceiling. The newsroom stretched the length of the building and was directly across the hall from the composing room on the third floor. Off the first-floor lobby were offices for Reuters and United Press International, along with a floral shop and the Press Galley, a greasy spoon and local hangout where reporters met contacts, employees grabbed coffee on their way to the elevators, and workers from nearby office buildings stopped in for lunch.

Alan Forsyth did stints as a copy editor at both the *Free Press* and the *News*, beginning in 1980. At the *Free Press*, Forsyth worked on the third floor with around ten other copy editors on the "rim" of the U-shaped copy desk, with the lead editor in the "slot" in the middle. At the *News*, Forsyth remembered, the L-shaped newsroom on the second floor was a larger, more open space, but still noisy. The two newsrooms were intensely competitive with each other. The *Free Press* had flourished, especially in the 1970s, under its brilliant, mercurial executive editor Kurt Luedtke. In the 1980s, however, the *News* emerged from a long torpor to produce its best journalism in years and become, in Forsyth's view, arguably the better paper.[20]

At the *Free Press*, Forsyth sent his finished copy to the slot editor, who with a single keystroke transmitted it to the profoundly transformed composing room. With the movement to cold type and digital layout, the Detroit Typographical Union Local 18 had over the course of several contracts negotiated a series of specific exceptions to its jurisdiction. In 1974 it bargained a landmark agreement that surrendered the computer entry of all news and editorial copy and single-column classified ads. The union retained only the inputting of display ads and their related codes, formatting, and final page makeup. The incumbent printers received lifetime job guarantees, and management gained a free hand to downsize the composing room.[21]

According to one estimate, in 1970 it took about 1,100 printers to typeset both the *Free Press* and the *News* using hot metal. Twenty-five years later, around 100 employees accomplished the same job on computers.[22] By the 1990s, the only new hires in composing were a handful of part-timers like Barb Ingalls, who started work in July 1994. Married to a United Auto Workers member, the thirty-eight-year-old Ingalls had never before worked in the newspaper industry. A year after hiring in, she was on strike. "Don't come to me for career counseling," she quipped.[23]

As late as the 1970s, both papers maintained integrated production sites downtown, and old-timers could recall how the *Free Press* building's lower floors would vibrate when the basement presses roared into action. Down the street, one former union representative recalled, "on a Saturday night you could walk in the *News'* old Lafayette building and you couldn't see from one end of the pressroom to the other, that's how thick the ink mist was. When you finished a shift, you spit black." With all the noise from the machines, workers in the pressroom risked significant hearing loss by the time they reached retirement.[24]

In September 1979, Knight-Ridder executives presided at the opening of a new $50 million printing plant on a twenty-two-acre site at the foot of Tenth Street along the Detroit riverfront. The new plant came complete with six seven-unit Goss Metroliner offset presses, making the *Free Press* then the largest paper in the nation to be printed with offset.[25] Six years earlier, the *News* had moved its presses and mailroom to its new $40 million facility in Sterling Heights. To save money, the *News* had chosen to install Goss Headliner Mark V letter presses, but was later forced to do several expensive modifications to convert those machines to a form of offset.[26]

Of all the workers in newspaper production, the press operators retained the most features of craft labor. Management hired from a union list, and members maintained work standards in shops across the metropolitan labor market. Many were second or even third generation in the trade, and they embodied southeastern Michigan's industrial culture of manufacturing and metalworking. Jack Howe came from a family of tool and die makers in Howell, about fifty miles from Detroit. He started as an apprentice at the *Free Press* in 1963, got his journeyman's card in 1967, and then went to the *News*, working his way up through the union until he became president of Graphic Communications International Union (GCIU) Local 13N in 1993.[27] By that time, however, the pressroom was shrinking, its apprenticeship program was inactive, and the papers wanted more cuts in staffing.

In the mailroom, the demand for labor followed the volume of advertising, which varied by season or even by the day. As in similar seasonal or spot labor markets, employers often turned to their own employees' personal and family networks to find reliable workers on short notice.[28] Anyone starting out had to begin on a part-time or "permit" basis, with no benefits, working on call maybe only a day or two every two weeks at first. Ben Solomon's father helped him get a mailroom job in 1973, when Ben was just eighteen years old. The young Solomon spent four and a half years as a part-timer before making it to full-time. "Every Monday in the old rotary phone days where you had to keep dialing and dialing, I would have black rings on my fingers from trying to get through to the office" to see if there was work, he recalled.[29]

As in the pressroom and the composing room, the companies hired mailroom workers from a union referral list. Jim St. Louis was an active member and officer of the mailers union, Local 2040 of the International Brotherhood of Teamsters. A native of Detroit, he had followed his father and his grandfather into the business. Like Solomon, he was eighteen when he started in 1977, working on a part-time basis. "But it was a decent hourly rate," St. Louis said.

> And if you stuck that out, you would eventually move up the list that when you got to the top of the list, if they needed full-time workers, then you would be next in line for that full-time job. And a lot of people would come and go because they wouldn't wait. And you would find that it was more people who had families in there who would say, "Stick it out, it's worth the wait. It's a good job once you get it." And it was a good job.[30]

On any given day, up to three hundred full- and part-time workers might be called in for the combined day and night shifts at the two newspaper plants, and on Saturdays the number might rise to four or five hundred. Much of the mailroom labor involved operating the machines that put advertisements and other special supplements into the papers. The machines featured a series of "heads" or "buckets" located around a circular or oblong conveyor called a "merry-go-round." Workers stationed at each head would feed preprinted inserts into the machine, which dropped them into the opened papers as they moved along in the buckets.[31] St. Louis explained the process:

> You have a skid next to you of all, let's say it was a Sears [insert], and in this skid there's maybe five thousand Sears products, same circular, and you would take them off by the handful and shuffle them, as we called it, so you're fanning them out, straightening them, getting the air out of them. Sometimes you have to put 'em in there, different ways for different parts. Sometimes curl up, curl down, put a hump, you know, you're actually literally feeding this machine so that it reaches out and grabs one and drops it in each paper and it goes by.[32]

The work was physically demanding, but more than just machine-tending; the fragile newsprint was often subject to paper jams or mechanical failure. Some stations were more difficult than others, and workers would help each other out or rotate positions during shifts to reduce the risk of wrist or back injury. "We always got extra people because [the newspapers] wanted the boat to sail smoothly," recalled Solomon. "And the management was always pretty good up to that point about giving us enough people to make the floor run." Frontline supervisors were themselves often former mailers who maintained cordial relations with the union leadership. "[Management] did the paperwork, but the [union] chairmen actually took care of the floor. They took care of what we needed, how it was going to get done, basically, and everything else."[33] Between the hiring list and the informal regulation of work on the shop floor, the mailers also functioned much like a traditional craft. In fact, at one time the Detroit mailers had been affiliated with the International Typographical Union, and like the printers, local leaders still used the name "chapel" to refer to their bargaining unit.

From the mailroom the papers were shipped out from the loading docks by workers like Tom Breyer, whose wife, Janice, was a clerical worker for the newspaper agency. A member of Teamsters Local 372, Tom Breyer worked as a pool driver and jumper, commuting from his home in Grosse Pointe Farms to printing plants and distribution centers throughout the metro area. His job description called for him to be able to lift and carry two thousand or more bundles of papers weighing an average of thirty-two pounds per bundle, or the equivalent of thirty-two tons per day. Occasionally, Breyer might have to do a split shift, working from 2:00 AM to 6:00 AM and then again from 10:00 AM to 2:00 PM in a warehouse some thirty-five miles from his home. Other times, he recalled, "I would go in at three on Saturday afternoon, work three to eleven and then eleven to seven, and it was not overtime because three to eleven was the Saturday shift and then eleven to seven was the Sunday shift. So you worked sixteen straight hours, and those were tough too."[34]

Finally, delivery to the stores, racks, and carriers was supervised by district managers like Leo Jenkins, Mike Fahoome, Paul Kulka, and Dennis Nazelli. Under the buy-sell system, the papers externalized the cost and risks of delivery. District managers were like small-business persons: they were responsible for handling the books and taking care of any and all problems on their routes. Mike Fahoome grew up in Detroit and in 1975 got a job with the *News* in one of the toughest districts in the city. "People would take the job, and they would last maybe six months if they were lucky," Fahoome remembered. "Every night I used to come home and tell my wife to call them [and say] I quit, because I'd been putting in fifteen, sixteen hours. But after the first year, when I filled all the routes, it started to get a little easier, and over a period of time I developed a good relationship with the dope addicts and everyone in the city where they stayed away from my kids and I stayed away from what they were doing."

The Arab American Fahoome was a strict manager but also developed a strong loyalty in his young African American carriers. "If there was a problem [with collections], I would take the child out and I'd knock on the doors myself and I'd get that money, or I would reimburse the kid and get rid of the customer because if he's a no-pay he doesn't need to have a child out there delivering and paying for his paper." As a result, Fahoome won regular incentive prizes from the papers, and at one point he took a company-sponsored trip to Florida with all twenty-five of his carriers, while their parents or family members covered their routes.[35]

Other district managers cultivated similar relationships and took an active role in the local community. Leo Jenkins met with parents and schoolteachers in his Detroit neighborhood, and Paul Kulka managed a youth baseball program in suburban Sterling Heights. To keep his carriers motivated, Dennis Nazelli would take them to Tigers games or play ball with them himself in a local park. One of his charges was a kid named Randy Karpinen, who was always handy around the district station. When Karpinen turned nineteen, Nazelli helped him get a job as a jumper on the loading dock.[36]

CONCLUSION: THE LABOR OF THE ENTERPRISE

In all of these working relationships, the employees of the *News* and the *Free Press* embodied the social being and collective use-value of the enterprise, the soul of the daily newspaper in Detroit. Their labor bridged the economics of the industry and the patterns of interaction in everyday urban life. As changes in technology and business practice altered relations in the workplace, so too did they affect the newspapers' presence in the local civic ecology, their organizational footprint, and their popular identity.

By the late 1980s, an era in Detroit newspaper history was coming to a close. With the creation of the JOA, the management at the papers was rapidly transformed. At the *Free Press*, "management of the production operations, advertising, [and] circulation all became a function of the Detroit Newspaper Agency," Neal Shine observed. "And so the only management functions that were retained by the *Free Press* were managing the editorial staff. That didn't change. Management of everything else changed. It became effectively Gannett management."[37]

The new leadership immediately implemented major structural changes, dropping the morning edition of the *News* and cutting back on outstate circulation. "The joint operating management didn't care very much about that circulation because it was expensive to deliver it," said *Free Press* business editor Tom Walsh. "And the advertisers didn't care about it because the advertisers that were mostly buying were in the three-county metro area."[38] Before the JOA, Gannett had claimed a daily circulation of 670,000 at the *News* compared to less than 650,000 for the *Free Press*. Four months after the JOA began, the *Free Press* led 639,000 to 526,000, a loss of more than 140,000 for the *News*.[39]

The structural changes were difficult enough, but they were also accompanied by a new level of antagonism, especially at the *News*. Mike McBride was a Detroit native and a seventeen-year newsroom veteran as a reporter and editorial assistant at the *News*. Gannett's arrival "had kind of shaken up the culture there," he recalled. "Their approach to journalism, for one thing. In general, reporters there thought it was a lower level of journalism. Two, they were bringing in a lot of editors from their smaller newspapers, and many of the reporters and longtime writers at the *News* felt that we were getting people without the level of experience or skill in those positions that needed to be there."

Equally important, the new management clashed with the union culture in Detroit. McBride noted, "I think Gannett and [*News* publisher] Bob Giles, in particular, I think they were so used to work environments where they just dictated the terms and conditions that when they came into Detroit where there's a long-standing labor union tradition, and in many ways a very highly professionalized workforce, much more than what they were used to working with before, it was something that they did not adapt to very easily, or very well."[40] Nor did they intend to adapt to it. Ben Burns was the executive editor at the *News* during the 1980s; he left the paper after it was purchased by Gannett and later became head of the journalism program at Wayne State University in Detroit. "I learned early on about the Gannett culture and what those guys were going to do," he recalled. "I think they intended to get major concessions, and if they didn't get major concessions in negotiations, they were going to get them by a strike."[41]

It would take several years to become a reality, but the introduction of the JOA would decisively alter the organization of the newspaper workplace in Detroit. Gannett and Knight-Ridder had won their antitrust exemption on the premise that the *News* and the *Free Press* provided a vital public service and that the journalistic goal of preserving both papers merited special privileges from the government. What obligations then did they have to their employees, to their readers, and to the values of the public sphere in Detroit? Who were the stakeholders in that process, what kinds of changes would be made, and how would they be decided?

In their daily operations, the newspapers were deeply embedded in the life of the metropolitan community. But they were also private enterprises and employers in business to make a profit. In a capitalist economy, the capacity for labor, or the ability to show up for work every day and carry out one's duties, is also a commodity, an object to be bought and sold in the labor market. The rules for negotiating such transactions, the laws of collective bargaining, and the institutions governing the relations among the parties now take us into the realm of the state, discussed in part II. In that realm also the Detroit strike signaled a landmark change as it traced the arc of a declining New Deal system and the ascendance of an anti-union regime of industrial relations in the United States.

PART II | The Institutional Regulation of Labor

Chapter 4 | Proper Channels: U.S. Labor Law and Union– Management Relations

THE WORLDS OF THE WORKPLACE and the neighborhood, or industrial relations and community life, appear to our twenty-first-century eyes to be almost entirely separate. To an observer in late nineteenth- or early twentieth-century America, however, the links between these worlds would have been obvious. In the 1880s, the Knights of Labor attracted a cross-class alliance of small producers in a mass movement that sprang up in cities and towns throughout the country. Later, the craft unions in the American Federation of Labor (AFL) organized skilled workers into urban building trades and central labor councils to regulate local labor markets.[1] The Industrial Workers of the World (IWW) and other nascent factory unions grew out of immigrant working-class neighborhoods in the years before and after World War I, and during the 1930s the Congress of Industrial Organizations (CIO) emerged from the port cities on the East and West Coasts and the mill towns and auto hubs of the Northeast and Midwest. As late as 1946, citywide general strikes erupted across the nation, in Stamford, Connecticut; Rochester, New York; Pittsburgh, Pennsylvania; and Oakland, California.[2]

If that history seems distant to us now, the difference is more than just time. The post–World War II dispersal of industry and the long-term shift to suburban residence undoubtedly affected the forms of popular communal action, as political scientist Robert Putnam has argued.[3] On the other hand, advances in communication and transportation have also reduced the physical barriers to organization, and in urban service sectors the "workplace" can now encompass an entire metropolitan area. If the worlds of labor and community appear separate to us now, a crucial factor in that differentiation is their legal and institutional regulation by the state.

Government policy and labor law have been powerful factors affecting relations not only on the job but also between the workplace and the urban community. In the United States, the watershed moment in this history begins with the period before the 1930s and the New Deal revolution that followed. In a break with the past, the New Deal reforms recognized workers' rights to organize and established a limited framework for the democratic governance of industrial labor markets. The legal and administrative structure that was created, however, also privatized relations between employers and unions, separating workplace conflicts from their historic ties with the local community.

Within the New Deal framework, industrial relations within unionized sectors temporarily stabilized in the postwar decades in a broad set of formal and informal arrangements, or institutional "accord."[4] Even at its peak of influence, however, the accord was accompanied by a parallel, anti-union path of development. By the 1980s and 1990s, the New Deal system began to break down and the anti-union regime gained ascendancy. The conflict between the two opposing orders exploded in a series of bitterly contentious strikes, including the strike in Detroit. The former boundaries of struggle became blurred, and disputes spread out across the state and, once again, into the community.

Part I of this book traced the historical development of changes in the organization of the newspaper business, in the urban community, and in the labor and technology of producing and distributing a metropolitan daily newspaper. Those changes increased the pressures on the employment relationship, but did not by themselves preordain a confrontation between management and labor in Detroit. Rather, as I argue, the resources and incentives available to actors for managing conflict depend on the institutional context. By the 1990s, that context served to channel the actors, not toward a settlement, but toward the polarization that emerged in the newspaper strike.

LABOR RELATIONS IN THE UNITED STATES: THE NEW DEAL AND THE POSTWAR ACCORD

Prior to the 1930s, American unions confronted a legal environment that historians have described as "judicial repression."[5] For decades, federal courts had repeatedly struck down workers' rights to organize and act collectively, as violations of property rights and combinations in restraint of trade. With little administrative capacity to regulate industrial relations, government authorities typically entered into labor disputes as an external, blunt force. In the event of a major strike, conservative judges would issue swift injunctions that declared further protest to be an unlawful disruption of public order. All too often, then, strikes ended with the deployment of troops. In the landmark struggles of the period—of the steelworkers in Homestead, Pennsylvania, in 1892; in the nationwide Pullman rail strike of 1894; and in the mining strikes in Couer d'Alene, Idaho, in 1899 and Ludlow, Colorado, in 1912—the use of military power resulted in tragic losses of life.[6]

By contrast, the 1935 National Labor Relations Act (NLRA, or Wagner Act) marked a radical departure. As legal scholar Ellen Dannin notes, Congress recognized that corporate law had already "enhanced employer power by transforming them from individuals into collective beings, while leaving employees with only the power of the individual."[7] To rectify the imbalance, the Wagner Act declared it the policy of the United States to encourage the practice of collective bargaining, and it protected workers' rights to organize for the purpose of negotiating terms and conditions of employment or other mutual aid or protection. Protecting the right to organize and bargain collectively, section 1 of the law states, promotes commerce "by removing certain recognized sources of industrial strife and unrest, by encouraging practices fundamental to the friendly adjustment of industrial disputes as to wages, hours, and other working conditions, and by restoring equality of bargaining power between employers and employees."[8]

Under the NLRA, the federal government established an administrative system for legally recognizing union representation and managing industrial conflict. Over time, this relationship was articulated as a model of industrial pluralism, with unions as the democratically chosen representatives of workers, labor and management acting jointly as "legislators" in bargaining, the contract as the rule of law in the workplace, and legally sanctioned procedures for grievance and arbitration as a judicial system of due process and enforcement.[9] The law recognized the employment of labor as a relationship between *collective* actors and codified a form of dialogue between them. The result was a historic democratization of the American workplace and economy, embodied in the institutional arrangements of the postwar labor accord.

As the system took hold, its institutional mechanisms "locked in" a form of labor-management relations within the new workplace regime. At the same time, however, the procedural infrastructure that was created effectively channeled the resolution of labor disputes away from other actors in the local community. To be sure, American employers only reluctantly embraced the principle of unionism, both before and during the era of the accord.[10] But the New Deal system itself possessed institutional limits that not only hastened its decline but also shaped the terms of post-accord conflict and held fateful consequences for the development of industrial cities like Detroit. To highlight these "unlocking" mechanisms, we can focus on (1) *who* could gain access to the rights and benefits of unionization, (2) *what* could be negotiated, and (3) *how* disputes could be settled under the law.

These mechanisms allowed the "layering" of a non-union employment path alongside and in opposition to the unionized core.[11] Gradually, corporations began to shift employment and resources away from areas and sectors with established New Deal–style labor institutions in order to avoid unionization. The turning point came in the 1980s, when the management strategy of union avoidance grew into more aggressive efforts at displacement, even in traditionally unionized industries. Against the new employer offensive, unions were forced to reinvent the forms and tactics of strike mobilization.[12]

The Limits of the New Deal System: Who Gains Access?

Under the NLRA, American unions did gain considerable power to regulate their labor markets in the postwar era. In organized sectors, "pattern" bargaining with the leading employers standardized conditions and took wages out of competition among firms. Inside the firm, managers typically retained control over new hiring, but contractual provisions for seniority, promotion, recall, and due process for discipline and discharge helped stabilize employment and gave a hard-won job security to workers who had previously been exposed to arbitrary dismissal and often wild fluctuations in the availability of work. Union contracts also raised standards at non-union employers, who often improved conditions in order to avoid organizing efforts among their own employees. Nevertheless, divisions quickly emerged between higher-wage jobs in the unionized "core" of the corporate economy and a broad range of less stable, low-wage, non-unionized jobs in competitive sectors on the periphery.[13]

These divisions often overlapped with or reinforced existing patterns of discrimination in the labor market. At the behest of southern Democrats in Congress, the NLRA itself excluded agriculture and domestic service, which remained the largest employment sectors for African Americans as late as 1940.[14] In the skilled trades, most AFL craft unions were racially exclusive by custom or rule, while in manufacturing, minority workers commonly obtained only the lowest-paid, most dangerous jobs, and with low seniority they were typically "last hired, first fired." Some unions, notably those allied with the CIO and the left, worked to overcome these barriers, but many others did not.[15] The lack of access to good jobs aggravated problems of minority unemployment and poverty in central cities like Detroit, deepening the divide between urban black and suburban white civic and cultural spheres.[16]

The Limits of the New Deal System: What Gets Negotiated?

Second, employers and the government set strict limits on the kinds of issues that could be subject to collective bargaining. Decisions by the NLRB and the courts distinguished "mandatory" subjects covering issues of compensation and work rules from "permissive" issues, on which the parties could agree, but were not required, to negotiate.[17] From the start, managers adamantly resisted union efforts to bargain over permissive issues related to the direction and control of the firm. The question was effectively settled by the 1950 contract between the United Auto Workers and General Motors, in what sociologist Daniel Bell, writing in *Fortune* magazine, called the "Treaty of Detroit." The union won higher wages and benefits in exchange for improvements in productivity, while ceding to management the control of strategic decisions beyond the shop floor.[18] Thereafter, the typical collective bargaining contract included a "management rights" clause, reserving to the employer exclusive rights to determine investments in production and technology; the design, quality, and pricing of products and services; where to locate, expand, or close down plants and facilities; and all other matters not explicitly covered by the contract.[19]

In addition, bargaining was limited to those work sites and units with either voluntary employer recognition or NLRB certification and was typically conducted at the level of the plant or firm, not at the level of the industry. As a result, employers could and did erode bargaining units by reclassifying jobs and transferring work away from union jurisdiction. The 1947 Taft-Hartley Act excluded supervisors from protection and allowed states to ban the "union shop," and more than a dozen states, mainly in the South, quickly did so. Within the industrial core, companies began to relocate their factories away from unionized urban centers to suburban and rural areas, to the less-unionized southern states, and to other countries around the world.[20] In a remarkably short interval, the process of deindustrialization turned the once-powerful manufacturing cities of the Northeast and Midwest into the abandoned, distressed regions of the Rust Belt.

The effect of these boundaries was to support a rival, non-union path of development and give employers a crucial exit option. Taft-Hartley and judicial decisions denied labor rights to workers in expanding white-collar sectors of the economy, leaving unions concentrated in an eventually declining blue-collar sector. For emerging technical and professional occupations, employers could seek to have employees classified as managers or supervisors under the law, making them "exempt" from union protections.[21] Ultimately, the parallel layer of non-union labor would approach the norm even in traditionally unionized industries, increasing the pressure on those firms still committed to collective bargaining.[22] By the 1980s, the union avoidance strategy had developed into its own industry, providing an array of nationally known business consultants, law firms, industrial psychologists, and private security "strike management" services.[23]

The Limits of the New Deal System: How Are Disputes Settled?

Finally, unlike many other industrialized nations, the system of labor relations in the United States had another distinctive feature. Except in rare cases of national emergency, the government did not intervene in the bargaining process to ensure settlements. The law only set the ground rules for negotiation, and contracts remained voluntary agreements between unions and management. Yet the integrity of the process required that both parties be free to walk away from the table; indeed, otherwise the employment relationship would approach the character of involuntary labor.[24] Thus, the language of the NLRA explicitly protected the right to strike.

The law acknowledged the legitimate role of economic pressure as an incentive for management and labor to resolve their differences. The underlying threat of economic sanctions like strikes or lockouts served to push the two sides to compromise and move incrementally toward agreement through the bargaining process. The U.S. Supreme Court affirmed this relationship in its 1960 decision in the *Labor Board v. Insurance Agents International Union* case:

> The presence of economic weapons in reserve, and their actual exercise on occasion by the parties, is part and parcel of the system that the Wagner and Taft-Hartley Acts have recognized. . . . The two factors—necessity for good faith bargaining between parties, and the availability of economic pressure devices to each to make the other party incline to agree on one's terms—exist side by side.[25]

The system had built-in incentives to come to terms, and the strike remained a last resort. Work stoppages imposed pain on both sides: employers lost production and profits, and workers lost wages and their means of subsistence.[26] Nonetheless, though the law was intended to reduce industrial strife, it relied on the right to strike as an essential guarantee of the free exchange of labor.

Almost immediately, however, Congress and the courts began to erode the statutory protection for the right to strike. Although workers could not be fired for striking, the Supreme Court in its 1938 *Mackay Radio* decision ruled that if employees struck to achieve economic contract terms like wages and working conditions, the employer could hire "permanent" replacements and was not obliged to give the strikers their old jobs back when the strike was over. For most workers, of course, it made little difference whether one was fired or permanently replaced, and in time the decision would profoundly alter the balance of power between the two sides. For employers that could operate freely using permanent replacements during a strike had far fewer incentives to reach agreement at the bargaining table.[27]

The *Mackay* doctrine allowed firms not only to avoid unionization in new facilities but to displace unions in existing ones. For much of the postwar period, employers generally accepted the status quo ante in sectors where unions were well established. Conflict was contained within institutional boundaries, and restrictions on unions' sympathetic action under Taft-Hartley further bounded and compartmentalized disputes, turning public attention and responsibility away from what became framed as private market transactions.[28] Strikes were "civilized"; federal courts prohibited most "wildcat" strikes during the life of the contract and refused to protect strikes for permissive demands challenging managerial control.[29]

By the 1980s, however, even the limited protections for the strike were collapsing. In 1981, President Ronald Reagan summarily fired the striking federal air traffic controllers and busted their union, the Professional Air Traffic Controllers Organization (PATCO). As federal employees, the controllers were not covered by the NLRA, and Reagan's action had no direct effect on the law governing private-sector employers. The outcome of the PATCO strike, however, announced a fundamental change in the American government's attitude toward workers' rights. As subsequently implemented by Reagan's appointments to the NLRB, this new stance marked a critical juncture in the role of the national state in regulating labor disputes.[30]

With this opening, employers in traditionally unionized industries quickly adopted more aggressive tactics, seeking to end the practice of pattern bargaining and drive down the cost of labor. In the workplace, however, the transition to a post-accord labor regime was neither immediate nor peaceful. Rather, as their competing institutional paths crossed and grated against each other, the tensions between the old and new orders became concentrated in particular industries and locales. This can be seen in two highly contentious struggles of the period: the 1983 Phelps Dodge strike and the 1990 *New York Daily News* strike.

SHOCK AND AWE: IMPOSING
THE NEW ORDER

In the private-sector economy, the critical turning point was the 1983 strike of a coalition of Arizona copper mining unions, led by the United Steelworkers of America (USWA). In that year, the Phelps Dodge Corporation broke with other major copper producers and refused to agree to pattern contract terms. The miners then walked out, in a strike that began in June at the company's mines in Ajo, Bisbee, Douglas, and Morenci, Arizona. Determined to break the unions, the management hired permanent replacements and continued to operate the mines, using strategies developed by specialists at the University of Pennsylvania's Wharton School of Business. As they crossed the strikers' picket lines, the replacements were defended by Arizona state police and National Guard troops equipped with riot gear, tear gas, armored cars, and guns firing wooden bullets, while union meetings were infiltrated by agents of the state undercover Arizona Criminal Intelligence Systems Agency.[31]

To coordinate the litigation related to the strike, the Steelworkers brought in one of their top legal consultants, attorney Duane Ice. A native of rural Michigan whose slow midwestern drawl belied his tenacity, the thirty-six-year-old Ice was a partner in the Detroit labor law firm of Miller, Cohen, Martens, and Ice, which had earned a national reputation representing steelworkers, coal miners, and unions in the skilled trades.[32] In August 1983, Ice met with key union officials in Arizona and explained to them the recently issued U.S. Supreme Court decision in *Belknap v. Hale*. That decision allowed permanent replacements to sue if they were laid off in favor of returning strikers, reinforcing Phelps Dodge's position that the replacements were permanent from the outset. Moreover, as Ice pointed out, under existing law, if the strike lasted for more than one year the replacement workers, and not the strikers, could then vote to decertify the union.

In October 1984, aided by NLRB regional director and Republican appointee Milo Price, the replacements in the Phelps Dodge mines did exactly that. As journalist and historian Jonathan Rosenblum wrote in his account of the strike:

> When requests for decertification petitions began to come into the Phoenix NLRB office after one year into the strike, according to an NLRB source, Price took a direct role in distributing and filling out the petitions—a practice that had never before been observed. On a Friday afternoon in July 1984, Price ordered one investigator to drive the four hours to Morenci to help process petitions. . . . In a break from normal procedure, the board accepted decertification petitions simultaneously from employees and from the com-

pany. Prior to the Phelps Dodge strike, the board dropped company filings when it received one from union members. When the board allowed both in this strike, it effectively provided Phelps Dodge a kind of decertification insurance.

The results of the decertification election were released in January 1985: by a combined vote of 1,908 to 87, the replacement workers had voted to abolish the unions at all of the company's Arizona mines. The miners' strike formally came to an end in February 1986 when the unions' last legal appeals were finally exhausted. Shortly after the decertification vote, Rosenblum wrote, "Phelps Dodge gave another presentation at the Wharton School that included a forty-five minute videotape on how it broke the unions."[33]

The victory of Phelps Dodge was followed by a series of bellwether strikes in the 1980s—of New England paper workers, midwestern meatpackers, interstate bus drivers, and others—in which the employers' use of permanent replacements led to bitter defeats for the unions.[34] Soon even profitable employers began to demand steep concessions, in effect daring workers to strike, knowing that the outcome might easily result in displacing the union.[35] As employers pursued radical restructuring plans during the 1980s and early 1990s, the struggling unions found little aid from the federal government under the administrations of Ronald Reagan and George H. W. Bush. The result was a dramatic drop in the total number of strikes nationally as the meaning of the strike was transformed from a strategic bargaining mechanism and protected legal right into a high-risk protest tactic in defense of the principle of unionism itself.

The Impact on Negotiations: Impasse and Implementation

The newfound ease of replacement dovetailed with accumulating case law that allowed employers to unilaterally implement their last offer upon reaching impasse in bargaining. The previous mechanisms that once encouraged settlement were now reversed: employers gained incentives to reach impasse quickly and impose their preferred conditions, while unions often scrambled to stave off impasse and prevent implementation.[36] This dynamic was vividly illustrated in the 1990 strike at the *New York Daily News*, owned by the Chicago-based Tribune Company. The *Daily News* management hired Robert Ballow, of the Nashville, Tennessee, law firm of King and Ballow, to conduct negotiations with the unions representing its newsroom, production, and distribution employees.[37]

Known for an "uncompromising, point blank negotiating style," Ballow's typical approach was to open with a set of maximal demands that were often virtually suicidal for the union and to present them, in effect, as a final offer. At the same time, the employer would conspicuously beef up security and make it clear that it was already preparing to hire permanent replacements. The unions then had to make a choice: agree to Ballow's demands or risk declaration of impasse, or worse, strike and be permanently replaced and decertified. The result, as one sympathetic observer put it, frequently "ended with unions being effectively broken—if not actually decertified, then forced to accept contracts that make a mockery of union power."[38]

At the *Daily News*, Ballow's contract proposal eliminated nearly all rules governing working conditions, staffing levels, seniority rights, and even union security; offered a sweeping management rights clause; and asserted the right to cut hundreds of jobs without specifying an exact number.[39] Meanwhile, the newspaper more than tripled its internal security force and arranged for the standby services of an additional one thousand contract personnel. Supervisors cracked down on discipline in production and circulation, firing workers for even minor incidents or infractions of the rules. Anticipating a strike, management developed detailed contingency plans for each department to be ready to publish without missing a single day. More than one hundred replacement drivers and crew members were recruited and trained, and for months, along with other core replacements, they were lodged in nearby hotels at company expense and paid each day to be on call if needed. Altogether, the newspaper spent an estimated $34 million to $40 million on negotiations and pre-strike preparations.[40]

Against these tactics, the *Daily News* unions strained to avoid both impasse and a strike by maintaining negotiations, absorbing hits, and staying on the job. "We're going to wince, squirm, and blink a little," said one local union leader, "but we have jobs, and we're going to protect those jobs."[41] With the support of the AFL-CIO, the unions brought in Samuel McKnight, a forty-five-year-old Detroit labor attorney and a highly regarded expert in newspaper labor relations. McKnight urged the unions to hold tight while he laid the groundwork for a circulation and advertising boycott. The mobilization of public support, he believed, together with the millions of dollars per week it was costing the company to prepare for a strike, could persuade the management to seek a compromise.[42]

The two sides settled in for a siege war. All through the summer of 1990, the unions parried in negotiations while Ballow refused to make counterproposals, threatened to declare impasse, and began laying off scores of workers.[43] In October, an incident at the paper's Brooklyn printing plant led to a spontaneous walkout of a group of employees. The newspaper swiftly deployed permanent replacements, prompting the long-awaited strike. The company managed to produce the paper with replacements, but the unions successfully disrupted newsstand sales (which in New York accounted for up to 80 percent of *Daily News* circulation), and advertisers left for the rival tabloids *New York Post* and *New York Newsday*. Still, management refused to alter its bargaining stance, and the strike was at last ended in March 1991 when the Tribune Company agreed to sell the paper.[44]

The standoff in the *Daily News* negotiations crystallized the transformations that had occurred in collective bargaining. McKnight later remarked that "impasse and implementation [were] the dominant consideration of virtually every negotiation" in which he participated. The prospect of impasse and implementation was "so attractive to employers and so menacing to unions and workers" that it had reduced the language of collective bargaining to "a list of words and phrases that unions can never use and employers must always use," such as "deadlock," "bottom line," "best offer," and "final offer."[45]

The Labor Movement: Strategic Responses

Confronted by these new conditions, American unions developed at least two counterstrategies, from both inside and outside the framework of the NLRA. First, although the law permits replacement of "economic" strikers seeking better wages and working conditions, it forbids the permanent replacement of workers who strike against employers' unfair labor practices (ULPs). Such strikers are entitled to reinstatement when they end their strike, and employers that refuse to take them back may be liable for back pay. These provisions offered the chance for a procedural check in bargaining, as employers might be deterred from unfair or unlawful declaration of impasse. Although the process of adjudication might take years, the prospect of massive liabilities for back wages could be used to restore a balance of power in negotiations.

By the late 1980s, unions had learned to ensure that strikes were linked to employers' unfair labor practices in order to gain some protection against permanent replacement. The strategy led to some notable labor victories, including a UAW strike at Colt Firearms in Hartford, Connecticut, which ended in 1990 with a $13 million back pay settlement and the buyout of the company by a coalition of private investors, the union, and the State of Connecticut.[46] For the most part, however, the ULP strike remained a defensive tactic, but it highlighted the fact that the central conflict in many strikes had shifted from the specific economic issues on the table to the future of the bargaining relationship.

A second, more highly public counterstrategy goes beyond the simple work stoppage and aims at mobilizing support from the surrounding community. This has taken various forms, from consumer boycotts to demands for state intervention to demonstrations and civil disobedience, all designed to open up the political space for action and to frame individual disputes in terms of larger cultural meanings and collective identities. In urban labor markets, these forms of mobilization may be described as a kind of community-based or "metro" unionism, taking advantage of geographic union density and gaining resources from the fabric of local civil society.[47]

Among the better-known examples of these efforts have been the Service Employees International Union's Justice for Janitors campaigns.[48] The strategy has developed especially in service sectors with spatially anchored or locally organized employers, such as large hospitals and hotels, citywide restaurant or janitorial contractor associations, and state-subsidized nursing homes and home health care agencies, all of which draw on low-wage, urban, minority, and often immigrant workforces. Under such conditions, local unions might well have the resources and density to organize and bargain effectively within urban and regional contexts.

The strategies of metro unionism and the ULP strike both grew out of the institutional limits of the postwar accord. The segmentation of union and non-union labor markets distanced unions not only from unorganized workers but also from other groups in the urban community. Employers' ability to exit gradually made non-union conditions the standard in many industries, even in those with formerly high union densities, putting the survival of the remaining unionized shops at risk. Finally, the shift in federal policy left unions less able to rely on traditional legal protections for workers' rights. The erosion of their former power forced some unions to adopt alternative strategies and reconstruct their strike leverage by using the law and reaching out to community groups previously left out of collective bargaining disputes.

The decade of the 1990s witnessed major industrial strikes of coal miners in Appalachia, aluminum workers in West Virginia, and food processors, tire makers, and heavy machinery workers in Decatur and Peoria, Illinois, among others.[49] Each strike included some combination of the new tactics, yet most occurred in smaller manufacturing towns or remote mining areas, often distant from wider media attention or public impact. At the same time, as sociologists Steve Lopez and Ruth Milkman have shown, new community-based organizing drives were emerging from the urban margins, where accord-era institutions were historically weak (as among immigrant janitors and construction workers in Los Angeles) or had already collapsed (for example, Pittsburgh nursing home workers amid the ruins of the steel industry).[50] In Detroit, however, traditional industrial unionism remained unusually strong. There the local newspaper unions operated in a highly populated urban setting, drawing support from workers, consumers, and government officials across a metropolitan area with comparatively high union density.

In the postwar era, American unions gained an institutional foothold in the core sectors of the economy under the NLRA, while a layer of union avoidance grew alongside and apart from the New Deal system. The balance of power between the two paths shifted in the early 1980s after the critical junctures of the PATCO and Phelps Dodge strikes. In response, unions adopted alternative tactics like the ULP strike and metro unionism. The combination of these strategic trends set the stage for the newspaper strike in Detroit, where the alignment of actors and conditions prefigured a powerful collision of opposing forces.

THE COLLISION COURSE: WHY DETROIT?

Economically, the Gannett Company's 1986 purchase of the *News* from its longtime local owners was the decisive trigger event that brought the postwar union avoidance path directly into the Detroit newspaper market.[51] Gannett already operated around 80 percent non-union throughout the chain, primarily in single-paper markets in small and medium-sized cities across the country.[52] In Detroit the formation of the JOA with Knight-Ridder eliminated business competition between the *News* and *Free Press* and created a new monopoly coalition to confront the unions at the bargaining table. With a majority on the DNA board, Gannett officials dominated the contract negotiations, while Knight-Ridder remained at best a junior partner.

More than Knight-Ridder, Gannett's management had a reputation for hard bargaining, particularly with the Newspaper Guild. As one labor journalist wrote, "Gannett sends the same corporate team to each contract negotiation, the team puts an offer on the table that includes, among other nettlesome issues, giving the company complete control over wages—and then says the offer is final."[53] Executives at Gannett were determined to bring costs in Detroit into line with their other papers, but they would have to do it on-site. Although classified as manufacturing, newspaper publishing combines features of several sectors: relying on close relations with local consumers and advertisers, the industry employs a range of professional, clerical, production, and transportation workers. Their spatial embeddedness makes newspapers less footloose than other enterprises and less able to seek lower wages through relocation or the threat of plant closure.[54]

And Detroit was not like Gannett's other markets. Despite a generally unfavorable national environment for unions, the area continued to possess significant resources favorable to labor and grounded in the norms of the accord. First, Detroit was a stronghold for two powerful unions that virtually defined American labor in the postwar era. More than half of the unionized newspaper workers were members of the International Brotherhood of Teamsters, and Michigan Teamsters Joint Council 43 was the former province of the legendary James R. "Jimmy" Hoffa, whose son, James P. Hoffa, would become president of the IBT in 1998. The Detroit area was also home to the United Auto Workers' international headquarters and several of its regional administrative divisions, and the union was bolstered by the resurgence of the auto industry in the 1990s. Southeastern Michigan as a whole counted more than 600,000 union members in 1995, trailing only greater New York, Chicago, and Los Angeles, and networks of local UAW and other union activists participated in an organizational culture of solidarity throughout the region.[55]

Second, the concentration of political and institutional resources was no less notable. Locally, labor's electoral clout ensured support from government officials, and long-standing ties with area civic organizations brought endorsements from civil rights, faith-based, and other community leaders. Moreover, by 1995 the unions could also take advantage of the political opportunity provided by a more sympathetic NLRB under the presidency of Democrat Bill Clinton. Indeed, the NLRB Region 7 office, based in Detroit, was considered to be particularly skilled in and positively disposed toward the principles of industrial unionism.[56]

In Detroit the economic power of two large national corporations, Gannett and Knight-Ridder, collided with the institutions of industrial unionism and the culture of class solidarity in the region. Here, more than anywhere else, the competing postwar paths of collective bargaining and union avoidance clashed directly with each other. The result was one of the largest and longest strikes in the United States in decades, one that would spread out into the courts and the streets and last for more than five years.

CONCLUSION: A SIGNAL JUNCTURE

During the postwar era in the United States, labor-management relations were largely contained within a stable institutional framework or "accord." Under the law, collective bargaining was decentralized and limited to bread-and-butter economic issues, depoliticized under formal procedural rules, and relatively insulated from the local community. Within this framework, American unions achieved unprecedented power, and American workers gained basic rights and a voice in the workplace. At the same time, however, the limits of the accord allowed the emergence and growth of an anti-union path that would eventually displace the New Deal system.

The process of displacement accelerated in the 1980s and 1990s, destabilizing the former institutional boundaries between the workplace, government, and the community. Confrontations between unions and employers were deroutinized, and strikes turned into high-stakes, wide-ranging struggles over the very terms and future of the bargaining relationship. Together, the tactics of metro unionism and the ULP strike reopened the questions of who had an interest in collective bargaining, what could be negotiated, and how settlements could be reached. As the rival institutional regimes came increasingly into contact with each other, their contradictions became sharper and often burst into explosive and costly episodes of conflict.

The Detroit strike was such an episode. When the two largest newspaper corporations in the nation sought to restructure the terms of employment at the *News* and the *Free Press*, they faced a labor movement grounded in the historic terrain of metropolitan Detroit. In the newspaper strike, the two sides each invoked different and conflicting institutional norms: the companies pursued a neoliberal agenda of corporate restructuring and management autonomy, while the unions organized to defend New Deal principles of collective bargaining. The collision of these institutional paths opened up battlegrounds in the form of both the extensive litigation and the high level of popular mobilization in the strike. The outcome would signal the consolidation of the ascendant anti-union regime, while highlighting emergent tactical innovations in workers' collective action.

From the standpoint of history, a showdown may have seemed inevitable. The newspaper strike followed strategic trends and precedents that had been developing since the 1980s and even featured some of the same participants as in the earlier struggles. But for many of the individuals involved, the precise contours of the conflict, and the choices they would confront, would only become visible through the progress of the events. The following chapters in part II explore the conditions on the ground at the newspapers, including the restructuring of the workplace under the joint operating agreement and the contract negotiations leading up to the critical year of 1995 and the start of the strike.

Chapter 5 | The Path to Confrontation: The Newspapers' Joint Operating Agreement in Detroit

THROUGHOUT THE 1980S AND 1990S, the business pages of American newspapers buzzed with talk of corporate restructuring, employment downsizing, and a new "lean" style of organization. Repeated waves of mergers and acquisitions made whole departments of large firms redundant as established companies reinvented themselves to maximize shareholder value, and managers and workers alike often scrambled to find their way on unfamiliar terrain.[1] Social scientists and journalists have amply documented these dislocations, but under the free market ideology of the time they seemed somehow necessary and unavoidable, like the imposition of a law of nature. In fact, the changes taking place reflected the deliberate choices made by a range of actors, not all of whom shared the same interests.

So it was in Detroit. The restructuring of the newspaper workplace under the joint operating agreement (JOA) was not an adaptation to an existing order, but an attempt to write the rules for a new one. At the outset, the lack of advance planning and cooperation made the implementation of the merger a nightmare, and despite its monopoly status the new enterprise failed to earn a profit in its first several years of existence. New actors entered the scene, representing opposing trends and tactics and opening the way to a more direct conflict at the bargaining table. As the pressure increased, it channeled the two sides toward an even larger confrontation.

From the start, the negotiations for the JOA set a new tone in relations between the companies and the unions. In part, this reflected the cast of characters on both sides, particularly the new management leadership coming from Gannett. The interactions between the parties, however, also signaled emerging conflicts between deeper institutional forces that were played out in the nuts and bolts of bargaining strategy, contract enforcement, and labor law. The formation of the JOA put these forces in direct contact with one another, and the 1992 contract negotiations offered a preview of the collisions to come.

CORPORATE RESTRUCTURING: THE NEWSPAPER AGENCY

At the very least, Gannett's arrival in Detroit inaugurated a change in the management culture at the *News*. With its national reputation for news reporting, a fiercely competitive urban market, and an 80 percent unionization rate among its employees (compared to 20 percent for Gannett as a whole), the *News* stood in sharp contrast with the other papers in its new parent company's chain.[2] Now Gannett and Knight-Ridder proposed to manage the business affairs of both the *News* and the *Free Press* under the joint operating agreement announced on April 14, 1986. The two papers would combine their production, circulation, advertising, accounting, and marketing operations into a single entity called the Detroit Newspaper Agency (DNA).

Under the agreement, the newsrooms would remain separate, and on weekdays the *Free Press* would have exclusive rights to the morning edition while the *News* would publish in the afternoon. On weekends the papers would have a joint masthead, splitting coverage by departments but preserving independent editorial pages. Gannett would have a majority of three on the five-member DNA board, with two seats going to Knight-Ridder. For the first five years of the one-hundred-year agreement, Gannett would receive slightly more than half the profits, and after that they would be split evenly between the two national corporations. Gannett chair Allen Neuharth selected William J. Keating, Gannett's general counsel and a former Republican congressperson from Cincinnati, to be the first chief executive officer of the DNA.[3]

Conflicts over the merger began even before the JOA was officially approved. Gannett and Knight-Ridder wanted as little union presence as possible in the new agency, but they expected to have to bargain with the Teamsters and the production crafts. They took a much harder stance, however, with the Newspaper Guild, which represented the newsrooms along with a group of janitorial workers at the *News* and more than three hundred advertising, circulation, marketing, and clerical jobs at the *Free*

Press. Employees in the latter jobs would now be under the DNA, and Keating made it clear that management would oppose any effort by the union to represent them.

It was not the first time the papers had stonewalled the Guild. Lou Mleczko (pronounced Muh-LETCH-ko) was president of the Guild's Local 22 in Detroit. A longtime journalist, a Detroit native, and the son of an autoworker, Mleczko had led the successful 1974 newsroom organizing drive at the historically anti-union *News.* Mleczko and his colleagues had won that fight, but unlike the *Free Press* decades earlier, the *News* had successfully excluded its editors and office staff from the Guild bargaining unit. On June 10, 1986, Guild attorneys met with Keating and Gannett labor relations counsel John Jaske in hopes of reaching an agreement on the Guild's jurisdiction at the DNA. The Gannett executives saw no need to compromise. "There's nothing the Guild can do to hurt us," Keating reportedly said. That night Local 22's Representative Assembly voted unanimously to request public hearings on the JOA.[4]

More than a year would pass before those hearings even began. Not until after Judge Morton Needelman had rendered his December 1987 opinion against the JOA did the publishers begin serious negotiations with the six local unions representing the bulk of the newspaper workforce. The Teamsters Local 2040, representing the mailers, and the Graphic Communications International Union (GCIU) Locals 13N and 289M, including the press operators and engravers, ultimately settled for the promise of no initial layoffs and a package of benefits for voluntary severance. The printers' International Typographical Union (ITU) Local 18, however, acceded only after Gannett negotiators threatened to withdraw from the papers' 1974 lifetime job agreement with the union. The district managers and field circulation workers in Teamsters Local 372 were forced to absorb job losses, but won pension improvements and the renewal of an agreement not to contest the district managers' status as employees under the NLRA. The employers also agreed to include more than one hundred "inside" circulation office workers from the *News* in a single bargaining unit with Local 372.[5]

The agreement with Local 372, however, meant that the Guild circulation workers at the *Free Press* were likely to be laid off. The Guild's sole remaining leverage was its legal challenge to the JOA, but now more than a few Local 22 members were frightened that the *Free Press* really would close. A dissident caucus of *Free Press* journalists filed a lawsuit to force a vote on the union's stance, and one columnist publicly criticized union leadership in the pages of the paper. More than four hundred Local 22 members attended each of two union meetings in February 1988, yet despite heated debate, the members voted overwhelmingly to continue the opposition to the JOA.

Talks between management and the Guild finally broke off in March, but by this time the pressure was also mounting on Knight-Ridder. In July, Knight-Ridder newspaper division president Tony Ridder and *Free Press* general manager Bob Hall arranged to meet, independently of Gannett officials, with Newspaper Guild national president Charles Dale and Local 22 administrative officer Don Kummer in Washington, D.C. Ridder and Hall refused to recognize the Guild's jurisdictional claim, but eventually promised that no more than seventy-five Guild members and none of Local 22's janitorial members at the *News* would be laid off. After an all-night session on July 22, the two sides reached a deal that included early retirement benefits and a half-million-dollar fund for retraining displaced workers. Local 22's membership remained sharply divided over the issue of the JOA, but the union's Representative Assembly narrowly ratified the settlement on July 25.[6]

With the unions now lined up in support, the U.S. Attorney General's Office approved the JOA on August 8, 1988. Yet another year would pass, however, while Michigan Citizens for an Independent Press pursued its lawsuit to the U.S. Supreme Court. After three and a half years of protracted litigation and negotiation, the JOA was finally launched on November 27, 1989. The papers now faced enormous tasks of internal reorganization: the new DNA had to merge and coordinate procedures in its business offices, printing plants, mailrooms, and circulation sites across the metropolitan Detroit area. As many as five hundred employees were slated to be laid off, and those who remained had worked without contracts for more than two years. In March 1990, less than five months after the DNA's official start-up, chief executive Keating left Detroit and returned to his former home to take over the *Cincinnati Enquirer*. He was replaced by Gannett manager Joseph Ungaro, who himself lasted little more than a year.[7] If the process of authorizing the JOA was contentious, the parties now entered into an even more difficult process of determining what kind of enterprise the Detroit newspapers would be.

AT THE TABLE: ACTORS AND ISSUES

With the creation of the Detroit Newspaper Agency, the conflicting national trends in workplace governance came to a head in the Motor City. Typifying the new lean-and-mean corporate style that became prominent in the 1980s, Gannett managers dominated the DNA administration and brought with them years of experience with radical restructuring programs, tough negotiating methods, and aggressive legal strategies. In Detroit, however, they encountered a set of labor unions that remained confident of their power and unwilling to give up without a fight. Local union leaders were themselves sophisticated bargainers and knew how to work within the framework of the NLRA. Acting in their organizational roles, individuals on both sides brought competing institutional norms and trends to bear in their relations with each other at the newspapers.

On the management side, the two most important figures from Gannett were Frank Vega and John Jaske. The forty-two-year-old Vega took over as chief executive officer and president of the DNA in May 1991. A native of Tampa, Florida, Vega was a protégé of Allen Neuharth, a circulation expert, and a member of the select corporate task force that had successfully launched *USA Today*. Short and stocky, with a large, voluble personality, Vega cultivated a reputation as a hard-nosed, chain-smoking, blue-collar boss who nonetheless wore expensive sweaters and enjoyed a good round of golf. Brought in to turn things around in Detroit, he participated in negotiations especially with Teamsters Local 372.[8]

Vega sat in sharp and sometimes uneasy contrast with Jaske, the senior vice president of labor relations and assistant general counsel for the parent Gannett corporation. Methodical and intense, with a gaunt face and receding hairline, Jaske was a brilliant strategist whose professional demeanor was described by others as "glum looking" and "stark, cold, [and] emotionless."[9] Responsible for labor matters at all Gannett properties, Jaske technically deferred to Vega on local issues, but in practice acted as chief spokesperson in the negotiations for the DNA and for the *News* editorial unit.[10]

No counterpart to Jaske existed within the Knight-Ridder corporate hierarchy until 1998, when Marshall Anstandig assumed that role.[11] At the DNA, the *Free Press*'s Tim Kelleher carried over as senior vice president of labor relations. Portly, cheerful, and sarcastic, Kelleher had been at the newspapers since 1982, knew the contracts and the unions, and acted as the historical memory for the employers. Attorney John Taylor from the *News* became director of labor relations and later senior legal counsel under Kelleher. Also at the *News*, editor and publisher Robert Giles came to Detroit in 1986, moving up the corporate chain from Gannett's Rochester papers.[12]

For the newspaper workers, Don Kummer and Lou Mleczko remained at the head of the Newspaper Guild Local 22, having guided the union through the struggle over the JOA. In the mailers union, Teamsters Local 2040, the lean, self-controlled Alex Young led a new generation of leaders elected in 1991. For the press operators, longtime union officer Jack Howe succeeded to the presidency of GCIU Local 13N in 1993.[13] Along with Robert Ogden of the engravers and Sam Attard of the printers, the local union heads formed the Metropolitan Council of Newspaper Unions (MCNU), under the leadership of Alfred "Al" Derey, a thirty-year employee of the papers who won election as secretary-treasurer of Teamsters Local 372 in 1989. With his silver hair, baritone voice, and deliberate manner, Derey was less a commanding general than a consensus-builder on the Council. His role, as he saw it, was to act as a "fireman," putting out fires when necessary and serving as "designated javelin catcher" for the media.[14]

Supporting the unions were two highly experienced attorneys who had participated in some of the landmark labor struggles of the previous decade. Coordinating strategy for the printers and later the MCNU was Sam McKnight, late of the 1990 *New York Daily News* strike, aided by his small firm of Klimist, McKnight, Sale, McClow, and Canzano in suburban Southfield. Representing the Guild and the press operators was Duane Ice, who had worked with the Phelps Dodge copper miners in the early 1980s and argued the Guild's case in the hearings on the JOA.[15] In addition, Local 372's Al Derey retained Frank Kortsch, an ambitious, outspoken young lawyer out of Milwaukee with ties to the Detroit-area Teamsters. Kortsch was more volatile and less experienced than McKnight and Ice, but he had won several grievance arbitrations for Local 372 against Gannett, and Derey relied on him in the negotiations.[16]

Anxious to get the DNA formally under way, the companies quickly signed contracts in 1989 that gave modest wage increases to all units but left other provisions temporarily more or less intact. Over the next five years, however, substantial differences between the two sides would press hard against the established institutions of labor-management relations that bound them together. In the sometimes arcane details of bargaining and contract enforcement there were crucial principles at stake, and the points of contention were often not so much about the specific issues in question as about the very scope and meaning of the bargaining relationship. These pressure points were revealed particularly in disputes over (1) unit boundaries and union jurisdiction, (2) the responsibility to bargain in good faith, and (3) the process of negotiating economic change.

On the Front Lines: Jurisdiction and Unit Erosion

At Gannett, senior vice president and assistant general counsel Jaske was intimately familiar with these matters. Jaske had started his career with a law firm in Baltimore, and in 1976 one of its clients, the Hearst-owned *Baltimore News-American*, was involved in an unfair labor practice case with the Typographical Union. The *News-American* and its rival *Baltimore*

Sun wanted to buy out a number of printers who had lifetime job guarantees under the collective bargaining agreement. The companies, however, sidestepped both the existing contracts and the union by unilaterally making the offer directly to the individual employees. In ruling on what one observer later called a "colossal blunder" for management, the administrative law judge, Thomas A. Ricci, found the action to be a flagrant violation of the statute.[17] As Judge Ricci wrote in his decision:

> After the employer has bargained with the union about such [terms and conditions], and signed a fixed contract precisely detailing the agreed-upon conditions, it may not thereafter deal with its employees individually, or unilaterally, without the approval of their bargaining agent . . . economic considerations appropriately govern the thinking of both parties when the collective bargaining agreement is negotiated; once it is made the parties are stuck with its terms. If either could change it at all for economic reasons there would be no purpose in having any collective bargaining agreements.[18]

Almost immediately afterward, Jaske left Baltimore and took a job with Gannett.[19] But the issue stayed with him, and he wrote about it in a law journal article published in 1982. He remained especially indignant toward the provision of lifetime job guarantees and speculated as to "how additional rights can be obtained by newspapers who have given their employees [this] ultimate concession." He wrote that management "has sought additional flexibility in the jurisdiction clause of the labor agreement" and, at smaller papers, "will simply be able to demand jurisdictional changes before employees can get a pay raise." Larger papers might have to give further incentives to introduce labor-saving machines, but Jaske raised the question of "whether a lifetime job guarantee carries with it the implication of a particular rate of pay or other terms and conditions of employment which would allow [the employer] to take the posture that, while it would not change the job guarantee, its wage proposal would be minimum wage or even zero."[20]

In other words, even if the jobs were guaranteed, employers might be able to remove from them all meaningful content. On its face the strategy might sound extreme, and it also carried with it several legal hazards. While employers had some rights to transfer work out of a bargaining unit, changes in the scope of the bargaining unit affected the union's statutory right to represent the relevant employees. Ultimately, the National Labor Relations Board reserved the right to clarify unit boundaries; the union could voluntarily agree to negotiate them but was not required to do so, and as a permissive subject the employer could not lawfully declare impasse on the issue and impose its demands.

The problem was illustrated in a 1982 case involving the Newspaper Printing Corporation, a joint operating agency of the *Nashville Banner* and *Nashville Tennessean* that Jaske argued successfully before the U.S. Sixth Circuit Court of Appeals. The company had proposed a contract clause defining the bargaining unit and the union's jurisdiction as "work performed in the composing room." The "jurisdiction of the union and bargaining unit work and/or composing room work," the proposal continued, would expressly exclude all work done on or by computers and the newer, emerging methods of pre-press production. In effect, the new language appeared to draw a box around the typographers' unit, separating it from the clear direction of technological change in the industry.[21]

The company did not move from this proposal, and a federal mediator declared an impasse in October 1977, allowing the employers to impose the terms unilaterally. The union filed an unfair labor practice charge, and in 1980 NLRB judge Peter Donnelly ruled against the company. Judge Donnelly was particularly skeptical toward the employer's "contention that there has not been any change or modification in the scope or definition of the unit, and that the new work jurisdiction provisions did not 'disenfranchise' any employee entitled to representation, but were necessary changes to provide the flexibility to operate its new equipment in an economic and efficient manner." In his analysis, the judge wrote: "This contention does not withstand even cursory review."

The full NLRB in Washington upheld the judge's ruling, but a federal Appeals Court panel disagreed. In their decision, the three-member appellate panel emphasized the legitimate interest of the employer in seeking language that "sensibly separated the concept of unit jurisdiction and work jurisdiction." Overturning the NLRB order, the court went on to say, "We find that the Company was careful to preserve the unit description while changing the jurisdiction clause about which it did have the right to bargain to impasse. . . . Members remain 'composing room employees' and, thus, remain part of the unit regardless of whether all of the work is transferred to editorial employees or elsewhere."[22]

The NLRB later revisited the issue in its 1993 *Antelope Valley Press* decision, where it adopted a new test for evaluating an employer's bargaining proposal. If the employer insisted on a change in the unit description, the Board ruled, that would affect the union's right to represent those employees and would be unlawful. However, if the employer did not seek to change the unit description but only demanded the additional right to transfer work out of the unit, then that would be lawful. The employer could not insist that the persons performing the work would *never* be part of the bargaining unit, and the union maintained the right to contend that they should be—for example, through a unit clarification petition or ULP charge before the NLRB.[23] Together, the rulings seemed to indicate a way for companies to achieve a major restructuring of their unionized work-places: as long as negotiators did not redefine the bargaining unit, they were free to demand drastic changes in the union's jurisdiction.

The point was not lost on the assistant general counsel for Gannett. During the negotiations for the Detroit JOA, Jaske proposed nearly the same language to the printers union, asserting management's right to introduce new technology and assign work to non-unit employees "provided that all active composing room employees continue to be assigned to composing room work."[24] In Detroit, however, Local 18 had signed a memorandum of agreement (MOA) with the newspapers in 1974, giving up much of its traditional work in exchange for guaranteed job security. Under the MOA, and in subsequent collective bargaining contracts, the union had carefully crafted a series of exceptions to its jurisdiction while retaining its original all-inclusiveness. As technology and job assignments evolved, the union reserved its rights to perform those jobs that it had not explicitly waived, wherever they might be.

Nevertheless, the newspaper management in Detroit continually sought to move work away from the union. In 1989, with the start of the JOA, supervisors were forced out of the bargaining unit at the behest of the employer. In 1993 the union charged the DNA with assigning unit work to non-unit supervisors, telemarketers, and employees in the marketing development department, including two unit members who had voluntarily transferred there and performed the same tasks as they had in the composing room. In finding for the union, independent arbitrator Joseph Girolamo observed: "It is really beside the point that many of the present employees will not be adversely affected by the removal of work from their jurisdiction. The bottom line is that the Parties, even though they agreed to guaranteed job security, also negotiated rather specific provisions concerning the work which was retained by the Bargaining Unit."[25]

In each of these disputes, management asserted that the changes were necessary to achieve economic efficiencies and that it should have the undivided authority to implement them. While not necessarily denying the economic claims, the unions continued to insist on preserving the integrity of contractual agreements and the collective bargaining relationship. The company could make changes, but it would have to negotiate those changes with the union representing the workers whose jobs would be affected.

Impasse and Unilateral Implementation

The issues in the jurisdictional disputes highlighted the strategic importance of management's ability to bargain to impasse in order to impose conditions. Both sides understood this clearly, well before the JOA even went into effect. On April 11, 1988, Michael Rybicki, an attorney with the nationally prominent management labor law firm of Seyfarth, Shaw, Fairweather and Geraldson, wrote a letter to Tim Kelleher of the *Free Press*, shortly after the JOA negotiations with the Guild had broken down. "It is essential," Rybicki wrote, "that the Free Press either reach an agreement or impasse with the Guild prior to implementation of the J.O.A." Rybicki doubted that an agreement would be possible, so the letter offered "some comments and suggestions concerning bargaining to impasse."[26]

"Unions in general," Rybicki warned, "and the Guild most particularly, understand the significance of a legal impasse and have proven extremely creative in their efforts to deny employers the right to post conditions." He complained that "a favorite tactic of the Guild to forestall impasse is to request all sorts of information and claim that it cannot 'bargain intelligently' until it has had an opportunity to review the requested material." The letter noted the likely criteria that would have to be met to prove impasse before the NLRB. "As a general rule," Rybicki advised, "unless and until all important mandatory subjects have been discussed, it is difficult to establish an impasse. . . . This means that negotiations concerning economic issues with the Joint Council will have to be brought to a head. The final proposals to the Guild must be presented as a complete package including economic." The letter left no doubt that the *Free Press* should seek impasse as a primary strategy. "Obviously, the Company needs to proclaim negotiations are at an impasse and present a final offer to the Guild as soon as possible."[27]

Of course, the Guild did settle with Knight-Ridder before the JOA, but the strategy of bargaining to impasse remained a powerful weapon in the newspapers' arsenal, allowing them the option of taking unilateral action. A similar dynamic arose concerning another point of contention for the Guild, namely, management demands for merit pay. In 1990, Jaske was victorious in a case before the NLRB involving Gannett's *Cincinnati Enquirer*. As chief negotiator for the paper, he had proposed to eliminate wage minimums and classifications for Guild unit members and substitute a system of pay increases based exclusively on merit evaluations. In addition, Jaske wanted an end to arbitration, "because of abuse of the process by the Union in the past," and the removal of any provision permitting strikes by unit employees. Although the no-strike clause was later withdrawn, the NLRB general counsel argued that the demands constituted an "insistence on unilateral control of all wages" and amounted to a *"per se* refusal to bargain" on management's part.[28]

Many Guild contracts across the country allowed for merit pay above the minimums, but without any negotiation on base rates, and without any right to due process or appeal on evaluations, it was hard to see what role remained for the union to bargain collectively for wages or represent workers beyond what individuals could do for themselves.[29] In this case, however, the judge and the board rejected the general counsel's argument. The board ruled that, because the employer did not insist on unilateral control of wage *reductions*, or of wages for new hires, the general counsel did not prove that it sought unilateral control of *all* wages. Although the conduct cited might constitute an element in a pattern of bad faith, it was not per se a violation, and the complaint was dismissed.

Negotiating Economic Change: Individual Unit and Joint Bargaining

Faced with increasing pressure on their units, the newspaper unions developed their own creative responses to the problems of downsizing and reduced bargaining leverage. Having lost the battle to control training in the new skills and technology, the unions developed a defensive strategy of accepting job cuts or reduced jurisdiction in return for compensation for the increased workload to the remaining employees. Tom McGrath was the director of the Newspaper Division for the International Brotherhood of Teamsters, with more than four decades of experience in the business. "If you were willing to make a major concession in the form of savings to the company, you could get something in lieu, as a quid pro quo," he explained. "Gannett wanted to get out of contract practices they had found out was just killing them, and they wanted to trade off getting rid of those things for extra money. So the company was in the same bargaining mode as the unions, and that caused them to be very, very inventive in their bargaining, all sides."[30]

In Detroit similar arrangements had been in place at least since the printers' lifetime job agreement in 1974. That same year, the press operators gave up more than one-quarter of their contractual staffing levels in exchange for what were called productivity or "P" days. Jack Howe explained: "For every day you worked you got one fifth day's pay which you could take off in time or you could just take the money, and it was like [up to] forty personal or forty productivity days a year."[31] Concessions like these cost the newspapers money, but in the long run saved them even more, and they continued to offer them. Thus, in 1991 the printers gave up the inputting of text for display ads in exchange for additional personal absence days.[32]

The 1992 contracts were full of such trade-offs. The press operators' Local 13N gave up sixty full-time positions and got a $31 weekly bonus in the second year. The small photoengravers unit gave up twelve jobs, or more than one-third of its membership. The mailers' Local 2040 received a first-year lump sum payment of $700 in return for sixty-five full-time job reductions and agreed to a voluntary buyout plan. Finally, a major reorganization of the delivery system resulted in compensation ranging from $20.08 to $92 per week for members of Teamsters Local 372.[33]

The unions distinguished these individual unit agreements from negotiations on across-the-board "economic" subjects like wage increases, health insurance, and the like. Since the 1970s, the unions had gradually moved toward a more stable joint bargaining stance on such matters, though occasionally the Teamsters or press operators might still break away and settle first. In any case, by the 1980s the Detroit papers had come a long way from the turbulent, strike-prone years of the 1950s and 1960s.[34] Even before the JOA, the days in which the unions could whipsaw the employers against each other had long passed. The last ones to try were the Teamsters. On the eve of the 1980 Republican Party convention in Detroit, Local 372 struck the *Free Press*, hoping to get a better contract. But after two weeks they accepted a deal no better than what they had before they went out. From then on, management actually held the upper hand: if it could reach a complete contract with one of the stronger locals first, the remaining units would invariably follow on the same terms.[35]

In 1989 the DNA and the unions agreed to bargain individual and joint issues separately, though concurrently, at the request of management. For the following contract, negotiations with Local 372 on the delivery restructuring commenced in October 1991, three to four months before talks began with the other unions. The DNA wanted to divide the home delivery of papers from single-copy distribution to stores and racks so that Teamster district managers would no longer handle both out of their neighborhood stations.[36] Given the complexity of the reorganization and their mutual backgrounds in circulation, Local 372 head Al Derey developed an especially close working relationship with DNA chief Vega.[37] The 1992 meetings were also the first to include both Vega and John Jaske, and the relations between the two men soon became strained. As Derey recalled:

> There came a time during those negotiations that Jaske felt that it was his job to negotiate it. And a conflict arose between both Vega and John Jaske. All the way to the point that Vega, through a fit of being mad, I guess, put him in his place in front of the unions and said, "I'm running the show. Shut your mouth." If people would know John Jaske, that is not the type of statement to make to this individual. . . . He forgets nothing.[38]

Meanwhile, the DNA beefed up its security and operating capacity in anticipation of a possible strike. Vega assigned his executive assistant, Alan Lenhoff, to the operations department to develop a detailed strike contingency plan. Lenhoff consulted with managers at newspapers across the country, and hired Asset Protection Team, Inc., a subsidiary of the private strike management firm Vance International, to review internal security. An emergency headquarters was slated for the Sterling Heights printing plant and barracks-like accommodations, complete with sleeping cots and washing machines, were set up inside the plant. Surveillance cameras and new fencing were installed on the downtown buildings, and extra guards appeared at newspaper facilities. Altogether, the publishers spent $2 million on preparations for a strike.[39]

On March 19, 1992, Jaske informed the printers union committee that the DNA had over 1,400 applications for replacement positions in distribution and would interview job-seekers in other areas as well. "We intend to publish," he told them.[40] That same day, Derey wrote a letter to Vega asking for joint bargaining on economic issues, but in a written reply on April 9, Vega declined.[41] By mid-April, Local 372 had walked out of negotiations over Jaske's proposal to split off the "inside" clerical circulation workers and bargain a separate contract for them.

Even as the tensions escalated, however, Derey felt that Vega still wanted to reach a deal. "Vega didn't want a strike," Derey said later, but "[Vega] did not think that Jaske could handle the unions in Detroit and avoid a strike."[42] At Vega's request, he and Derey met privately in late April at the Sweetwater Tavern in downtown Detroit, where they agreed to set aside joint issues until after the individual negotiations had been concluded.[43] With the focus now on individual unit concerns, Derey and Vega concentrated on the distribution system and completed a settlement in a matter of days.

In Derey's words, "We were able to change the entire circulation department around from a storefront type of distribution to a warehouse type of distribution." The 368 district locations were consolidated under approximately 26 distribution centers across the Detroit area, and the company offered buyouts of $70,000 plus ten years of paid health insurance.[44] It was an impressive feat of bargaining, and across the industry observers took note. "They rewrote the method of delivering—the whole distribution of that paper changed from one day to the next," said the IBT's McGrath. "It was a massive, massive agreement and massive changes. It was trend setting. . . . So yeah, Vega had a claim to fame, he was totally responsible for that."

Vega's deal with Derey changed the dynamic in the negotiations for the other unions. McGrath continued: "[Vega] pulled the rug out from [under] Jaske, because then Jaske, who was playing very hard and rough at the table, had no real emphasis to convince the powers-that-be within Gannett that they should go and play hardball, and so Vega's agreement with the drivers effectively cost Jaske his position at the bargaining table. . . . With the agreement [Gannett] figured they had with the drivers, that was enough to make that a very successful bargaining session. . . . They had what they thought they'd never get."[45]

Eager now to bring the remaining talks to a close, Vega pleaded with the MCNU heads in joint bargaining to accept a wage freeze and take lump-sum bonus payments instead. According to union leaders, he promised that if the unions gave ground now they could come back at the next contract when the papers were making money and "pick my pocket."[46] In the end, the unions agreed to no increases in base pay and bonus amounts of $1,200 the first year and $1,000 each in the second and third years, with a $1 per shift contribution to benefits in the third year. The previous contracts expired on April 30, and all negotiations were concluded less than a week later.

CONCLUSION: CRISES POSTPONED

The two-stage joint bargaining model produced a settlement in 1992, and both Vega and Derey could take credit for successfully avoiding a strike. However, even though the contracts were signed, at best they merely postponed many of the individual issues still hanging over the other units. The press operators' agreement included language requiring the two sides to meet during the second year and continue to discuss pressroom staffing, with potential adjustments tested in the third year, subject to arbitration.[47] The mailers' contract had similar provisions. The DNA wanted to close the "Funny Farm," the old *Free Press* mailroom annex located on Clayton Street in southwest Detroit, and move the work to a new $22 million inserting facility it was building at its Sterling Heights plant. As Local 2040 president Alex Young described it, staffing for the new facility "would be negotiated during the contract so when they opened the expansion we'd have negotiations specifically to deal with the moving of people and how many people and all of those kind of things. . . . During the '92 contract, we were never able to reach agreement on how that was all going to happen."[48]

Finally, Gannett management at the *News* proposed to the Guild the elimination of all contractual pay raises in favor of a system of merit-only increases. Since 1974, Local 22 had agreed to allow merit increases over and above the negotiated base rates, but *News* publisher Giles wanted newsroom raises to be entirely separate from the across-the-board wage hikes that the Guild negotiated with the other members of the MCNU.

The merit pay issue dominated the bargaining at the *News* and was the last item left in dispute between the papers and the unions in the 1992 negotiations. Lou Mleczko remembered that "the Council held strong and said if the Guild doesn't want merit pay, then we support the Guild on that and we're not going to be able to announce an overall settlement until that issue is off the table. And subsequently they pulled it off the table."[49]

The 1989 approval of the JOA marked the formal juncture between the forces of corporate restructuring and the power of organized labor at the Detroit newspapers. In turn, the 1992 contracts saw their first real collision in the workplace. Each side attempted to negotiate the contractual rules governing the new agency, and their struggle was fought out in the fissures of a declining New Deal institutional order. As it was, the DNA was still losing money, and there would be demands for more concessions. But already the relations between management and the unions, and between the newspapers and the community, were starting to change. At the bargaining table, the unions now faced the monopoly power of the DNA under Gannett. On the job, Teamster members like Leo Jenkins and Dennis Nazelli would no longer lead teams of teenage carriers from their neighborhood storefronts; instead, the papers would be delivered from industrial warehouses by adults driving motor vehicles.

Moreover, the DNA's new warehouse system not only reduced costs but also increased its ability to operate with replacement workers during a strike. Before 1992, former *News* journalist Bryan Gruley observed, "the DNA could not hope to replicate the complex machinery of drivers, jumpers, district managers, and other Teamsters that moved papers from the printing plants to coin boxes and people's doorsteps every day. Knight-Ridder and Gannett could conscript nonunion journalists from their other papers to write and edit stories, but they could not hire someone who could quickly learn to navigate a coin-box-and-convenience-store route through Lincoln Park."[50] The next time, that would no longer be true.

The 1992 contracts left many unanswered questions, and union leaders did not fail to recognize the threat. As McGrath later noted, "Jaske had played pretty tough there [in 1992] . . . he went right down to the wire, but he couldn't pull the trigger. He might have loaded the gun, but he couldn't fire it, and so Jaske was forced to settle and give a lot of things to people that he hadn't wanted to or hadn't planned to and thought were wrong. And after that bargaining, it was clear that Jaske had set about saying, 'That will not happen to me again,' and came into the next bargaining with lots and lots of theories and plans about how not to get trapped and how to take and fight 'em if necessary and he had that as part of his repertoire."[51]

Local 2040's Jim St. Louis agreed. At a ratification meeting for the 1992 contract, he spoke to his members: "I said, I want to talk to you about the next one. And I said, they are coming to get us. I'm warning you right now. . . . And I said, you go take your overtime and you go take your extra days and you go put it in the bank, because come next contract in '95 they're gonna come at us with both barrels and they're, in my opinion, they were already getting ready to make a strike."[52]

Chapter 6 | Extraordinary Measures: Planning for War

IT SEEMED LIKE PERFECT TIMING. On November 1, 1994, eight labor unions representing 2,600 workers struck at the *San Francisco Chronicle*, the *San Francisco Examiner*, and their joint operating agency. The Bay Area newspapers chose to continue publishing during the walkout, resulting in a bitter and sometimes violent confrontation that lasted for two weeks. In Detroit, DNA executives were gearing up for their own upcoming contract negotiations and felt that the San Francisco strike might offer a valuable preview. "[We] thought this was an opportunity for our individuals to see firsthand a strike situation that was ongoing in our industry," said Tim Kelleher, DNA senior vice president for labor relations. They decided to send two of their top people, Alan Lenhoff and John Anthony, to go and check it out.[1]

The forty-four-year-old Lenhoff was director of planning and development and one of the bright stars on the DNA management team. A graduate of the University of Michigan, former editor of the campus *Michigan Daily*, and self-described "card-carrying liberal," he had started at the *Free Press* in 1979 as a business writer covering the auto industry. From there he moved into management, serving as an executive assistant to the publisher of the *Free Press* and then as assistant to the chief executive of the DNA, where he coordinated the strike planning in 1992.[2] Anthony was the newly appointed director of security for the Newspaper Agency. A retired Federal Bureau of Investigation agent who specialized in bank robberies, foreign espionage, and violent crime, Anthony was a tough, no-nonsense lawman who had spent two decades in the FBI's Detroit office. Hired as a contractor by the DNA in September 1994, he was especially valued for his extensive contacts with local law enforcement agencies across southeastern Michigan.[3]

Lenhoff and Anthony spent five days in California investigating the *Chronicle* and *Examiner* strike. They met first with senior officers of Huff-master, Inc., a private strike security firm based in Troy, Michigan, and retained by the San Francisco publishers. They also visited the newspapers' main offices and printing plants, observed evidence of property damage, took notes, and photographed picketers at various sites. The two men spoke with the in-house security director at the papers and conferred with police departments in San Francisco and at the suburban plant locations. Huffmaster officials showed Anthony an edited video compilation of strike events, including clashes between strikers and police, and later sent a copy of it to him in Detroit.[4]

When they returned, Lenhoff and Anthony were determined to keep control of matters in their own house. Well before their trip, however, it was already clear that the 1995 contract negotiations at the Detroit papers would be anything but ordinary. As never before or since, the companies committed enormous resources to ensure that they could operate and break any possible strike. Their efforts included not only strengthening internal security but systematic outreach to local law enforcement agencies. The massive buildup of forces set the context for a declaration of "war" long before the first formal bargaining sessions even began in March 1995.

That declaration took shape in the development of the employers' opening contract proposals for the 1995 negotiations. Those proposals called for substantial changes in the organization of the workplace and in many cases were designed to undermine the unions' bargaining power or diminish their representation at the newspapers. Recognizing that their demands might provoke a strike, the DNA made special efforts to reach out to the Sterling Heights Police Department (SHPD). Their close contact and cooperation throughout the process allowed the DNA to influence the views of the SHPD command staff and the formation of the police department's internal policy.

THE BUILDUP:
DNA STRIKE PLANNING

Jim St. Louis was right. At the DNA, strike preparations began virtually the instant the 1992 contracts were signed. On May 12, 1992, without informing the unions, the newspapers quietly filed a memorandum with the U.S. Department of Justice, asserting their right under the JOA to publish a combined daily edition of the *News* and *Free Press* in the event of a work stoppage. In Detroit, key supervisors were formally debriefed and asked to review and critique the 1992 strike plan. Over the next two years, Lenhoff and other managers traveled to and consulted with papers in Akron, Baltimore, Camden, Cleveland, and San Jose to discuss strategy and gain insights from their experiences.[5]

On the basis of that research, Lenhoff significantly revised the 1992 plan. The results were compiled into two thick three-ring binders, organized by department. Each department was ordered to create checklists of tasks with timelines and managers responsible for their completion. In the circulation department, the plan listed more than three hundred separate tasks, such as mapping out carrier and truck delivery routes for replacement workers and hiring locksmiths to change the locks on warehouses. In finance, procedures were set up to collect money from customers, arrange for check-cashing privileges for out-of-town replacements, and establish a "petty cash" fund to provide bail money to nonstriking workers in case of their arrest. For production, supervisors would be trained to operate the presses and mailroom machines, and an off-site hiring and training center was established for replacement workers. The plan anticipated where employees were going to park, how much they would pay for parking, and how they would get into the buildings. Lenhoff even included details such as how to fill vending machines and get hot meals on-site for replacements working overtime during the strike.[6]

The DNA's core executive planning group included Lenhoff, Kelleher, chief executive Frank Vega, and chief financial officer Gary Anderson. They initially met monthly, starting in earnest in July 1994. After he was hired in September, Anthony also assisted in the evaluation and selection of private strike management contractors. For security they chose Asset Protection Team, Inc. (APT), which they had used as a consultant in 1992. Over the previous decade, APT had made its reputation in strikes in the coal industry and at Caterpillar, Inc., and APT's parent company, Vance International, provided security for Gannett's corporate headquarters in Virginia.[7] To provide truck drivers and transportation security, the group chose locally based Huffmaster, Inc., the lead firm in the San Francisco strike. "We encountered [Huffmaster] when John Anthony and I went to San Francisco in 1994 during their strike and thought they did a pretty good job there," Lenhoff said later. "We came back and said, 'Why put all our eggs in one basket? Let's have a local firm.'"[8]

Finally, the DNA planners determined that all newspaper production would be concentrated in the *News*'s North Plant in Sterling Heights. Although the *Free Press*'s Riverfront printing plant in Detroit had more efficient and modern offset presses, the Sterling Heights site had better highway access and property security. In addition, as DNA counsel John Taylor later wrote, "it was felt that the employers would receive better police support from the Sterling Heights police than from the Detroit law enforcement officials."[9]

By January 1995, the initial team from APT began arriving in Detroit, including task force leader George Beach and David Walworth, site commander for the North Plant. They set up headquarters on the vacant (and now restricted) second floor of the downtown *Free Press* building and spent the next two months evaluating overall needs for exterior lighting, fence construction, and site security. In coordination with Anthony, they prepared their own detailed strike plan, indicating which DNA facilities would be in use and how guards would be posted and deployed. Anthony organized a system to videotape picket line activity and arranged to record and file incident reports in an "evidence room" to be set up near their headquarters in the *Free Press* building.[10]

Meanwhile, Anthony met with more than a dozen area law enforcement agencies, including the police departments in Detroit and suburban Farmington Hills, Livonia, Westland, Taylor, and Lincoln Park; the sheriff's departments in Wayne, Oakland, and Macomb Counties; the Michigan State Police; and the federal Bureau of Alcohol, Tobacco, and Firearms (ATF) and the FBI.[11] In January, former FBI agent Jim Harrington called Chief Thomas Derocha of the Sterling Heights Police Department to arrange a meeting between Derocha and Anthony. The meeting took place on February 17 over lunch at the Steak and Ale Restaurant in Sterling Heights; present were Anthony, Kelleher, Derocha, and Sterling Heights police captain James Owens.[12]

The DNA representatives discussed the upcoming contract talks with their unions, as well as recent newspaper strikes in Pittsburgh and San Francisco and the potential for violence in Sterling Heights. Kelleher said that if a strike occurred, they intended to print and distribute the newspapers, and they expected to have complete freedom of ingress and egress to their facilities. Anthony was designated as the security liaison for the DNA, the two sides exchanged contact information, and the DNA picked up the tab.[13]

The newspapers' strike planning was systematic, thorough, and far beyond anything they had ever done before. Company executives had determined that a work stoppage was likely and that if it occurred they would operate with replacements. Following precedents in the 1990 *New York Daily News* and 1994 *San Francisco Chronicle* and *Examiner* strikes, they developed detailed contingency plans for every department and hired experienced strikebreaking security firms. Aware of the controversy their actions might generate in a city like Detroit, they deliberately chose to concentrate production in the more politically favorable Sterling Heights, and they made a concerted effort to enlist the cooperation of local law enforcement.

They also assumed an extraordinary level of antagonism toward their unionized employees. Perhaps that was not surprising, for the employers intended to make major contractual changes during the 1995 negotiations and might reasonably have expected their actions to provoke a strike. By the time Anthony and Kelleher left the restaurant in Sterling Heights on February 17, however, the DNA had not yet made a single formal contract proposal to any of the members of the Metropolitan Council of Newspaper Unions. But they had made sure they were going to be ready when they did.

THE STAKES OF THE GAME:
MANAGEMENT'S GOALS

After years of losses, the DNA had finally made a profit of $55 million in 1994, and business observers projected it to post a return of $70 million for 1995.[14] For their part, the unions had negotiated previous rounds of job cuts and rule changes, and they expected to see demands for more. As in the past, they wanted compensation in exchange for concessions and were eager to boost base wage rates that had been stagnant since the approval of the JOA. "We've given at the office," said the Guild's Don Kummer in December 1994, "and now it's our turn."[15] Company managers, however, viewed the 1995 contract talks as an extension of their unfinished agenda of workplace restructuring. Rather than reward employees for past sacrifices, the newspapers wanted even more cost reductions in production and distribution.

Many of the issues at stake were the same ones left outstanding from 1992. On the eve of negotiations, however, at least one crucial change occurred on management's side. In December 1994, the federal Securities and Exchange Commission (SEC) filed insider trading charges against Thomas Farrell, president of Gannett's New Media Group, and five others, including the DNA's Frank Vega. Among other allegations, the complaint said that Farrell had illegally disclosed the pending takeover of a Rochester, New York, savings bank to Vega in April 1993, while the two were in Florida on a golf vacation. Vega then purchased 6,500 shares in the bank under Farrell's advice to buy stock in small amounts over time to avoid notice. Farrell later pleaded guilty, while Vega signed a consent order agreeing to testify about his actions and to pay $98,338 in disgorged profits and fines. Despite the scandal, Vega kept his job as DNA chief, but he was immediately dropped from Gannett's Newspaper Operating Committee, the group of top corporate executives who met routinely to discuss newspaper division strategy. He remained a force in Detroit, but the 1995 contract talks would be dominated by Gannett's lead negotiator, John Jaske.[16]

As the time for contract renewal approached, a flurry of confidential memoranda circulated among the newspapers' departmental and labor relations management, focused on bargaining goals and sometimes simply titled "Strike Planning Issues."[17] On January 8, 1995, composing room supervisor Larry Ross wrote to DNA senior legal counsel John Taylor regarding "Things We Will Want in the Near Future." Ross urged the DNA to have telemarketing employees create display ads and send them directly to production, bypassing the composing room entirely. The marketing development department should also create their own "spec" ads to order for customers, Ross argued, while proposed "service desks" could receive client-produced display ads. "It should be a Management decision and of no concern to the Union," Ross wrote. ". . . In this manner, *nothing* has to come into Composing *before* this ad is published."[18]

Ross foresaw similar changes in the practice of code input and scanning of original artwork, which "should be done where ever the Detroit Newspapers feels it can be done most efficiently. . . . [It] should be a Management decision based on good economics and productivity and not involve the bargaining units." As the DNA moved forward with electronic pagination, he continued, "both from the Newsroom side and from the Production side, I see [the unions'] involvement in the placing of display ads diminishing dramatically, not to mention very, very quickly, in huge numbers."[19]

The changes Ross proposed, of course, were precisely the sorts of issues that Local 18 had grieved in 1993 and that were currently pending before arbitrator Joseph Girolamo. Adopting them would mean a drastic departure from previous agreements between the newspapers and the union, and Jaske understood clearly what that meant for the negotiations. "We must clean up the remaining jurisdictional barriers to new technology," he wrote tersely in a March 6, 1995, confidential memo to Gannett vice chair Doug McCorkindale.[20] Throughout his career, Jaske had battled the printers union, using the language of jurisdiction to reduce the scope of union representation. Now he would have the opportunity to do so again.

In the newsrooms, the *Free Press* anticipated no major workplace changes. But the *News* revived its controversial 1992 merit pay plan and further sought to reclassify certain employees as professionals exempt from federal wage and overtime laws. Its initial proposal to the union specified that "all future pay increases to bargaining unit employees will be on the basis of merit utilizing the Company's performance appraisal

system." In addition, it said that "News Department employees who qualify as professional within the meaning of Federal wage and hour laws
may, at their option, apply annually to be salaried and exempt from overtime. Any employee so applying may be offered a salary."[21]

Under a waiver from Local 22, over half of the *News* editorial staff had
received merit raises during the life of the 1992 contract.[22] But the union
saw the new proposal as a radical departure from past practice and a
threat to its function as a collective bargaining agent. As a former *Free
Press* journalist observed, "Gannett wanted to allow and encourage reporters to shift from hourly to salaried status and then bargain individually, while remaining nominally in the union. The Guild saw this as diminishing its collective strength, an invitation to slow suicide."[23] Ben Burns,
the director of the journalism program at Wayne State University and a
former executive editor of the *News*, concurred. While sympathetic to the
merit pay proposal, he acknowledged its impact on the union. "It would
emasculate the Guild," he told a reporter. "It destroys the ability of the
Guild to bargain for all its employees."[24]

The *News*, however, was determined to pursue the plan. "[*News* pub-
lisher] Bob Giles very much wants to stick to a proposal for merit pay in
the editorial department," Jaske wrote in his memo to McCorkindale. "I
agree with him."[25] With his record of success at the NLRB in the *Cincinnati
Enquirer* case, Jaske understood how to negotiate the issue within the sub-
tleties of the law. At the *News*, he would not hesitate to advocate forcefully
for it.

In the pressroom, the DNA had won significant job cuts in 1992, going
from units-plus-five (meaning a standard of two workers per press unit,
plus five supervisory and apprentice positions) to units-plus-two. The
company wanted more reductions, but much of what it regarded as excess
staffing was now covered at overtime.[26] In years past, "full time pressroom reductions [had] been on the basis of a buyout, and we shared a
relatively small percentage of the savings with the remaining employees,"
Jaske wrote to DNA executives.[27] This time the emphasis would be on the
control of hiring and the elimination of overtime.

By far the largest number of proposed job cuts affected the Teamster
units. In the mailroom, mechanization had reduced the demand for labor,
but the need for workers still fluctuated based on the number of advertising inserts. Each week an estimated number of employee shifts were filled
or "hired" from union lists. There were approximately three hundred full-
time journeyman mailers on the hiring "board" who were guaranteed five
mandatory shifts per week and who could bid on a percentage of additional shifts at overtime rates; perhaps three-fourths of all full-time mailers earned some overtime pay. In addition, around fifty part-time mailers

on the "A" list had to be available for, but were not guaranteed, full-time work. Finally, several hundred part-time employees on the "B" list worked on call and would often come and go, although some stayed with the job for years.[28]

Under this arrangement, the union in effect managed the supply of labor for the company in the mailroom. "We supplied any supplemental help that they needed over and above the full-time people through our hall," Local 2040's Alex Young recalled. "But at any given time, we always had to have a list of that many people because when you get into October and the Christmas season, you needed to have the additional one hundred people because the workload would fluctuate so much."[29] Over the years, management had also cut back on supervisory jobs and ceded much of the scheduling and direction of work to the union. "They kept eliminating supervisors and pushing the work onto either the union or the union stewards or the union membership," Jim St. Louis observed. "They'd throw it at the union steward and say, you do it."[30] These local practices made the Gannett corporate negotiators furious: "The employees think they work for the union rather than the company," Jaske complained in his March 6 memo to McCorkindale. "This has, and will continue to cost us a great deal of money unless we get control."[31]

With $22 million invested in new inserting machinery at the Sterling Heights plant, Jaske wanted to downsize the full-time staff and replace them with lower-paid part-timers. "Mailer manning is excessive, and this should be a strike issue," he wrote to McCorkindale. "Average salaries in the mailroom approach fifty thousand dollars per person. . . . Future extra hires whose main job is to feed the inserter should be paid much, much less than the current $16.00 per hour."[32] In fact, DNA payroll data for 1994 showed that average annual gross pay for full-time mailers was only $43,780. Part-time casual or substitute employees, who made the same base wage but without benefits, accounted for about one-fifth of all work hours and averaged from $6,047 to $9,302 annually.[33]

The payroll figures included overtime pay, but for the union the question of overtime was about more than money. Paying additional hours as overtime allowed the DNA to avoid hiring more full-time mailers, thereby saving the company the cost of benefits. On the other hand, converting the work to part-time threatened to reduce the number of full-time positions. St. Louis explained:

> That was our protection from them saying we'll just have a hundred full-timers and a thousand part-timers. . . . We knew that formula made them lay out the cost of fringe benefits versus the cost of the overtime. And so, when they came to us and said, we want to eliminate that overtime cost, we said,

fine, we'll be happy to do that, but we need protection against you dwindling this board of full-timers down to nothing and bringing everybody in on a part-time basis.[34]

The core of the mailers' bargaining came down to the issue of staffing. Union leaders wanted to preserve the supply of good-paying, full-time jobs for the future, while the company mocked their concern for "the unborn mailer." As the negotiations went on, Jaske wrote to the DNA management: "We need to set manning minimums that are very close to what we have proposed and then discuss: 1. How we achieve the reductions, and 2. What, if anything, we pay for the reductions and to whom."[35]

Lastly, in the circulation department the DNA wanted to continue the massive restructuring of operations begun in 1992. The company tried to institute a system of part-time drivers under the 1992 contract, but an arbitrator ruled against them.[36] Now the focus shifted to the carriers. A confidential February 8, 1995, memo in the circulation department identified the number-one priority: "Moving from [independent carriers] to Agents with the overall perspective that staffing efficiencies could be had in the way of a DM [district manager] handling both products [*News* and *Free Press*]; no reliefs needed for regular DM day off, fewer DM's handling a smaller force of agents."[37]

The agent plan was intended to replace the old buy-sell system. Carriers would be converted from independent operators to company agents and paid a set fee, while the DNA would take over billing and collections and gain access to account data on its subscribers.[38] Between 1989 and 1995, the newspapers had already reduced the number of carriers by 80 percent, from 14,000 to 2,800, as they shifted from youths to the system of adult carriers in cars. Now the number would be reduced again by as much as half, and the delivery areas correspondingly increased.

Although nominally aimed at the carriers, the agent plan had serious implications for the Teamster members in Local 372. The DNA wanted to cut scores of Teamster jobs, leaving fewer district managers to supervise carriers across much larger delivery areas. The non-union carrier-agents would also be allowed to perform work formerly done by union members, further eroding the bargaining unit. Finally, because the district managers would be directing company agents instead of independent operators, the DNA might have a better chance at having them reclassified as supervisors under the law and removing them from the union entirely.[39]

For years the Teamsters and the newspapers had negotiated a side letter in which the employers agreed temporarily not to contest the status of the district managers before the National Labor Relations Board.[40] To revoke that agreement now would undoubtedly be seen as an extraordinary act of aggression against the union. Nevertheless, Jaske wrote McCorkindale, "I would prefer to see us only have a one year contract covering the district managers and then take them out of the union next year. However, I do not believe Frank [Vega] will insist on it."[41]

Altogether, it was an ambitious bargaining agenda for the newspapers. For each of the units, however, there were "poison-pill" provisions that the unions would have a very hard time swallowing. Some of the proposals would, in effect, bypass the union or undermine its capacity for collective bargaining. Others would cut union jobs and replace them with lower-paid, non-union labor. Far from making up for lost ground, management seemed to demand continued sacrifice from the unions at a time when the papers were no longer losing money. But in no case was the problem simply about wages. The 1995 negotiations were about changing the relationship between the employers and their unionized employees. That was a far more wrenching change, and one perhaps requiring a greater show of force.

In February, Jaske submitted his monthly report to McCorkindale, covering labor relations at forty-six Gannett locations. For "Detroit Newspapers," he wrote, "We have virtually completed first proposals for all 14 bargaining units," including several small units of skilled trades like electricians and garage mechanics. "Negotiations will begin in a few weeks. We are also working on strike planning." Jaske's full report mentioned at least fifteen other Gannett workplaces with ongoing collective bargaining negotiations. None of the reports from the other workplaces indicated any strike planning.[42]

The DNA sent its first proposals, with more than three hundred separate items in all, to the unions on February 20. In his cover letter, the DNA's Tim Kelleher announced that the newspapers "will not be engaging in joint or pattern bargaining with any of the unions."[43] Individual meetings with Local 13N for the pressroom units and Local 2040 for the mailers began on March 9 and 10, respectively.[44] Less than two weeks later, on March 20, Captain Owens of the SHPD issued a memo to his operations division command staff. "A lack of progress in labor negotiations may result in a strike this summer, involving employees of the Detroit Newspaper Agency. This includes workers from several unions in both the Detroit News and the Detroit Free Press," Owens wrote. "The newspaper agency has arranged for a team of staff members including the Strike Security Coordinator [Anthony] to meet with representatives of this Division to consider the same." Owens ordered his lieutenants to attend the meeting, with overtime paid for those officers not on duty. At the time of Owens's memo, the newspapers had held two bargaining sessions with the press-room units and three with the mailers. They had not yet met with either the printers or the Guild.[45]

ARMING FOR BATTLE: THE DNA AND THE SHPD

Regardless of how negotiations were in fact going, the DNA's strike preparations rapidly accelerated. On April 3, the company signed contracts with Huffmaster and its affiliate, Alternative Work Force, Inc. (AWF), for services to be made available on May 1. The Huffmaster contract called for the provision of 33 supervisors and administrative staff, 182 transportation security officers, 83 two-man mobile response teams, 52 hotel security officers, 16 evidence and documentation personnel, and 25 downtown shuttle officers, to be assembled in the Detroit area by April 28. The DNA agreed to pay a $125 prep fee per security person, $125 per hour for managers, and $17.75 per hour for each security guard. The contract estimated needs for 37 nineteen-passenger vans, 70 full-size four-door cars, and 3 minivans, as well as 180 video cameras, 233 mobile radios, and 90 cellular phones, all paid for by the client.

Huffmaster's duties were to guard property and vehicles; secure access; inspect, report, and photograph the strike; and maintain the chain of custody of evidence. AWF agreed to provide 259 CDL-A truck drivers, up to 240 home delivery workers, and 64 diesel mechanics, electricians, and engineers. AWF coordinators, drivers, and skilled craft workers were each charged at $35 per hour, and home delivery workers at $17.75 per hour. For both contracts, the DNA agreed to pay for time and cost of travel to Detroit as well as hotel or motel accommodations and per diem of $35 a day.[46]

In Sterling Heights, Chief Derocha, Captain Owens, and their lieutenants met with Anthony, APT's George Beach, and Huffmaster senior manager Woody Goodnight at an Italian restaurant, Filippa's Wine Barrel, on March 31. Anthony gave an update on the progress of negotiations and mentioned possible strike dates. He, Beach, and Goodnight briefed the Sterling Heights officers on their security plan, the location of company facilities, and their respective duties and assignments, using a large diagram of the *News* printing plant. They discussed the Pittsburgh and San Francisco strikes, described Huffmaster's role in San Francisco, and reiterated the possibility for violence.[47]

The police commanders were impressed. Chief Derocha later testified that "this was probably much more significant in terms of potential demands on us than what we had anticipated; that here was material on file from prior strikes which would create a preparatory blueprint of sorts."[48] The officers were given contact information for law enforcement agencies in the Bay Area, and Derocha assigned Lt. Frank Mowinski to be strike coordinator for the Sterling Heights Police Department.

For the thirty-six-year-old Mowinski, it was a career moment. A graduate of Sterling Heights High School, twice divorced, and the father of one son, he had joined the Sterling Heights department in 1981, working his way up the ranks from patrolman to sergeant in the traffic division. On the day of the Filippa's meeting, he was actually due to be promoted to lieutenant; his job as strike coordinator would be his first major assignment. Mowinski took to the job with diligence and zeal, gathering information from the police departments and private security involved in the San Francisco strike, reading documents, and doing research on easements, parking, and traffic around the *News*'s North Plant.

At the DNA's invitation, Mowinski, Owens, and other SHPD officers toured the North Plant on April 12, observing the layout of the office, warehouse, pressroom, and mailroom areas.[49] Following the March meeting, Anthony sent to Sterling Heights a copy of the Huffmaster video of the San Francisco strike. Chief Derocha found the tape particularly disturbing, and over the next several months he oversaw an unprecedented mobilization of capacity within the Sterling Heights Police Department.[50] On May 1, Mowinski sent the results of his research to Owens. In a ten-page, single-spaced memo entitled "Impending Strike at the Detroit News Plant," he began by defining a "Mission Statement":

> This Department will maintain its impartiality in labor disputes. It recognizes that negotiation, collective bargaining and strikes involving picketing are legal methods of peacefully settling labor disputes. This Department's role will be to provide for the safety of the citizens, employees of the DNA, members of the labor union along with the officers of this Department and any other government agency assisting them. The Department will maintain order during this process.[51]

The memo went on to discuss the logistics of the North Plant site, tactical needs and resources, and contact persons at the papers and the unions. It also included detailed summaries of the experiences of the Bay Area police departments in the San Francisco strike. Within the report, however, were contradictory statements as to the SHPD's role in any potential dispute. Under "Intelligence," Mowinski noted that the North Plant "will be the only Detroit News operating plant during the strike. All other Detroit area plants will be closed." Mirroring the DNA's demand for unrestricted access, he continued, "our officers' main duty will be to allow vehicles to safely enter and exit the facility." Finally, Mowinski noted that, "in the past, both the DNA and the Unions have extended negotiations [beyond the April 30 contract expiration date]. The DNA does not project a strike to take place until after the second week of May. Updates will be provided on the process of negotiations."[52]

Mowinski's report became the basis for his five-page "Contingency Plan for Impending DNA Strike," delivered to Owens on May 6 and implemented on May 8.[53] The plan spelled out equipment needs, the duties and placement of field forces and vehicles, arrest procedures, and parking provisions in the event of a walkout. A special section on "Confrontation" contained legal orders for declaring an "unlawful assembly" and methods for the dispersal of picketers. In addition, as part of their training, an abridged version of the Huffmaster video was played for operations division personnel during their mandatory roll call meetings.[54]

On May 8, Chief Derocha sent a copy of the action plan to Sterling Heights city manager Steve Duchane. Attached to it was a confidential memo in which Derocha identified several "Key Issues." "Our primary focus and responsibility," Derocha wrote, "is that of maintaining access to and egress from the facility for management personnel, temporary workers and materials. This will have to be accomplished amid large numbers of vocal and potentially violent picketers." Nowhere under the "Key Issues" in Derocha's memo was there any mention of impartiality, the right to protest, or the safety of citizens.[55]

CONCLUSION: COME HELL OR HIGH WATER

In the 1995 negotiations, the DNA and Gannett wanted to make major changes, not only in the structure of the workplace but in the relationship of the newspapers with their unionized employees. They knew these demands might provoke a strike: internal company documents discussing bargaining goals made explicit references to "strike planning." To prepare for that likelihood, the DNA management committed to a decision to operate with replacements, developed comprehensive contingency plans across all departments, and hired outside, professional strikebreaking security firms. They anticipated that their actions might cause havoc, and they intended to be ready for it.

Perhaps most remarkably, in the winter and spring of 1995 the DNA initiated a relationship with the Sterling Heights police command that would develop into a pattern of collusion. Starting well before negotiations even began, the DNA attempted to persuade the police that a strike was likely, that it would be violent, and that the SHPD would need to develop anti-riot capacity to ensure the company's overriding right to its property. Their campaign was successful: on May 8, Captain Owens wrote to all operations division personnel that "the potential for the kind of violence which recently occurred in newspaper strikes in both San Francisco and Pittsburgh must be considered highly possible here also."[56]

Notwithstanding the formal "Mission Statement," SHPD policy early on showed a bias toward DNA priorities. Lieutenant Mowinski's May 1 report and Chief Derocha's confidential May 8 memo to city manager Duchane both stressed the "main duty" or responsibility to guarantee ingress and egress at the North Plant. Moreover, the DNA shared with the SHPD confidential information on strike planning and negotiations, including the fact that only the Sterling Heights plant would remain open in a strike and even the dates on which the DNA anticipated a walkout. The police in turn did not share this knowledge with the unions and did not even meet with them until May 5, after the action plan was already virtually completed.[57]

As Derocha had said, the SHPD took the information the newspapers gave them as a "blueprint," and Mowinski used those materials to draft his report and action plan. The Huffmaster video was literally incorporated into the mandatory training for SHPD officers, even though the video was the edited product of a DNA contractor, hardly an impartial source. In addition, buried within Mowinski's May 1 report was a recommendation from the San Francisco Police Department: "Closely monitor Huffmaster Security as they were found to instigate disturbances with strikers (security being suspected in damaging striker vehicles.)"[58]

Despite the warning, however, the momentum within the SHPD continued to grow. In his May 8 memo, Captain Owens wrote that "various equipment which may be needed has also been given careful consideration and is in the process of being selected and shipped to this Department."[59] On May 9, Mowinski obtained invoices from a supplier for new helmets, shields, clear-out grenades, plastic double-cuffs, and other items costing a total of $4,549. Unwilling to wait for a city purchase order to be processed, Mowinski procured the items on credit at ninety days same as cash.[60]

The shields and helmets were delivered, and on May 31 they were used in a four-hour training session conducted on the grounds outside the Sterling Heights city hall. On a sunny, spring suburban morning, around seventy-five officers in riot gear showed up to practice crowd control, mobile formations, and field tactics, under the direction of a paid expert consultant, Sgt. William Jones of the Detroit Police Department. "We're doing some tactical training now in preparation of a possible, rather major strike at the News plant," Derocha told a reporter, as curious onlookers passed by on their way to the public library and the courthouse. "We're hoping for the best, but preparing for the worst."[61]

"A lot was made of the fact that we planned for the strike," the DNA's Frank Vega said later, comparing it to hurricanes in his home state. "If you live in Florida, and a hurricane's coming, do you just sit there and do nothing? No, you board up your windows, you go buy water, you get batteries, you get a generator. If a storm is coming, you get prepared for it."[62] The residents of Florida, however, did not have the ability to negotiate agreements with the earth's climate, and the benign imagery of natural disaster relief obscured the political reality of police and guards marching in riot helmets and shields. The DNA prepared for the worst because it was determined to get what it wanted, whatever that might take. There were other ways to avoid a walkout. The postwar system of labor relations was designed to encourage settlements, and a strike was meant to be a last resort. The system worked best when both sides accepted its core values and principles. In Detroit in the spring of 1995, however, the newspaper companies were moving in a decidedly different direction.

Photo 1. John Jaske (*right*) and Tim Kelleher attend a hearing at the National Labor Relations Board office in Detroit. Jaske was assistant general counsel and senior vice president for labor relations for the Gannett Company, Inc., the parent company of the *Detroit News*. As chief negotiator for the *News* and the Detroit Newspaper Agency (DNA), he was the most powerful figure on the management side. Kelleher was senior vice president of labor relations at the DNA and a chief media spokesperson for the newspapers. Copyright Rebecca Cook.

Photo 2. Frank Vega, chief executive officer of the DNA, photographed standing on top of his desk in his office. Vega became the public face of the company's resistance to the strike, but he had little control over the contract negotiations that led to and prolonged it. Copyright daymonjhartley .com.

Photo 3. Metropolitan Council of Newspaper Union (MCNU) leaders on stage at Action! Motown '97 in Hart Plaza on June 21, 1997. From left to right: Lou Mleczko, president, Detroit Newspaper Guild Local 22; Don Kummer, retired administrative officer, Detroit Newspaper Guild; Bernie Schenk, president, Photoengravers Local 289M; Jack Howe, president, Pressmen's Union Local 13N; Al Derey, secretary-treasurer, Teamsters Local 372 and chair of the MCNU; Sam Attard, president, Local 18, Detroit Typographical Union; Alex Young, president, Teamsters Local 2040. Copyright *Detroit Sunday Journal*/Patricia Beck.

Photo 4. Labor attorneys Duane Ice and Sam McKnight. Both were experienced lawyers and veterans of some of the landmark strikes of the 1980s and 1990s. Ice had worked with Arizona copper miners in the 1983 Phelps-Dodge strike, while McKnight was an advisor to the unions in the 1990 to 1991 strike at the *New York Daily News*. Copyright Rebecca Cook.

Photo 5. Attorneys from the National Labor Relations Board in Detroit during the hearings on the principal unfair labor practice charges against the newspapers. From left: assistant general counsel Ellen Farrell; supervising attorney Amy Bachelder; attorneys Linda Rabin Hammell, Blair Simmons, and Mark Rubin; and regional director William Schaub. Copyright Rebecca Cook.

Photo 6. Private security forces stand on the roof of the *Detroit News* building in downtown Detroit, overlooking demonstrators on the street below. The newspapers spent an estimated $40 million for security during the course of the five-and-a-half-year-long dispute. Copyright *Detroit Sunday Journal*/Patricia Beck.

Photo 7. Off-duty Sterling Heights Police Lt. Jack Severance kicks striking press operator Frank Brabanec at the DNA's Sterling Heights printing plant on August 19, 1995. The DNA had initiated private meetings and coordinated with the Sterling Heights Police Department (SHPD) months before the strike began. Copyright daymonjhartley.com.

Photo 8. Police use pepper spray against picketers at the Sterling Heights printing plant. After the strike started, the DNA donated more than a million dollars to suburban governments to cover the costs of police protection and overtime, and even paid for shields and equipment delivered to the SHPD. Copyright daymonjhartley.com.

Photo 9. A DNA delivery truck parked at the Sterling Heights plant was set on fire and destroyed during Labor Day protests on the night of Monday, September 4, 1995. The DNA used images of the fire in ads to show alleged violence by strikers, but an investigation by Macomb County Prosecutor Carl Marlinga found it unlikely that strikers were responsible, since at the time the truck was behind the plant gate and surrounded by security guards. Copyright daymonjhartley.com.

Photo 10. Private security guards hired by the newspapers attack picketers outside the gate at the Clayton Street distribution center in Detroit on Sunday, October 1, 1995. One of the picketers, Vito Sciuto, was struck on the head by a security guard wielding a heavy wooden stick. He suffered a fractured skull and brain damage and required surgery to reconstruct his face and eye. Copyright daymonjhartley.com.

Photo 11. Leafleters outside a local furniture store chain urge customers not to patronize the retailer because it placed advertising in the struck newspapers. The unions appealed to the community to support a circulation and advertising boycott of the newspapers, extending the struggle beyond the workplace to include commercial and residential areas throughout metropolitan Detroit. Copyright George Waldman, DetroitPhotoJournalism.com.

Photo 12. Protestors took their message to DNA chief executive Frank Vega's home in suburban Grosse Pointe Farms, Michigan, while an armed security guard (*left*) stands at the home's gated driveway entrance. The community campaign brought civic demonstrations and collective action into local streets and neighborhoods and challenged the normal boundaries between public and private urban space. Copyright *Detroit Sunday Journal* / Patricia Beck.

Photo 13. Detroit City Council President Maryann Mahaffey (*left*) and striking Detroit *Free Press* columnist Susan Watson walk to Central United Methodist Church in Detroit, along with other participants of the Fast for Justice and Peace at the Detroit Newspapers, on October 1, 1996. Watson was coeditor of the weekly strike newspaper the *Detroit Sunday Journal,* and for many became the voice and conscience of the strike. Copyright *Detroit Sunday Journal*/Patricia Beck.

Photo 14. Religious leaders from the Readers United coalition conduct civil disobedience at the headquarters of the *Detroit News* in downtown Detroit. Seated in front are Rev. Ed Rowe (*center*) and Rev. Bill Wylie-Kellerman (*right*). Standing in rear (*left to right*): Rev. Nicholas Hood III, Marietta Jaeger Lane, Sister Margaret Hughes, Ann Maneinski, Gerry Sellman, and Sister Cathy Desantis. Copyright George Waldman, DetroitPhotoJournalism.com.

Photo 15. Members of the United Auto Workers (UAW) block the entrance to the *Free Press* building on Lafayette Street, March 28, 1996. Sixty-five non-striking union leaders were arrested that day, including UAW Region 1A director Bob King (*center*) and seventeen area UAW local union presidents. Copyright *Detroit Sunday Journal*/Patricia Beck.

Photo 16. Strikers and supporters sit down in front of the *Detroit News* building in a nonviolent protest during Labor Day weekend, on August 30, 1996. The newspapers used photographs of the scene like this one to identify and fire the strikers for participating in the action. Front row (*left to right*): Gary Rusnell, Emily Everett, Nancy Dunn, Susan Watson (*holding Dunn*), Harry Collins. Second row: Dia Pearce (*in baseball cap*), Allan Lengel, Shawn Ellis, Frank Prainito. Third row: Millie Kenyon, Rick Stringer, Bob Ourlian (*in white baseball cap*), Kate DeSmet, Dick Coil, Rick Torres. In the center at rear are AFL-CIO secretary-treasurer Richard Trumka, AFL-CIO president John Sweeney, and Bill Boarman, president of the Printing, Publishing, and Media Workers Sector of the Communications Workers of America. Copyright George Waldman, DetroitPhotoJournalism.com.

Photo 17. Action! Motown '97 demonstrators march down Michigan Avenue from the old Tiger Stadium, in the background at top right. The peaceful, orderly procession to Hart Plaza took at least two hours, with marchers stretched out over a mile along the city streets. Estimates of the crowd for the day ranged from 60,000 to 100,000 persons. Copyright George Waldman, DetroitPhotoJournalism.com.

Photo 18. Striking newspaper workers and supporters join hands and sing during Action! Motown '97 at Hart Plaza in Detroit on June 21, 1997. (*From left*) Detroit Newspaper Guild members Toni Martin, Emily Everett, and Luther Jackson (*center*). Jackson was a San Jose Newspaper Guild member and former *Free Press* business reporter and administrative officer for the Detroit Newspaper Guild. Copyright *Detroit Sunday Journal*/Patricia Beck.

Photo 19. Elected officials from twenty-four area city councils and county commissions from Wayne, Oakland, and Macomb Counties convened at a summit conference, sponsored by Religious Leaders for Justice at the Detroit Newspapers, to encourage a settlement of the dispute. Representatives of Detroit Newspapers management were invited to participate in the conference, held on May 18, 1998, at Sacred Heart Seminary in Detroit, but declined to attend. Copyright *Detroit Sunday Journal*/Patricia Beck.

Photo 20. Members of the Teamsters Locals 2040 and 372 count ballots from an election ratifying the contract with the newspapers, December 17, 2000. The contracts did not allow fired strikers to return to work, and charges of unlawful discharge by the newspapers remained in litigation for over five more years. Copyright George Waldman, DetroitPhotoJournalism .com.

Chapter 7 | War of Position: The 1995 Contract Negotiations

THEY KNEW IT WAS NOT going to be easy. The leaders of the Metropolitan Council of Newspaper Unions approached the 1995 negotiations warily, anticipating a struggle. They knew their power was not what it once was: the *News* and *Free Press* now enjoyed monopoly power in the DNA, while advances in technology had made it easier to produce and perhaps even deliver a newspaper during a strike. The 1992 contract had bought a provisional and uneasy peace, but relations on the job had since deteriorated, leading to numerous grievances and arbitrations. Now the newspapers were demanding more concessions, and militarized guards were beginning to assemble on the second floor of the *Free Press* building on Lafayette Street.

At least one factor, however, was working in the unions' favor: they were united. In the old days, organizational or personal rivalries would inevitably weaken or split apart the union coalition. The generation of leaders who came to the table in 1995, however, had developed an unusual trust in and solidarity with each other. "Our personalities just seemed to click, and for some reason, as the pressure increased, we got tighter instead of falling apart," the press operators' Jack Howe observed. "And we helped one another. We went to each other's union meetings to explain what was going on with our own segments. We invited members from other locals to come to our meetings, and I mean it was a very open relationship with the council."[1]

They would need all the help they could get. Conventional economic theory assumes that both management and unions engage in rational cost-benefit calculation and act within standard institutional channels or routines. In brief, strikes occur because the parties simply fail to agree on well-defined issues at the bargaining table. As the events unfolded in Detroit, however, it became apparent that the two sides were really playing under very different sets of rules.

Under the leadership of Gannett managers, the newspapers adopted the norms and logic of the postwar union avoidance path. In negotiations they deployed tactics of hard bargaining, impasse, and implementation in order to override the unions' resistance to their demands. As in the Phelps Dodge and *New York Daily News* strikes, they made massive preparations to operate with replacement workers, and they radically intensified their security forces. Finally, they actively courted the command staff of the Sterling Heights Police Department to ensure their cooperation and neutralize the impact of any strike.

By contrast, the unions remained committed to New Deal principles of collective bargaining. Convinced that their organizational survival was at stake, they ultimately chose to strike in a desperate effort to preserve their rights and protections under the old system. Deprived of the traditional mechanisms for reaching agreements, however, the unions also turned to alternative tactics, filing unfair labor practice charges to protect their right to strike and reaching out for public support through the circulation and advertising boycotts.

The two sides began meeting in March 1995. They were unable to achieve a settlement before the previous contracts expired on April 30, however, and under a temporary extension the negotiations continued into the summer. As the talks began to break down in May and June, the unions filed unfair labor practice charges in three principal areas covering negotiations with the printers union, the Newspaper Guild, and the joint bargaining with the MCNU. When the strike finally began on July 13, it marked the opening of a signal juncture in the history of labor relations in the United States.

HARD BARGAINING: THE START OF THE 1995 NEGOTIATIONS

The 1995 negotiations opened on a sharply antagonistic note, beginning with the Teamsters Local 2040 mailroom unit. In Local 2040's first bargaining session with management on March 10, Gannett lead negotiator John Jaske announced that the DNA had tentatively concluded that unless mailroom productivity improved, it would shut down the $22 million inserting operation it had only recently installed at the Sterling Heights North Plant and outsource the work. Local 2040 leaders were surprised, but saw this as a monumental bluff. Immediately after the meeting, they sent an update to their members advising them to stay calm and to resist the DNA's attempts "to climb into all of their employees' heads and steer them in whatever direction they want."[2] The union gave its own initial proposal to the company, but a week later DNA chief Frank Vega sent a letter with a sixty-day formal notice under the federal Worker Adjustment and Retraining Notification (WARN) Act to Locals 2040 and 372, the units that would be affected by the proposed closure.[3]

At their next bargaining session on March 29, Local 2040 president Alex Young brought up the WARN notice. "We have a legal obligation to discuss both the decision and the impact of that decision," Jaske answered blandly. He reported that the DNA was considering a bid to transfer the work to a firm in Allentown, Pennsylvania, a move that might put more than two hundred DNA mailers out of work. Young proceeded cautiously, asking what the union could do. According to the company's typewritten bargaining notes, Jaske replied:

> "We don't know, we can't say this is a *fait accompli*. If you have any suggestions we are legally and practically obligated to discuss it with you."

The conversation continued:

> "Is your decision tentative or final?" Young asked.
>
> "It is what it is," said Jaske.
>
> "We think you have an obligation to tell us."
>
> "We have our obligation to bargain with you over the decision and will do so in good faith. If you have proposals, we will listen."
>
> "I'm lost, I don't know what to say."[4]

The thirty-seven-year-old Young was dumbfounded but moved carefully; not only had the DNA dropped its bombshell, but now Jaske expected the union to bargain against itself, forcing up concessions that the company might or might not choose to accept. Local 2040 bargaining team member Jim St. Louis was furious. "We made a proposal to cut costs, and your response is to send a letter. . . . Are we to assume that our offer is off the table?" Union leader John Peralta was equally frustrated. "Why can't you tell us up front about the decision?" he asked. "Folks would like to make plans to get on with their lives." Jaske merely replied, "I have the legal obligation to keep the issue open. I can't come to the table with a decision made. I don't have any suggestions as to what you can do. If you have no proposals or suggestions, we can discuss the impact."[5]

Union leaders remained skeptical; the DNA purportedly intended to truck newspapers more than five hundred miles from Allentown to Detroit, across the Allegheny mountains and through winter weather over the Great Lakes. "This is Michigan, that's Pennsylvania," Young said later. "It's a perishable product. It snows."[6] Nevertheless, the threat of the closure hung over the mailroom negotiations until early June, when a tentative deal on staffing was reached and the WARN notice withdrawn. Even the DNA's Tim Kelleher admitted, "It would be—not foolish—but kind of a dumb decision on our part to have built that [insertion facility], put the money into it, then shut it down and go someplace else." But the threat served its purpose, Kelleher said, because "unless we get some movement from the mailers, there's no sense in leaving that room open."[7]

The DNA's stance with the mailers set the tone for the talks with the other units and, along with the papers' visible reinforcement of security, convinced the MCNU leaders to step up their own mobilization. They had previously met with David Hecker, executive assistant to the president of the Metropolitan Detroit AFL-CIO, to discuss strategy in late 1994. In January 1995, they opened a contract campaign fund and retained Sam McKnight, who already represented the printers, to assist in joint activities. By mid-February, Hecker was coordinating the MCNU's action committee and overseeing a program of one-on-one internal membership organizing as well as research on potential community allies and advertisers in the papers.[8]

By April, little progress had been made in the negotiations. As a precaution, the unions asked their members for strike authorization votes, a standard procedure to give additional leverage to the leaders at the bargaining table.[9] In May, the MCNU opened a campaign headquarters in office space above the Anchor Bar, a traditional newspaper watering hole on West Fort Street near the *News* and *Free Press* buildings. Hecker was joined by national AFL-CIO representative George Curtin, and together they set up a speakers' bureau and a phone bank, developed pledge cards for subscribers to cancel their home delivery, and began contacting advertisers for a potential boycott.[10] "We were going out almost every other day," Alex Young recalled, "to a UAW local or machinists local or somewhere, giving speeches, building up support and collecting [subscriber] boycott cards."[11] According to Hecker, the idea was that

> you don't want to strike, so you try to do everything else. And that is reaching out to elected officials to get them to make statements and send letters, et cetera, on our side . . . building up the database of advertisers and keeping advertisers in touch with what was going on so they knew, well, it may be in your interest to talk to the papers, because eventually we might ask you to

pull your advertising if this doesn't work out. It was getting pledge cards, I remember, from everyday folk, that if there's a strike, or I think it said, if the unions ask, not even just a strike, we will stop, we will boycott the paper.[12]

Months before the strike started, the dispute was already escalating beyond normal institutional channels. The MCNU reached out through the infrastructure of labor and civic organization in the region to communicate with subscribers, advertisers, elected officials, and religious and community groups. Aiming at the revenue streams for the newspapers, the unions took their campaign to independent businesses and the reading public. Meanwhile, the newspapers mobilized their own local outreach, coordinating security plans with the Sterling Heights Police Department and other law enforcement agencies.

In late April, the DNA settled three-year contracts with several small, separate units of machinists and other skilled trades altogether representing around one hundred workers. The contracts included wage increases of 4 percent the first year and 3 percent the second and third years, prefiguring the economic offer the papers were prepared to make to the other unions. On April 30, however, the contracts covering the 2,500 employees represented by the MCNU expired without any successor agreement. The two sides decided to extend the old contract's terms and conditions on a day-to-day basis, while bargaining continued toward a new contract.[13]

In an effort to jump-start the process, MCNU chair Al Derey asked DNA chief Vega in May to reinstate the joint bargaining format on economic issues that had worked successfully in 1992. Vega appeared to agree, but significant problems remained in the individual unit negotiations, especially with the printers on the issue of jurisdiction and the Guild on merit pay. In both of those cases, the company eventually declared impasse and implemented its proposals, causing the unions to file unfair labor practice charges. Finally, even the promise of joint economic bargaining collapsed, leaving the parties utterly at odds with each other.

BAD FAITH? IMPASSE, IMPLEMENTATION, AND JOINT BARGAINING

On May 9, Derey and Local 372 president Dennis Romanowski caught up with Vega at the DNA headquarters during a caucus in the negotiations. Up to that point, Vega had had relatively little direct role in the talks at the table, but he invited the union leaders into his office and told them of his desire for a speedy settlement. Derey suggested that they adopt the two-stage joint bargaining procedure, reserving common, across-the-board economic items until after each unit had resolved its individual issues. Vega said that he was agreeable, but that the request had to come from Derey, not Vega. Later that day Derey sent a letter to Vega confirming their conversation.[14]

The following day the MCNU leaders met and identified thirteen subjects to be reserved for joint bargaining, including wage increases, health insurance, vacation and holidays, a 401(k) plan, and other items. Derey then called Vega to discuss the list, and Vega said, "It sounds to me like the same as last time," and he asked Derey to put it in writing. On May 11, Derey hand-delivered a letter enumerating the thirteen subjects and signed by the principal officers of all six unions in the MCNU. Vega received the letter and told Derey that joint bargaining would commence on the issues cited after "a tentative overall agreement on non-economic issues."[15] The unions hoped that they could focus now on their individual unit issues, such as staffing, buyouts, and the restructuring of work. Yet, almost immediately, other problems erupted. According to Derey, when he told Jaske on May 11 of his agreement with Vega, Jaske replied, "You can do any fucking thing you want."[16] In a bargaining session that same day, Jaske declared an impasse on jurisdiction with the printers.

The Printers and Jurisdiction

In the DNA's initial proposal to Local 18, the very first item demanded a "non-exclusive" jurisdiction clause, asserting the company's unrestricted right to assign work done by the printers to employees in other areas not currently in the unit. Jaske, of course, had identified jurisdiction as a priority for the printer negotiations in his March 6 memo to Gannett vice chair Doug McCorkindale, but he also knew that it was a hot-button issue for the union, as their 1993 grievance on the matter was still pending before arbitrator Joseph Girolamo. At the first bargaining session on March 22, Local 18 president Sam Attard reacted strongly against the proposed jurisdiction clause and said it would emasculate the contract and destroy the printers' bargaining unit.

At their April 27 meeting, union negotiators told Jaske that the jurisdiction proposal was a permissive subject, affecting the definition of the bargaining unit and the union's ability to represent it. The union's claim was important, because if the proposal was a permissive subject, then the union was free to refuse to discuss it—and they promptly did just that. At the meeting, Jaske denied that the proposal involved any change to the unit definition and said it would not affect the printers' lifetime job guarantees. He warned, however, that a refusal to bargain over it would deadlock the negotiations.[17] In that case, an impasse would exist and the company could unilaterally implement the proposal.

The two sides met again on May 11 in a conference room at the *News* building downtown. This time, the printers' committee was joined by MCNU leaders Derey, Jack Howe, Don Kummer, and Robert Ogden, along with Ron Ruth of Local 18's international union, the Communication Workers of America (CWA). The union produced a written statement citing the printers' 1974 memorandum of agreement and claimed that it was wrong for the company to try to abrogate that agreement now. The statement accused the company of surface bargaining, saying, "We believe the company is bargaining in bad faith by insisting on negotiating this permissive subject before it will negotiate on any other point." Jaske replied that the DNA considered the proposal to be a mandatory subject covering operational efficiency and reiterated promises to provide "composing room work to all employees covered by the job guarantees in the composing room."[18] As the meeting came to an end, Jaske said that the negotiations appeared to be deadlocked.

On May 22, arbitrator Girolamo issued his decision, upholding the union's position on jurisdiction. Jaske refused to comply with the ruling, however, contending that it applied only under the now-expired previous contract and that his current proposal was effectively implemented by his declaration of impasse on May 11. At the June 15 bargaining meeting, Local 18 attorney Sam McKnight asked Jaske to implement the arbitrator's award first and said the union would then be flexible in bargaining changes in work assignments. Jaske again refused, saying the DNA did not want to risk the costs of compliance only to undo it weeks later and resume its present practice.[19] As McKnight later testified, "I said, 'You've just told us that any bargaining we engage in over your view of Item 1 of your proposals would be meaningless because, after a couple weeks, the union is either going to completely capitulate to your demands, or you're going to implement them. So there's no point in even going through that exercise. Bargaining would be absolutely futile.'"[20]

In this and in two more sessions in June and July, Jaske repeatedly insisted that the printers would continue to have jobs, although he conceded that the proposal could allow the employer the right to transfer all unit work to persons not now in the unit. For their part, the union believed Jaske was trying to "build a wall" around the composing room and that honoring the lifetime guarantees did not prevent the DNA from wiping out whole sections of the MOA. On June 22, McKnight filed an unfair labor practice charge against the DNA for refusal to provide information. On the day the strike began, July 13, the charge was amended to bargaining in bad faith.[21]

The Guild and Merit Pay

While the printers struggled with the DNA, the Guild faced its own problems in negotiations for newsroom employees at the *News*. The company's opening contract proposal featured fourteen items, including proposals for mandatory television appearances for reporters without additional compensation, a plan to encourage employees to shift to salaried professional status exempt from federal overtime laws, and, once again as in 1992, merit pay tied to performance evaluations.[22] The union initially responded by claiming that the overtime exemption proposal was an illegal subject of bargaining, prompting the *News* to file an unfair labor practice charge against Local 22 for refusing to discuss it.

The central issue in the Guild negotiations, however, was merit pay, and Jaske was prepared to stick with it to impasse if necessary. On April 25 the *News* offered a modified plan that included a 1 percent across-the-board wage increase and an additional larger percentage set aside in a "merit pool" based on the minimum wage rates for each job category. Like the language in the 1990 *Cincinnati Enquirer* case (but unlike the previous *News* contract), the union would have the right to grieve but not arbitrate an employee's performance evaluations. Anyone already over the contract minimum (and most were) would have their pay determined solely by merit. As for the details of how the plan would be administered, Jaske gave only vague promises of future explanation.[23]

Later that day, Jaske and *News* publisher Bob Giles met privately and agreed to base merit percentages on individuals' actual wages rather than the contract minimums. They faxed the proposal to the union, but the faxed document failed to mention the change in the merit base. At the May 3 bargaining session, Guild leader Don Kummer told Jaske that his members were not interested in the plan as it had been described to them, but he did not rule out further discussion. Jaske responded that there was little chance of reaching an agreement without merit pay, and he then rejected, point by point with minor exceptions, the Guild's entire fifty-six-page contract proposal. Afterward, Giles issued memos to the *News* editorial staff on May 3 and on May 10 claiming that the Guild "flatly rejects the merit pay proposal" and accusing it of refusing to bargain.[24]

"It appears that the negotiations are deadlocked," Jaske wrote to Kummer on May 24.[25] Guild negotiators were mystified. "We were still trying to get a better handle on the [merit pay] proposal, because we still had a lot of questions about just about all the phases and aspects of it," Mleczko later testified.[26] At the June 14 meeting, Kummer asked about the overtime exemption proposal, and Jaske replied that management would make all determinations of employees' professional status and in-lieu-of-overtime salary, though he refused to provide a list of unit employees the *News* considered to be eligible for the plan. In response to Kummer's questions, Jaske finally disclosed the change in the base for calculating merit pay; however, he refused to state the dollar value of the merit pool, even though the *News* had produced an internal document in April with those exact computations projected for each contract year.[27]

As in the *Cincinnati Enquirer* case, Jaske and Giles appeared to want to exclude the Guild from any meaningful role in setting wages for newsroom employees. Instead, they would bypass the union and deal directly with staff through the overtime exemption and the merit pay plan. They knew the Guild would resist these proposals, and they seemed anxious simply to declare a deadlock. In bargaining, Jaske was reluctant to specify details or even to provide facts that the *News* already had, while Giles was quick to blame the union in memos to *News* employees. The Guild was reduced to asking questions about proposals it did not like or understand in order to stave off impasse and implementation. Mleczko said later, "We kept saying, 'We're not at an impasse, you're not providing us even basic information that we need to make sense out of this, let alone agree to it.'"[28]

Kummer wrote Jaske on June 16 to ask for another meeting, suggesting July 3 as the earliest possible date. Local 22's international union had scheduled its national convention in Boston from Saturday, June 17, to Sunday, June 25; Kummer and Mleczko were committed to attending and would not return until Monday, June 26. Jaske was incensed. "In view of the deadlock in the negotiations resulting from your refusal to bargain on our overtime and other proposals, I see no justification for delaying negotiations until the week of July 3," he wrote Kummer on June 20, adding, "Unless you can assure me that you intend to modify your position on those issues, we will have no choice but to implement our last offer to you."[29]

Eight days later, Giles sent *News* employees a two-and-a-half-page memorandum, edited by Jaske, explaining the merit pay and overtime proposals in more detail than any document the Guild leaders had yet received at the bargaining table. The June 28 memo noted that nearly 90 percent of the 176 professional staff would qualify for merit pay based on performance evaluations of "outstanding" or "commendable." Giles concluded his notice by stating: "The deadlock in the negotiations has resulted from the refusal of the Guild to bargain on these proposals." Without mentioning Kummer's pending request for a meeting, he added, "Union negotiators have been at a convention and unwilling to meet."[30]

Now back in Detroit, Kummer faxed a June 29 letter to Jaske, again asking for another bargaining session. In his reply, Jaske indicated his availability at 10:00 AM on Monday, July 3, and faxed the letter to the Guild office on Friday, June 30 at 8:07 PM, after the Guild officers had already left for the weekend. Kummer and Mleczko saw Jaske on Monday at 1:00 PM at a meeting involving the Guild's maintenance unit, but Jaske said nothing about his letter or his proposal to meet that morning. According to Mleczko, neither he nor Kummer even knew of it until they saw Jaske's letter later that afternoon.[31]

The MCNU and Joint Bargaining

If the MCNU leaders hoped that Derey's agreement with Vega on joint bargaining would help save the negotiations, as it had in 1992, they would be disappointed this time. On June 7, Jaske warned in a letter to the Guild that the *News*, like the DNA, had established a firm deadline of June 30 for the completion of all negotiations.[32] In bargaining, Jaske and Kelleher began blurring the two-stage format, raising economic proposals in the individual unit talks. When reminded by union leaders that such topics were reserved for later, they would agree to hold them for joint bargaining, "if we ever get there."[33]

Concerned about the status of the talks, Derey called Vega in mid-June to ask for a written confirmation of their negotiating agreement. Vega answered in a letter, drafted by Jaske but signed by Vega, dated June 14 and hand-delivered to Derey outside Vega's office in the *News* building downtown. The letter asserted, for the first time, that joint bargaining was contingent on the completion of all individual issues by a fixed deadline. "In view of the lack of progress in negotiations and our desire to finish negotiations by the end of the month," it stated, "we will continue to deal on economic issues individually with each union. However, if we can finish all non-economics in sufficient time prior to June 30, we will meet jointly."[34]

Derey responded by denying that there had been any conditions on the May 10 agreement, and he angrily accused Vega of reneging on the deal, calling him a "goddamn liar."[35] At the June 15 bargaining session with the printers, Jaske repeated the June 30 deadline and his intention to bargain all items now, economic and non-economic, owing to the slow progress in individual negotiations. "If you don't want to continue bargaining, just say so," he said, "and then we'll do what we have to do."[36] Speaking for the union, McKnight asked the DNA to reconsider and said that to revoke joint bargaining would throw "a tremendous monkey wrench into the entire bargaining process between all six unions and the company." "You've got our proposal," Jaske replied.[37]

By agreeing to separate the individual and joint bargaining, Vega had made an important concession to the unions; in turn, Jaske gained considerable leverage from merging them back together again. The mixed messages to take up joint sessions "if we ever get there" sowed confusion among the unions, disrupting their bargaining strategy. The move also provided an opportunity to split the MCNU: if any one union signed a complete contract first, all the others would be forced to agree to essentially the same economic terms, making joint bargaining irrelevant.[38] Finally, merging individual and across-the-board issues would undermine the practice of providing separate economic compensation for job cuts and other union concessions. The savings from staff reductions could then be used to cover buyouts *and* wage increases, with money left over for the newspapers' bottom line. In bargaining, the unions were forced to absorb the risk of producing a sufficient surplus for the company before it would absolutely commit to no layoffs. Derey explained:

> Jaske said, "We'll see." I took that as meaning, we'll see how much money is left. You know, if there's not enough money, there won't be any buyouts. Well, what happens is, you have layoffs then. That's just a whole different issue. I said, "What you're doing is you're taking our money, our jobs, and you're giving us about 60 percent back through the back door." . . . He wanted us to pay for our own raises, plus give up.[39]

The DNA now stepped up the pressure, threatening to withdraw proposals if no agreement was reached by June 30. In individual negotiations with the mailers on June 16, Jaske offered a proposal that included a three-year contract with annual across-the-board wage increases of 4 percent, 3 percent, and 3 percent, provided the union ratified the deal by the end of the month. Similar offers were made to the press operators on June 16 and to the printers on June 22, and in each case the union insisted that the issues were reserved for joint bargaining. On June 27, the MCNU filed an unfair labor practice charge against the DNA for unilaterally reneging on the joint bargaining agreement.[40]

High Alert: Marshaling the Troops

As the negotiations gradually broke down, both sides increased their mobilization in anticipation of a strike. The MCNU lobbied politicians for expressions of public support, and city councils in Detroit, Sterling Heights, and Warren, Michigan, as well as county boards of commissioners in Wayne and Macomb Counties, passed resolutions urging fair settlements. Internally, union organizers began planning picket line logistics and arranging for food aid, credit counseling, and continued health insurance for members in the event of a walkout.[41] Local 2040's Jim St. Louis worked on the advertising boycott, calling department stores and merchants in the region. He recalled, "I used to get mad at [McKnight]. I would say, 'Okay, we're ready. If we need to go, we're ready.' And he would constantly tell me, 'You're not ready.' And then he had three more things for me to do."[42]

At the DNA, management kept up a neutral public image. "We don't make strike preparations," Kelleher told a reporter in late May. "It's the unions who prepare for a strike. Our goal is to negotiate and reach an agreement."[43] Kelleher was perhaps disingenuous: among other things, he and other top DNA officers had been tutored in media management and public speaking, including practice sessions with mock press conferences. "Our key spokespeople were trained, and we learned to prepare and stick to our key messages to control what went out," DNA media liaison Susie Elwood later recalled.[44] The company had also stocked up on newsprint at its Sterling Heights plant and was continuing to spend money on security. According to its contract with Alternative Work Force, the DNA was already paying AWF a premium of $10 per day per person for each additional day replacements were made available after May 15. By June, hundreds of private contractor employees were being housed in hotels and motels across southeastern Michigan.[45]

In Sterling Heights, DNA security chief John Anthony kept in regular contact with Captain Owens and Lieutenant Mowinski of the SHPD concerning the progress in bargaining and the DNA's security deployment.[46] In May and June, Mowinski wrote a series of "updates" on the situation to all SHPD operations division personnel. His May 30 memo stated: "Negotiations are still going on according to the Detroit News [sic] Agency. There is a 50–50 chance of striking. If a strike does occur, it will likely happen on a Friday night. If it is not negotiated by June 30, the Detroit News will initiate a lockout."[47]

As the deadline neared, Mowinski again sounded the alarm. "According to sources at the Detroit News Agency, there is still a 50–50 chance that the strike will take place at any time," he wrote on June 23. "Negotiations are still continuing but not going well. The Detroit News Agency still plans to lock out employees on June 30, 1995, as previously stated."[48] Four days later, Captain Owens ordered all operations division command officers to attend a mandatory staff meeting on June 27 regarding the "Detroit News strike."[49] Finally, in a memo co-signed by Owens and dated June 27, Mowinski elaborated on "the Impending D.N.A. Strike":

> The Detroit News Agency stated that negotiations are reaching an impasse for the June 30th deadline. If a contract is not negotiated as of the 30th, the D.N.A. will not lock out the workers as they have previously stated. They do

intend to not honor the expired contract and initiate their own working rules. The unions were notified of this action.

The D.N.A. expects the unions to walkout rather than work under the new rules. Since then, numerous pressmen have been removing their tools from the plant this week. This walkout is expected to take place on Friday, June 30, 1995 at 6:00 pm.

Preparing for this action, Security will be strengthened over the next few days. You will be notified of any changes as I receive them.[50]

"We don't intend to lock anybody out," DNA spokesperson Kelleher declared publicly the following week.[51] Nevertheless, the SHPD's readiness closely tracked the signals from the DNA. Indeed, Mowinski's May 30 memo was dated a week *before* Jaske's letter to the Guild informing them of the June 30 hard deadline. By the end of June, the SHPD understood that the DNA expected the contract termination to provoke a work stoppage and even anticipated the date on which it would occur. Nowhere in Mowinski's memos, however, did he refer to any communication with the unions about the "impending strike."

THINGS FALL APART: THE COLLAPSE OF NEGOTIATIONS

As the negotiations approached the eleventh hour, events began to accelerate rapidly. On Monday, June 26, the newspapers told the MCNU that they would no longer extend the previous contracts past 6:00 PM on Friday, June 30. The move was strategically aimed at the unions' institutional standing; employees would continue to work, but the company would cease arbitration of new grievances, stop requiring new hires to join the union, and no longer collect union dues through its payroll. That Friday the company allowed a forty-eight-hour reprieve, but on Sunday evening, July 2, the newspapers canceled their contracts with the unions.[52]

Meanwhile, from June 29 to July 5, managers at the *News* immediately carried out more than eighty crash performance evaluations of newsroom employees (forty of them on July 3 alone), a number equal to more than half of all those conducted to date for the year.[53] At a press conference on the morning of July 5, Giles announced the implementation of the merit pay and other proposals. Over the next six days, the *News* sent out 171 merit pay determination letters to members of the Guild bargaining unit. On July 11, the Guild filed unfair labor practice charges for unlawful implementation and failure to bargain in good faith.[54]

The day after the *News* imposed terms on the Guild, the MCNU met and agreed to set a strike deadline for July 13. McKnight arranged for all the local union heads to sign a statement condemning the employers' bad-faith tactics and pledging to honor each others' picket lines in the event of an unfair labor practice strike.[55] Leaders from all the unions met collectively with the DNA on July 7. Derey suggested that they go offsite for round-the-clock bargaining sessions, and that weekend the parties assembled at the downtown Pontchartrain Hotel, across from the Detroit River.[56]

By this time the mailers and the press operators had in fact worked through most of their individual staffing issues, having agreed to job cuts. Both unions were very close to a settlement, pending the resolution of compensation from the DNA for the reductions and the onset of joint bargaining.[57] For the printers, in their final session on July 10, Jaske again proposed a three-year contract with the 4/3/3 percent formula. In addition, he included a "me-too" clause if any other union should get a better wage offer, implying that Local 18 might feel competition with its partners in the MCNU. McKnight was not amused. If Jaske really wanted to get an agreement, he said, then "the one thing he should do right now was to honor [their] commitment and reserve the common economic items for joint bargaining."[58]

The action now came down to the DNA negotiations with Teamsters Local 372. As the leader of the largest and most powerful newspaper union, Derey wanted to keep Local 372's issues for the end, when he could exercise the most leverage for his own members and for the MCNU. Working with his attorney, Frank Kortsch, Derey maximized his bargaining demands. "The company understood that Derey had blocked them successfully," Teamster newspaper division director Tom McGrath recalled. "Derey was using the need of the company to get an agreement with him so they could close the contract as his major hammer, and that's why he had them roadblocks all over. . . . 'If I just keep 'em all boxed in, if he can't get by me, they can't live without me in a contract, I'll get what I want,' and that was his theory."[59]

From July 9 to July 12, the two sides bargained over job reductions, pension contributions, and the effects of the proposed conversion of independent carriers to agents. On Tuesday, July 11, the *Free Press* reported that the DNA wanted to cut fifty-nine district manager jobs for a savings of about $14.1 million, about half of which would go to pay for buyouts and higher wages. Meanwhile, the union approached the company off the record to ask for a long-term agreement on the status of the district managers under the NLRA. The DNA replied that in exchange the district managers would have to agree to continue working regardless of what the other unions did.[60]

On Tuesday, Derey presented a compensation package keyed to the much larger size of the districts under the agent system. The following day, however, the DNA charged that the total cost of Local 372's proposals was $71 million. The company further claimed that, with pay raises and severance costs, the proposed fifty-nine job cuts (along with twenty-six additional related positions) would produce savings of no more than $5.1 million. The Teamsters disputed the figures and in negotiations agreed to about half of the proposed district manager cuts, but Jaske rejected the offer. Derey then rejected the agent system proposal and refused to meet again until the DNA countered on district manager pay.[61]

At that point Jaske refused to move any further, leaving more than one hundred specific items still outstanding. As Derey later admitted, "Our proposals, three days before we struck, were probably $70 million . . . we don't deny that. What we deny was that that would have stayed on the table. Every contract, three days prior to an agreement, there's a lot of money on there from both sides, there are a lot of cuts and a lot of money. And it was not our intention to get that kind of money."[62]

Derey's strategy assumed, however, that the DNA was still willing to bargain over the remaining one hundred items. Ultimately, Derey relied on his personal relationship with Vega to trump any moves made by Jaske. As McGrath observed, "Derey felt that Vega and him were buddies. . . . They hated one another, except that when I would be in a caucus or anything with Derey, when it came to Vega he would say, 'I could out see him, I think I can get that done.' He still harbored in his mind that notion that he had made this relationship with Vega that would see him through any kind of problem."[63]

Unlike 1992, however, Vega no longer had that kind of power in the negotiations. Derey's approach backfired this time because Jaske could now plausibly argue to his Gannett superiors that there was no possibility of a deal. McGrath explained:

> So what they thought was their strong bargaining position was what was killing them because . . . the amount of issues that [Local 372] was demanding and the cost of what that would be, because Jaske, who's a very bright guy, costed out every item you're demanding from him, so he would say this thing would cost [$71 million], it's all over. Give 'em the paper, we might as well close the door, that kind of thing. So [the union] made Jaske a hero [to Gannett], and it served his purpose, because this time Jaske was going to control the bargaining, and he was going to lead the parade. Vega had a veto power, but he had to overcome Jaske's arguments where, as I tell you, they were absolutely impossible to overcome.[64]

With the Local 372 talks stalled, Jaske made a final round of attempts to break off and sign separate agreements with the other unions. On July 12 he offered a complete contract to the press operators.[65] "They approached me and it was the same [offer as with the printers], and we told them no," Local 13N's Jack Howe recalled. "We could see exactly what they were doing."[66] In the weary hours at the Pontchartrain near the end, Jaske and Kelleher approached the mailers' Alex Young:

> It was like eleven, twelve o'clock at night, and John Jaske and Tim Kelleher called me and Jim St. Louis out into the hallway . . . they said, "We're willing to give you this, but we think there's going to be a strike tomorrow and you're probably going to honor the line, aren't you?" Now, that might not be the exact words, but that's what happened. And we told them that if one of the units strike, we will honor the picket line. And that's how our bargaining ended that night.[67]

At the *News*, there was little effort even to bother negotiating with the Guild. On July 11, as attorney Duane Ice was at the table seeking information, Giles issued another memo to the staff covering the proportion of unit employees eligible for merit pay, the average raises for those rated "outstanding" and "commendable," the range of percentage merit increases, and other items. Again, Jaske previewed the document but did not disclose the information to Guild bargainers, despite Ice's specific questions to him.[68]

Bob Ourlian was a reporter for the *News*, a Detroit native, a nine-year veteran at the paper, and a member of the Local 22 bargaining team. He remembered the Guild's last bargaining meeting before the strike:

> [Giles] had no apparent responsibility for anything, and in fact, even if you addressed a question to him at a bargaining session, he would not respond. Or if he responded, it was just very tentative and preliminary, and he would defer over to Jaske. . . . And so at this last session, Jaske was called out of the room. He left Giles sitting there. Giles sat there uncomfortably for what seemed like half an hour, and eventually he just collected the papers, stood up, and walked out of the room as well—left us sitting there, not knowing which way to proceed. And Duane Ice, who I believe was with us then, said: "I guess that's the end."[69]

On Thursday the unions pushed back the strike deadline from 6:00 to 8:00 PM, to allow for a last-ditch mediation by Detroit mayor Dennis Archer. The parties met that afternoon at City Hall, with the mayor shuttling back and forth between them, for three and a half hours before breaking up around 6:30 PM.[70] At the papers' downtown newsrooms, the employees waited to hear the results. "There was an uneasiness all day," said *Free Press* newsroom secretary Jocelyn Faniel-Heard, "and people were, you know, getting their things together, notes and that kind of stuff."[71] *Free Press* editor Nancy Dunn was also working that evening:

> I remember standing at one of the layout tables. We were trying to figure out what we were going to do with one of the special sections; we were trying to redesign one of the features or entertainment sections, and I remember we were standing there, and there was a manager there, I don't remember exactly who it was, but we all said, well, let's just hope that this doesn't last long, and you know, we can come back here next week and we can work on this. . . . We all kind of shook hands and said, see you soon kind of thing.[72]

In the *News* building, the atmosphere was somewhat different. Around midnight the night before, managing editor Christina Bradford had approached a bank of mail slots for newsroom employees on the second floor. Angry at the unions for setting a strike deadline, and in violation of federal law, she systematically removed copies of union flyers that Guild bargaining team member Ourlian had just inserted in the slots. She also tore down union notices and other information from two bulletin boards reserved for the use of the Guild, again in violation of the law. The following day, July 13, copies of the notices that Bradford had removed the night before were back up on the boards and in the mail slots.[73]

CONCLUSION: PARTING COMPANY

From the sidelines, DNA chief Vega could barely contain himself. On the eve of the strike, he charged that the Teamsters' demands would drive the newspapers back into the red after they had just regained profitability. "We made a profit last year and a bit of money the year before that," he told a reporter from the *News*. "They [the union] basically think it's like the old days, and they're going to get a piece of what we've got, and it ain't going to be that way."[74] The day after the strike began, he was more subdued. "I am deeply saddened by this turn of events," he said. "We thought we made one of the best offers that's been made to any union around the country."[75]

Indeed, the DNA's proposed wage increase of 10.3 percent over three years was reasonably generous, as the company repeatedly stressed in its public statements before and after the walkout began. Yet, the economic offer was accompanied by conditions that entailed drastic changes in the nature of union representation at the newspapers. The issues that led the unions to strike were not simply a matter of higher wages and benefits. Although hinging on technical and often far from transparent legal criteria, they went to the heart of the collective bargaining process and the relationship between the employer and the employees. "They sit there telling you it's a 4 percent, 3 percent, [and] 3 percent," Teamster member Tim O'Malley told a television news reporter a week before the strike. "That's not really the problem. The problem is with the things that they introduce, when it's all over with, we're not going to have enough membership to survive."[76]

Altogether, the newspapers and the unions engaged in more than sixty bargaining sessions in the spring and summer of 1995, and their differences were hardly the result of miscommunication. On the contrary, union leaders saw clearly what was happening in the negotiations even as they seemed powerless to alter management's course of action. The strategic choices they made were not irrational; rather, the two sides were simply playing by different sets of rules. Their decisions and behavior at the bargaining table reflected a broader historic collision of two opposing institutional logics.

Under those circumstances, the assumptions of the traditional strike theory no longer held. The unions' organizational security was undermined by proposals that directly threatened their jurisdiction and their capacity to represent and bargain for their members. The Guild could scarcely calculate the costs and benefits of proposals for which the *News* refused to provide information, and the give-and-take of bargaining was destabilized by the employers' expressed willingness to declare impasse. The integrity of the entire process depended on a New Deal institutional order that was deeply eroded by the ascendant anti-union regime. The unions saw that correctly as well, and so prepared to act outside traditional channels.

The DNA's termination of the contracts on July 2 marked the collapse of the old system in the workplace. With the removal of key organizational and procedural protections, the MCNU leaders feared losing all control of events on the ground. "The DNA was threatening to cancel the arbitration process, the union security provision, and the dues checkoff," Derey said later. "The DNA knew this was an act of war . . . [because] if you do this, one supervisor firing the wrong guy could cause a walkout, and we're going to be out there. I said, 'Don't put yourself in this position. Don't put us in this position.'"[77]

Three days later, the *News* implemented the merit pay proposal on the Guild, prompting the MCNU to set a strike deadline. Given the pressure in the negotiations, however, why did the other unions rally together in unity? Why did skilled press operators and blue-collar Teamster leaders strike to defend white-collar professionals when their own organizational interest might have led them to break off and accept separate settlements, as in previous decades? The MCNU leaders had developed a high level of personal confidence in each other, and for each of the units there remained significant problems in the final offers Jaske had put on the table. But union leaders were also convinced that any one of them who cut a deal would undoubtedly become the target the next time, and in any case their entire relationship with the newspapers was already at risk now. Lou Mleczko recalled:

> It was clear to all the Council officers that the demands that the company was putting on regarding work rule changes, larger reductions of employees, and other significant cutbacks in the collective bargaining agreement were going to be soon implemented unilaterally on [the other unions] . . . and that if the strike hadn't been triggered by the merit pay that was being used, a week or two down the road there would be an issue in the Pressman unit or the Teamsters unit that would have triggered one of those units going out on strike.[78]

Jaske had bargained extremely hard in 1995, and in contrast to the 1992 negotiations, he succeeded in making nearly every move that he wanted. As a consequence, however, the unions could see no other alternative but to strike. "They set their goals so high on achieving concessions, that there was no way for the unions to climb that ladder," Kummer said in a television news interview. "We couldn't reach the agreements they were asking and then go back and have our members approve it. . . . The company's take-aways are so significant that we couldn't agree to them."[79]

Desperate to preserve their rights and refusing to concede, the unions stuck to their deadline, placing their faith in the ULP charges and in the boycott. "This is a union town," Derey said publicly a week before the strike. "We believe the subscribers out there will support us."[80] Unfortunately for the MCNU, the middle of July was among the worst possible times for a walkout. The slow summer season for advertising in the papers dulled the immediate economic impact of the boycott, the major weapon on which the unions relied. The company's determination to publish with replacements, and the unions' dependence on the legal process to adjudicate the ULPs, made it unlikely that the conflict would be resolved soon.

On the evening of July 13, DNA security chief John Anthony was standing in the lobby of the *News* building along with DNA chief financial officer Gary Anderson. "All of a sudden," Anthony recalled, "all of the Guild people started flooding down the stairs by the hundreds with their personal effects and out the door." The mass exodus followed the company's plan exactly. Anthony explained:

> Everything was ratcheted up right to the level to launch. . . . As soon as the strike was announced, [APT] people went right to key locations in the building, and then the plan was, and it worked perfectly, was to align with management because we didn't know everybody that was in there, we didn't know who should be left behind, and just like a toilet flushing, just work your way down and everybody goes out. . . For those several hours, every building, the two buildings [downtown], the two plants, were flushed clean of everybody except security and management.[81]

For the newspapers, the striking employees were now perhaps little more than a problem of waste disposal, a hazard to be controlled. Just before the strike, a group of Detroit-area religious leaders issued a letter urging the two sides to seek peace. The letter, signed by Roman Catholic auxiliary bishop Thomas Gumbelton, the Rev. Wendell Anthony of Fellowship Chapel, and Rabbi Ernst Conrad of Temple Kol-Ami, among others, said, "Management must realize that a labor struggle at the two newspapers can only divide our community."[82] The religious leaders were not mistaken. The struggle for control at the papers would last for more than five years and incite a bitter civic war across multiple institutional arenas in the state and in urban civil society.

PART III | The Spaces of Conflict

Chapter 8 | Worlds Collide: The Start of the Strike

IT WAS RIGHT out of central casting. About an hour or so before the strike began, a violent midwestern thunderstorm rolled into southeastern Michigan, bursting with lightning and rain and turning the July evening sky an ominous shade of purple and green. "That whole day was one of the tensest days I had ever experienced at work," said *Free Press* reporter Bill McGraw. "There was that electricity in the air, literally and figuratively, so it was just a very strange and tense night."[1] Reporter Michael Betzold, McGraw's colleague at the *Free Press*, agreed. "There was a sense that this rift had happened in our ordinary lives that was accentuated by the weather," he recalled, "like the skies opened up and that's sort of how it felt, suddenly everything was new and different."[2]

The strike had begun, but the ways in which the struggle took shape would do much to determine its outcome. The chapters in part II of this book explained *why* the strike happened at the particular historical juncture that it did. The following chapters in part III show *how* the Detroit strike signaled the extent to which the social and institutional terrain of labor conflict had changed. In conventional social science theory, strikes were often seen as routinized displays, fully incorporated into the framework of the postwar labor accord. In the newspaper strike, however, the course of events would be anything but routine.

From the start, urban civil society was both a strategic resource and a dynamic medium for collective action in the strike. The unions relied heavily on the embedded culture of labor in the region—for the unity among striking workers on the picket line, for material aid from the wider union movement, and as the key to the circulation and advertising boycotts. Civil society, however, was not the only theater of conflict. The community campaign remained intimately tied to the economic balance of power, and the advertising boycott depended on the disruption of service

151

to keep advertisers, the newspapers' main source of revenue, out of the paper.

Consequently, the workplace remained a crucial site of direct action, especially at the Sterling Heights North Plant. The companies deployed enormous resources in order to continue operating, and they gained a significant economic advantage with the hiring of permanent replacements. That decision forced a crisis, however, particularly among the striking journalists at the *Free Press*, and virtually destroyed any remnants of moderation on the part of the employers. The battle between the two sides turned into a civic war, reaching a dramatic peak with the picket line protests around the Labor Day weekend and its aftermath.

SOLIDARITY IN ACTION:
MOBILIZING THE STRIKE

The start of the strike unleashed an extraordinary popular mobilization that spread throughout the Detroit metropolitan area. "We had so many fronts," said Kate DeSmet, a religion reporter and a seventeen-year employee at the *News*. "There wasn't just one central picket line, so we were all over the metro area, which was a huge area. And there were guys picketing probably thirty, forty, fifty miles away from me who I didn't picket with, but when we got together at a strike function, we would be able to be on the same page immediately."[3] Reporter Bob Ourlian did his picket duty at the *News* building downtown. "I became a picket captain," he recalled. "Just assign people, sign people up, turn in sheets, and make sure people got their strike pay and all that kind of thing. That was usually a four- to eight-hour shift every day. And then frequently, in the evenings, I would check on the evening picket crews and then also go around and check on the picket lines at different distribution centers."[4]

Walking a picket line can be tedious work, marching day after day in heat, cold, or rain, hours of repetitive activity pierced by moments of intense confrontation. Yet many strikers described experiencing a powerful sense of emergent solidarity that dissolved the social distance between workers of diverse economic status and location. "There were people picketing next to each other, and it was really hot out," said striking *News* photographer Rebecca Cook. "It didn't matter if you were the person who collected the trash or if you were the person who wrote the columns, took the photos or did the layout, or drove the trucks. They were all together."[5]

Free Press editor Nancy Dunn remembered "people that became my friends that I met, that I never knew before, people who worked as circulation district managers, pressmen, and people from the other newspapers that we didn't know, the other newsrooms." She continued:

In a sense it was almost an adventure, and I hesitate to say that because there's so much economic tragedy and family tragedy and ruin that comes out in a situation like that, but there was something very important, I think, that came out of the experience of actually feeling the solidarity instead of just—I mean, it was a word that I never understood until the strike. Then I understood what solidarity meant, not just because of the picket line experiences, when you realize that you are standing together, walking together, shouting at scabs together, suffering together, dodging trucks together. I mean . . . we were in a war. I mean, dodging pepper spray together. That's not something that I ever expected that I would be exposed to as part of my career as a journalist.[6]

Solidarity extended beyond the striking workers: organizational and material aid for the strike poured in from the labor movement in southeastern Michigan. In July the Michigan Federation of Teachers and the United Auto Workers called on all their locals to have their members cancel their subscriptions to the papers. The UAW distributed hundreds of thousands of copies of the strike newsletter *The Detroit Union* to its members and banned rack sales of the *News* and *Free Press* in its unionized auto factories, a move that alone cut the newspapers' circulation by 25,000. Members from the dense network of UAW local unions in the area participated in strike assistance committees and joined picket lines at the papers' printing plants and distributions centers.[7]

UAW Region 1A, with sixty local affiliates located in the southwestern "downriver" suburbs, was especially active in support of the strike. Led by director Bob King, Region 1A had already sponsored a series of weekly "labor crisis" meetings where local leaders from the UAW and other unions would come together and discuss current news and concerns. When the newspaper strike started, King assigned staff organizer Michele Martin to work full-time mobilizing support activities among UAW members. As head of the Rapid Action Disciplined Deployment (RADD) team, Martin organized turnout for picket lines and rallies and coordinated leafleting campaigns at car dealerships and Firestone and Belle Tire outlets to get them to stop advertising in the newspapers.[8]

Other unions also contributed resources and money. In the first few months, the Detroit Federation of Teachers gave $10,000; UAW Local 594, representing seven thousand General Motors factory workers in Pontiac, Michigan, raised $11,274; and the Greater Detroit Building Trades Council contributed close to $40,000. Unions of all kinds chipped in. The Asbestos Workers Local 25 donated $1,000, as did members of the Detroit Federation of Musicians Local 5 at the Detroit Symphony Orchestra.[9] Support came from across the industrial Midwest and Great Lakes region. Union members in Toledo, Ohio, delivered 1,500 hams and several truckloads of produce to the food bank at the Teamsters Hall on Trumbull Street. Minnesota trade unionists gave $10,000 and, as part of the ad boycott, leafleted the Minneapolis store of the Dayton's department store chain. In late September, the Pennsylvania Conference of Teamsters delivered two semi-tractor-trailers carrying forty tons of food, and Conference president Johnny Morris promised to deliver more.[10]

Nationwide, the strike became a cause célèbre within the newspaper industry and in the larger labor movement. The national AFL-CIO obtained pledges of $1 million from its member unions for the campaign and announced a national boycott against major retailers that continued to advertise in the papers.[11] The Toledo Newspaper Guild pledged a donation of $10,000 to the MCNU; the president of the New York Newspaper Guild came to Detroit and personally presented a check for $2,500; and locals of the Guild and the Typographical Union in Hawaii sent checks for $5,000 and $1,000, respectively.[12] Traveling striker emissaries collected $3,500 at state AFL-CIO conventions in Boston and Providence, Rhode Island, and Local 6 of the New York Hotel and Restaurant Workers donated $5,000.

Locally, participation in the strike and the boycotts flowed in and out of multiple levels of urban civil society. The Detroit United Way announced that it would not place its $250,000 worth of United Fund advertisements in the newspapers and asked the papers to withdraw from a job fair it co-sponsored at Oakland Community College in October. In November, twelve Detroit high schools declined to take part in a student journalism program sponsored by the *Free Press*.[13] The Salvation Army distributed free food to strikers at its churches in Royal Oak and Pontiac, while the Vegas Super Markets in Warren, Center Line, and Harper Woods offered strikers a 20 percent discount on groceries and other items.[14] Gas stations and convenience stores posted signs announcing their refusal to carry the papers, and fewer than half of the three thousand regular home delivery carriers showed up for work.[15] Tony Fera, owner of the Little Professor Book Center in Dearborn, told a reporter: "We're backing the union and the drivers. Those drivers have been with us for years. They've been doing us favors all year. They bring us extra papers when we run out."[16]

Other gestures of solidarity seemed to rise out of the cultural woodwork of the community. Don Pilette, a part-time Wayne State University journalism teacher and retired *News* systems editor, handed out hot dogs and sandwiches to picketers every weekday for months. Seventy-one-year-old retired autoworker Louie Hill went door to door asking his neighbors to join the boycott. Chrysler worker David Hewlett and his wife Linda, a former CWA member, saved for months and bought $1,600 worth of toys and clothes for strikers' families at Christmas.[17]

Awareness of the strike became a part of the common experience of everyday life in the city. A. J. Hartley was director of publishing technology at the *Free Press*, a management position. He continued to work while his wife, Patricia Cybulski Hartley, an editorial assistant at the paper, went on strike. "You really couldn't drive in many neighborhoods in the metro area without running across yard signs [saying] No NEWS OR FREE PRESS WANTED HERE [or] NO SCAB PAPERS," he recalled. "I mean, the church that we went to every Sunday, part of the prayers of the church were for the striking workers." At one point Hartley went out of town on a business trip and paid at the airport parking lot with his company credit card. "I didn't even realize at the time it had THE DETROIT FREE PRESS imprinted on it, and, you know, I had the woman at the gate give me five minutes of grief. I think there were pockets of that all over the metro area."[18]

In the public sphere, a political battlefront opened up that stretched from the national and state arenas to the trenches of local municipal and county governments. President Bill Clinton ordered his executive staff members to decline interviews with the *News* and *Free Press*, and in Michigan leading Democratic Party politicians refused to speak to strikebreaking journalists.[19] Former Detroit mayor Coleman Young wrote an August 11 letter to DNA chief Frank Vega calling on him to "end this bitter, destructive labor impasse" and blasting the agency for creating the potential for "long-term, irreparable harm to both newspapers, to your employees, and most importantly, to this community."[20] The six MCNU unions and the national AFL-CIO formally asked U.S. attorney general Janet Reno to rescind the antitrust protection for the newspapers' joint operating agreement, citing the newspapers' "secret" 1992 amendment claiming the right to publish a combined strike edition. City councils in Detroit, Sterling Heights, Warren, and St. Clair Shores passed resolutions urging Reno to investigate the matter, and in November former mayor Young, Detroit City Council president Maryann Mahaffey, councilor Sheila Cockrel, and four other plaintiffs filed a class action suit seeking to declare the joint edition unlawful and to invalidate the JOA.[21]

Other local government actors joined in support of the newspaper boycott. City councils in Melvindale, Hazel Park, and Garden City voted to pull their legal notices from the papers, and Melvindale directed its local police to enforce littering laws to end the random delivery of papers to residents who canceled their subscriptions. The city of Taylor, home of the UAW Region 1A headquarters, halted action on a property tax abatement slated for a warehouse owned by the DNA.[22] In Grosse Pointe Farms, where both Frank Vega and Bob Giles resided, the city council denied a request to allow street vendors to sell the Sunday edition of the papers at a major intersection in town. The attorney for the DNA pleaded that many

retailers refused to carry the paper and that home delivery had been sporadic since the strike, but the council unanimously rejected the plan.[23] In
December the Wayne County Board of Commissioners banned the papers
from receiving county advertisements worth an estimated $497,000 annu-
ally and directed the county executive to take steps to prevent the sale of
the papers in county-owned or -leased buildings, including the Detroit-
Wayne International Airport. Wayne County executive Edward McNamara wrote a letter to county employees urging them to donate to a striker
relief fund and charging the newspapers with having "betrayed the trust
that led many of us to support the JOA agreement. Their stance throughout the strike indicates they have little interest in dealing with their unions
honorably."[24]

The Limits of Mobilization:
Union Organizational Capacity

Despite the widespread show of popular support, the strike suffered from
serious weaknesses. Notwithstanding the unions' preparations, the action
lacked a comprehensive plan, and the timing of the deadline was abrupt.
The first night, strikers complained of disorderly communications, poor
coordination, and even a lack of picket signs. Striking journalist John Lippert was a member of Guild Local 22 and covered the labor beat at the *Free
Press*, including the negotiations with the newspapers before the strike.
"The union leaders viewed the [strike] deadline as an impetus for intensified bargaining, and as a short-term response to anxious workers demanding some kind of action," he wrote later. "They did not set it because they
wanted a strike, or expected one, or had a plan for how to win it."[25]

Mobilizing the walkout was by itself an enormous undertaking, and
organizational challenges arose constantly. The newsroom buildings,
printing plants, and other potential picket sites were miles apart, and the
strikers themselves often hailed from far-flung suburbs. Trucks delivering
the Sunday morning papers left in the middle of the night, requiring
round-the-clock picket duty. When it did not rain, daytime temperatures
were sweltering as they reached almost 100 degrees in July and August.
Sam Maci was a press operator and the secretary-treasurer for Local 13N.
"It was just miserably hot," he recalled. "I had a large-sized van, so I
cranked the air up, and I'd take it around, let people sit in it who wanted
to cool off, 'cause we had brought bottles of water for everybody, too . . .
[just] see how they're doing, let 'em cool off a little bit in my van."[26]

Financially, the support from the wider labor movement helped, but it
was also desperately needed. The International Brotherhood of Teamsters
strike fund was practically broke, and members of Locals 2040 and 372

received no strike pay for the first several weeks. In September a special Michigan-Ohio Teamsters Strike Fund kicked in with weekly payments of just $55, supplemented by additional funds raised from the national AFL-CIO.[27] Guild members started out with $150 per week in benefits; Local 22 executive officer Don Kummer had also socked away money to pay members' health insurance, but the funds were exhausted after ten months.[28] The Communications Workers of America created a program for other CWA local unions to send monthly checks to its affiliate Guild and Typographical Union members, and by the spring of 1996 more than 120 CWA locals across the country had "adopted" strikers.[29]

Nevertheless, many striking workers experienced severe economic hardship and deep personal struggles. Sixty-year-old press operator Tom Waldron, a forty-three-year veteran at the papers, went through $20,000 in savings to maintain health insurance for his wife, who was crippled with arthritis. Teamster Randy Karpinen had to borrow money from his parents to pay his mortgage and ran up $12,000 in credit card debt. The MCNU set up a striker assistance program under the Community Services Office of the Metro Detroit AFL-CIO to help strikers facing eviction, repossession, utility shutoffs, or other creditor actions.[30] "We went through our savings," Leo Jenkins recalled. "We maxed out our credit cards trying to live. Financially it was devastating, which caused a whole bunch of other kinds of problems too. When your finances is whacked, your relationship is whacked. It was rough. I mean, we went from middle-class to poverty."[31]

Others did what they could to support themselves. Teamster Tom Breyer was unemployed for five months before getting a position as a maintenance worker at a Catholic church in Troy. He worked a second shift for eight hours, went home, and then picketed from 4:00 to 8:00 AM. The engine in Alesia Cooper-Cunningham's car broke down, and she could not find employment. Her sister co-signed a loan for the repairs, and in the meantime Cooper-Cunningham took a job in a fast-food joint across the street from where she was staying.[32] Striking *News* food editor Robin Mather spent forty hours a week at the Holiday Market in Royal Oak and another forty hours each week as the Guild's scheduling coordinator. *Free Press* assistant features editor Renee Murawski worked two jobs, temping during the day and serving as a hostess in a chain restaurant in the evenings. Photographer Jetta Fraser freelanced, using her own or borrowed equipment. Her income was only one-fifth of her prestrike wages, but her credit union allowed her to pay only the interest on her car loan.[33]

Altogether it was an extraordinary collective effort and personal sacrifice, and in many ways it actually succeeded. Circulation dropped precipitously: in the first few days the papers printed less than one-quarter of their normal run, with almost no home delivery.[34] "We had difficulty getting the paper out in Macomb County," DNA spokesperson Susie Elwood admitted. "My guess is that may be due to the strong union membership there."[35] A *Washington Post* article estimated that, in the first month, at best 65 percent of papers got to homes that paid for them, while the *Wall Street Journal* reported that in some areas carriers were delivering papers to any home with a porch or a driveway, blanketing block after block with unwanted or unpaid-for papers.[36] Bales of papers turned up indiscriminately dumped in garbage bins and ditches, and the city of Farmington Hills complained that DNA employees were unlawfully dropping off bundles of undistributed copies at the noncommercial municipal recycling center.[37]

Perhaps no one knows how many papers were actually delivered during the first several months; the DNA did not permit the independent Audit Bureau of Circulation to verify distribution until the following year.[38] Advertisers, however, drew their own conclusions. Data from Knight-Ridder and the market research firm Adtrack showed that ad lineage fell by one-third, while October revenues from run-of-press ads in the *Free Press* were nearly $7 million lower than the previous year.[39] Automobile classified ads—normally one of the newspapers' largest sources of revenue—fell by almost half. Retailers like Sears, JCPenney, Montgomery Ward, and major local grocery stores turned to direct mail and other media to distribute their preprinted circulars, and the small, local chain of suburban *Observer* and *Eccentric* papers saw its business rise from 1.2 million to 3.2 million inserts per week. At its peak, the unions claimed that more than 230 advertisers were avoiding the *News* and the *Free Press*, while those that remained received rates discounted by up to 65 percent.[40]

In the first few months at least, the unions effectively succeeded in their mobilization campaign against the newspapers. The level of resistance caught the publishers by surprise, and together Knight-Ridder and Gannett acknowledged losing $92 million from the strike in the first six months.[41] Workers and community residents showed an extraordinary solidarity with the newspaper strikers, in the largest popular demonstration of labor support in the Detroit area in decades. Unfortunately for the unions, however, that support was still no match for the resources the papers were willing to devote to breaking the strike.

PUSHING THROUGH: THE NEWSPAPERS' STRIKE OPERATIONS

On July 13, DNA planning director Alan Lenhoff's systematic operational plan for the newspapers was finally put into action. The newsrooms immediately merged their weekday publication under a joint masthead, as the publishers had announced in their 1992 memo to the U.S. Justice Department. More than five hundred existing non-union editorial and other employees were redeployed in other departments, and corporate "loaners" were flown in from elsewhere in the two chains. The out-of-town transfers were processed at intake centers throughout the city, where they received job assignments, identification cards, and payroll authorizations; Knight-Ridder alone recruited 140 staff members from other locations and paid their living expenses plus a $750 weekly bonus. The first week, employees slept inside the newspaper buildings on cots, couches, and office floors and ate hot meals prepared by an outside vendor with a crew of forty, working from the cafeteria in the downtown *News* building.[42]

Although its printing presses were more modern and efficient, the Riverfront Plant in Detroit was closed and production was moved to the Sterling Heights North Plant. The DNA set up a dormitory inside the plant to keep security personnel billeted on the premises, while other employees parked in rented lots at remote sites and were shuttled to and from work across picket lines in fifteen-passenger vans. Contractors drove the trucks filled with papers from the North Plant to the distribution centers, escorted by guards with video cameras riding alongside them in cars. Adult carriers were brought in from out of state, and each carrier was sent out on a route equipped with a car, a cellular phone, $1,000, a beeper, and a map. In all, DNA vice president for human resources Randi Austin later reported, the company rented six hundred cars, occupied one thousand hotel rooms, and put nine thousand cellular phones into use.[43]

"There were a lot of things that didn't happen according to plan," Lenhoff observed, "but we gave ourselves a lot of options."[44] The first week, home subscribers were not even charged for delivery. Neighborhoods of special interest to advertisers received "saturation" service; simply giving every house a paper was easier than having substitute carriers try to figure out specific delivery addresses.[45] Vandals damaged an average of two thousand newspaper racks per week, so the company turned to street hawkers and offered commissions to churches to let them sell Sunday papers near their congregations. The papers themselves were physically thin, short on ads, and full of wire copy, yet somehow the DNA managed to produce and distribute enough issues of the joint edition to claim that they never missed a day of delivery.[46]

From the beginning, however, the flashpoint in the system became the entry and exit of vehicles from the Sterling Heights North Plant. Under an agreement with the police, all gates to the plant were closed except for the south entrance on Mound Road, where the SHPD set up a command post on the center island across from the gate. Chaos soon erupted, however, as police in helmets and shields physically confronted strikers, using pepper spray to disperse the crowd. Fourteen strikers were arrested in the first two days, at least three were injured, and one lost several teeth.[47] To control the process, the SHPD had DNA trucks and vans line up in convoys in the left-hand flare lane on the northbound side of Mound Road. On an hourly basis, officers would stop traffic, cross the street in a V-formation, and clear the driveway, allowing vehicles to move in and out of the gate.[48]

The tensions at the North Plant seemed to epitomize the aggressive atmosphere that spread quickly over the strike. On the first night, July 13, striking mailer Steve Munson was picketing at the plant. At the request of union leaders, he got in his car and began following a DNA truck to see where it was taking newspapers for distribution. As he was doing so, he noticed two vehicles with security guards in them following him. The guards' vehicles rammed into Munson's car several times, forcing him off the road into a ditch. Huffmaster guard Paul Nevil later pled guilty to a charge of reckless driving in connection with the incident and was sentenced to twenty days in jail.[49]

On July 16, Sterling Heights police found and seized twenty-five nightsticks and a supply of pepper spray from guards inside the plant, a violation of the DNA's promise that private security forces would carry no weapons.[50] In a July 17 memo to SHPD chief Thomas Derocha, Lt. Frank Mowinski complained of these and other "flagrant and intentional" violations. When passing through the gates, Huffmaster employees verbally and physically taunted and "incited the strikers to the point of endangering our officers' safety."[51] In addition, Mowinski wrote, Huffmaster personnel sought out unauthorized confrontations with strikers beyond the plant gates. Employees in two Huffmaster vehicles showed up at a union representative's home to harass him, while another followed a union member on the road for more than fifteen miles from Meadowview to Telegraph Road and Interstate 696. So many problems with the Alternative Work Force contractors were reported that the DNA replaced the firm on July 18, while the Huffmaster guards were not terminated until August 8.[52]

With their jobs and livelihoods at stake, striking workers responded in kind. Picketers showered line-crossers with verbal abuse and threw rocks and swung picket signs at vehicles. Police reported arrests of union members for unarmed robbery of papers, breaking windows on company vans, and other property damage and disorderly conduct. Hundreds of vehicle tires were flattened as "star nails," four-pronged nails with one point that always stood up, were scattered anonymously in company driveways and parking lots.[53]

Union leaders disavowed any violence and set explicit rules for picket line behavior. They could not control the conduct of every individual striker, however, much less that of non-union protesters, including the sectarian political groups that showed up at picket lines. Early on, striker Randy Karpinen was picketing at a warehouse with his fellow Teamster Dennis Nazelli. "I picked up a rock, and I said, 'Dennis, tell me why I shouldn't throw this through that window of that truck?'" Karpinen recalled. "Here it is just late at night, these guys in the warehouse, they're taunting, you know, 'You're not gonna get your job back, you're not gonna do this' . . . and he just said, you know, 'Just drop your rock, just stay calm,' and you know, 'We don't need that.'"[54]

As the strike went on, the clashes in Sterling Heights grew more intense, particularly on Saturday nights before the delivery of the Sunday edition. When a crowd of about three hundred pickets refused to clear the Mound Road gate on August 19, police charged into the crowd with riot shields and nightsticks. Television news video showed forty-five-year-old striking press operator Frank Brabenec, dressed in shorts, T-shirt, and sneakers, being dragged by police and kicked repeatedly by an off-duty Sterling Heights police officer. Four strikers were arrested, and one suffered a broken arm. The following weekend, police and pickets again squared off at the entrance to the plant. More than sixty officers gathered on the Mound Road neutral ground as their commander ordered the strikers to give way, shouting over a bullhorn, "You are an illegal assembly. Let the vans go through." After a hastily negotiated truce, the crowd stepped aside shouting, "Shame, shame, shame," while police escorted DNA vehicles in and out.[55]

Despite the growing confrontations, the DNA continued to push ahead without regard for expense. Before the strike, company executives claimed that extending the contracts cost them $150,000 per week in lost savings from job reductions not yet implemented.[56] Once the strike began, Wall Street analyst Tod Jacobs estimated that it cost the employers $600,000 per day in the first few weeks. The DNA's Tim Kelleher disputed the figures, but joked, "Nobody knows how much it's costing us because right now, our accountants are running our mailroom."[57] As planning director Lenhoff later mused, "I kept waiting for someone to say, 'Stop! You're spending too much.' No one ever did."[58]

THE FAILURE OF CORPORATE PATERNALISM: THE FREE PRESS AND PERMANENT REPLACEMENTS

Whether or not they ever questioned the cost, at the corporate level there was no doubting Gannett's determination. "There's no blinking, no questioning, no wavering," said Gary Watson, president of Gannett's newspaper division, to a gathering of *News* managers and staffers in Detroit on July 19.[59] With the unions now out on the street, Gannett negotiator John Jaske saw a strategic opportunity. On July 26, he wrote letters to three of the unions in production and distribution, ratcheting up his position at the bargaining table. To the press operators and the mailers, Jaske withdrew the offers of compensation for reduced staffing and streamlined work practices. "It is unclear at this time whether we will ever need the staffing levels that we needed prior to the strike," he told the press operators' Jack Howe. Because circulation had fallen during the strike, Jaske suggested to Local 372 that even more district manager jobs might be cut. "We will have to re-evaluate both the size and number of districts based on new circulation needs," he wrote. "We, obviously, cannot continue our commitment to only reduce 59 districts. Many fewer districts may be appropriate."[60]

At the *News*, the air of antagonism between management and strikers also ran high. "These people [strikers] were assholes, and that's on the record," said *News* business editor Nolan Finley. "You should have stood here for three, two or three days, and listened and watched how these people behaved. The people who were coming in this door, you know, saleswomen and non-bargaining-unit HR employees, who were being just called every despicable, racist, sexist name in the book by people who thought somehow the high moral cause they were engaged in justified this low behavior. You wouldn't have to stand there two or three days before you lost all sympathy for them."[61]

"We have taken a very aggressive management position here in our relations with the unions all along," *News* publisher Giles told the media in September.[62] The *News* started advertising for replacement hires as early as July 26.[63] "There was incredible pressure applied by the newspaper to force, try to force people, entice people to cross the lines," Bob Ourlian recalled. "Columnists were constantly threatened with losing their columns; beat reporters were threatened with losing their beat. They were told point-blank: 'If you don't come back, you will not be able to write about X if you ever do come back.'"[64] In the main office of the *News*, a sign on display in the newsroom declared proudly: TWICE THE WORK, HALF THE STAFF, AND NONE OF THE WHINING.[65]

The End of Moderation: The Free Press

At the *Free Press*, however, things were somehow thought to be different. Publisher Neal Shine still presided over the newsroom, having come back after a brief retirement in 1989 and a two-year bout with cancer. Many midlevel editors and supervisors were actually part of the union, dating back to its original organization in the 1930s, and managers and journalists alike said that they "felt part of a family."[66] Urban affairs reporter Bill McGraw was hired by Shine in 1977. Like Shine, he had grown up in Detroit's East Side Irish Catholic parishes, and he shared his boss's love for the city's history and for the newspaper. "It's a cliché to say it was a family atmosphere. It wasn't always a family atmosphere for everybody," McGraw noted, "but it was more of a family atmosphere than the way I understand a lot of workplaces. . . . In general, the *Free Press* bent over backwards to accommodate people's personal situations," long before that was required by law or became a common practice in American corporate life.[67]

McGraw also believed that Knight-Ridder, unlike Gannett, was relatively benign in its treatment of unions, and he felt that the *Free Press* had more respect for the principle of collective bargaining. "The [Guild] local at the *Free Press* had very few grievances with the management over the years," he recalled. "At the *Free Press*, the management did nothing in the run-up to the strike, they did nothing like what we understood was going on at the *News*."[68] *Free Press* managers also did nothing, however, to stop or restrain the Gannett executives, who dominated the decision-making in the process leading up to the strike. "The way the negotiations were conducted is they [Gannett] weren't calling and saying, 'What do you think we ought to do about this?'" Knight-Ridder chief executive P. Anthony Ridder later admitted. "It was more we [Knight-Ridder] were saying, 'What the hell is going on?'"[69] With the strike now under way, Gannett once again was calling the shots. Knight-Ridder was persuaded to go along, and the *Free Press* management fell into line.

On Tuesday, August 8, the paper issued its ultimatum: in a letter signed by Shine and seven other *Free Press* executives, the newspaper warned striking newsroom employees to return to work by 10:00 AM on Thursday, August 10, or face permanent replacement. The letter bluntly stated that any strikers who failed to return by the deadline and were replaced would be eligible to come back only as new vacancies allowed, and that the company would be "under no obligation to make the replacement leave to give you back a job."[70] The threat worked—on deadline day, some three dozen *Free Press* journalists, including several star columnists, joined about forty others who had already crossed the picket line. By August 24, the newspaper claimed that 117 out of 265 striking *Free Press* employees had returned to work.[71] In July, popular sports columnist and broadcast commentator Mitch Albom, author of the soon-to-be-published best-selling book *Tuesdays with Morrie*, had proudly told his television audience, "You're looking at a man on strike." By early September, he was back at the newspaper.[72]

A little more than a year earlier, the *Free Press* had editorialized in favor of a bill in the U.S. Congress that would have banned the hiring of permanent replacements during strikes. "The right to strike is essential if workers are to gain and preserve fair wages," the editors noted in an opinion published on June 24, 1994. They continued:

> But the use of strikes was undermined during the 1980s, as more and more businesses took advantage of a 1938 U.S. Supreme Court decision that created a loophole in labor law—firing workers who strike over wages is illegal, but permanently replacing them is not. . . . Workers who engage in legal strikes over economic issues increasingly risk losing their jobs, and that threat hovers over labor negotiations.[73]

Under a Republican filibuster, the bill banning permanent replacements died in the Senate. With the "loophole" still available, the *Free Press* now chose to use that weapon against its own employees.

Free Press executives later contended that they gave the order to return because they wanted to save the paper and feared that, unless they resumed independent publication, corporate interests would move to close it. "I was deeply afraid," said deputy managing editor Carol Leigh Hutton, "that if the *Free Press* couldn't hold up its end and publish, that we would just be sucked under and the *News* would take over. . . . I believed, and I know that many of my associates who were still in the room, that if we didn't find a way to make this happen, our newspaper would be gone and that was it."[74] Publisher Shine agreed. "I knew that if the *Free Press* was not able to publish the newspaper, I was terribly concerned that Knight-Ridder would say, 'That's it, we don't need this aggravation,'" he recalled. "Nobody said, 'Do this or the paper's gone,' absolutely not. I knew that we needed to publish the paper. . . . There was a question of making the *Free Press* viable, and that was the only way to do it."[75]

Hutton and Shine may have believed they were saving their newspaper, but sources at the parent corporation denied that they ever considered shutting down the *Free Press*, which, as the morning paper, enjoyed the dominant position and a circulation advantage of more than 50 percent over the *News*. The *Free Press* itself reported on July 22 that "Knight-Ridder, Inc., owner of the *Detroit Free Press*, does not want a long newspaper strike and has no interest in leaving Detroit or making it a one-newspaper town, Chairman P. Anthony Ridder said Friday." The author of the article, *Free Press* editor Tom Walsh, quoted Ridder as saying: "Detroit is the fifth or sixth largest market in the country, and we have the largest newspaper in that market. It's an important market for us, and we think it provides good opportunities for the future."[76]

"We, Knight-Ridder, very much wanted to [publish separately] as soon as we could, and we were pushing to separate them," Ridder later re-called. "I don't remember that Gannett was really resisting us on that, but I remember that we didn't want a joint paper. We wanted to keep that to the bare minimum amount of time."[77] In fact, speculation focused more strongly on the possible closure of the *News*, which publisher Giles de-nounced as "reckless [and] without foundation in fact," in a July 16 front-page editorial on "Why Keeping Two Daily Newspapers in Detroit Is Sim-ply Good Business."[78] Under the JOA, the companies shared revenues from the two papers evenly, and having both brand names available pro-duced a total market penetration greater than either one alone could achieve. As former *News* executive editor Ben Burns later wrote: "[The] financial facts don't support the idea that Frank Vega, who is the head of the Detroit Newspaper Agency which runs the business sides of the news-paper, would let one of the newspapers die."[79]

In any case, from the start of the strike the *Free Press* management sought to separate relations in the newsroom from the unions represent-ing the workers at the DNA. They were quick to blame the Teamsters for the walkout; Hutton later claimed that at the time she did not even know about the Guild's unfair labor practice charge at the *News*.[80] "The issues between the *Free Press* and its Guild members don't seem formidable com-pared to the unresolved problems with the other unions," wrote Shine in a "Page One" opinion piece on July 17. "But tell Guild people on the picket line that this is not their strike and they will insist that it is," he added in-credulously, "[and] that they exist in solidarity with the other unions."[81]

A few weeks later, *Free Press* executive editor Heath Meriwether was even more strident, accusing Guild leaders of having "yoked their mem-bers to the issues of the other unions, which include work rules and pro-cedures that create inefficiencies that simply aren't acceptable in today's world."[82] Privately, managers called reporters and columnists personally and lobbied them to cross the picket line. "Some of the managers said di-rectly to people, 'What are you doing out there with these truck drivers?'" striking *Free Press* music writer Gary Graff remembered. "You know, 'You've got a college education, you've got a career, a reputation . . .,' and so on and so forth. And they really played that card very well."[83]

Some of those who did cross expressed anger about risking their jobs to strike alongside less-educated blue-collar workers. "My own feelings are that I'm just appalled by the notion that we have to be chained to the Teamsters on this," said *Free Press* television critic Mike Duffy, who led a brief opposition effort within the Guild before returning to work on his own.[84] Many striking Guild members, however, had experience with unionism in their families or communities, believed in its legitimacy, and saw it as a defense of professional integrity and autonomy. *Free Press* reporter Patricia Montemurri had grown up in Dearborn Heights, the daughter of Italian immigrants, in a family of autoworkers and union members. For Montemurri, the newspapers did not act very differently from any other corporate employer toward her, notwithstanding her University of Michigan journalism degree. "It's very easy for them to take advantage of your professional dedication to getting news and telling a story," she remarked. "That's why I belong to a union, that's why I expect to be paid overtime, and all that was threatened."[85]

Others saw participation in the strike as rooted in their sense of vocational identity and moral duty. Striking *Free Press* editor Nancy Dunn thought that "most of the people who went into the newspaper business went into the business because they believed in the power of newspapers to do good, and when they start to do things either deceptively or illegally, or immorally, then you just don't stand with them if you really believe, if you went into the business for that reason."[86] Reporter Michael Betzold felt that the strike was a test of his journalistic relationship with his subjects and readers. "Detroit is a city about the labor movement and working people, and how are we going to write about this area and these people if we're standing in opposition to them or identifying ourselves with corporate or professional interests as opposed to the interests of working people? To do so, it seems, would be defying not only the cultural nature of Detroit but the whole history of Detroit."[87]

Dual Workforces: Replacing Union Members

On Wednesday, August 30, the *Free Press* made one more attempt to win back the striking newsroom workers. Negotiators presented a contract proposal that would let all Guild members return, but only if the union voted to accept it by the following Tuesday; even so, some returning strikers might still not get their same jobs back because the paper had already begun hiring replacements. The proposal offered some modest economic concessions, including a slightly higher ratio of across-the-board versus merit pay increases and no phase-out of guaranteed wage raises, as in the paper's earlier proposal. It also offered the option of a fully paid health maintenance organization insurance plan, as opposed to partially paid Blue Cross coverage, and a "me-too" clause if any other union should get better benefits. But the offer came with conditions that included a significant rollback of the structure of union representation at the newspaper.

The offer was presented as a complete settlement: to accept it would mean the *Free Press* unit had renounced joint economic bargaining with the MCNU, and returning journalists would have to walk past the picket lines of the other striking workers, including their fellow Guild members at the

News. The proposal called for thirteen union members to be moved out of the bargaining unit and into management, and it established an open shop, ending more than fifty years of agreements that had required workers covered by the Guild contract to belong to the union. Finally, management demanded that the Guild agree by 10:00 AM on Friday to put the offer to a membership vote, and copies of the proposal were sent directly to *Free Press* employees with a letter from executive editor Meriwether.[88]

The last demand effectively bypassed the negotiating committee and sidelined the union from any meaningful negotiation over the proposal, a fact highlighted when the union learned of its public release only after receiving it in a fax from a local television station. On the Friday deadline, the Guild rejected management's proposal in a brief meeting in the lobby of the *Free Press* building. With the threat of permanent replacement hovering over the negotiations, striking photographer and Guild bargaining committee member Daymon Hartley handed back to Meriwether a stack of the letters the paper had sent to employees. Said Hartley, "Our response was not to respond, and to say, 'Stay out of our union.'"[89]

By the end of August, all three employers were actively replacing their striking employees. Between August 1 and December 31, the *News* hired eighty-four journalists, nearly four times as many as they had hired in the year before the strike. During one stretch, the *Free Press* took on an average of one new person per day, and both papers employed younger, less-experienced journalists than they had hired before the strike.[90] One of the new hires at the *News* was Ron French, a reporter from the Fort Wayne, Indiana, *Journal-Gazette*. French had never before worked in a unionized newsroom, and he was impressed by the Detroit papers' determination to break the strike.

> Anything, everything was charged to the company. People were driving company cars to and from work. They were passing them out. It was . . . "Just go ahead and drive a company car. We have plenty of them, more than we have workers. Go ahead and just drive them back and forth." Because they were doing anything they could. It was obvious that the corporations had said that the checkbook's open. "Do whatever you have to do to keep these people happy who are helping us out." You see that sort of attitude coming in and you get the impression these people are serious. There's no way they're going to give up to the union.[91]

Because unfair labor practice charges were pending against them, the DNA and the *News* at first avoided calling their replacements "permanent." But unlike the newsrooms, the DNA made little effort to bring striking union members back, instead choosing to replace them en masse. The company posted job advertisements nationwide and claimed that in six weeks they received more than fifty thousand phone calls and conducted eight thousand interviews. Reference-checking and testing of interviewees were waived, and on peak days the DNA hired between fifty and one hundred people.[92] By August 12, eight hundred replacements had been hired; two weeks later, the number reached more than eleven hundred. Out of approximately two thousand Teamsters, mailers, press operators, and printers, only about one hundred crossed picket lines.[93]

The systematic hiring of permanent replacements brought an immediate outcry of community protest, most notably from Detroit-area religious leaders. More than one hundred local pastors, rabbis, and religious sisters signed a statement from the Interfaith Committee on Worker Issues condemning the hiring of permanent replacements. A similar statement appeared as an advertisement in the *Michigan Chronicle*, a local African American newspaper, signed by the Rev. Wendell Anthony, president of the Detroit NAACP, and the Rev. Robert Smith, pastor of New Bethel Baptist Church. A landmark Detroit church, New Bethel was the home of the late Reverend C. L. Franklin, a prominent minister and father of the singer Aretha Franklin.[94]

At a meeting on August 15, Catholic auxiliary bishop Thomas Gumbleton, Episcopal bishop R. Stewart Wood, Rabbi Irwin Groner of Congregation Shaarey Zedek in Southfield, and Rabbi M. Robert Syme of Temple Israel in West Bloomfield joined together in calling for an immediate halt to the hiring of permanent replacements. Finally, while proclaiming his neutrality in the strike, Roman Catholic cardinal Adam Maida, head of the 1.2 million–member Archdiocese of Detroit, issued a statement on August 16 saying: "In this instance, the hiring of permanent replacement workers from outside the organization is not an acceptable solution. If striking workers are threatened with being permanently replaced, this practice seems to undermine the legitimate purpose of the union and to destroy any possibility for collective bargaining."[95]

But the newspapers did not look back. Despite its reputation as the "Morning Friendly," the *Free Press* adopted a hard-line policy of permanent replacement. Many striking *Free Press* workers were appalled by the management's actions and could not believe that they would abandon employees who had given years and even their careers to the paper and who had stayed with it through the crises of the newspaper war and the formation of the joint operating agreement. In the midst of this crisis, however, the managerial culture of corporate paternalism offered no protections for striking workers and no resistance to the path of polarization charted by Gannett.

Few experienced a deeper sense of betrayal than reporter Bill McGraw, who felt disappointed most of all by Shine. In an editorial published in the strike newsletter *The Detroit Union*, McGraw personally chastised Shine, whom he had admired as the embodiment of the paper's distinctive character, for signing the August 8 letter. Invoking their common religious beliefs and ethnic Detroit roots, he exhorted Shine to take a stand "by speaking out, by stopping his accomplices on the third floor from conducting their fire sale of *Free Press* jobs, by demanding that the companies bargain in good faith," or, failing that, by resigning in protest.[96] Shine did none of those things. There was no longer any moderate voice on the management side—all three employers were united. The leading editorial spokesperson for the companies was now Giles of the *News*, who told the *St. Petersburg Times* on August 27, "We're going to hire a whole new work force and go on without unions, or they can surrender unconditionally and salvage what they can."[97]

A "UNION TOWN": LABOR DAY WEEKEND 1995

The companies had thrown down the gauntlet, and for strikers like Local 372 member Paul Kulka, the very identity of their community and its historic labor culture were at stake. Kulka grew up on the East Side of Detroit and had hired on at the *Free Press* in 1968, working his way up from jumper to driver and relief man and finally to district manager. He recalled:

> You can talk about cowboy scripts and all this other stuff, but it was like the bad guys came to your town and now they are trying to take it over. And are you just going to let them take it over, or are you going to fight with everything you got? And that's exactly the way I felt. They weren't going to come in here after I've worked for this company for twenty-six years and just take it over and throw me out the door.

With the Labor Day holiday coming up, the local union movement prepared for some of the largest mobilizations yet in the seven-week-old strike. "The attitude was an attitude of, they're pushing it and they are going to test to see how strong the unions are here in Detroit," Kulka added. "We felt it was a union town, and there's no way they are going to bust the unions here."[98]

The growing animosity in the strike was amplified in the volatile atmosphere of Sterling Heights. On August 28, SHPD Lt. Frank Mowinski wrote a memo to Chief Thomas Derocha. "In response to your earlier directive," Mowinski said, "the DNA was advised that escorts in and out of the News plant will stop as of 1900 hours on 08-26-95." Mowinski reported a conversation he had had with Kevin Johnson, a Vance security supervisor in the plant, who said that if the police would not provide escorts, the DNA intended to open the lines into the plant using Vance personnel. The company also immediately deployed an additional eighty guards, equipped with riot helmets, bullet-resistant vests, and the same type of shields as those used by the SHPD. "The DNA deploying 80 guards in full riot gear to open gate(s) at the News plant would cause violence and injury to citizens, strikers, security, and our officers," Mowinski warned Derocha. "It would also cause a confrontation between the strikers and the DNA vehicles, causing extensive damage to property."[99]

Mowinski's fears came to pass that weekend. On Saturday, September 2, a crowd of around four hundred had gathered by the late afternoon at the North Plant. When Sterling Heights police attempted to clear access to the plant gate, the picketers refused to leave. The officers used pepper spray on the crowd after being pushed back across the street amid a hail of bottles, cans, and bricks. At 5:00 PM, a much larger group of strikers and sympathizers rallied at the UAW Local 228 headquarters in Sterling Heights, about a mile from the North Plant. As the rally broke up, a half-mile-long procession of demonstrators marched down all four lanes of Mound Road to join the pickets at the gate, where the crowd swelled to around three thousand. The police called for backup from neighboring towns, and ultimately some three hundred officers from more than twenty law enforcement agencies were amassed on Mound Road. Despite repeated requests from the DNA to clear the gate, however, the SHPD declined to wade into the huge crowd, citing safety concerns.[100]

Around 2:00 AM and again at 4:30 AM, newspaper trucks attempted to leave the plant but were met with bricks, bottles, and picket signs, and several vehicles' windshields were smashed. DNA chief financial officer Gary Anderson and Gannett negotiator John Jaske were both at the plant that night. Around 4:00 AM, they ordered a convoy of semi-tractor-trailer trucks to leave from the north gate facing 16 Mile Road, contrary to their agreement with police. As Jaske later recalled, "We decided, because the heaviest amount of the mass picketing and violence was concentrated [on Mound Road] and going after the police who were generally on the median and so on, that we would try to in effect sneak out the back."[101]

The gate was around ten feet high and thirty to forty feet wide; a group of around seventy pickets who stood in the driveway outside had chained and padlocked the fence shut.[102] Without informing the police, Jaske and Anderson decided to use a truck to crash the gate open. Jaske later described the scene: "So the first driver, whether he backed up, I don't think he did, but he rammed that gate and tried to break the chain. Well, what happened was, the chain was stronger than the bottom hinges, and the gate flips up like this, and he's stuck. So everybody's got to back up, and the gate falls down."[103]

Union witnesses said the truck accelerated toward the gate at up to thirty miles per hour, which company sources denied; a forty-year-old Teamster member was injured when he was briefly pinned under the collapsed fence. There was no police presence nearby to ensure public safety; the DNA had intended that its security guards would follow the truck out of the gate and clear the strikers from the driveway by themselves, again in violation of their agreement with the SHPD. Within minutes, however, hundreds of other pickets rushed to the area from Mound Road and set upon the stopped truck and three other vans now blocking the entrance, smashing windshields and causing other property damage. Not until 8:30 AM Sunday, when the crowd of pickets had eventually dwindled to around fifty, did a convoy of trucks finally leave the plant through the Mound Road gate.[104]

The protesters had stalled, though they did not actually stop, the delivery of the Sunday paper, but union leaders publicly declared a victory and promised to return the following weekend. On Monday, September 4, an estimated five thousand unionists gathered in Detroit for the traditional Labor Day parade down Woodward Avenue, including AFL-CIO president Thomas Donahue and Service Employees International Union (SEIU) president John Sweeney, then challenging Donahue for the labor federation presidency. The marchers turned west onto Lafayette Avenue and went past the *Free Press* offices to a noon rally in front of the *News* building, where U.S. congressperson John Conyers and the Rev. Joseph Lowery, head of the Southern Christian Leadership Conference (SCLC), spoke in support of the strike.[105]

That evening as many as three hundred pickets arrived at the North Plant, including many non-union protesters. Facing them on the Mound Road median were at least one hundred police officers from Sterling Heights and other suburban municipalities. Among the participants that night were Lt. Frank Mowinski and striking mailer Ben Solomon. As the SHPD commanding officer at Mound Road, Mowinski declared the assembly to be unlawful and gave the orders to the crowd to disperse. Again and again, during a five-hour standoff, police forayed into the crowd using shields, batons, and pepper spray; each time they were pushed back by strikers throwing sticks, rocks, and other objects.

Some of the protesters found a cache of discarded five-inch steel rods behind a nearby machine shop and began hurling them at the police and at security guards inside the plant grounds. A television camera operator was injured after being hit when a guard tossed one of the rods back at the demonstrators, and news video footage recorded the *plink! plink!* sound of metal landing on pavement. By that night, Mound Road was strewn with broken glass, trash, and bits of concrete, while pickets fell to their knees choking under a cloud of pepper gas. For Mowinski, the most important assignment of his career was escalating out of his control. In turn, Solomon would end the night gassed, beaten, arrested, and detained for almost nine hours without medical care. Around midnight, police used tear gas to disperse the crowd, and delivery trucks finally slipped out of the plant about an hour later.[106]

At least one demonstrator was hospitalized after exposure to the gas fumes, while a plant security guard reportedly suffered a broken leg when he was run over by a speeding delivery truck. Police made twenty-three arrests, more than half of whom were not newspaper strikers. Fifteen people, including Solomon, were charged with unlawful assembly, five others with inciting a riot, and the remainder with disorderly conduct and resisting or interfering with an arrest, including an Associated Press photographer who was dragged away while taking pictures of police beating a demonstrator.[107] During the night, a DNA truck parked at the plant was set on fire and destroyed. A DNA internal review failed to find any suspects, but an investigation by Macomb County prosecuting attorney Carl Marlinga's office determined that it was unlikely that strikers were responsible, since at the time the truck was behind the plant gate and surrounded by security guards. A videotape showed debris in the cab of the truck that caught fire and spread rapidly, indicating that an accelerant was used. No charges were filed, but according to Marlinga, the circumstantial evidence pointed to "someone who was already on the DNA side of the fence."[108]

Altogether, the Labor Day weekend protests were the most serious disruptions the newspapers had yet experienced in the strike, and they caused particular problems for DNA chief executive Frank Vega. While Vega had all along hoped to avoid a walkout, he did not control the company's actions at the bargaining table and could not now broker an end to it. At the same time, he was responsible for maintaining the DNA's operations, and any failure to deliver the papers would be seen as his failure. With his own position at stake, Vega pursued a policy of total war against the strike. Frustrated by the siege in Sterling Heights, he ordered Lenhoff to find a way to use helicopters if necessary to airlift papers out of the plant.[109]

On Tuesday, September 6, the DNA filed for an injunction seeking to limit the number of pickets at the North Plant to no more than six at each gate. Macomb County Circuit Court judge Peter Maceroni, however, withheld a ruling on the condition that both sides promised to maintain peace and obey the law.[110] That Saturday, September 9, an estimated two thousand demonstrators turned out on Mound Road, including religious supporters and members of the autoworkers, steelworkers, teachers, restaurant employees, and building trades unions. For ten hours, the pickets blocked the entrance to the plant. After two unsuccessful attempts to clear the way, police chief Derocha decided not to try a third time to move the crowd.[111] With the DNA trapped inside the plant, Vega called in the air force. Lenhoff, who personally supervised the operation, described the scene:

> At about 8:00 PM, the first helicopter flies over the plant and lands on a big field behind it that we own that's kind of in the area of the plant . . . [then] another helicopter and another helicopter and another helicopter, and between 8:00 PM and 4:00 AM we took out papers on helicopters. We had basically everybody out of the pressroom out on this field handing papers down a long line like a bucket brigade, loading up these helicopters. And we had, we were dispatching them to little airfields. For the most part, they were unlit grass airfields or small airports in suburban communities. And I was talking to our circulation people on an aviation phone, talking in code, telling them where the papers were coming and how many . . . and all told, I think we got out 120,000 or 130,000 papers that way.

The action was costly, and the total number of papers flown out was a fraction of even the reduced strike circulation, but Vega had made his point: the DNA would do anything to break the strike. As Lenhoff remarked, "It was a message the company gave both to the strikers and to its own employees that we were too committed to allow them to shut us down, and no matter what they were going to do, we were going to find a way to counter it."[112]

Despite the dramatic show of will, however, some three-quarters of the next day's Sunday edition remained inside the plant awaiting delivery. Again, Jaske was on the premises that night, and at 11:30 PM he called Derocha, expressing frustration over the delay at the south gate.[113] Derocha said that he thought it was too risky for him to intervene, as he later testified, because "it was clear that we would not be able to [clear the entrance] without having to do the impractical and that is probably have to arrest everybody that was there."[114] Later that night, around 250 pickets were milling around the driveway when Jaske called Derocha again and said that he intended to have a convoy of trucks exit the gate. Derocha told Jaske that he would not stop the trucks, but that he would not use police resources to protect them; under the circumstances, he told Jaske, he felt it was poor judgment to try to leave the plant. "The company said they wished to get their trucks out," Capt. James Owens of the SHPD told a reporter the next day. "We didn't recommend it. They chose to get out anyway."[115]

At 3:50 AM, the DNA informed police that trucks would be exiting the Mound Road gate at 4:15 AM. Despite an advance notice of twenty-five minutes, the SHPD gave no warning to the crowd of persons in the driveway.[116] At 4:15, while Jaske stood watching from the rooftop of the North Plant, the gates swung open and a caravan of eleven tractor-trailers and one car drove through the crowd. The first three or four trucks moved slowly, at perhaps five miles per hour, as startled pickets scrambled out of the way and began throwing rocks and swinging signs. The remaining trucks sped through at twenty to thirty-five miles per hour while police officers stood passively across the street.[117] "The trucks came out at a high rate of speed and didn't stop," said Sgt. Scott Lucas of the SHPD. "No one was run over." Several minor injuries were reported, but the SHPD did not pursue the vehicles or issue any citations for reckless driving, instead blaming the pickets for refusing to yield to the trucks.[118] Striker Kate DeSmet was at the scene and witnessed the events. "It was like when you're in a near car accident and you're just in this involuntary shaking in your system, and I stood there shaking, looking at this building and thinking, they want to kill me, they want to kill all of these guys, what, for a thirty-five-cent newspaper, for God's sake."[119]

CONCLUSION: PICKET LINES AND PICKET SIGNS

The following Tuesday, September 12, DNA lawyers were back in court seeking an injunction, this time before Judge Raymond Cashen, who had taken over the case. Cashen issued his ruling the next day, restricting the total number of pickets allowed in the Mound Road driveway to ten, although no limits were placed on the number elsewhere around the plant. Vehicle drivers were required to blast their horn or flash their headlights when entering or leaving the plant, and pickets were ordered to leave when so warned and to desist from throwing sharp objects in the driveway.[120]

The injunction immediately changed the dynamic of protest at the North Plant, as the unions now faced substantially greater legal risks in physically resisting the company and the police. Union leaders were unwilling to violate the court order through mass civil disobedience, for example, and they did not believe the majority of their members were actually ready to go to jail and possibly sacrifice their jobs. The unions themselves were hardly prepared to take such steps, but they also believed that they had significant strategic alternatives. The circulation and advertising boycotts were in full swing, the companies were spending millions of dollars to fight the strike, and the legal machinery of the unfair labor practice charges was just getting under way. The MCNU heads did not want to jeopardize those efforts and risk the public support that they perceived they had.[121]

For those first two weeks in September, however, Paul Kulka's "union town" had battled the SHPD and the newspapers, significantly and forcefully disrupting the DNA's efforts to operate during the strike. But the company had fought back, violating its agreements with police, sending trucks into crowds of pickets, and showing a disregard for public safety. The DNA "didn't intend for anyone to get hurt," said company spokesperson Susie Ellwood. "But our position is that we have a lawful right to enter and leave our facilities." County prosecutor Marlinga demurred. "There are legal, non-violent ways to deal with people who break the law," he said. "One of the ways that is not open to Detroit Newspapers is to use physical force to endanger human life."[122]

In Sterling Heights, a private labor dispute between unions and management had become an all-out civic war, drawing in the coercive force of local police authorities and tearing at the fabric of social relations in the community. "That was an amazing time for me," Kulka said later. "I bet you I knew a dozen cops that were across that street right there at that time." Kulka worked as a district manager in Sterling Heights, and among the police officers on duty he recognized neighbors and parents of kids he knew from the city's youth sports programs:

> And they were sick about it, most of them. The majority of them were sick about it. But there were your gung-ho-ers. And you know, they'd come push us across the line, the street, try to break us up. And we'd push them right back across that island. That was an amazing time because here I am, the director of baseball and softball in Sterling Heights, that I'm fighting for my job . . . all the six different unions were all there, holding up their picket signs, fighting for their jobs.[123]

For their part, the Gannett managers in particular seemed to take an aggressively personal interest in combating the strike. Giles publicly taunted the unions and even told strikers who crossed picket lines, "If you go back to work, you surrender."[124] Vega reveled in the nickname given to him by the strikers and gave out T-shirts with DARTH VEGA printed on them to the replacements.[125] Jaske, a senior corporate executive at Gannett, played the role of a daring field commander at the North Plant, giving orders against police advice in the predawn hours and watching from the rooftop as trucks exited the gates. As a confidential company memo on strike operations from mid-September concluded, favorably: "Quote of the day: 'Those DNA guys sure got a lot of chrome'—one of our contract drivers, after watching the helicopters at the North Plant take off full of newspapers."[126]

As much as the managers might have enjoyed the credit, however, the events at the North Plant could not be attributed to any one individual's personality or will. The militarization of security and the hiring of permanent replacements were already familiar steps in what was by then a standard post-accord business model for operating during strikes.[127] The violent clashes in Sterling Heights were all too predictable and signaled the local fallout from the collision between the norms and institutions of New Deal unionism and the insurgent corporate anti-union agenda. The companies did not anticipate the level of resistance shown by the strikers, and they did not plan on losing more than $90 million in the first six months.[128] The newspaper executives were free at any time to step back from the confrontation, but once they had set themselves on their path, they seemed determined to follow it regardless of the cost to themselves, their employees, or the community.

After Judge Cashen's ruling in the injunction, the main sites of picket line confrontation would move on to other locations. By mid-September, however, the DNA had weathered the Labor Day storm of popular mobilization and had almost completely replaced its workforce in production and distribution. On September 18, sixty-seven days after the start of the strike, the newspapers resumed publication of separate weekday editions of the *News* and the *Free Press*.[129]

Chapter 9 | Law and Violence: Permanent Replacements and the Control of Collective Action

WHY DID THEY NOT step back? What incentives drove the newspapers to escalate their war against the unions, and what mechanisms reinforced their determination? How did the historical context allow them to make the choices they did, and what resources did they mobilize in pursuit of their objectives? The answers, I argue, lie in the erosion of the larger New Deal order. With the rise of the anti-union regime in the 1980s, the law no longer served to steer the actors toward a peaceful, negotiated settlement. Rather than absorbing conflict within institutional channels, the new regime actually raised the likelihood of repression and violence, especially when employers hired permanent replacements during strikes.

In particular, the increased use of permanent replacements after 1981 led to significantly longer and more contentious strikes. Economists John Schnell and Cynthia Gramm found that when employers permanently replaced strikers, the probability of settlement fell by approximately 30 percent.[1] With fewer incentives to settle, strikes that did occur were more likely to turn into long wars of attrition and a sheer test of force. A study of more than three hundred major strikes by economists Peter Cramton and Joseph Tracy showed that walkouts lasted an average of 217 days when permanent replacements were hired, almost seven times longer than when no replacements were used. In addition, 46 percent of the contract negotiations involving major violence were associated with the use of replacement workers.[2]

More than a strategic bargaining mechanism, the use of permanent replacements threatened to punish workers with the loss of their jobs for exercising their statutory rights under the NLRA. The effect was to sharply tilt the balance of power in negotiations, undercut the process of collective bargaining, and potentially push labor disputes into unregulated class warfare. "Hiring permanent replacement workers can represent a fundamental attack on strikers' economic security and lifestyles," legal scholar Seth Harris observes. "As a result, some strikers suffer acute physical and mental health problems, marriages dissolve, friendships end, and communities are split. Others turn to violence against the replacement and line crossers, commonly known to strikers as 'scabs.'"[3]

Sadly, all of these dynamics were present in the Detroit strike. In this chapter, I begin with a brief review of the right to strike and the dilemmas raised by employers' use of permanent replacements, dilemmas that tend to break more toward polarization than a negotiated settlement. In this case, the newspapers chose to use repressive methods to exclude and expel the striking workers and restrict their collective action. Such measures aimed to strip away the economic pressure of the picket line, threatened the destruction of the unionized workforce, and cast a coldly cynical air over the interaction between the two sides. By the late fall of 1995, the clashes between strikers and security forces had become ever more volatile and vicious. The employers, however, offered no moves toward compromise but rather used the strike as an opportunity to restructure their operations.

IRRECONCILABLE TERMS: THE RIGHT TO STRIKE VERSUS PERMANENT REPLACEMENT

The right to strike is explicitly protected in the language of the NLRA: workers cannot be fired for choosing to walk out. Starting from the Supreme Court's 1938 *Mackay* decision, however, the courts have imposed increasing limits on the rights of strikers to return to work. Under *Mackay*, if employees are striking to achieve "economic" contract terms like wages and working conditions, they can be "permanently" replaced. In that case, they are not guaranteed their old jobs when the strike is over; the employer is not obliged to displace the permanent replacements and may take back the strikers only as new vacancies allow. Moreover, the employer can refuse to reinstate strikers if their old jobs have been abolished owing to reduced business or production levels and if the returnees are unable to perform other required jobs.[4] This creates a dilemma for the union: even if it offers to end the strike, it may be forced to bargain for terms that do not include all of its members going back to work.

Hiring permanent replacements, however, also creates a dilemma for the employer, which practically speaking now has two workforces: the replacement one in the workplace and a striking one on the street. The situation makes settlement with the union more difficult; if and when the strike is resolved, one set of workers obviously must go. Under the Supreme Court's 1983 *Belknap v. Hale* decision, if the employer promises the replacements that they are permanent, then the replacements may sue for breach of contract if they are laid off in favor of returning economic strikers. Once an employer chooses to hire permanent replacements, in other words, it may be locking itself into its decision well past the end of the strike.

The result actually rewards opportunistic behavior by the employer, which can then maximize its demands on the union even if it prolongs the strike, knowing that it has already unilaterally achieved more favorable employment terms with the replacements.[5] By September 1995, that option appeared to be the newspapers' preferred choice in this case. As Tod Jacobs, analyst for the New York investment firm Sanford C. Bernstein and Company, wrote: "Having endured the strike this long, we believe management would likely not revert to previously expected agreements, but would press for maximum headcount reductions, perhaps as much as 500 to 600 heads."[6] In a report issued in early October, Knight-Ridder chief financial officer Ross Jones confirmed Jacobs's analysis. "Whatever the short-term cost of the strike to us and our partner [Gannett]," Jones predicted, "it will be recouped in long-term savings from operating with a smaller and more efficient workforce."[7]

The Detroit unions, however, had not lost all of their rights. If a strike is called to protest an employer's unfair labor practices, then the employer may lawfully hire temporary but not permanent replacements. Unfair labor practice strikers are entitled to immediate reinstatement to their former jobs once the union makes an unconditional offer to return to work. The employer must take them back and, if necessary, discharge any temporary replacements to make room for them. Employers that refuse to reinstate unfair labor practice strikers commit an additional unfair labor practice and may be liable for back wages starting from the date of the unconditional offer to return to work. All of that is contingent, however, on a legal process to determine whether the original unfair labor practices have in fact occurred.

That process can be lengthy and complex. It begins with the filing of an unfair labor practice charge with the regional office of the National Labor Relations Board, which then assigns an agent to investigate. If the investigation finds reasonable cause to support the charge, the agent will first try to settle the case, but if no settlement is reached, then the regional director issues a formal complaint. Short of any interim settlement, the case goes to trial before a federal administrative law judge (ALJ). Attorneys from the NLRB regional office prosecute the case on behalf of the NLRB general counsel, while the charging party may also have legal representation and present evidence at the trial.

If the ALJ finds that the employer has committed unfair labor practices, the employer may appeal the decision to the NLRB in Washington, D.C. Even if the Board upholds the judge's ruling, the general counsel must petition the federal Court of Appeals to enforce the Board's order if the employer refuses to obey. In that way, the employer may secure judicial review of the Board's decision, and the case may be appealed all the way to the Supreme Court.[8] The determination of unfair labor practices can thus take years, while the strikers remain uncertain whether they will ever get their jobs back.

As many labor law scholars have argued, the practice of permanent replacement radically undermines the statutory right to strike and its function in collective bargaining.[9] In Detroit, *News* publisher Bob Giles's August 27 boast that "we're going to hire a whole new work force and go on without unions, or they can surrender unconditionally and salvage what they can," accurately reflected the newspapers' position.[10] "Before we ever hired a replacement worker, we said they would not be replaced if strikers returned," said *Free Press* deputy managing editor Carole Leigh Hutton. "We used to send a letter to the new hires to make it clear that this was not temporary, we hired them into a real job."[11] As John Taylor, DNA general counsel and director of labor relations, later wrote, "The *Mackay* Doctrine was an essential element in the Detroit Newspaper strike. Permanent replacements were hired and the newspapers were not required to rehire the strikers at the end of the strike."[12]

Closing the Door: The Impact on Negotiations

During the first several months of the strike, each of the local unions continued to meet intermittently and bargain with the newspapers, but with no significant progress. By the end of August, NLRB Region 7 director William Schaub Jr. had issued complaints in two of the three principal unfair labor practice charges in the Detroit case: the illegal impasse claim on the printers' jurisdiction, and the failure to bargain in good faith against the DNA on joint bargaining. If the charges were proven, Schaub said in a public statement, the strikers would have rights of reinstatement as unfair labor practice strikers.[13] At the beginning of October, leaders of the international unions and their advisers began informally to raise the possibility of the Detroit locals making an unconditional offer to return to work.[14] Such a step would start the clock on any back pay liability and might exert pressure on the newspapers to settle an agreement.

The local union heads in the MCNU, however, strongly opposed the idea, as did many of their members. They felt that the strike mobilization still had considerable leverage and momentum and that returning without contracts would amount to the "surrender" the newspapers apparently wanted.[15] Teamsters Local 2040 president Alex Young recalled:

> We were highly involved in the boycott and knew that we were having an impact on them, and we weren't interested [in returning to work] at that point in time. . . . It's like, "unconditional"? We're going to come back on our knees and you get everything you want? That's not negotiations. I mean, that's what my mind was saying to myself at the time, so I think the timing of it and everything else, it made you dig in your heels.[16]

Instead, local union leaders made a conditional offer to return in an attempt to jump-start the negotiations. On October 5, the MCNU presented its new "principles of settlement." The offer proposed that all striking workers return to their former jobs under the previous contracts, while intensive bargaining for new agreements would resume for a thirty-day period. At the end of the thirty days, the parties would submit all remaining unresolved issues to binding arbitration. The unions acknowledged that "recent revenue losses may initially result in modified re-employment opportunities or buyouts" and as a sign of good faith offered to negotiate job cuts and rule changes to produce $15 million in labor cost savings under the new contracts. The MCNU further pledged to commit itself, with the support of the local labor movement, to a concentrated effort to rebuild the newspapers' circulation and advertising if the negotiating principles were accepted.[17]

The DNA immediately rejected the offer to return to work, saying that it would not fire the replacement workers.[18] On October 27, Gannett lead negotiator John Jaske and DNA vice president Tim Kelleher sent a written reply to the unions. "Because of the higher productivity levels we have achieved and the loss of some business, we don't need nearly as many workers," their letter warned. "In some areas, less than half our former staffing level is needed. In addition, we do not plan to displace our current workforce." Jaske and Kelleher also rejected the thirty-day bargaining proposal and insisted that "we are still very far apart." At the same time, the DNA felt little need to move toward compromise with the union: "Since the strike started on July 13, we have had 45 negotiation sessions, but we've seen no new proposals that are any more realistic than the previous ones. Our current offers fairly reflect how we are and must continue to run our business. Until you recognize and accept that reality, we're, frankly, not optimistic about reaching an agreement."[19]

Less than two weeks into the strike, when its duration and long-term impact on the newspapers were as yet unclear, Jaske had already withdrawn offers to the Teamsters and the press operators and projected permanently reduced staffing.[20] Now the company claimed entrepreneurial justification for reductions far greater than anything they had expected to achieve through negotiations before July 13. If the policy of permanent replacement created a dilemma of two workforces, the newspapers had clearly decided how they intended to resolve it and were actively taking steps to eliminate the striking workforce. In bargaining, Jaske told the unions that the Riverfront Plant in Detroit would remain closed for the foreseeable future, limiting the number of jobs still available.[21] To the media, the DNA's Frank Vega bragged, "In the pressroom, we had 265 guys walk out of here. We now know we can run with 118 pressmen. So, 140 people are never going to see the inside of this building again. And that's the *best* case for the union."[22]

While it reduced costs for the newspapers, however, the sudden and drastic restructuring of the workplace only deepened the antagonism with the strikers, who remained on the street outside the employers' facilities. Company managers were aware of the danger of this situation but had planned for it in advance and now used it to their advantage. "We will not take back any striking employee who has been terminated for serious misconduct during this strike," Jaske and Kelleher wrote in their October 27 letter.[23] Rather than trying to resolve the conflict, company policy focused on maintaining security and control.

CONTROLLING COLLECTIVE ACTION: THE DNA AND OFFICIAL REPRESSION

"We will win this strike by mass action and community sentiment," declared MCNU attorney Sam McKnight on the day the injunction was issued covering the Sterling Heights plant.[24] McKnight's words were not mere bravado, and the DNA did not take lightly the power such tactics represented. A basic element of the company's approach involved restraining and controlling collective action by the strikers and their supporters, with the assistance of local government and federal law. This was done in at least three ways: by direct financial payments to the SHPD and the City of Sterling Heights to preserve their goodwill, by attempting to influence the SHPD's methods of law enforcement, and by actively firing their own striking employees for even minor incidents of alleged picket line misconduct.

An Ongoing Business Expense

At the beginning of the strike, Sterling Heights police had complained that the DNA was violating its agreement by having vehicles enter and leave continuously at unauthorized times and gates and without police escort. As a result, SHPD Lt. Frank Mowinski initiated a procedure of hourly windows where convoys of trucks, vans, and cars could move through the Mound Road south gate.[25] DNA executives, however, were unhappy at the limits placed on their access to the plant. In response, DNA chief financial officer Gary Anderson asked security head John Anthony to set up a meeting with the authorities in Sterling Heights in order to "voice our displeasure at the fact that we were unable to enter and leave our facility as we felt we had a right to, which was at any point in time."[26]

On Tuesday, July 18, less than a week into the strike, Anderson and Anthony met with SHPD chief Thomas Derocha and Capt. James Owens in Derocha's office. Anderson raised his objections to the access procedure, whereupon Sterling Heights city manager Steve Duchane entered the room. Duchane was angry and told the DNA officials that they didn't realize the financial strain on the city caused by having "the super bowl of labor disputes" in their town.[27] Anderson then suggested that the DNA "would look at making a contribution to offset a portion of the cost that was being absorbed by the city and its citizens."[28] Duchane got up to leave and said he would give Anderson a detailed breakdown of the figures.[29]

The following day Duchane sent a letter to the newspapers itemizing $116,921.57 in overtime charges for police department and other city personnel from July 13 to July 17.[30] Meanwhile, Anderson met with DNA chief Vega and argued for paying the money. As Anderson later testified, "I briefed him [Vega] on the events of the meeting and recommended to him very strongly that we take away any reason or any basis from which we would have—that we would lose the protection of the police department in providing us with access to and from our facility, and I recommended very strongly that we look at eliminating any extra costs to the citizens of that community."[31] Vega agreed. The next day, July 20, Anderson's office prepared a check made out to the City of Sterling Heights for the amount of $116,921.57, and Anthony hand-delivered it in a sealed envelope to the SHPD.[32]

It was not the way the DNA normally made payments of more than $100,000, and it was only a first installment. Duchane kept sending similar letters, each time stating the updated costs of overtime the city had incurred owing to the strike. Repeatedly the DNA made out a check for the exact amount, to the penny, and hand-delivered it, usually within days, to Sterling Heights. On July 24, Duchane wrote Anderson a corrected statement of costs through July 17, showing a balance of $50,956.42. Two days later, Anderson sent a check for that amount. "We understand the difficult position that your community has been placed in and appreciate the fine efforts provided to us by your departments," Anderson wrote in a cover statement attached to the payment. Duchane's July 31 letter reported actual overtime costs of $69,225.08 for the seven-day period ending July 28. The DNA's check for $69,225.08 was dated a week later, August 7. The payments to Sterling Heights went on regularly in this manner for more than a year, totaling nearly $1 million in all.[33]

By mid-August, word of the arrangement had reached the unions and the public; not until then did Duchane start sending copies of his letters to the MCNU. The newspapers claimed that the money was a donation by the company as a good corporate citizen and was intended to improve public relations. But internal DNA check requests signed by Anderson explicitly stated that the reason was for purchasing "security services," and the checks were drawn not from a tax-deductible charitable account but from a strike-related account used for security expenditures. DNA executives later denied under oath that the payments were charitable contributions and described them instead as an "on-going business expense" and a "cost of doing business."[34] The checks were specially prepared by hand and returned to Anderson before being quietly delivered to Sterling Heights. Neither Vega nor Kelleher, one of the principal media spokespersons for the papers during the strike, could recall any public relations campaign by the papers to promote awareness of the DNA's largesse.[35]

Nonetheless, the checks did serve to improve relations with officials from the City of Sterling Heights and the SHPD. Subsequently, the DNA expanded the effort to include police departments protecting company property in other suburban towns, including Oxford, Farmington Hills, Novi, and Lincoln Park, among others. With Anderson's consent, Anthony told police chiefs that the DNA would consider requests to reimburse their strike-related expenses, but Anthony kept no records or files on these conversations, nor was the policy ever written down or memorialized in internal company documents. Ultimately, the DNA paid out more than $690,000 in 1995 and 1996 to municipalities and police departments other than Sterling Heights.[36]

Knowledge of the payments did not improve relations, however, with the unions, which were instantly outraged. "The best police department money can buy," sneered the MCNU strike bulletin *The Alliance*. On the picket line, strikers and supporters chanted "Bought and paid for!" and mockingly called the Mound Road median "Treasure Island" for all the overtime pay that police earned there.[37] SHPD chief Derocha admitted that the money caused friction with the strikers, but insisted that it did not bias his officers, although no further training was provided to them to clarify department policy or reinforce neutrality once the contributions became known. According to Anthony, some weeks after the strike began Lieutenant Mowinski asked him if the DNA would purchase additional helmets, face guards, and shields for the SHPD; Anthony agreed and paid a vendor approximately $2,000 for the equipment.[38] That autumn, when Sterling Heights police confronted strikers at the North Plant, part of the riot gear they possessed was indeed bought and paid for by the newspapers.

Selective Law Enforcement: Unlawful Assembly

Since the start of 1995, the DNA had made a determined effort to cultivate the sympathy of the SHPD and influence its perception of events. In the months before the walkout, the company succeeded in persuading the SHPD command that any strike would be violent and that riot control tactics would be required from the first night. This educational campaign bore fruit with the drafting of Lieutenant Mowinski's May 6 "Contingency Plan for Impending DNA Strike," especially in the section titled "Confrontation." "When confronted by a large disturbance or riot," the section read, "the objective will be to funnel the strikers to Center Drive [south of the plant off Mound Road] and to their vehicles to facilitate an orderly exit." The plan laid out a specific procedure to accomplish this goal: "An order to disperse will be given to the crowd as follows":

> "I am (rank and name), of the Sterling Heights Police Department. I hereby declare this to be an unlawful assembly, and in the name of the State of Michigan, command all persons so assembled at (specific location) to immediately and peaceably disperse. If you do not do so, you will be arrested. Michigan' [sic] Statute on Unlawful Assembly prohibits remaining present at an unlawful assembly."[39]

This procedure was used at the Mound Road south gate from the first night of the strike on July 13. When the strikers occupied the driveway, the police declared an unlawful assembly, came across the street in formation, and, using shields and pepper spray, dispersed the crowd as indicated in the plan. For the first few weeks, no one was actually arrested for unlawful assembly; the goal appeared to be mainly to remove the pickets.[40] As the strike went on, however, the resistance intensified as the Labor Day holiday approached.

In late August, Captain Owens called Anthony, asking for copies of state or federal statutes related to strikes, and Anthony replied that he would contact the DNA's attorneys and get back to him. On August 24, Anthony faxed to Sterling Heights a packet of documents with a signed cover letter that read: "Jim: Attached are relevant MI Statutes. I spoke with our attorneys and I am informed there are no federal laws re strikes. Some federal statutes address 'the right to strike,' etc., but nothing on point.

Federal law re illegal acts during a strike are duplicates of state statutes. Any additional help let me know!"[41] The documents identified actions for which strikers or picketers could be arrested, including unlawful assembly, but made no mention of individuals' rights under the National Labor Relations Act, the cornerstone of federal labor law that explicitly protects workers' concerted activity and the right to strike.[42]

Why would the SHPD, a public law enforcement agency, seek legal advice from a private corporation and a party to a labor dispute that the SHPD was responsible for policing? Why did the police department not seek guidance on state statues from the democratically elected county prosecutor, the equivalent of a district attorney and the chief public law enforcement officer in Macomb County? Whatever the reason, for the first time in the strike the SHPD began arresting persons for unlawful assembly during the Labor Day protests. Fifteen people, including Ben Solomon, were booked on the charge, the majority of them apprehended after the police used tear gas to disperse the crowds. Several persons had already left the immediate area and were arrested while standing on the opposite side of Mound Road.[43]

As a felony offense, the charge of unlawful assembly required the SHPD to submit warrant requests to the office of County Prosecutor Carl Marlinga, who promptly denied all of them.[44] In a September 8 letter to Chief Derocha, Marlinga explained the reasons for his action. "Initially it is important to give deference to the legal principle that picketing a place of business in the course of a strike is legally protected activity," Marlinga wrote, citing federal statute and case law. He continued:

> It is your duty to respond to individual acts of violence and other lawlessness by making arrests of the individuals who are guilty of such acts. It is not legally permissible, however, to use the individual acts of violence as a basis for declaring the strikers to be engaged in an unlawful assembly. The law provides a mechanism for the NLRB and/or the courts to determine whether there has been a sufficient level of violence to justify the curtailment of picketing activities. Unless and until such legal process is placed in your hands by the NLRB or a court of law, it is not appropriate to issue a general order to tell the picketers to leave the premises.[45]

The charge of unlawful assembly required proof of an illegal violent act and individual guilty knowledge and intent to participate, shared with at least four other persons. But in the United States, Marlinga reminded Derocha, all guilt is individual, and therefore the police report had to indicate either that the accused person committed an act of violence or that they aided and abetted an act of violence. Nor could the SHPD bootstrap a charge of refusing to obey an improper order by failing to disperse. "A person standing next to an accused, who is out of the line of ingress and egress, and who is not participating in an act of violence still has a right to be there," Marlinga wrote. "It is, therefore, not possible to order such person to 'disperse' nor is it possible to arrest that person on the theory that he or she will engage in similar conduct."

The newspapers had the right to petition the NLRB or a state court to enjoin the picketing owing to violent or illegal activity. Without such authority, however, the SHPD could not on its own simply break up a picket line and force everyone to leave. "Telling picketers to 'disperse' is not a valid order," Marlinga explained. "They have a legal right to be there, so the order to leave is not proper. If police officers use force to enforce an illegal order, so the strikers would be justified in using an equal amount of force to resist the illegal actions of the police. This is obviously a situation to avoid."[46]

The DNA did finally go to court to petition for an injunction on September 6. As tensions rose at the North Plant in July and August, however, why did the company not seek to enjoin the pickets sooner? According to Gannett vice president Jaske, the newspapers did not trust either the NLRB or the judicial system in southeastern Michigan to rule in their favor. "We were concerned that we would not get anywhere in an injunction action even though the violence was horrendous . . . we thought we'd lose," Jaske said. "We finally said, 'Look—win, lose, or draw, even though we think in this jurisdiction we're going to lose, we gotta take a shot. The NLRB will do nothing.'"[47]

If the DNA feared losing at the NLRB or in a court of law, it had by contrast already developed a close working relationship with the SHPD. From January through August, the DNA had so influenced the environment in which the SHPD acted that police command officers even consulted with the company on applicable laws under which to arrest strikers. Only when the mass protests around Labor Day exceeded the SHPD's capacity to maintain order did the newspapers finally plead their case before a judge in open court. After receiving prosecutor Marlinga's September 8 letter, the SHPD submitted no more warrant requests for unlawful assembly. Instead, arrests for violations of local ordinances and misdemeanors were channeled through the non-elected office of the city attorney, in Sterling Heights a private law firm serving under contract with the city.[48]

Purging the Workforce: Employee Discharges

The newspapers did not need to wait for the police to arrest strikers in order to take action against them. From the beginning of the strike, the company adopted an aggressive policy of firing employees for alleged strike-related misconduct. Sixteen striking workers were fired for misconduct in the first three weeks, and ultimately more than two hundred were discharged.[49] Many of the discharges were eventually reversed, but only after years of litigation, and many fired workers never got their jobs back.

NLRB administrative law judge Richard Scully heard consolidated complaints involving 121 disciplinary actions taken against about eighty-five strikers, and in his decision he reviewed the applicable legal principles under NLRB case precedents. The employer may not apply a double standard to behavior by strikers versus nonstrikers or replacements, and the misconduct must be such that, "under all the surrounding circumstances, it may reasonably tend to coerce or intimidate other employees in the exercise of rights" under the NLRA. The standard is an objective one and does not involve an inquiry into whether any particular employee was actually coerced or intimidated. Moreover, an employer need only establish an "honest belief" that an employee has engaged in the misconduct for which he or she is discharged. Judge Scully explained:

> The employer's burden of establishing its "honest belief" is no more than that and does not require it to prove that the striker did in fact engage in misconduct. It does, however, require more than the mere assertion that it had such belief. There must be some specificity, linking particular employees to particular allegations of misconduct. The employer's "honest belief" may be based on hearsay sources, such as, the reports of nonstriking employees, supervisors, security guards, investigators, police, etc. Whether or not the employer had an "honest belief" is judged on the basis of the evidence available to it when it took the disciplinary action and it need not attempt to get the striker's side of the story before doing so.[50]

In its preparations for the strike, the DNA went so far as to predraft the pleadings and other court documents needed to pursue charges of illegal union conduct.[51] Once the strike began, the newspapers set up a separate disciplinary procedure, coordinated by general counsel Taylor, exclusively for strike-related actions. DNA security personnel or specially hired private agents would investigate allegations of misconduct, and nonstriking employees were encouraged to make complaints. An incident report form was developed, and the DNA offered to pay for expenses like vehicle damage, provided they were strike-related. Once the information was collected, it was forwarded to Taylor, who took affidavits from witnesses, reviewed videotape shot by security, and personally observed picket line activity. If he felt that action was required, Taylor would forward the file with his recommendation for a final decision by top executives at the DNA, the *News*, and the *Free Press*.[52]

Using this system, the newspapers fired scores of strikers for serious misconduct, including allegations of punching and spitting on picket line crossers, vandalizing property, throwing rocks and star nails, and threatening persons with physical harm. Some strikers were fired several times for separate incidents. At the same time, some of the offenses seemed rather less than serious. Teamster member Larry Skewarczynski was fired for squirting clear water from a toy water pistol and accidentally hitting a security guard in the eyes on July 29, 1995. Striker Gary Tebo was part of a group leafleting outside a Sterling Heights car dealership in April 1996. In retaliation, the manager of the dealership turned on the property's landscape water sprinklers, soaking the leafleters. Tebo then kicked the head off one of the sprinklers, causing $150 worth of damage for which he later pleaded guilty to malicious destruction of property.[53]

The unions contested many of the firings, and dozens of them were found to be unlawful after review by the NLRB. Mike Fahoome, recording secretary for Local 372, was fired for allegedly threatening carrier Charlene Krauss on September 5, 1995. In an unsworn affidavit signed three weeks after the incident, Krauss asserted that Fahoome had threatened to blow up her vehicle. When she testified under oath at the hearing, however, she repudiated her earlier statement and claimed that she "didn't say half the stuff that was in there." *Free Press* photographer Damon Hartley was fired for nonviolent incidents on August 19 and September 5, 1996, solely on the basis of the company's interpretation of ambiguous video recordings. In his decision on the case, Judge Scully wrote, "The Respondent's officials simply looked at the videotape, saw what they wanted to see, and pronounced it serious misconduct."[54]

In other cases, Judge Scully found instances of fabricated evidence, collusion by company witnesses, reports filed months after the fact, and disparate treatment.[55] Not all of the firings came before the NLRB. Part-time mailer Jamie Slawick was discharged for allegedly throwing orange juice and coffee at a guard on September 17, 1995. Slawick denied that she was anywhere near the picket line on that day, having just given birth in a hospital four days earlier. She later sued the DNA for libel, and a Wayne County Circuit Court jury awarded her $106,000.[56]

While many of the dismissals were eventually overturned, the process of litigating them took years. The hearings on the 121 incidents before Judge Scully were held on 53 separate dates between September 22, 1997, and September 23, 1998, and the judge did not issue his ruling until December 17, 1999. Appeals in the case to the NLRB in Washington were not decided until June 30, 2004, more than three and a half years after the strike itself was settled. Along with the hiring of permanent replacements, the newspapers' aggressive discharge policy functioned to eliminate the striking workforce and prevent them from returning to the workplace. That included much of the union leadership: by December 1998, five of the six local union presidents in the MCNU had been fired.[57]

DESCENT INTO VIOLENCE

As the possibilities for compromise faded in the autumn months of 1995, the battle on the streets turned even more bitter and volatile. With the injunction covering the Sterling Heights North Plant, the focus of union picketing shifted to the warehouses and distribution centers scattered throughout the metropolitan area. On Sunday, September 24, a crowd of up to three hundred people gathered outside the gate at the distribution center on Clayton Street in southwestern Detroit, facing around a dozen police officers. Nearby, protesters found an apparently abandoned pickup truck, and they managed to push it into the large driveway to block access to the gate. Around 1:00 AM, a semi-tractor-trailer truck approached the entrance, but was quickly surrounded by a wall of pickets and forced to back up and leave. The protesters then flipped the pickup truck over, but more police arrived, cleared the driveway, and had the truck towed away. Another semi arrived around 3:30 AM, but left without attempting to pass, and a half-hour later police pushed the crowd aside to allow three cars into the center. The crowd eventually dwindled to some fifty persons, police made five arrests for misdemeanors, and at 6:00 AM the driveway was cleared to allow a semi and three other vehicles to enter.[58]

The following week the Clayton Street center was again the site of confrontation. This time, 150 to 200 people were present on Sunday, October 1, along with approximately forty Detroit police. Shortly after 2:00 AM, the police were escorting a semi-tractor-trailer and two vans through a crowd of picketers to the gate. Suddenly, without warning and in violation of their agreement with police, fifteen to twenty Vance guards in shields and riot gear burst through the gate. The guards charged in a V-formation for about thirty to forty feet into the crowd, knocking down protesters and pinning them between the guards and police. At least four people were injured during the melee, and the Newspaper Guild's Don Kummer was hit in the chest by a police baton. Police later cleared the driveway, and at least eight picketers were arrested, but protesters burned tires and other debris outside the gate, and around 5:00 AM a car parked inside the fenced lot at the center caught fire.[59]

One of the injured strikers that night was Vito Sciuto, a twenty-eight-year-old mailer, father of two young children, and member of Local 2040. Sciuto had stopped to help a fallen striker when he was struck on the head by a security guard wielding a heavy wooden stick. He suffered a fractured skull and brain damage and required surgery to reconstruct his face and eye; photos of Sciuto's shaved head showed stitches zigzagging across the top of his skull. No one was arrested for the assault, and DNA spokesperson Kelleher defended the Vance guards for moving beyond the gate. "If it happens again, I'd expect security guards to react the way they did," he said. "They have to protect our property and the people in those vans."[60]

Sciuto was not the only casualty at the hands of the newspapers. Just two nights later, on September 3, thirty-eight-year-old striking mailer James Mikonczyk was picketing at the Clayton Street center. Around 4:00 AM, a convoy of trucks left the gate, while Mikonczyk and other strikers hovered near the street. The driver of the fourth van in the convoy was thirty-five-year-old Brian Carter, a suspended Detroit police officer. As he approached the picketers, Carter turned onto the road without stopping and struck Mikonczyk, rolling over him with both the front and back wheels. Neither Carter nor the remaining drivers in the convoy stopped to help Mikonczyk, who lay in the street for forty-five minutes before an ambulance arrived. Carter returned after delivering his papers and was arrested and released by police pending a warrant, but no charges were brought against him and no disciplinary action was taken by the DNA.

Mikonczyk suffered a broken hip, leg, and arm and was hospitalized for six weeks. The DNA issued a statement saying that the injury was unfortunate, but blaming the strikers: "We have said over and over again since the strike began that the practices used by the picketers are, in many cases, illegal and likely to have disastrous results." As Mikonczyk lay in the street, his fellow picketers became enraged and began throwing rocks at the Vance guards pressing close to the fence. Four of the picketers were arrested, and all four, including Mikonczyk's brother Dennis, were fired.[61]

After the incidents at Clayton Street, the DNA closed the facility and moved its operations to Sterling Heights.[62] For the next several weeks, the unions continued to mobilize protests at other distribution centers in Oak Park, Troy, Harper Woods, Farmington Hills, Taylor, Lincoln Park, and Dearborn. At varying locations, crowds of two hundred to three hundred pickets would assemble on early Sunday mornings and block access to the centers for several hours before departing and allowing trucks to pass by around 6:00 AM. Some of the protesters threw rocks, star nails, and firecrackers; broke windows in buildings; flattened tires; and caused damage to vehicles and the portable floodlights that guards had installed to shine on the crowds. But the demonstrations were mostly peaceful, and police made few arrests.[63] The distribution center protests succeeded in disrupting delivery of tens of thousands of Sunday papers, delaying them by several hours in their respective areas. Each center, however, represented only a fraction of the total Sunday distribution, and despite the pressure, the DNA remained entrenched in its position.

Meanwhile, individual acts of fear and violence continually erupted in an uncivic war across the metropolitan area. On October 8, Sterling Heights police stopped a replacement worker who drove through a group of picketers at the North Plant, nearly hitting some of them. Officers discovered that his driver's license was suspended and then found a loaded crossbow in the front seat, hidden underneath a towel.[64] On October 29, police in Berkley arrested six strikers in an incident outside the Carpenters' Hall on 12 Mile Road. The strikers had caught two security guards spying on them, smashed in the windows of their vehicle, and injured one of the guards.[65] On November 1, a pipe bomb exploded inside a newspaper rack, and an unexploded bomb was found in an adjacent rack around 2:45 AM in Shelby Township.[66] In Ferndale, two men were arrested for placing a Molotov cocktail on a striking Teamster member's porch on November 29 in what police said was part of a vendetta related to the strike.[67]

On October 2, the unions filed a federal civil rights lawsuit in U.S. District Court against the DNA, its private security firms, and the City of Sterling Heights and its officials. The suit alleged that the defendants conspired to deprive union members of their rights during the strike, and it sought at least $15 million in damages and injunctive relief to prevent further harassment of strikers. "We're saying there has been a massive conspiracy by these parties to undermine the rights of free speech and assembly of these workers," said attorney Sam McKnight at a press conference announcing the suit. MCNU head Al Derey added, "The DNA does not own Detroit or Sterling Heights. Today we are reclaiming our cities and our rights."[68]

The DNA responded six weeks later, just prior to the Thanksgiving holiday with its anticipated heavy advertising volume. On November 15, the company filed a counterclaim alleging conspiracy by the unions under the federal Racketeer Influenced and Corrupt Organizations (RICO) Act. The suit accused the unions of an "on-going pattern of extortion, robbery, arson, and interference with commerce" and demanded triple damages and attorneys' fees as provided under the RICO legislation. "Because of the triple damages and the expenses of litigation, nearly all of these cases settle out of court," attorney Don Scharg told a *Free Press* reporter. "So it does pose a serious threat to the unions."[69] The lawsuits would remain outstanding for more than five years, until the strike itself was settled in December 2000.

CONCLUSION:
INSURMOUNTABLE OBSTACLES

The Detroit strike illustrated several of the contradictions embodied in the new anti-union regime. The decline of traditional legal protections for the right to strike transformed its economic function in collective bargaining, reducing the incentives for employers to settle through the process of negotiation. Once the newspapers hired permanent replacements, they effectively locked themselves into a policy of total war against the striking unions. Whatever their intentions before the walkout, the employers seized on the opportunity to radically downsize employment and unilaterally establish their preferred conditions with the replacements. That "reality" became the DNA's absolute condition and new status quo for bargaining with the unions, which in turn had few motives to accept the employers' demands. "The company has dug in its heels and, as far as we're concerned, has been totally inflexible," the Guild's Lou Mleczko told the Associated Press in November. "We gave them some new conditions to try to settle this strike and they rejected those, but they have not come back with any counterproposals."[70]

Instead, the newspapers simply announced their plans to move on with the replacement workforce, offering little to the strikers beyond complete and abject "surrender." As Jaske wrote to Gannett vice chair Doug McCorkindale in late December: "Now that the unions know that their only alternative is surrender, there is an increased likelihood that we will have one or more of them offer to unconditionally return to work. . . . Until the unions make an unconditional offer to return to work, the law is clear that we can pay replacement workers less and have different terms and conditions of employment for them."[71] The decision to use permanent replacements, however, set up an inevitable conflict with the striking workforce, aggravating tensions on the picket line and increasing the likelihood of violence.

The employers' choice virtually required them to engage in repression of the strikers' activity, with the help of strategically selected law enforcement authorities. Given the civic culture of labor solidarity in southeastern Michigan, the DNA initially tried to avoid democratically accountable venues like the elected county prosecutor's office and open procedures in district court. Instead, it relied on informal ties with suburban police departments to control the strikers' immediate physical presence and on federal law to deny them the right to return to their jobs. The results were daunting. "I never thought in Detroit I would see the level of raw power demonstrated against ordinary working people," said striking *Free Press* copy editor Bill Hanson. "It was literally impressive and frightening at times. There were certainly things that happened among union pickets that I didn't support or approve of, but they were far fewer and less severe than the very mechanized, organized, uncivil behavior from the management side."[72]

Over time, the flashpoints of conflict and pressure shifted as the strike went on. After the September injunction in Sterling Heights, the struggle on the picket line moved to the distribution centers. The DNA withstood the challenge, however, and toward the end of the year it became clear that the conventional workplace locations were no longer the main focus of mobilization. For Thanksgiving, the unions unexpectedly kept a low profile and emphasized plans for leafleting aimed at holiday shoppers.[73] Picketing continued, but in the days ahead the unions would put more emphasis on the community campaign and the unfair labor practices case.

"When you can keep this number of people on a picket line when it's raining and cold, I think that tells you something about their resolve," the press operators' Jack Howe said in late October.[74] Nevertheless, the injunction and the RICO suit had a discouraging effect on the MCNU's willingness to pursue picketing and demonstrations at the North Plant and the distribution centers. With the winter approaching, the prospects for a settlement appeared as gray and dim as the Michigan sky. In November and again in December, the United Auto Workers international union presented holiday checks of $150 to each of the striking newspaper workers. The two thousand or so strikers were hardly more than the number of workers at a single medium-sized assembly plant, and with relative peace in the auto industry, the UAW could afford it, but the generosity was not lost on the strikers.[75] By that time, however, dozens of employees, including many journalists, had already retired or begun to leave town in search of work. The papers themselves seemed like they would never again be what they once were. On December 6, *Free Press* publisher Neal Shine, in poor health, announced his retirement as of the end of the year.[76]

As the days grew short, local civic leaders made one more effort to find a resolution. On December 19, Detroit mayor Dennis Archer, Roman Catholic cardinal Adam Maida, and U.S. senator Carl Levin joined in a public plea to the parties to resume negotiations before Christmas. Archer offered to mediate the discussions, and Maida appealed "to all people to put their best heart forward and put aside differences . . . to embrace one another for the good of the community and for those who are suffering."

Newspaper executives agreed to meet, but cast doubt on the chances for a breakthrough. "We have been willing and we are still willing to give it a try," said Tim Kelleher. "But Christmas? I can't say."[77]

The following day the two sides met for four hours in the mayor's office, as DNA negotiators reiterated that the strikers were permanently replaced and that the Riverfront Plant would remain closed. The newspapers demanded that the unions agree to several conditions. First, any contracts had to reflect the current staffing levels unilaterally imposed by management, including the reduction of some 650 positions at the DNA. In addition, the employers refused to displace the 1,400 replacements to make way for the workers still on strike, and they refused to allow amnesty for strikers accused of picket line misconduct. If the unions accepted these terms, the newspapers said, they would offer to provide a $2 million fund to retrain and relocate the strikers. "We've laid out how we intend to operate," Jaske said during the meeting. "If you accept the present, this is the future."[78] The companies further noted that 289 of the striking workers were eligible for retirement, and they suggested that the national unions also contribute to the retraining fund.

It was not clear how many strikers the newspapers immediately expected to take back; when asked in October how many jobs remained unfilled, Kelleher said, "Probably less than 200, including the two newsrooms."[79] In the meeting in the mayor's office, however, Jaske reportedly told those present that, except for twenty pressroom employees, *all* the striking workers had been permanently replaced.[80] In any case, the companies' proposal clearly encouraged union members either to relocate or to retire, consistent with the goal of eliminating the striking workforce. "What's being offered the unions is not peace with dignity," a disappointed Mayor Archer said after the meeting. "The unions came to the table to bargain in good faith. But management has effectively said 'it's over.'" The Guild's Mleczko called the offer "heartless and cruel." He said, "They told the unions, the mayor, the cardinal, the senator, and the community effectively to drop dead."[81]

The next day, Archer spoke to striking reporters. "The replacements could not have been there to work, nor could there have been two newspapers, if those same strikers had not been the ones who gave up money and time to cause the JOA to come into existence," he said.[82] Executives at Gannett were more sanguine. On December 21, Jaske wrote a memo to McCorkindale, Gannett chair John Curley, and Gannett newspaper division president Gary Watson. "As you have heard," Jaske wrote, "yesterday's meeting was obviously a 'set up' by the Mayor to either force us to get rid of the replacements or give us a PR hit. We did not and he did." On a brighter note, Jaske attached a draft of an agreement with the NLRB that the unions would have to sign to avoid a complaint on charges of picket line misconduct. "Either way we will get good public relations," he observed. Jaske ended the memo with a hearty season's greeting to his Gannett colleagues: "HAPPY HOLIDAYS!"[83]

Chapter 10 | Theaters of Engagement: Civil Society and the State

THE START OF THE NEW YEAR marked another turning point in the development of the strike, one that again signaled the changed landscape of industrial conflict in the United States. By January 1996, the newspapers had effectively countered the traditional forms of strike mobilization used by the unions. In the alliance with the Sterling Heights police, the aggressive policy of firing picketers, the injunction at the North Plant, and the pursuit of the federal RICO charges, the companies used a combination of law enforcement and judicial repression to contain the strikers' collective action. Constrained by these barriers, the unions were compelled to find new and different ways to bring pressure on the employers. As they did so, the conflict pushed past the conventional boundaries of labor disputes and entered into new areas in civil society and the state.

Searching for leverage, the unions both broadened the scope of the struggle and drove it deeper into the urban community. With the founding of the strike newspaper, the *Detroit Sunday Journal*, and in their corporate campaign against Knight-Ridder and Gannett, organizers sought to appeal to a wider public and force the employers to move at the bargaining table. At the same time, the intensification of the advertiser boycott and the adoption of ambulatory and residential picketing enlarged the spaces of protest and tested the limits of legitimate action. As they moved further into the terrain of civil society, the unions encountered other actors seeking their own voice and role as stakeholders in the dispute. One of those actors, the loose coalition called Readers United (RU), raised pointed questions about the responsibilities of the newspapers and their civic function in the community.

While the unions and other community-based actors organized on the streets and in the neighborhoods, the employers used different means to try to shape public opinion about the strike. An old joke in the news business warns against picking a fight with someone who buys ink by the barrel, and the Detroit papers, especially the *News*, did not shy away from using their own pages to promote their position. Even as they drew criticism from the journalism profession, the papers were able to powerfully frame the public perception of both the strike and the underlying issues in the dispute. The two sides not only contended in the community but also fought a legal battle over the regulation and control of collective action. Part of the struggle was a battle over how the struggle could be carried out, and state authorities were called upon to police the borders of what could be regarded as public and private space and the places where civic demonstration and dialogue could occur.

Finally, the state was the venue for determining the official meaning of the strike or what it was supposed to be about, whether it was an "economic" or an "unfair labor practice" strike. The charges in the case charted the historic collision of actors playing under different institutional rules, with the newspapers exploiting their opportunities under the ascendant anti-union regime and the unions defending their rights under a declining New Deal order. The trial itself illustrated the breakdown of that order, as the institutions intended to reinforce negotiation gave way to litigation instead.

LABOR AND COMMUNITY: EXPANDING THE SPACES OF ENGAGEMENT

From the outset, the public representation of the strike was a problem for the unions. Striking journalists, especially, were dismayed by what they saw as an early lack of effective media outreach, and in July 1995 a group of Guild members on their own began posting stories to an online forum they called the *Detroit Journal*. At the unions' strike headquarters, *Free Press* reporter Joe Swickard took on the role of union spokesperson for other news media. But "management obviously was much, much better prepared and had gone to school on it," Swickard recalled:

> And television news, which was about the only news at that point, would speak to management people in very controlled, calm situations. They'd meet in offices sitting down and somebody looking very businesslike, whether it was a man or a woman, it was very well presented. A lot of times what TV news seemed to be doing to balance talking to management was then just finding the first person that would speak to them on the picket line. And it might be some really pissed-off Teamster or mailer in cutoffs and a T-shirt saying, you know, "Fuck the boss." And we were losing the image battle, it was very difficult right from the start.[1]

Initial discussions about starting a union strike newspaper were tabled because MCNU leaders feared both the costs and the diversion of energy from the picket lines and the boycott.[2] By the fall, however, the idea had gained support from new AFL-CIO president John Sweeney and Newspaper Guild president Linda Foley, who helped secure $500,000 in start-up funds from the Teamsters and other international unions. Housed in a former military recruiting station on East Jefferson Avenue in Detroit and printed at a plant near Flint, the *Detroit Sunday Journal* published its first issue on November 19, 1995. Striking union members provided the labor for the production, distribution, and business operations, with circulation ultimately reaching two hundred delivery routes and more than one thousand sales outlets. By July 1996, the paper was financially self-sustaining, with a press run of 165,000 per week, according to advertising director and striking *News* editorial assistant Mike McBride. By the end of the year, it was the largest weekly and third-largest Sunday paper in the state.[3]

Immediately, the *Sunday Journal* became a significant journalistic presence in the Detroit metropolitan community. Led by *News* and *Free Press* veterans, including co-editors Norman Sinclair and Susan Watson, features editor Rob Musial, and circulation director Joe Merritt, the scrappy tabloid covered local, state, and national politics, business, entertainment, and sports, as well as news about the strike. Watson, a popular columnist and advocate, became the best-known voice in the paper and personified for many the "conscience and soul of the strike."[4] Describing herself as "an incurably nosy middle-aged journalist with age spots on my hands, stretch marks on my stomach, and ink in my veins," she wrote in an early issue:

> My beliefs are simple: I believe that only a fool keeps her mouth shut when someone is trying to destroy her; only a coward shuts her eyes when she knows that a bully is picking on someone half his size; and only a handful of saints escape the temptation to close their eyes and seal their lips in the face of adversity.[5]

The *Sunday Journal* offered a crucial alternative to the newspapers' accounts of the strike and was an important force in the unions' efforts to reach out to a larger public. Developing this goal, the unions both broadened their strategy with a national corporate campaign and deepened their outreach into local civil society. In February the AFL-CIO announced support for a circulation and advertising boycott of Knight-Ridder's *Miami Herald* and Gannett's flagship *USA Today* newspaper. The boycott, formally initiated in late March, aimed in part to persuade hotel chains and airlines to stop providing free copies of *USA Today* and included participation by the Teamsters, Hotel Workers, and Flight Attendants unions, among others.[6]

In April, around twenty strikers and supporters attended Knight-Ridder's annual board meeting at a downtown hotel in Miami. Among others, Watson, *News* editorial assistant Alesia Cooper-Cunningham, DNA district manager Shawn Ellis, and the Rev. Ed Rowe of Detroit's Central United Methodist Church addressed the board members and CEO P. Anthony Ridder, while another 125 local labor supporters rallied outside. "The strike won't pay for itself, if ever, until the next century," said *Free Press* maintenance worker Ernestine Traylor. "How much are you willing to lose in Detroit?" Ridder replied by repeating the conditions from which the newspapers would not move. "First, we will not fire the replacement workers," he said. "Second, we will not resume featherbedding practices. Third, we will not force anyone to rejoin a union. That means we will recognize the union, but we will operate as an open shop." Ridder insisted, however, that he remained eager to settle the strike. The next day *Free Press* bargainers in Detroit declared an impasse with the Newspaper Guild and imposed conditions including merit pay and an open shop.[7]

A few weeks later, an even larger group descended on the Gannett board of directors meeting in Arlington, Virginia. Five hundred people, including International Brotherhood of Teamsters president Ron Carey and Detroit city council president Maryanne Mahaffey, gathered and marched in support of some fifty strikers attending the three-hour-long meeting. Inside, Shawn Ellis's thirteen-year-old daughter Laura spoke and asked board member Rosalyn Carter when the strike could end, but Gannett chair John Curley ruled her out of order. Reverend Rowe got down on his knees and appealed to the Gannett officials to "take the moral high ground" and find a compromise. "You cannot ask a union to negotiate its own demise," he said. Curley was not moved. He told the strikers, "When you asked for $100 million [sic], you took away from us any position of ever being able to bargain." Turning back this demand was so important to the company, he said, that the cost of the strike in lost profits and readers was "irrelevant."[8]

The corporate campaign ranged across the country as groups of strikers traveled from city to city to raise funds and awareness and to participate in actions against the two chains. Teamster member Ellis and striking press operator Tom Waldron went to Milwaukee in February to speak at a meeting of the Milwaukee County Labor Council, which agreed to contribute $250 per month to help support the strikers. In March, Waldron was in Boulder, Colorado, where he demonstrated in front of the Knight-Ridder-owned *Boulder Daily Camera*, along with members of the Boulder

County Labor Council and the Denver branch of Jobs with Justice. In June, Guild member Jocelyn Faniel-Heard was among the Detroit strikers joining 150 unionists in Macon, Georgia, protesting at Knight-Ridder's *Macon Telegraph*. Led by Atlanta Labor Council president Stewart Acuff, the protesters represented the AFL-CIO, the Communication Workers of America, the Graphic Communications International Union, and the Georgia State Employees Union.[9]

Closer to home, strike organizers redoubled their efforts on the advertiser boycott, targeting local car dealerships especially and aided by activists from the UAW.[10] In January, nine metro Detroit auto dealers pledged to stop advertising in the papers after a two-week round of intensive leafleting. The following month four more dealerships pulled their ads, bringing to 106 the number of car dealers supporting the boycott, according to union figures. Meanwhile, UAW Local 412 in Warren sent a letter to dealers and other retailers announcing that UAW members at Chrysler were being urged to spend their $3,200 profit-sharing checks only at firms that were avoiding the struck papers, and UAW vice president Richard Shoemaker made a similar appeal to members who were receiving profit-sharing checks at General Motors.[11]

On the picket line, the unions refocused their activity onto street sales and home delivery. In January, MCNU attorney Sam McKnight wrote to seventy-five local law enforcement agencies informing them of plans to begin "ambulatory picketing" of newspaper carriers in residential neighborhoods. "The striking unions have a federally protected right to engage in ambulatory picketing of vehicles and/or carriers distributing the Detroit Newspapers," McKnight wrote, "ambulatory picketing of vehicles and carriers is lawful and it is *not* a violation of Michigan's 'stalking' statute."[12] Launched on February 11, the mobile pickets followed newspaper carriers door to door, leafleting households that received the papers and gathering data on their circulation. The unions prepared careful instructions for the picketers, including a list of dos and don'ts and even the proper distance and tone of voice for the scripted talking points. Police in Dearborn and Taylor received legal opinions from their city attorneys okaying the tactic, and according to sources on both sides, no incidents were reported the first weekend.[13]

Finally, the Teamsters International union brought in veteran organizer Eddie Burke to act as overall strike coordinator, managing staff from the various unions and the AFL-CIO.[14] A key strategist in the United Mine Workers' successful 1989 strike at the Pittston Coal mines, Burke restructured the Detroit campaign to provide more extensive coverage of the metropolitan area and bring pressure on multiple fronts. "These people [the newspapers] plan to wipe you off the face of the earth," he told a gathering of strikers in May. "The only way to prevent that is to take the volume of what you're doing and turn it up." A week later, several hundred striking union members received three days of training in nonviolent direct action tactics, assisted by members of the UAW Rapid Action Disciplined Deployment (RADD) team.[15]

During the spring and summer months, strikers poured into suburban residential streets demonstrating and chanting, "Scabs in the Hood!" at the homes of executives Frank Vega, Tim Kelleher, and Bob Giles, columnists Pete Waldmeir and Mike Duffy, and others. In one neighborhood in Warren, marchers passed out two hundred lawn signs and signed up one hundred subscribers to the *Detroit Sunday Journal*.[16] Pickets also targeted gas stations and street hawkers selling the Sunday edition of the newspapers. On May 19, hundreds of strikers in platoons swarmed hawkers at over seventeen locations, from 12 Mile Road in Southfield to East Jefferson Avenue near Grosse Pointe Park. On June 16, Susan Watson and a crew of pickets in Detroit were joined by U.S. congressional representative John Conyers Jr. The group stopped at several gas stations along Seven-Mile Road and persuaded the owners to remove the papers, leaving only after Conyers convinced the merchants to pose for a group photograph with the strikers.[17]

In the first half of 1996, the strike mobilization expanded into new territory. Forced to go beyond a focus on central workplace locations, the unions pushed their actions deeper into the community and outward toward a larger public sphere. In so doing, they challenged the distinctions between the private economy and the public good, the boundaries between commercial property and civic space. Whether in distant cities and corporate sectors or in local streets and residential neighborhoods, the unions searched for venues where they could confront the newspapers and demand a response. The process tested the conventional limits of the newspaper workplace and its relationship with the field of urban civil society.

The Subaltern Speak: Other Actors in Civil Society

The unions were not the only ones organizing on the urban field. Other groups maintained their own presence and spoke from independent moral traditions and authority. In January, Roman Catholic auxiliary bishop Thomas Gumbleton addressed a rally of three hundred strikers on Martin Luther King Jr. Day, along with representative Conyers and the

Rev. Wendell Anthony, president of the Detroit branch of the NAACP. "If King were alive today, where would he be?" Gumbleton asked. "Rev. King would be on the picket line at the *News* and *Free Press*, supporting the strikers."[18] Bishop Gumbleton and members of an informal coalition called Religious Leaders for Justice at the Detroit Newspapers circulated a letter deploring the "use of violence, both personal and institutional, by anyone involved on either side," and calling the permanent replacement of strikers "morally objectionable and a breach of the ethical teachings of our faith traditions."[19]

The letter appealed for support for the newspaper boycott, and by mid-February it had been signed by more than two hundred Detroit-area religious figures, including the Rev. Robert Smith of New Bethel Baptist Church, Rabbi Ernst Conrad of Temple Kol Ami, retired Episcopal bishop H. Coleman McGehee, and the Rev. Faith Fowler of Cass Community United Methodist Church. At a press conference on February 13, the Rev. Odell Jones of Pleasant Grove Baptist Church said that the newspapers had made the permanent replacements a roadblock to settling the strike. "It's time to remove that obstacle," he said, "by recognizing that striking workers have a legal, moral, and ethical right to return to their jobs at the conclusion of a strike."[20] On February 25, St. Michael Catholic Church in Sterling Heights, one of the largest suburban parishes with 3,800 members, printed the entire text of the letter in its Sunday bulletin. By mid-April, the list of signatures had grown to 800, and the coalition announced that Reverend Jones and Reverend Rowe would travel to Miami and present the appeal at the Knight-Ridder annual meeting on April 23.[21]

Another civic coalition emerged in the fall of 1995, calling itself Readers United. A network of religious and secular community leaders in Detroit, RU included core members Clementine Barfield, founder of the antiviolence group Save Our Sons and Daughters (SOSAD), and longtime local activist Grace Lee Boggs. Led by the Rev. Bill Wylie-Kellerman, a Detroit native and United Methodist pastor, and Jeanie Wylie-Kellerman, editor of *The Witness*, a national magazine owned by the Episcopal Church, the members of RU asserted a unique community interest in the strike and raised demands on both the newspapers and the unions. In their opening statement, they challenged the DNA to negotiate with the unions, dismiss the permanent replacements, and "stop the belligerent and provocative violence of Vance security and DNA drivers." Starting in early October, the group held several protests outside the *Free Press* building in which they burned newspapers to show symbolic support for the strike.[22]

Readers United also called on the strikers to undergo immediate training in nonviolent direct action, on the model of the United Mine Workers at Pittston. In addition, they asked for the creation of an alternative strike paper to serve the community's needs for quality journalism. "Those of us who will not buy a newspaper produced by 'permanent replacement workers' are operating in a news vacuum," the RU leaders wrote. "We need information about community health concerns, schools, city hall, the police, cultural events." In late October, RU members met with MCNU chair Al Derey and lobbied Guild president Foley for a strike paper, adding to the momentum that led to the creation of the *Sunday Journal* in November.[23]

Frustrated by their limited support role, Readers United went even further the following spring. The group initiated a series of ten nonviolent civil disobedience demonstrations at the newspapers' downtown offices, organized in waves occurring from March through May 1996. Each wave focused on a different group within the community, and organizers explicitly asked that strikers not participate in civil disobedience but attend a legal picket and support rally held at the same time. The first action on March 6 drew some seven hundred demonstrators, and police arrested twenty-four religious and community leaders for peacefully blocking the entrances to the *News* building on Lafayette Street. Among the arrestees were three bishops, two Baptist pastors, Detroit city council president Mahaffey, Selma Goode of the Jewish Labor Council, and Marian Kramer of the National Welfare Rights Council.[24]

The March 6 event was followed on March 14 by a women's action, timed to honor the celebration of International Women's Day on March 8. Forty-four women activists were arrested, including Gloria Woods, president of the Michigan chapter of the National Organization of Women (NOW), Detroit city councilor Sheila Cockrel, and former state senator Lana Pollack.[25] A week later, retired UAW president Doug Fraser led a contingent of twenty-two labor activists who were arrested for their blockade of the *News* offices. On March 28, sixty-five nonstriking union leaders were arrested at the *Free Press* building, including UAW Region 1A director Bob King and seventeen UAW local union presidents.[26] The actions resumed at the *Free Press* on April 11, with two hundred demonstrators and twenty-four arrests of local elected officials and political activists, including Detroit city councilor Mel Ravitz, Wayne County Commission members Edna Bell and Kenneth Cockrel Jr. and Commission chair Ricardo Solomon, state representative Martha Scott, and longtime community organizer General Baker Jr. Subsequent waves featured civil disobedience actions by educators, veterans, and retirees, among others. Altogether, 288 people were arrested in the nonviolent protests organized by RU against the newspapers.[27]

The actions of the religious leaders and Readers United brought new voices into the public dialogue around the strike and raised issues not normally considered to be a part of industrial relations. In the midst of a labor dispute, they recalled the journalistic mission of the newspapers, articulating a vision of their civic function and social compact with the community. As the RU leaders said in their opening statement, "[A newspaper] creates a product that is woven together from our lives; we lend it our stories and our names in exchange for accurate information. A newspaper both draws from the community and creates opportunities for the community to come together."[28] Likewise, the group argued, the unions' struggle for justice also had a meaning for and relationship with the community. Reverend Wylie-Kellerman recalled an early meeting of RU leaders with the MCNU at which SOSAD's Barfield spoke. "She made a really passionate pitch that this strike could be a service to the community," he said. "In a city that was fraught with violence, you could teach students how to engage in social change and social struggle in a disciplined, nonviolent way."[29]

As the unions sought allies in the community, so too did community actors step forward to claim a role of independent stakeholders in the strike and in its outcome. "With respect to the papers," Reverend Wylie-Kellerman wrote in an op-ed published in the *Sunday Journal* in August, "the Detroit community is at the point where we must be asking: What is the purpose and vocation of a newspaper? What, in plain language, is a paper for?"[30] In different ways, both the unions and the community leaders tried to expand the scope of public engagement and discourse in the strike. Meanwhile, the newspapers worked just as diligently to exclude wider participation by community groups, to defuse their issues, and to control the terms of public debate.

THE NEWSPAPERS AND THE FRAMING OF PUBLIC DISCOURSE

Entrenched in their position, the newspapers showed no interest in altering the shape of the playing field in the strike. Company executives ignored most local civic and elected leaders and attacked those who dared to side with the strikers. DNA bargainers brushed off Mayor Archer's attempts to facilitate a settlement, while CEO Frank Vega denounced city council president Mahaffey for her attempts to intercede between pickets and Detroit police at the distribution centers. Tim Kelleher curtly dismissed the Readers United protests, saying, "These people just want their names in the paper and their picture in the paper."[31] Vega even discounted the entire Detroit-area union community supporting the circulation boycott. "A lot of people stopped taking the paper, and they may have been union members," he told the *Chicago Tribune* in February 1996. "But I'm not sure how many union members shop at Neiman-Marcus. Most of them shop at Sam's Warehouse," which did not advertise in the *News* or *Free Press*.[32]

Perhaps the most strenuous voice on the management side was *News* publisher Robert Giles. Don Gonyea, a Detroit correspondent for National Public Radio, recalled that Giles "was definitely very aggressive on making sure the newspaper management's spin was out there. . . . He was definitely a lightning rod."[33] In August 1995, Giles wrote a letter to religious leaders defending the newspapers' hiring of permanent replacements. "We all remember the lessons of recent history," he said. "The Communist Party's unions were compulsory; Solidarity was voluntary."[34] That statement drew a rebuke from Solidarność president Marian Krzaklewski in Gdansk, who wrote: "We, in Poland, lived that history and we ask that it be respected and not be turned on its head as part of an anti-union propaganda campaign. . . . Instead of permanently replacing workers, robbing them of their jobs and their futures, which can only make negotiations more difficult, we urge you to bargain in good faith."[35]

After the Readers United protests started in 1996, Giles wrote a *News* column on March 10 on the philosophy of civil disobedience in the work of Henry David Thoreau and Dr. Martin Luther King Jr. "Spokesmen for the protesters last Wednesday called forth the memory of Dr. King," he wrote, "but it is difficult to find any legitimate or rational connection between the civil rights movement as a form of civil disobedience and the protests in support of the newspaper strikers. The civil rights movement sought to create change and reform. The newspaper strike seeks to resist change and reform."[36] Partly in response to Giles's remarks, Martin Luther King III came to Detroit three weeks later and spoke to a crowd of 250 strikers and supporters at New Bethel Baptist Church. The thirty-eight-year-old son of the slain civil rights leader told the audience to continue their protest and led them in singing "We Shall Overcome." King said that the newspapers had ignored Detroit's rich history of labor and civil rights organizing and that if his father were alive he would encourage the employers to negotiate an end to the strike. He called Giles's column "totally backward" and "the epitome of white arrogance," but Giles conceded nothing in his position. Reached for comment after the event, he said, "If his father was alive and understood the issues, he wouldn't be demonstrating on behalf of those workers. The strike is not about undoing any wrongs. These workers had good pay, good benefits, and a good offer from the company."[37]

The Media Blitzkrieg: The Newspapers' Strike Coverage

Hardly indifferent to public opinion, company officials used different means to try to shape popular perceptions of the strike. While the unions drew on their historic ties with local civic leaders and grassroots organizations, the employers relied instead on a media war conducted largely in the pages of their own newspapers. Journalists and critics across the nation cited the noticeable bias in the papers' coverage of the strike. In July 1995, the *Washington Post* scored the early joint edition of the paper, saying that "its partisanship is evident in its coverage of the strike, which at times seems like company agitprop masquerading as news, presenting the conflict pretty much as a collision between modern management imperatives and regressive union demands."[38] In November, the *Columbia Journalism Review* gave a "dart" to both the *News* and the *Free Press* for their "strikingly tilted news." Once the strike started, the journal editors observed,

> readers might have expected that the papers would cover the bitter dispute with the same fairness and balance given to previous hometown labor issues, such as those involving the United Auto Workers and the Big Three in Detroit. What readers got instead, however, were daily bundles of stories, editorials, columns, photos, and ads pushing the management line. . . . Fortunately, less self-serving coverage was available on local TV, most notably on WXYZ—a lesson not likely to be forgotten by newshungry Detroit when the strike finally comes to an end.[39]

Local journalists were especially critical of the content in the *News*. "Since the papers started printing separate editions, it appears the *News* often uses its stories as a corporate mouthpiece," said *Oakland Press* business writer Jennifer Bott, noting in addition the use of letters from the editor on the front page.[40] WDIV-TV (Channel 4) media critic Ric Bohy, a former *News* reporter who left in 1988, accused the *News* of "using [the] news hole for propaganda, for blatantly slanted coverage of the strike, to crush the strike, to serve its own purposes."[41] Jonathan Friendly, a former *New York Times* media writer and head of the journalism program at the University of Michigan, was less harsh, but said: "There were times when [the *News*] went over the line, when the [*News*] was looking for more negatives [about strikers] than a balanced account would offer. . . . I think there has been a tendency to discount some of the news coverage because a lot of it felt overblown."[42]

Sources from inside the newsroom reported editorial pressures to adhere to the company point of view. In July 1995, *News* Washington correspondent Bryan Gruley went to Detroit to fill out the staff and help cover the strike. After writing several pieces without incident, Gruley noticed that a quote from a striker criticizing the publishers was removed from one of his stories. "They said it was for space," Gruley recalled. "I said, 'I don't want my byline on these stories.' They sent me back to D.C." Similarly, *Wall Street Journal* writer Jason Anders was an intern at the *News* when the strike started. He co-authored three stories on the walkout, but then asked to be taken off the beat. "I was uncomfortable with the way the stories were being handled and finally insisted that I not be involved with the stories anymore," he said later. "[The] stories were being edited to reflect a specific tone. . . . A few of the newsroom editors I felt were consistently pushing for stories that had an anti-union bent to them."[43]

News publisher Giles defended the paper's practices and claimed that they were necessary to counteract pro-union bias in local radio and television news. "We have covered the strike very aggressively and one of the things we have focused on is the violence," Giles told the magazine *Editor & Publisher* in March 1996. "The unions, in our judgment, really have had a sort of platform [from broadcast news] to present their positions without any meaningful challenge. . . . To some extent, we feel the newspaper has to balance the story." Giles singled out local National Public Radio outlet WDET-FM, complaining that it had given a "very, very sympathetic treatment of violence that resulted from [strikers'] actions. . . . For a long time they refused to suggest that by blocking the trucks trying to come in and out of Sterling Heights or distribution centers, [strikers] were violating state law."[44]

"Oh, that's just bullshit, and you can quote me on that," replied WDET-FM's news director Roger Adams. "We've been round and round and round, me and Bob. We have included in every story the fact that by standing in front of gates, the strikers are violating state laws of egress and ingress into a business. We have never condoned violence and we point out that, yes, strikers are violating laws." He added, "But then when 11 huge semis come barreling out of [the newspaper plant] gates at 30 miles per hour with picketers two feet away"—an event that Adams said he personally witnessed—"yes, we'll say that is reckless and dangerous."[45]

Violence was a central theme of the newspapers' overall public relations campaign in the strike. The DNA ran television ads featuring video footage of the truck burning at the North Plant, even though the Macomb County prosecutor determined that whoever set it could not have come from the union side of the fence.[46] Many violent clashes did occur, of course, but the companies possessed powerful means for framing the interpretation of the events in the video and photographic images taken by security forces and in their editorial presentation in the papers. "It became the picture of the strike, and that was unfortunate," said union attorney Duane Ice. "It made it appear that the strikers were the aggressors, and what got lost in those convenient videos of picket line conduct is the larger dispute. The larger, aggressive conduct of the employers to stop bargaining, impose conditions, encourage people to take other people's jobs, and unprecedented aggressive behavior by employers, got lost." The DNA, the Reverend Wylie-Kellerman added, "could run a truck through a crowd, which is a pretty violent act, and make it look and feel like strikers are hitting a truck with picket signs. Well, they are [hitting it]. Where the real violence is there, is a question. . . . This was a very bloody strike and, you know, virtually all the blood was striker blood."[47]

The *News* managed to find violence even in events that had not yet occurred. In May 1996, Readers United announced a nonviolent protest by retirees in support of strikers and their children. They invited community members to attend and to bring their children to the 4:30 PM action on Thursday, May 9. On Sunday, May 5, the *News* ran a story on the front page of its metro section with the lede, "Backers of the Detroit newspaper strike plan this week to bring children to the picket line, which has been marked by obscenity, lawlessness and racial and sexual intimidation. Children are on the pickets' bill for Thursday, which has evolved into a day for protestors to break the law and get arrested." Nowhere in the unsigned, 106-line story did it say that the planned action was explicitly "nonviolent," nor did it explain who "Readers United" were or what their message in the protest was. The story earned a condemnation from Jack Lessenberry, political columnist for the Detroit weekly *Metro Times*, in a piece he wrote titled "Papers Not Fit for Your Cat Box."[48]

Permanent Replacements: Union "Privilege" and Racial Diversity

Beyond the story on the picket line, the newspapers also carefully framed the underlying dispute and management's role in it. Company spokespersons generally ignored or belittled the unions' unfair labor practice charges and continually repeated the $71 million cost estimate of the Teamsters' demands, even well after the union had formally withdrawn the proposals from the table.[49] Another much-used talking point was that five of the papers' eleven unions had ratified contracts in April 1995 without a strike, compared to the seemingly intransigent unions that walked out. Left unsaid was that the five unions together represented only around one hundred employees in units where the employers were not seeking major job changes. The six striking units, by contrast, represented twenty-five hundred employees who performed most of the labor in the papers' major editorial, production, and circulation departments.[50]

A particularly important theme in the newspapers' public statements was the conflation of the hiring of permanent replacements with the elimination of "featherbedding" and the racial diversification of the papers' workforce. In a full-page "Open Letter to Our Community" published at the start of the strike and signed by Vega, Giles, and *Free Press* publisher Neal Shine, the newspaper executives wrote:

> For years, the unions have dictated many of the practices in our workplace that are traditionally the responsibility of management, often requiring us to operate in extraordinarily wasteful, unproductive ways. For example: Our union contracts dictate how many people we must use to perform many jobs—even when those staffing requirements exceed common sense and standard practices in our industry. In some production areas, the work pace is so leisurely that some workers actually find time to sleep on the job—or to leave the premises during their shift.[51]

The statement did not mention that in negotiations before the strike the DNA had reached tentative agreements with the mailers and press operators on staff reductions and that those issues were not the sticking points that led to the walkout. Teamster warehouse worker Tom Breyer admitted that some of his fellow employees slept at the workplace, but they did so on their own time between split shifts. He explained:

> I might go be assigned to way out in Plymouth, and I would work 2:00 AM in the morning till 6:00 AM and then have off from 6:00 AM till maybe 9:00 AM or 10:00 AM, and then you would work 10:00 to 2:00. So that's what they called a split shift. . . . And if you were any distance from home, what are you going to do? You just stayed there at the distribution center. . . . I know during the strike the company said these people in the warehouse were sleeping. Well, they were, but they didn't explain that they were on their own time, these split shifts, which were terrible. . . . If I was going to Plymouth, I would leave here at 1:00 AM in the morning to be there at 2:00, and I wouldn't get back until maybe 3:00 the next afternoon, and you got paid for eight hours.[52]

Nevertheless, "sleeping on the job" became an archetypal anecdote in management's framing of "featherbedding." Union work practices were also explicitly tied to ethnic nepotism. "Sometimes, when we have job openings, our contracts allow the unions to do the actual hiring," said the "Open Letter," which was also published in the *Michigan Chronicle*, an African American newspaper in Detroit. "Those jobs get filled with the friends, neighbors and the relatives of union leaders, regardless of whether they are suited for the job. And we can assure you these kinds of practices do not help develop a diversified workforce."[53]

For decades the companies had made use of such informal practices as a convenient method of recruiting spot labor, and hiring more black workers was not a demand that management had pushed during the negotiations. Far from seeking to expand the total range of opportunities, the DNA was now actively reducing the number of full-time jobs in production and distribution. In addition, several senior managers themselves had relatives working at the papers, including DNA counsel John Taylor and vice president Tim Kelleher, whose son Joseph reportedly earned $17.50 per hour working in the North Plant mailroom during the strike.[54] Before publisher Neal Shine retired, the *Free Press* hired his thirty-two-year-old son, Dan Shine, as a reporter. "I made sure [executive editor] Heath [Meriwether] and [managing editor] Bob [McGruder] wanted Dan because of himself, and not because of me," Neal Shine said.[55]

By the fall of 1995, the papers were openly declaring their loyalty to the permanent replacements, portraying them as the more deserving employees. In response to the unions' conditional offer to return in early October, the DNA issued a statement that "firing our hard-working new employees or bringing back those guilty of strike misconduct are [*sic*] not in the cards."[56] By November, managers began to link the replacements more explicitly to racial diversity. As Vega said in an interview, "We do have a different culture here now. Over 57 percent of new people hired are minorities. In many of the union shops, the minority percentage was in single digits, and in some cases zero," though he did not say which units those were. "So all of a sudden, we have a very different work force in terms of the cultural issues that deal with different backgrounds."[57]

In fact, during the first months of the strike company executives had quietly reached out to church leaders in both white and black neighborhoods to promote opportunities with the struck newspapers. In August, DNA circulation chief Rob Althaus wrote a letter to pastors urging them to sell the Sunday papers. "Here's a *fantastic* opportunity to raise extra funds for a variety of purposes," the letter said. "Gather a few people together to sell the *Sunday Detroit News and Free Press* after services outside the church each week to members and passersby."[58] Top managers also met publicly and privately with selected community groups, including inner-city black clergy. The DNA's Alan Lenhoff recalled:

I think we might have spent some time with the Reverend Jim Holley [of the Little Rock Missionary Baptist Church]. He's one of the major movers and shakers. I can't remember who else we met with, but one of the sort of sub-issues that was going on here was that the black clergy knew that the unions that walked out were essentially white and suburban, and in some cases their contracts allowed them to control hiring. . . . You would look on our payroll list and there would be seventeen people with the same unusual last name in a row. It was a very cliquey thing. You had to sort of know somebody to get hired. . . . The black clergy looked at it and saw these white people who have been keeping us out of employment and really good jobs have walked out, and they didn't speak out on behalf of the newspapers, but their silence said a lot, and it clearly had come to their attention that when we began to hire replacement workers, that our workforce was a lot more diverse than it had ever been.[59]

At the DNA, "pre-strike, those [production workers] were 80 percent white, 18 percent black, 76 percent male, and 15 percent were Detroit residents," Meriwether told a community meeting in Detroit. "[Now] 57 percent are white, 38 percent black, 4 percent Hispanic, 60 percent are male and 39 percent are Detroit residents." Black strikers were disgusted by the papers' newly professed racial piety. "As a black man and an employee of the *Detroit Free Press* for 20 years, I resent the race card that is being played by this management," said Teamster district manager Crawford Webb.[60] In her *Sunday Journal* column, Susan Watson wrote:

My bosses go around town telling people that the workplace is more racially integrated than since the unions went on strike. What they don't tell you is that the company, not the unions, has always done the bulk of the hiring. The company is pitting black folks who desperately need work against strikers who are risking their future to preserve decent paying jobs, not just for themselves, but for all working class people.[61]

Most of the change occurred in the DNA's workforce; at the *News* the proportion of black newsroom employees remained about the same, and at Meriwether's *Free Press* it actually declined.[62] Data from the companies' employment records subpoenaed by the NLRB show that 2,025 replacements were hired at the *News*, the *Free Press*, and the DNA in the first eleven months of the strike up to June 20, 1996.[63] Of these, 48 percent were black and 46 percent were white. Twenty-four percent of the replacements—or 487 people—were hired as part-time or casual employees; however, a greater percentage of black replacements were part-time or casual (35 percent) compared to whites (11 percent). Moreover, nearly one-third of all replacement hires had been terminated by June 20, 1996, and black replacements were more likely to be terminated (40 percent) than white replacements (25 percent).

Racial differences also appeared within job classifications. Seventy-two percent of all replacement janitors and 61 percent of replacement "material handlers" (the equivalent of journeyman mailers) were black, while only 8 percent of replacement reporters were black. Nearly half (48 percent) of the 320 total replacement material handlers were hired part-time, but 57 percent of blacks in those jobs were brought in as part-time compared to 38 percent of whites. The DNA also paid lower wages to black replacement material handlers, with a mean hourly rate of $8.68 compared to $9.28 for whites in the same job.[64]

Such details were not generally disclosed, however, and overall the influence of the media campaign left public opinion divided about the strike. A statewide poll of nine hundred adults conducted in June 1996 for WXYZ-TV (Channel 7) found that 45 percent of respondents agreed that management was trying to bust the unions, compared to 23 percent who disagreed and 32 percent who were undecided. But 45 percent of those surveyed also said that the unions were mostly responsible for strike violence, compared to 12 percent who blamed management and 43 percent who did not know.[65] The papers' framing of race was also not without impact. Teamster member Webb felt that,

> basically, the company better utilized the black community against [the strike] than the unions were able to use on their behalf. . . . We have a very liberal portion [in Detroit] who are going to support the strikers. But if you had people who perceived this newspaper as being a white entity, I don't care how liberal you are, as a black you can see this is something that you are not a part of, now someone's opened a door up for you to be a part of it, so whose side are you on?. . . We appealed to [black ministers]. But what I found out was that there were people in their congregations who were getting these jobs. So you know, so hold it now, we didn't have this inroad before. So how do I sit and tell my people who are now working for the papers—and one of the members of my church got one of these jobs![66]

In their replacement hiring, the employers took advantage of the legacy of racial inequality in Detroit and easily drew upon the large, dependent, low-wage labor pool in the city. Their framing of the issue painted the permanent replacements as a more legitimate workforce than the strikers, rather than addressing questions about the practice of permanent replacement itself, its relationship to the ULP charges, or its effect on the process of collective bargaining or the community. On the one hand, the papers sought to distance themselves as much as possible from the strikers, while, on the other, they portrayed themselves as if they were brand-new enterprises with entirely new workforces. "We have hired 1,350 people, who I don't consider replacement workers at all," said Vega in November 1995. "These are new employees that are going to stay here as long as they want, as long as they do a good job." He added, "So in many ways, we're kind of starting a new company while we're fighting it out on the street every day."[67]

THE STATE I: REGULATING ACTION IN THE PUBLIC SPHERE

Alongside the struggle for public opinion, the unions and the newspapers fought an ongoing legal battle over the legitimate forms of collective action. The two parties engaged in a perpetual tug-of-war over the strikers' conduct on the picket line. On January 12, 1996, the MCNU signed an informal settlement agreement with the NLRB in response to the newspapers' charges of vandalism, mass picketing, and threats to employees crossing picket lines. In the voluntary settlement, the unions disavowed violence and promised not to engage in any illegal activity; however, within days the companies asked the Board to set aside the agreement and seek an injunction against the unions in federal court. On February 8, NLRB regional director William Schaub tossed out the settlement, and on February 27 he issued a formal complaint, charging union members with throwing star nails, blocking entrances, and hurling objects at company buildings. Schaub did not immediately seek an injunction, however, and declared simply, "All I'm saying at this point is, 'Stop doing it.'"[68]

The issue did not go away, and the companies continued to press for action against the unions. In July, four days before the one-year anniversary of the start of the strike, the NLRB in Washington, DC, voted to give Schaub the authority to seek an injunction against picket line misconduct. "This means if any union or union agent engages in violations of the injunction, they could be held in contempt, fined or jailed," said Schaub. "There are all kinds of sanctions possible here."[69] This time, on July 12, the unions signed a binding agreement, promising to refrain from violence, coercion, and threats against the newspapers and their employees. Union leaders subsequently distributed a list of "sixteen commandments" to their members, including prohibitions on everything from vandalism and mass picketing to name calling—other than "scab"—and even littering. After the agreement was signed, the demonstrations over the anniversary weekend were peaceful and comparatively mild. "We wanted it to be low-key," said Dia Pearce, chair of the Guild unit at the *News*. "The main thing we wanted everybody to see is that this is not a celebration for us."[70]

As with the picketing activity at the newspapers, the unions' leafleting of advertisers also became the object of constant litigation. In October 1995, the retailer Art Van Furniture filed an unfair labor practice charge against the unions, accusing them of picketing, blocking entrances, intimidating customers, and engaging in an unlawful secondary boycott of the company's eleven Detroit-area stores. In a settlement with the NLRB, the unions agreed to stop picketing at the stores and, at Schaub's insistence, to take a one-week hiatus from leafleting to "allow Art Van to get back to normal business operations."[71] As the boycott against car dealers advertising in the papers picked up in early 1996, DNA chief Frank Vega wrote a letter to dealers on January 26 offering DNA security staff and resources to help them prevent leafleting at their lots. "We are willing to absorb all legal costs to stop this interference with your business," Vega wrote. "We simply need you to help." In February, two press operators were arrested for blocking traffic while leafleting at a car dealership in Livonia. The owner later agreed to drop the charges and pay legal fees, however, when the union members requested jury trials and filed charges with the NLRB.[72]

All summer long, union protesters carried on a nonviolent guerrilla war with local police departments over leafleting and residential picketing. In Troy, Madison Heights, and Clinton Township, police officers ordered strikers to cease handbilling on public property, forcing union attorney David Radtke to write to municipal authorities and remind them of the strikers' constitutional and statutory rights.[73] In August, Troy police arrested strikers Mike Fahoome and Gus Peponis and Teamster organizer Mike Zielinski for refusing to disperse from a demonstration in front of the house of Paul Krause, a Teamster member who crossed picket lines and returned to work. Undaunted, the pickets showed up at Krause's home again the following week, after the Troy city attorney acknowledged their lawful right to be there.[74] The City of Sterling Heights passed an ordinance in September prohibiting targeted residential pickets after strikers marched on the homes of city manager Steve Duchane, police chief Thomas Derocha, and police lieutenant Frank Mowinski. On the day the ordinance took effect, the marchers were back in Sterling Heights to test the new rules. Because protesters kept moving and did not target a specific home, police said, they did not violate the law.[75]

In the fall, the MCNU unveiled a new tactic in the advertiser campaign. On October 6, more than one hundreds strikers and supporters, wearing T-shirts that said in bold letters PLEASE DON'T SHOP HERE, walked peacefully through a dozen stores in Shelby and Utica townships, just north of

Sterling Heights. A few weeks later, teams of leafleters were joined by around forty supporters in T-shirts at stores in Clinton, where they were met by squads of Vance guards videotaping their actions. By November, the DNA had filed a charge at the NLRB on behalf of four of the targeted retailers. The Board filed a complaint and sought an injunction against the walk-throughs in federal court, but the unions signed a consent agreement promising not to threaten or coerce advertisers to drop out of the newspapers. The unions maintained the right to hand out leaflets and otherwise communicate peacefully with customers, however, and pledged to continue the pressure in their campaign.[76]

As community actors became involved in the boycott and the strike, so too were they drawn into the ever-widening legal struggle. In June, just over a week after the UAW RADD team participated in nonviolent action training with the unions, the DNA amended its RICO countersuit to add the UAW as a defendant in its conspiracy charges. The company also asked the federal court for access to union records, in order to identify individuals accused in the suit.[77] In March, pursuant to an inquiry by the DNA, the NLRB opened an investigation of Readers United to determine whether it was acting as an "agent" of the unions. The implications of the investigation were serious: if Readers United was found to be an agent, its actions could be used against the unions in the company's NLRB charge on picket line misconduct, and Readers United itself could be subject to any injunction issuing from that complaint.[78]

"We feel it is 'in-your-face' to the labor board," said Tim Kelleher of the first RU protest. "The demonstrators locked arms and flouted a government ruling."[79] The unions quickly disavowed any connection to the group or its acts of civil disobedience. On March 19, the MCNU's Sam McKnight wrote a letter to NLRB investigator Mark Rubin. "With respect to the demonstrations sponsored by Readers United and/or NOW on March 6 and March 14, 1996," McKnight said, "the Unions deny sponsorship and responsibility for these events." After the March 6 action, he added, the unions "took the additional precautions of notifying members that the Unions had cancelled all picketing at the Detroit News Building during the Readers United demonstration scheduled for March 14, 1996. There is nothing else the unions can do."[80]

At Rubin's request, leaders from RU met with him at the NLRB's regional office on March 26, accompanied by civil rights lawyers Bill Goodman and Julie Hurwitz. "I am concerned about what this unique inquiry into a community group means for freedom of association and conscience," said Goodman. "This inquiry can be understood as an attempt to chill people's rights to speak out." The investigation was subsequently dropped, and Readers United continued their nonviolent protests. After the meeting, the RU leaders issued a statement criticizing the DNA. "The Company's implication that residents of metropolitan Detroit do not have a huge stake in this strike is naive and short-sighted. Their suggestion that people in this community could not think for themselves and act independently to hold the newspapers accountable is a substantial misunderstanding of the situation which they have created."[81]

In their legal contest over the conduct of the strike, the various parties fought a battle within the state over the regulation of collective action in the civic arena. Strikers and their supporters pushed the envelope on the legitimate forms of public protest, opening up space for mobilization while walking a fine line with official authorities. In turn, the newspapers pushed back hard against the unions, their allies, and actors in the community, demanding legal sanctions and using state enforcement actions to try to discredit protesters and their message. The battle over the conduct of protest, however, was only about the rules governing the forms of mobilization. The parties also struggled to define the meaning or content of the strike, and the rights of the strikers, in the trial to determine whether or not it was an unfair labor practice strike.

THE STATE II: DETERMINING THE MEANING OF THE STRIKE

The NLRB's unfair labor practice complaints against the newspapers effectively captured or crystallized the extent to which the two sides were operating according to different institutional rules. The process of litigation, in turn, would decide which of those sets of rules would prevail and how they would be applied in this case. Removed from the actual events of the preceding year, however, the trial before an administrative law judge had a certain artificial air about it. In the course of the proceedings, the attorneys on both sides worked skillfully to parse evidence and construct stylized legal facts as a basis for the judge's decision. The outcome would merely determine the rights of some two thousand striking workers and very likely the balance of power in the strike.

A hearing in the case was originally scheduled for October 31, 1995, but was postponed several times as new charges were filed and issued in consolidated and amended complaints.[82] By April 1996, there were nine charges in the case, including the allegations of refusal to give information and unlawful declaration of impasse by the *News* in the Guild negotiations, the illegal imposition by the DNA of its jurisdiction proposal on the printers union, and the employers' unilateral withdrawal from their commitment to joint bargaining. In addition, there were charges concerning the DNA's threats to permanently replace unfair labor practice strikers

and its unilateral setting of terms and conditions for the permanent replacements, among others.[83]

The trial finally began on April 15, 1996, in a small courtroom on the
third floor of the massive Patrick V. McNamara Federal Building on Michigan Avenue in downtown Detroit. Presiding was administrative law
judge Thomas Wilks, a Detroit native who had first joined the NLRB in
1960. Colleagues described him as smart and fair, "low-keyed, not flashy,"
and "a good, solid judge."[84] Representing the NLRB general counsel were
two senior staff attorneys, Amy Bachelder, a Detroit native and twenty-
year veteran with the Board, and Linda Rabin Hammell, who started at
the Region 7 office in 1979. For the unions, Sam McKnight appeared on
behalf of the Teamsters and Duane Ice represented the Guild. At the respondents' table sat John Jaske and, as the lead counsel for the employers,
Robert Battista. A partner in the prominent Detroit law firm of Butzel
Long, Battista seemed ill prepared and uneasy during much of the trial,
overmatched by the presence of his client, Jaske, at his side.[85]

The first day started inauspiciously. After an opening statement by
Rabin Hammell, Bachelder and McKnight told the judge that the newspapers had failed to turn over some three hundred pages of documents covered under the subpoenas duces tecum (commands to produce documents
or evidence) that were served on the companies in mid-February. Battista
explained that he had failed to file a required petition to revoke the subpoenas in a timely manner because he believed that the documents were
privileged and therefore he assumed they were simply not included in the
orders. The NLRB and union attorneys were aghast, and even Judge Wilks
was stymied. "It's unheard of in all my years of practice before the agency
and as an Administrative Law Judge that a privilege is not asserted in a
petition to revoke," he said. "The argument that a person upon whom a
subpoena is served *duces tecum* can make a judgment that, oh, it's assumed
that they don't want these documents because they're attorney/client
privilege, so I'm just going to redact them on my own, and then later on, a
week or so before trial, make that comment in a conference with the judge,
the first time the judge is hearing about this, and—it just baffles me, to tell
you the truth."[86]

Most of the documents were either authored by or under the review of
Jaske, as the lead negotiator for Gannett. The dispute led to two and a half
days of argument by the lawyers, extended chamber conferences, and the
examination of Jaske on the stand to clarify his role in the company. The
examination underlined the problem of Jaske's position as both an officer
of the Gannett corporation and its attorney in the proceedings, and his accounts as a witness sometimes threatened to blur the lines between factual
testimony and legal argument.[87] In the end, Wilks granted the petition to

revoke the subpoenas, but in July the NLRB in Washington reversed his ruling and ordered the companies to produce the documents.[88]

The prosecution of the general counsel's case began in earnest when the hearing reconvened on April 29. The task at hand for Bachelder and Rabin Hammell was to show that the newspapers had committed the alleged unfair labor practices and that those practices caused or prolonged the strike. First, they intended to show that the DNA's repudiation of its joint bargaining pledge constituted bad-faith bargaining. The law did not require the newspapers to bargain jointly at the outset, but once they had promised to do so, they could not unilaterally withdraw from the arrangement after negotiations had begun. In her opening statement, Rabin Hammell compared the bargaining process to a game of chess: the logic of a move is often chosen in anticipation of what the chessboard is going to look like later. The DNA's sudden repudiation of its prior commitment to joint bargaining, however, "dashed the legitimate bargaining strategies, plans, and expectations of the constituent unions of the Council, and was the significant factor contributing to the unions' decision to strike."[89]

With regard to the charge on the printers' jurisdiction, the general counsel's theory was three-pronged. First, the DNA's declaration of impasse and implementation of its proposal could be seen as a unilateral midterm change of the printers' 1975 memorandum of agreement (MOA) covering lifetime job guarantees and work arrangements. The MOA did not end with the expiration of any collective bargaining agreement and could not be modified without the union's consent. Alternatively, the proposal could be viewed as an attempt to alter the scope of Local 18's bargaining unit by limiting it within the four walls of the composing room. Such a change was not a mandatory subject of bargaining and therefore could not be unilaterally implemented. Last, the general counsel argued that the parties simply had not yet bargained to a good-faith impasse. As a result, the employer was not allowed to unilaterally impose its proposal whether the subject was deemed to be mandatory or not.[90]

In the case of the Guild, the general counsel argued similarly that no good-faith impasse had been reached when the *News* imposed its merit pay plan on July 5, 1995. There was inadequate disclosure of and insufficient bargaining about the details of the plan, and in addition, the *News* illegally refused to provide information about the proposal on overtime. Beyond that, the general counsel argued, the *News*'s conduct attempted to exclude the Guild from input into the determination of wage increases. Even if there had been a good-faith impasse, by its nature the merit pay plan "was the kind of proposal that arrogated too much discretion to the company," Rabin Hammell said later. "You can unilaterally implement a wage of $10.50 an hour [upon reaching a good-faith impasse], but to unilaterally implement the ability to unilaterally do anything you want is sort of like *too* unilateral."[91]

All of these unfair labor practices, Bachelder and Rabin Hammell argued, contributed to causing and prolonging the strike. In addition, the Board attorneys argued that, as unfair labor practice strikers, the striking employees should have been protected from permanent replacement. Hence, the employers' public threats to permanently replace them were unlawful and incendiary and had "a natural and foreseeable tendency to prolong the strike."[92] Finally, the general counsel asserted a new theory: the purposes and policies underlying the National Labor Relations Act should require an employer involved in an unfair labor practice strike to continue the preexisting terms and conditions of employment, even with respect to replacement employees. Existing case law on this point was not entirely settled, the general counsel acknowledged, but the attorneys contended that an employer should not be rewarded for violating the law. As Rabin Hammell explained at the trial:

> A rule contrary to the one that we propose would have the perverse effect of strengthening an offending employer's ability to weather a strike caused by its own unfair labor practices. For example, reducing terms and conditions unilaterally lowers labor costs, thereby allowing the employer to profit from its own misconduct. On the other hand, granting improved terms and conditions to replacements undermines the status and power of the striking employees' union. So, in short, we say that an employer whose illegal conduct has helped to cause a strike should not be given an economic weapon which will have the ineluctable effect of prolonging that strike.[93]

The general counsel presented its case on ten separate hearing dates through May and June, and the newspapers opened their defense on July 9. On the joint bargaining charge, the newspapers denied that economic issues like across-the-board wage increases were ever reserved exclusively for joint sessions, and they said that they never reneged on their promise. They claimed that they never said that they would not bargain jointly on economics if individual negotiations went beyond June 30, 1995, and the parties were still, in effect, in individual negotiations, and so they had not even gotten there yet.[94] Indeed, on March 4, 1996, Jaske had written to Local 13N's Jack Howe in part to ask whether he wanted to resolve certain issues now, "or wait for joint council negotiations?" Howe had replied that, some eight months into the strike and after nearly all of his members had been permanently replaced, Jaske's suggestion was "mind-boggling."[95]

For the proposal on the printers' jurisdiction, Jaske and Battista claimed that when the DNA started in 1989, it adopted the 1975 MOA's job guarantee provisions but not the work arrangements that were also in it. Since the DNA's proposal did not affect the lifetime job guarantees, the MOA had no bearing on the case. Second, the company invoked the NLRB's decision in *Antelope Valley Press* to argue that its demand was a mandatory subject and that the precise language of that demand did not imply a change in the bargaining unit. "I understand the issues with regard to jurisdiction and bargaining unit as they apply to the [printers union], and I understand the law," said Jaske under direct examination by Battista. "I've litigated this issue, negotiated this issue many times, litigated it to the Court of Appeals level, and you cannot change the bargaining unit with this or any union."[96] Third, the company lawyers said, a valid impasse existed because the union's insistence that it was a permissive subject meant that it continually refused to discuss it, demonstrating the futility of further negotiation.

As for the *News*'s imposition of merit pay, the lawyers argued that the "vitriolic and vituperative" opposition of the Guild membership to the plan underscored the valid impasse that existed over the proposal. The *News* complied with its duties to provide information, the plan itself met the criteria for a mandatory subject of bargaining, and the implementation was proper.[97] Finally, since the employers held that the strike as a whole was an economic and not an unfair labor practice strike, its actions with the permanent replacements were lawful and the general counsel's charges were moot.

The hearing dragged on in stops and starts through the summer and into the fall, with long recesses, postponements, and the scheduling of additional dates. The trial itself was like "kind of a mosaic," Rabin Hammell later recalled. "It had all these discrete parts, these various issues. It wasn't like one linear story to be told."[98] Much of the witness testimony concerned correspondence or negotiations that the company and union attorneys themselves had engaged in across the table a year earlier, so that more than once the examination devolved into factual disputes between those same individuals as to who had said what to whom. At one point McKnight changed hats from witness to counsel while still on the stand, in order to raise a point of privilege about his own testimony.[99] Wilks was uncomfortable with the move but allowed it, and in his decision he wrote: "In this regard, there is a great deal to be said for codes of ethics in some jurisdictions which preclude an attorney from litigating an issue on behalf of a client for whom he testifies as a witness in the same proceeding."[100]

Even when they did behave as witnesses, it was hard for the attorneys to resist introducing post hoc arguments or legal interpretations into their reconstruction of events. Jaske seemed especially prone to make argumentative points beyond the required response; when Battista questioned him about the Guild negotiations, Wilks admonished them both, saying, "I don't want to get into this after-the-fact theorizing. . . . Let's make sure if you ask a question that—and the witness answers it as to avoid a present day theorization of something that happened way back then."[101] As the trial went on, Jaske increasingly took over the control of the defense from his own lead counsel, examining witnesses on his own and acting as spokesperson before the judge. Toward the end, however, even he seemed to wear down after four straight days on the stand under lengthy grilling from Bachelder, Rabin Hammell, McKnight, and Ice.[102]

By the time the hearing finally concluded in early October, six months after it began and more than a year after the first complaints were issued, observers were hopeful that Judge Wilks might have a ruling sometime in early 1997.[103] Company executives, however, had already expressed public contempt for the NLRB and declared their intention to appeal. "Look, get this right, because I've been misquoted on it so many times," DNA chief Vega said in March 1996, before the hearing even began, "but there is no question in my mind—because this is Detroit—we probably have a snowball's chance in hell of those charges not being upheld here."[104] The following month Vega told the conservative Mackinac Center for Public Policy that "I've never heard the NLRB to be objective," while Gannett chair John Curley, at the company's annual meeting in May, said that the Board "generally operates as an arm of organized labor."[105] For the newspapers, the trial and the NLRB were only the first stages to get through before they reached their preferred venue in the federal court. Meanwhile, the striking union members remained out on the streets, their right to return to their jobs hanging on a legal process that might not be decided for years to come.

CONCLUSION: THE LIMITS OF LOCAL ENGAGEMENT

As the strike expanded and developed in 1996, it more and more came to signal the new terrain of labor conflict that had emerged by the mid-1990s. Forced to escalate their campaign, the unions deployed tactics from the repertoire of metro unionism, accelerating the consumer and advertising boycotts, reaching out into the community, and opening up space for collective action. At the same time, they defended their rights as strikers through the unfair labor practice case at the NLRB. Both sides adapted to the new forms of engagement: the newspapers fought back on the same terrain, promoting their own public representations of the strike, pursuing charges of misconduct on the picket lines and in the boycott, and even

threatening union allies with legal pressure. Altogether, the struggle signaled the extent to which contemporary labor disputes exceeded their traditional boundaries, spilling over into multiple areas of civil society and
the state.

While the scope of the struggle grew, however, it did not appear to get
any closer to reaching a settlement. Undeniably, the unions' mobilization
had an impact on the companies. In September 1996, for the first time
since the start of the strike, the independent Audit Bureau of Circulation
released its report on the *News* and the *Free Press*. The report, which covered the first quarter of 1996 only and not the second half of 1995, showed
a combined average weekday circulation of 576,698, a loss of 288,676 or 33
percent from the previous year. The Sunday average for the same period
was 769,594, down 29 percent from nearly 1.1 million one year earlier. The
declines were considerably more than the company's prior claims of 24
percent for daily circulation, and in blue-collar areas the drops were even
higher. In Wayne County, combined circulation fell by 39 percent, and in
Macomb County the drop was 42 percent.[106]

The newspapers also acknowledged declines in advertising revenue of
25 percent from prestrike levels, although the unions argued that the
losses were even greater. By June 1996, the unions claimed, a total of 1,395
advertisers had supported the boycott for at least thirty days during the
strike, while 715 continued to appear in the papers.[107] Estimates of the
overall financial losses for the companies ranged from $150 million for the
first two years to $250 million, including forgone profits.[108] The strike con-
tributed to a 19 percent drop in earnings for Gannett's newspaper division
in the third quarter of 1995 and a 7 percent fall in the fourth quarter.[109]
Knight-Ridder reported an 82 percent drop in its third-quarter profits for
1995, with the strike responsible for an estimated fifty cents of the fifty-six-
cents-per-share decline. Its losses continued into the next year, with the
strike accounting for perhaps two-thirds of the 34 percent decline in the
corporation's first-quarter earnings.[110]

Yet, managers at the companies were not moved. The strike put an
enormous bite on the finances of the two newspapers, but the parent corporations were both large enough and wealthy enough to tolerate losses
in the Detroit market and wait for the tide to turn. Profits from Gannett's
television and radio holdings allowed the company as a whole to post a
fourth-quarter gain in net income of $1.11 a share in 1995, while overall
revenue rose 9 percent, from $1.05 billion to $1.15 billion.[111] Knight-Ridder
was more vulnerable than Gannett, but in the bull market of the mid-1990s
its stock still closed at $68 a share at the end of March 1996, up from around
$56 a year earlier. Investors seemed to regard the strike as a sunk cost and

looked forward to greater profit margins down the road. "What's done is done," said industry analyst John Morton. "People on Wall Street are asking, 'What happens next quarter?'"[112]

"There has been a lot more community support for this than they [the newspapers] ever anticipated," said striking Guild member Bob Ourlian on the first anniversary of the strike. Still, he admitted, "it hasn't been enough to do the job."[113] At the local level, the employers skirted all attempts at civic mediation and maintained their repressive stance toward civic protest. In July, after a group of strikers visited his office, Detroit mayor Dennis Archer made another attempt to help resolve the dispute. The mayor summoned the two sides to City Hall, promised to provide rooms and staff support for negotiations, and volunteered to monitor the talks.[114]

Over the next several weeks, Archer continued to press behind the scenes for more progress and proposed to examine the DNA's claims that it hired poor Detroit residents as permanent replacements. If the claims were found to be true, a plan would be developed to assist these residents in finding other jobs, thereby removing the replacements as a barrier to settlement. The city government was about to undertake a major hiring push, and the mayor reportedly promised help from Blue Cross–Blue Shield in finding jobs for those who lived outside Detroit.[115] The unions also offered to create a three-person mediation panel to study the issues and make binding recommendations and said that the mayor agreed to nominate as members retired UAW president Doug Fraser, Wayne State University journalism department chair Ben Burns, and former University of Michigan president Robben Fleming. At a meeting on October 1, however, the newspapers categorically rejected the mediation plan. The DNA did not respond to the offer to help relocate the replacements, and the mayor withdrew the proposal.[116]

For the 1996 Labor Day weekend, representatives from the unions' internationals organized a rally at the *News* building to coincide with a visit to Detroit by AFL-CIO president John Sweeney, secretary-treasurer Richard Trumka, and other national labor leaders. The event was planned as a photo opportunity to build public awareness and support for the strike, and prior arrangements were made with the Detroit police that after the rally Sweeney and others would be arrested for civil disobedience. On Friday morning, August 30, organizers set up on the steps and sidewalk in front of the *News* building's main entrance on Lafayette Street, and around 9:00 AM a crowd gathered and soon swelled to several hundred.

At around 10:00 AM, Detroit police lieutenant James Noetzel ordered the front door of the building locked, following the usual police procedure with demonstrations at the *News*. The company complied by shutting off the electronic doors and barricading the glass, although traffic continued to enter and exit through the side doors of the building, which remained open and unblocked. For two hours, hundreds of demonstrators assembled in front of the entrance and listened to speeches by labor and civic leaders, and around noon between fifty and one hundred of them sat down on the steps and refused to move. Police then arrested twenty-one of the protesters for disorderly conduct, and after the nearby police bus was filled, they asked the rest of the crowd to disperse, which they did.[117]

The action was symbolic, peaceful, and orderly and stood in sharp contrast to the events of the Labor Day weekend at the North Plant the previous year. Among those arrested were Sweeney, Trumka, Newspaper Guild president Linda Foley, U.S. representative John Conyers, Detroit city council president Maryann Mahaffey, UAW Region 1A director Bob King, Bishop Thomas Gumbleton, Rev. Ed Rowe, and Readers United founders Jeanie Wylie-Kellerman and Rev. Bill Wylie-Kellerman. In addition, MCNU local union heads Al Derey, Jack Howe, Sam Attard, and Alex Young were also cited, while dozens of other strikers and supporters sat down and waited to be arrested but never were.

Although clearly aimed at winning public support, the nonviolent civil disobedience also technically violated the unions' agreement with the NLRB on picket line misconduct. Within a few weeks, the employers fired around thirty strikers for sitting down on the steps after the rally, regardless of whether they were actually arrested at the scene. All four of the MCNU heads at the action were fired, along with Teamster member Shawn Ellis and Guild members Bob Ourlian, Kate DeSmet, Nancy Dunn, and Susan Watson, among others. The termination of Watson, a thirty-year *Free Press* employee and the paper's only black general columnist, brought a special condemnation from JoAnn Watson (no relation), executive director of the Detroit branch of the NAACP, who called it "one more action of management against this community. We respect and admire [Susan Watson] and we stand with her in solidarity."[118]

For a year and a half, the strikers had fought and in many ways won the battle of Detroit. But the newspapers' response raised doubts as to whether the struggle could be decided at the urban metropolitan level. Already in mid-1996 there were debates within the local unions about what to do next, but support for the strike remained strong. By the end of the year, however, international union leaders became increasingly concerned about the cost and direction of the campaign. In February 1997, local Teamster leaders Al Derey and Alex Young flew to Washington, DC, to meet with International Brotherhood of Teamsters president Ron Carey and other IBT officials, while the other MCNU heads conferred with their respective leaders in the Communication Workers of America and the

Graphic Communications International Union.[119] As Guild Local 22 president Lou Mleczko recalled:

> In mid-February of '97, that was after another full year of running those boycott programs. It was only then that the Council along with the Internationals agreed that we've exhausted the boycott activities and things related to it as best as we can, because of the ongoing strike and the fact that people had to now be scattering and finding other employment. . . . After we finally went through the last advertising cycle and boycott activities pre-holidays, it became clear to the Internationals and the Council that we were going to have to change strategies. And that's when we made the decision to make an unconditional offer and start the clock running, the legal clock on unfair labor practice and those things.[120]

On Friday, February 14, Derey made the formal announcement at a press conference in Detroit. "Today, the Teamsters and other unions have made an offer—as required by law—to reclaim our jobs at both papers," he said in a prepared statement. "This bold move leaves the companies with only two choices: they can reinstate the unfair labor practice strikers—or start the meter running with back pay liabilities of up to $250,000 per day."[121] Derey insisted that the unions would continue to pressure the newspapers by maintaining the circulation and advertiser boycotts and by continuing to publish the *Detroit Sunday Journal*. The struggle would enter a new phase, and union leaders expressed a grim determination to fight. "This is simply a new strategy," said Derey, "against corporate giants that don't have souls."[122]

Chapter 11 | Waiting for Justice: The Return to Work and the End of the Strike

CONVENTIONAL THEORIES OF HOW workers mobilize during strikes developed especially in the 1970s and 1980s in American social science. Such theories often argued that labor militancy in the postwar United States had been incorporated into a stable system of legal regulation. Researchers claimed that "strike action in the U.S. prior to the late 1940s occurred in a wholly different environment than did insurgency after this point in time," as sociologist Holly McCammon notes. "During the late 1940s the context of workplace negotiations became 'institutionalized.' The U.S. state now granted workers a legal right to organize and bargain in the workplace and with this came a stabilization not only in union membership levels but also in the relationship between workers and employers."[1]

Ironically, this view reached its fullest expression just as those historic institutional conditions were being radically undermined. Dramatic changes began to appear in the 1980s, leading to the substantial *de*-stabilization of unions and the ascendancy of the anti-union regime. Those changes did not occur overnight, and conflicting institutional norms continued to exist in different organizational contexts and locales. In the Detroit newspaper strike, this uneven process of institutional grating and displacement was illustrated in the long, drawn-out litigation surrounding the unfair labor practice charges. The unions actually won their case before an administrative law judge and on appeal at the NLRB in Washington, D.C., but lost crucial decisions before judges in U.S. district and federal appellate courts. The results highlighted the historic decay in the role of the NLRB and the return of judicial repression in U.S. labor relations.

Conventional studies of strike mobilization also focused largely on behavior in the workplace and so gave little attention to action in the local

227

community or civil society. As unions began to turn to strategies of metro unionism, however, protest moved beyond the normal channels. Civil society gained renewed importance as an arena of conflict; in Detroit, for example, the largest single protest action occurred *after* the unions had offered to end the strike and return to work. If mobilization is no longer limited to formal channels, however, it is still not entirely free of any institutional ground. To achieve change, organizers must be able to pressure contending groups into some new framework or set of binding relationships. In Detroit, actors in the civic arena lacked access to effective regulatory mechanisms or leverage to compel the newspapers to respond, and the companies remained deaf to their appeals.

Once the Metropolitan Council of Newspaper Unions made the unconditional offer to return, the unions no longer had the economic weapon of the strike. Organizers had to find alternative means to sustain public awareness and support, and they did so spectacularly with the staging of the Action! Motown '97 demonstration in June 1997. The event represented the peak of popular mobilization and coincided with the decision by the administrative law judge upholding the strikers' unfair labor practice charges. Despite the popular show of solidarity, however, subsequent decisions by federal judges kept the campaign tied to an extended process of litigation. Mobilization continued, perhaps most notably in a spring 1998 community summit organized by religious and civic leaders. But as strikers slowly returned to work or otherwise dispersed, the unions were left with fewer options, especially after the U.S. Court of Appeals overturned the unfair labor practices case in 2000. Beaten but not broken, the unions finally settled contracts on management's terms, and by the end of the year the newspaper strike was over.

INSIDE GAME: THE UNCONDITIONAL OFFER TO RETURN

On February 19, 1997, the *News*, the *Free Press*, and the DNA formally accepted the unions' unconditional offer to return to work. Not surprisingly, however, the employers maintained their position that the walkout was economically motivated and not an unfair labor practice strike. Consequently, they refused to displace the replacements or take back more than a fraction of the returning strikers. "We will legally fight to the death to protect those people [the replacements]," declared *News* publisher Bob Giles, while at the *Free Press* executive editor Bob McGruder said that vacancies below the department head level were "just a handful—fewer than ten."[2] The newspapers continued to try to encourage strikers to seek employment elsewhere, and they again offered to create a $2 million retraining and relocation fund to help former strikers find jobs at other papers within the two chains. "This is clearly an offer made with reconciliation in mind," said Giles. "We believe it represents the kind of creative solution that many in the community have called for."[3]

The unions were not impressed and quickly labeled the newspapers' stance a lockout. "My reaction is that this is a kind of artful effort to put a nice face on a response that says 'drop dead' to the workers," said union attorney Sam McKnight. "If what they are doing looks like, walks like, talks like, feels like, and sounds like a lockout, that's what it is." Union leaders immediately asked the NLRB to seek a federal injunction to force the companies to reinstate all of the strikers immediately. The employers, however, framed the end of the strike as the end of the underlying dispute. To help ensure that outcome, in March the DNA declared impasse in negotiations with the Teamsters and the press operators, the largest remaining units where it had not already declared impasse, and unilaterally imposed proposals from its last offers.[4]

Managers at the *Free Press* were the first to begin actually calling back strikers, offering four newsroom jobs and one part-time clerical position to Guild members at the end of February. But following the law for economic strikers, the company only recalled workers for available openings and did not necessarily return them to their former jobs. Striker Jean Sarna, a food specialist, had been the director of the *Free Press*'s test kitchen and a former winner of a statewide Home Economist of the Year Award. Among the first to receive an offer to return, Sarna was hired back as a clerical worker and typist in the business news department. As *Detroit Sunday Journal* columnist Susan Watson wrote, "She will be doing many of the tasks previously performed by a union member who crossed the picket line during the strike and took Sarna's job in the test kitchen. That's right. Sarna gets the scab's former job while the scab keeps Sarna's prestrike job."[5]

The *Free Press* revised its offer when the Guild reminded management that Sarna was in a different job classification, but other experienced journalists received similar treatment. Music writer Gary Graff, a thirteen-year veteran at the paper and an active participant in the Detroit music scene, was offered a job as a general assignment reporter in the suburban Oakland County bureau; his former beat was held by a replacement.[6] Molly Abraham reviewed restaurants for nearly thirty years for both the *News* and the *Free Press*; her published guide to local eateries had gone through six editions before the strike. She was recalled in May and assigned to writing obituaries as a general reporter on the city desk, while the *Free Press* kept a line-crossing worker in her former job. After she returned, the paper added a second restaurant critic position and chose another line-crosser for it rather than Abraham.[7]

At the DNA, thirty-three members of Local 13N were back on the job by the end of April, including twenty-seven press operators, five paper handlers, and one plate-maker, but the latter two categories had their wages cut by one-quarter to one-third from the prestrike contracts. Most of the striking printers union members had lifetime job guarantees, and management chose to bring them back slowly in groups of sixteen employees per week. By May, seventy to eighty had returned, but the company refused to reinstate striking printers who were older than sixty-five or who had been hired after the lifetime guarantees were negotiated. Moreover, according to Local 18 president Sam Attard, the returning printers were forced to attend "a week-long 'orientation' where management officials subject the workers to as much verbal abuse, gloating and sarcastic treatment as they can get away with."[8]

Attard was allowed to accompany his members for the first four hours of the orientations, but at that point he was then escorted out of the building. The employees were then put in a room with fifteen computer stations where they were told that they could practice their skills, but they received no training. At the end of the week, they underwent a "computer skills assessment test"; the 60 percent or so who passed were assigned a wage rate of $17.30 to $18.00 per hour, while the rest were told that their rate was $12. Regardless of the outcome of the test, however, all of the returning printers were initially assigned no work at all but were left in a vacant isolation room in the *Free Press* building with nothing to do but talk, read, or play cards to pass the time. Workers sat on metal folding chairs at empty tables and had to ask permission to go to the washroom or get coffee. When DNA chief Frank Vega heard that they were playing cards, he ordered them to stop.[9]

In his 1982 law review article, Gannett's John Jaske had raised the possibility of a lifetime guaranteed job stripped of all meaningful content. Here his vision was at last objectively realized by the DNA. The returning printers were confined within the four walls of a composing room that had no work. "This isn't the composing room," said one of them, "it's the decomposing room."[10] Later, some of the workers were given quasi-production tasks taking old ads that were in an obsolete ad-composition program and putting them into a newer one, but Attard said that the union was "still concerned because they have put very few of our people into mainstream production." The same management that had accused the unions of "featherbedding" now preferred to have the printers sit idle rather than allow them access to the work of composing the newspapers or to their fellow employees. The decomposing room remained open until February 1998, at an estimated cost of more than $1 million, before the last twenty-four printers were finally integrated back into the DNA's composing room.[11]

The majority of the striking printers, however, at least formally had their jobs back. Five months after the end of the strike, no striking Guild members had actually returned to the *News*, and by September 1997 only two were back at work.[12] None of the striking mailers in Teamsters Local 2040 received offers to return from the DNA until August. By the peak of the holiday season in December, only sixteen had been recalled on a full-time basis, while another seventy or so were offered part-time work. All of the returnees were paid a base wage of $8 per hour, or about half of the prestrike rate.[13] Presented with those terms, most of the striking mailers refused the company's offer to return. Local 2040 president Alex Young explained:

> What [the DNA] are continuing to do is to take away people's right to recall for full time. . . . If our guys go back to work full-time, they get their seniority back. Then, in February, if there are layoffs, the scabs will be laid off. That's what the issue is here. The company is not living up to its obligation to call our people back to work as a result of the unconditional offer to go back to work.[14]

The employers maintained that their recall practices simply reflected their position that the strike was economically motivated, and that they had no duty or intention to displace the replacements for the sake of returning union members. The NLRB, however, disagreed. In early April, regional director William Schaub issued a new complaint against the newspapers for failing to take back all of the strikers. "I've always said these are unfair labor practice strikers," said Schaub. "Therefore, they're entitled to immediate reinstatement to their former jobs, even if it means displacing the new hires." At the DNA, executives already expected to appeal the entire unfair labor practices case, even though administrative law judge Thomas Wilks had yet to issue a decision. "Mr. Schaub is certainly entitled to his opinion," said DNA planning director Alan Lenhoff. "But we very strongly believe that, when these issues are finally decided, either by the full NLRB or in the courts, that it will be determined that this was not an unfair labor practices strike."[15]

DANCING IN THE STREET: THE ACTION!
MOTOWN '97 DEMONSTRATION

For the unions, the offer to return was simply a shift in strategy, dictated by the law and the balance of power in the campaign. The boycotts and protest actions continued along with informational picketing and publication of the *Sunday Journal*, but without the weapon of an actual strike, many local unionists feared a loss of momentum and public support. The previous summer, groups of strikers and supporters had begun to press for a national march and rally in Detroit, and in August 1996 several of them formed a loose coalition called the Action Coalition of Strikers and Supporters (ACOSS).[16] By the end of 1996, hundreds of strikers had signed petitions calling for a national march, and the idea was subsequently endorsed by the MCNU, the Metropolitan Detroit AFL-CIO, and dozens of local unions affiliated with the Teamsters, the United Auto Workers, and the United Food and Commercial Workers.[17] In February 1997, an informal delegation of strikers traveled to Los Angeles to lobby international union officials at a meeting of the AFL-CIO Executive Council. With the strike now ended, the group succeeded in persuading the federation leaders to support a national march scheduled for later that summer on June 20 and 21.[18]

AFL-CIO field organizer John Cox was assigned to coordinate a steering group made up of strikers and local activists, divided into eight different committees focused on logistics, media, and other aspects of the mobilization now called "Action! Motown '97." Packets of information were sent from national and state union offices to local leaders and members nationwide, and traveling crews of strikers spread the word in actions against Gannett and Knight-Ridder in other cities. On the still relatively new Internet, the event website received as many as two thousand hits a day.[19] Buses were chartered from Philadelphia, Chicago, and Milwaukee, and union members in San Francisco booked a plane to fly to Detroit. The march was framed as part of the national renewal of the U.S. labor movement under AFL-CIO president John Sweeney, and in April organizers predicted that the turnout might exceed the twenty-five thousand who attended a demonstration for strawberry workers in Watsonville, California, earlier that month.[20]

On Thursday, June 19, the day before the Action! Motown '97 program was slated to begin, NLRB judge Thomas Wilks issued his 113-page decision finding the newspapers guilty of unfair labor practices. The strikers were euphoric. "I'm happier than a pig in s——, although you can't print that!" Teamster Rick Schleeter told a reporter. "On a scale of one to ten," said Guild member Kate DeSmet, "this decision is a ten."[21] Reporter Bob Ourlian was at the *Sunday Journal* office when the news came in. As he recalled:

> We learned about it, I believe, on the phone and I think—I recall participating with, I think, Tom Schram, who was the editor of the paper then, and very quickly writing an article, and he and Steve Anderson, our editor-page designer, crafted a page of the *Sunday Journal* where the headline was

"GUILTY!" And so we put it all this together very quickly, and I think we just made a mock-up of the front page. There was a very large meeting going on at Teamsters Hall, and I don't know what that meeting was for, but a few of us went over there to convey the news of what had happened. And we walked in with this front-page mock-up that said "GUILTY" and just held it up like that, and the place just broke into roaring applause.[22]

Teamster organizer Mike Zielinski was in Grosse Pointe and immediately ran downtown for a spontaneous rally that converged on the *News* building. "I just remember people hugging each other and arms, you know, raised in triumph and victory signs. And it was just incredible! It was a validation of everything everyone had been through," he recalled. "And the timing couldn't have been better. With tens of thousands of people scheduled to arrive, already arriving, in Detroit for Action! Motown, it really gave a tremendous boost to the mobilization, and it felt like we were finally, finally going to achieve justice."[23]

The ruling gave an air of joyous celebration to the entire weekend, beginning on Friday, June 20. Organizers set up reception centers at the Teamsters Hall on Trumbull Avenue, the UAW's Dave Miller Building on East Jefferson, and at UAW Local 157 in suburban Romulus. Friday evening featured a teach-in at Wayne State University and benefit concerts for locked-out workers at local music clubs. Saturday, June 21, began with an interfaith religious service with Dr. Joseph Lowery, president of the Southern Christian Leadership Conference, and nonviolent protests at the Sterling Heights Police Department and at the home of DNA chief Vega in Grosse Pointe Farms. On a brilliant, sunny, hot Michigan summer day, the march stepped off in the afternoon from Michigan and Trumbull Avenues near the old Tiger Stadium, went down Michigan to Third Street, and then turned south toward Lafayette, parading past the newspapers' headquarters to Woodward Avenue and ending in a rally at the riverfront Hart Plaza.[24]

A sea of protesters filled the streets along Michigan Avenue from east of Trumbull to west of Rosa Parks Boulevard and on Trumbull from Fort Street to the Teamsters' headquarters north of Interstate 75. The peaceful, orderly procession to Hart Plaza took two hours, with marchers stretched out over a mile down the city streets; police estimates on the scene ranged from 60,000 to a peak of 100,000 persons. Organizers reported that members of forty unions from forty-five states, including New York, Maryland, Georgia, Kentucky, Texas, and California, attended the event, arriving by bus, train, plane, automobile, semi-tractor-trailer convoy, and motorcycle brigade. Visitors from twelve nations also came to show support, including Tristan Malle, president of France's National Federation of Journalists, and Jacques Girot, president of the National Federation of Newspaper Employees.[25]

"I would say that was one of my highest feelings of the strike, seeing all those people, you know, marching down the street, just block after block after block," said striking Teamster member Randy Karpinen.[26] The rally was the largest labor protest in the city in fifty years, since the April 1947 UAW demonstration against the Taft-Hartley Act in Cadillac Square. Now, against the backdrop of downtown, AFL-CIO president Sweeney addressed the massive crowd. "For 23 long months, this greatest of American union cities has rallied to uphold not only the workers and their unions, but to uphold the most important standard of corporate conduct we all rely on—basic respect for workers and the jobs they do," he said. "Brothers and Sisters, you have won the battle of Detroit." Later on in the program, AFL-CIO secretary-treasurer Richard Trumka spoke and said, "The questions raised by these workers and their unions go far beyond the gates of the Detroit News and the city limits of Motown USA. They are questions that go to the heart of the American way of life and they deserve an answer."[27]

The federation leaders' remarks expressed a point of view grounded at the intersection of the economy and civil society and affirmed values that bound the former to the latter. Sweeney invoked a workplace governed by cultural and communal standards of dignity and respect, while Trumka stressed the need to hold private enterprises like the newspapers accountable to a democratic public. Together they illustrated the clash between the norms of solidarity embodied in the labor movement and the logic of the free market as practiced by Gannett and Knight-Ridder. For the next several years, the contest between these opposing principles would be fought out on the uneven, crosscutting institutional terrain between an embattled New Deal order and the rising anti-union regime.

Coming just before the Action! Motown '97 weekend, Judge Wilks's decision also illustrated the power of the state to fix the meaning of events. Strikers expressed relief at the official vindication of their struggle: "I think this will lift the spirits and people will get some idea of what they're fighting for. It's been proven now," said striking press operator John Jackson. For Guild member Audrey McKenna, the ruling meant that, "from the moment this started, what, 708 days ago, that we did the right thing day in and day out. We got up in the morning and did the right thing."[28] McKenna's fellow Guild member Jocelyn Faniel-Heard was in the unions' strike headquarters on the day of the announcement. "I was in the speakers' bureau office, and usually anytime any good news came in, somebody would just rush down the hall and yell it out. And we'd all jump up and run up to the front to find out what, you know," she recalled. "But I remember we were all just like, oh thank you, God. Because now these people will see that we were not lunatics, you know? That had been the thing the whole time, that we were a bunch of lunatics."[29]

Together the ruling and the demonstration served notice to the public that the unions' fight with the newspapers was still very much on. Guild member and *Sunday Journal* advertising manager Mike McBride said that the rally was "a reminder to the advertisers that there is still a labor dispute in this town, especially the national advertisers who think this thing is over." At the same time, the giant march and rally underlined the independent role of mobilization in the community. Rev. Bill Wylie-Kellerman remarked that "Action! Motown is a way of affirming that the struggle is not just in the courts, but in the streets." And Guild member Jetta Fraser added, soberly, "I think it's always our strike to win, regardless of legal decisions, and that we need to be glad for those decisions but not expect the victory to come just from the efforts of lawyers in offices downtown."[30]

The events bolstered the strikers' resolve, but did not reduce the newspapers' antagonism toward the unions and the strike. As marchers went by the *News* building on Lafayette, replacement workers stationed in the windows overlooking Second Street leaned out and taunted the marchers by pointing, laughing, and making obscene gestures. Police had to order them away from the windows when a crowd began gathering underneath them.[31] The *News*, characteristically, could not resist headlining charges that "Some Throw Rocks, Trash *News* Racks in Downtown Detroit," and estimated the crowd size to be as low as seven thousand.[32] In turn, the *Free Press* received another dart from the *Columbia Journalism Review* for its coverage of Judge Wilks's decision. The *CJR* editors noted that typical headlines for the story nationwide included "Judge Orders Detroit Papers to Rehire Strikers" (*New York Times*), "Detroit Papers Ordered to Rehire Workers" (*Boston Globe*), and "Judge: Former Strikers Should Get Their Jobs Back" (*Miami Herald*). The *Free Press* headline for the story read: "Strike Ruled Unfair; Appeal Planned."[33]

JUSTICE DELAYED: THE WILKS DECISION AND THE DENIAL OF THE 10(J) INJUNCTION

The Wilks decision was not an undivided victory for the unions, and it actually rejected two of the charges in the consolidated complaint. First, the judge threw out the charge on the printers' jurisdiction on all of its grounds. Based on the Board's 1993 ruling in *Antelope Valley Press*, Wilks found that in bargaining Jaske had carefully avoided insisting that the employees to whom the printers' unit work was assigned would *never* be considered part of the unit or that the union would waive its right to seek to represent them through a Board petition, unfair labor practice charge, or other legal process. Furthermore, the judge wrote, "it is not relevant that [the proposal] theoretically gave the DNA the power to reduce the size of the unit or even alter its membership, as would any transfer of unit work."[34] As long as it did not change the unit description, it was a lawful and mandatory subject of negotiation and open to impasse and unilateral implementation.

The law here appeared to create a kind of shell game, with the employer able to constantly move work away from the union's jurisdiction and the union having to chase after it through administrative means. But in this case, the NLRB general counsel and the union had also argued that the printers' jurisdiction was protected by the 1975 memorandum of agreement (MOA), which could not be modified without the union's consent. Wilks found that the DNA had adopted both the lifetime job guarantees and the work arrangements in the MOA, but he introduced his own novel interpretation: because the MOA did not have a fixed end date on it, it did not fall under the protection of the law. The DNA was not prohibited from declaring impasse and imposing a midterm modification of the agreement, because there was no term. The union's insistence on May 11, 1995, that the MOA was a permissive subject, and its refusal to bargain changes in it, was therefore proof of a valid impasse.[35]

The judge also refused to uphold the charge that the employers had violated the law by unilaterally setting terms and conditions for the replacements different from those of the striking employees they replaced. The general counsel and the unions advanced several legal and public policy arguments for establishing a new precedent on this issue, but Wilks declined to address those, saying that they should be left to the full NLRB to decide. Wilks noted that existing law recognized management's right to set terms and conditions for economic replacements as a necessary incident of the right to hire them in the first place, and that, in general, a union could not represent both strikers and replacements. The general counsel and the unions argued that the newspaper strike was caused by the employer's unfair labor practices and therefore it should not "be able to profit by its own wrongdoing nor be permitted to withstand the strike by virtue of its financial savings from lower-paid replacements."[36] For Wilks, that shifted the argument from a conceptual representation issue to one of balancing economic forces, which was not a proper consideration for the Board.

Notwithstanding these setbacks, the Wilks decision was an outstanding win for the unions. The judge upheld the charges against the employers on joint bargaining, against the *News* on the overtime exemption and the merit pay plan, and on several related counts. As a result, Wilks concluded that the strike "was an unfair labor practice strike at its inception and was prolonged by subsequent unlawful threat[s] to permanently replace unfair labor practice strikers."[37] As union attorney Duane Ice said, the decision meant that "the strikers are entitled to return to work [and] the replacements have to go."[38] Now the question of how best to protect the strikers' rights would be the next major step and a crucial turning point in the course of the dispute.

Reasonable Cause, Just and Proper: The Petition for the 10(j)

Enacted as part of the Taft-Hartley amendments of 1947, section 10(j) of the National Labor Relations Act empowers the NLRB to petition in federal district court for a preliminary injunction against any party that "has engaged or is engaging in an unfair labor practice." In adopting the provision, Congress recognized that the Board's heavy workload and lengthy appeals process might make it unable "in some instances to correct unfair labor practices until after substantial injury has been done. . . . It has sometimes been possible for persons violating the Act to accomplish their purposes before being placed under any legal restraint and thereby to make it impossible or not feasible to restore or preserve the status quo."[39]

By the 1990s, such procedural delays were a serious problem. In 1996 the median time from an ALJ decision to the Board's final ruling was 217 days, with another 474 days on average needed to gain enforcement of the Board's order by the court of appeals.[40] To help strengthen the Board's remedial capacity, NLRB chair William B. Gould IV and general counsel Fred Feinstein adopted a policy in 1994 of more actively pursuing injunctions under section 10(j) of the Act. According to Gould, over the next four years the NLRB had a success rate of almost 90 percent, including wins and settlements, in seeking 10(j) injunctions.[41]

In the Detroit case, with a trial transcript of some three thousand pages (or more than five times longer than average), the prospect of further delay was considerable. In April, NLRB regional director Schaub sent a request for authorization to seek a 10(j) order to the Office of the General Counsel in Washington, D.C., based on the papers' refusal to reinstate all of the strikers after their unconditional offer to return. On July 1, the Board voted unanimously to authorize Schaub to petition for the injunction in U.S. District Court in Detroit.[42] In addition, Board chair Gould took the unprecedented step of releasing a written opinion in support of the request.

In his statement, Gould noted that most 10(j) cases arose after a complaint had been issued but prior to a ruling by an administrative law judge. In this case, however, Judge Wilks had already ruled, and his decision "serves as an important adjunct to our reasonable cause determination" that the employers' actions had caused and prolonged the strike. Now that the strikers had offered to return, Gould warned that the injunction was necessary to avoid further harm to them. "The strikers, like dismissed workers, may 'scatter to the winds,'" he wrote, "thus making ultimate relief at some point in the future an ineffective remedy. Indeed, the parties have asserted that many have already left the area in search of alternative jobs—and there is no reason to assume that this process will not continue."[43]

The injunction petition was assigned to Judge John Corbett O'Meara of the U.S. District Court, Eastern District of Michigan, appointed to the bench by President Bill Clinton in 1994. A Democrat and a former chair of the state party, O'Meara had spent most of his legal career representing corporate clients, frequently in labor matters, at the Detroit firm of Dickinson, Wright, Moon, Van Dusen, and Freeman. In April 1997, he had ruled against the suit filed by former Detroit mayor Coleman Young and others claiming that the newspapers violated antitrust law by publishing a combined daily edition during the first two months of the strike.[44] Yet NLRB and union attorneys decided not to object to his handling the case, not knowing who they might draw instead. As Duane Ice later recalled, "[Our] impression of Judge O'Meara was that he was a moderate judge, came from a corporate firm, but was a lifelong Democrat, and we thought we would get as fair a hearing from him as anyone. . . . [We] were just looking for a fair shot, and we thought with him we had as good a shot as any."[45]

A hearing in the case was set for the end of July.[46] On the companies' side, however, a new legal team had emerged. As early as April, former lead counsel Robert Battista and his colleagues from Butzel Long had been conspicuously absent; in their place the newspapers brought in local co-counsel Robert Vercruysse and, as the new lead, Andrew Kramer from the Cleveland law firm of Jones, Day, Reavis, and Pogue. A veteran management lawyer, Kramer was a coauthor of the landmark 1982 Wharton School manual *Operating During Strikes: Company Experience, NLRB Policies, and Governmental Regulations.*[47] Kramer and his fellow attorneys fought hard against the Board's 10(j) request and, in a highly unusual move, even deposed regional director Schaub. "The newspapers were arguing, successfully, that they needed to find out what was in Bill Schaub's mind to find out why he wanted to complain, why he thought there was reasonable cause to issue a complaint to start with," Board attorney Linda Rabin Hammell later recalled. "And yet I think they wanted to depose him to scare us, to scare him and to go on a fishing expedition. And O'Meara let them do it."[48]

To secure the injunction, the Board had to meet a two-pronged test: first, to show that there was "reasonable cause" to believe that the companies had committed unfair labor practices, and second, to show that it was "just and proper" to impose a temporary order to force them to reinstate the strikers even if it meant displacing the replacements. Under the relevant case law, the reasonable cause burden was "relatively insubstantial." The Board had only to show that the charges were not "frivolous" and to show "some evidence" that the violations did occur; conflicting evidence did not preclude a finding of reasonable cause. The District Court was not supposed to judge the entire case on its merits and did not have to rehear all of the evidence from the six-month-long trial. Rather, the court was supposed to defer to the Board's determination of the facts, and in this case it had the Wilks decision already before it.[49]

The "just and proper" criteria were more complex. Under the standard of the Sixth Circuit governing the District Court in eastern Michigan, relief was just and proper when it would restore the pre-violation status quo, serve the public interest, and further the remedial purpose of the National Labor Relations Act. Section 10(j) of the NLRA was not intended simply to vindicate the interests of private groups, but to serve the public interest by promoting the peaceful settlement of labor disputes through the collective bargaining process. "The public has a keen interest in a restoration of labor peace at their daily newspapers, whose embroilment in unfair labor practices has split and wracked this community," the Board said in its brief to the court. The companies' insistence on retaining the replacements had "created an insurmountable obstacle to reaching an agreement" and had allowed the employers to stonewall the unions and make regressive demands in negotiations. The NLRB cited DNA chief Frank Vega's statement that "it will be a cold day in hell before any mailers come back to work," and said that in November 1995 Vega had told employees that the companies would pursue the appeals for so long that the strikers in general "would either have to get other jobs, would retire or would be dead" before they would get their jobs back.[50]

The hearing finally commenced on August 1 at 10:00 AM in room 257 of the federal courthouse on Lafayette at Washington Boulevard, just across the street from the *Free Press* building. No witnesses testified at the session; the lawyers had filed briefs a week earlier and now made oral presentations before the judge. NLRB attorney Mark Rubin, arguing the case for the Board, said that the permanent replacements remained a barrier to a contractual settlement. "The newspapers' refusal to reinstate the strikers is causing the process to fail," he said. "What union could negotiate an agreement that leaves its members without good jobs?. . . The bargaining process is utterly failing because no progress is possible without reinstatement, and the company refuses to discuss the issue." The protracted strike and the lockout had strained the community, Rubin argued, and he accused the companies of trying "to starve the unions out" through delays. "The employers know they will probably be forced to reinstate the workers," he said, "but they know that the longer that process takes, the fewer will be coming back." When asked by O'Meara why the process of appeals shouldn't be allowed to run out, Rubin replied that it would undermine the Board's remedial power. "The papers haven't committed that they will obey the board's order," he told the judge. "In fact, it is clear they won't." The appeals process could take years and render the NLRB's decision meaningless as the unions weakened and the strikers simply gave up and moved away.[51]

Speaking for the newspapers, lead counsel Kramer said that the judge should let the litigation take its course. "I thought the rule of law is you at least have the right of appeal," he said. "That is a right we have." Kramer denied that the strikers were leaving the struggle and argued that the unions had to have been strong and well entrenched enough to carry on a strike for two years, a length of time determined, he said, by the unions alone. By contrast, he said, the employers would suffer more than $30 million in losses to reinstate the strikers, including an estimated $9.5 million in unemployment benefits for the displaced replacements. As for the delays, Kramer blamed the NLRB itself and said that the companies had asked the Board to expedite its hearing on the Wilks decision.[52]

Sam McKnight spoke for the unions. Between July 1995 and June 1997, he argued, the newspapers had rejected every effort by the unions, Mayor Archer, and other civic and religious leaders to reinstate the strikers and get the talks moving. "What does the company want?" McKnight asked. "The company wants to maintain its bargaining power . . . while it completes its mission of destroying the strikers." He said that he found it startling that Kramer had not used the words "settlement," "solution," "conclusion," or "resolution" and urged the judge to listen more carefully to the words of company executives than to the lawyers. He quoted DNA chief Frank Vega on the unions ("Those bastards will never get back in here") and noted that not a single mailer had yet been rehired, while only one reporter had returned to the *News*. Calling the newspapers "disciples of delay," McKnight said, "We are faced with a mountain of company arguments that they have the right to break the law and punish strikers until all of its appeals are exhausted. . . . These corporate giants have made it clear by their words and deeds that these workers and their unions are never coming back."[53]

"Not Good Process . . . Not Now": O'Meara's Decision

The hearing lasted only one day, and afterward the judge promised to have a ruling on the petition within ten days. On August 14, O'Meara issued his eighteen-page opinion, denying the injunction on both the reasonable cause and the just and proper grounds. In a critical move, O'Meara split the case against the newspapers in half, separating all of the violations adjudicated in the Wilks ruling (or what he called "Complaint I") from the April 1997 complaint, amended on July 2, for refusing to reinstate the strikers ("Complaint II"). Because the Board had based its request for a 10(j) on the refusal to reinstate, O'Meara set aside Wilks's decision on Complaint I and focused only on Complaint II. He then determined that the simple failure to reinstate the strikers was not itself illegal. The Board did not show reasonable cause that the companies had committed an unfair labor practice, the judge wrote, "because the refusal to reinstate striking workers is not an unfair labor practice without a final adjudication that the strike itself was an unfair labor practice strike." The Wilks ruling was not sufficient; the strikers would have to wait until the entire appeals process had answered "affirmatively and finally" whether unfair labor practices had occurred before the court would take action.[54]

O'Meara also rejected the petition on the just and proper standard. He denied that a failure to grant injunctive relief would erode union support, risk scattering former strikers, or create an impediment to bargaining. "No order of the court will predictably repair erosion and scattering which has occurred to date," the judge wrote. "The court does not recognize that speculation about further erosion and scattering can be a basis for concluding that failure to grant an injunction will frustrate the remedial powers of the Board." Finally, the judge found that retaining the replacements created no obstacle to the negotiations. "The parties have continued to bargain throughout the strike and remain unable to agree on hundreds of issues," he declared. "The Board has not provided evidence that the reinstatement issue has impeded bargaining progress."

O'Meara concluded by blaming the NLRB for the delays in the case, noting that the initial charges were filed even before the strike began more than two years earlier. "The Board now asks the court to plunge into this difficult and, in many ways, tragic, labor dispute and impose a final remedy two weeks after the case [Complaint II] was submitted to it at oral

argument." The judge scolded the Board for inappropriate procedure before dismissing the petition:

> Not good process. And not an appropriate use of section 10(j), and therefore
> not, as the court has ruled, "just and proper."
> The Board should expedite its review of this matter. It can be done. The
> reviewing court of appeals, if there is one, should also deal promptly with
> the issues brought to it. Only then should a remedy be imposed, if one is
> appropriate.
> Not now.[55]

Attorneys for the unions and the NLRB were astounded. Duane Ice
called the decision "extremely technical, hyper-technical," while Linda
Rabin Hammell later recalled that O'Meara "said we didn't have reasonable cause to believe the Act was violated—this after the [administrative
law] judge had already given us a win, and where the standard of proof is
so slender." General counsel Feinstein said that the facts "demonstrate
that an injunction is necessary to preserve the integrity of the bargaining
process," and NLRB officials quickly announced their intention to appeal
the ruling to the Sixth Circuit Appellate Court.[56]

Board chair Gould issued a statement expressing his "regret" at
O'Meara's decision and said that it appeared "to proceed upon erroneous
assumptions about fact and law." Gould reiterated that, "in most instances,
there has been no hearing, let alone an administrative law judge decision,
prior to the commencement or completion of a 10(j) proceeding." In this
case, however, Judge Wilks had already reviewed the facts and concluded
that the reinstatement issue impeded bargaining progress. On the law,
O'Meara had ruled that the reinstatement question could not be resolved
until there had been a "final" affirmative answer on the unfair labor strike
issue. "With all respect," wrote Gould, "this conclusion is in error and, if
accepted, would completely undercut Section 10(j). The striker reinstatement issue is one of liability rather than remedy."[57] Requiring the Board to
fully adjudicate a case before it could show reasonable cause ran counter
to the legislative history of section 10(j) and defeated the whole purpose of
temporary injunctive relief.[58]

O'Meara had said that no relief would repair any union erosion or scattering of strikers that had already occurred, and he refused to speculate
about any that might occur. Yet, in a July 6 affidavit, Local 2040 president
Alex Young said that prior to the strike his union "took in approximately
$20,000 a month in dues, assessments and referral fees. Currently the
union receives between $6,000 and $7,000 a month."[59] Indeed, the judge's

ruling seemed to allow that *no* degree of erosion or scattering, past or future, could be seen to affect the bargaining process or call for an injunction. But the refusal to reinstate the strikers did create obstacles to the negotiations, by making it difficult for the unions to communicate with their members and by forcing them to spend energy trying to get their members' jobs back, impeding progress on other issues.[60]

O'Meara also said that the parties had continued to bargain throughout the strike and remained unable to reach agreements. As the NLRB general counsel had argued, however, the employers' retention of the permanent replacements was precisely what empowered them to resist the unions at the bargaining table, making the negotiations almost meaningless. In a meeting with the DNA in May 1996, Teamsters International official Tom McGrath asked Tim Kelleher if there was *anything* the union could offer that would cause the company to bargain over reinstatement. Kelleher replied that the employers were not interested in bargaining over that subject.[61] With the newspapers flatly declaring that the strikers would not come back, what purpose was there in discussing contract terms? In their brief to the judge, the unions cited the statement of Sonny Shannon, international representative for the engravers local, regarding a bargaining session in October 1996. "I said to Jaske, What good are wages, hours and conditions if you didn't have jobs? Jaske just shrugged and didn't say anything."[62]

Beyond his idiosyncrasies as a judge, O'Meara's decision captured the ongoing conflict within the state, between the New Deal values embodied in the NLRB and the anti-union regime now anchored in the increasingly conservative federal courts. In the denial of the 10(j) petition, the court effectively displaced the Board's role of restoring the collective bargaining process and substituted a course of litigation that would inevitably return to the federal court of appeals for its ultimate resolution. The result tilted the balance of power toward those actors with greater resources and staying power—in this case, the corporations—and highlighted the erosion of the independence and authority of the NLRB. As Board attorney Sarah Pring wrote in a law journal article, "In a case where the employer openly bragged to reporters that it would 'go on without unions, or they can surrender unconditionally and salvage what they can,' the damage to the Board's ability to foster collective bargaining and maintain industrial peace should have been the court's main concern."[63] Instead, it focused on the employers' procedural rights as if the case were a traditional dispute between private groups, ignoring the public interest in sustaining the institutions of collective bargaining.

"Not good process," the judge said. "It can be done. . . . Not now." At the time of the ruling, some observers believed that it might take three to six more months for the full Board to reach a decision and seek expedited enforcement from the appellate court.[64] As it turned out, the case would remain in litigation for almost three more years. In 1995, DNA chief Frank Vega had predicted that the companies would drag out the appeals for so long that the strikers would eventually get other jobs, retire, or die. By and large, he was correct: talented journalists left the newspapers, taking with them years of professional experience, local knowledge, and public memory. Striking assistant features editor Renee Murawski, after fourteen years at the *Free Press*, got a job at *Newsday* on Long Island in New York and two years later joined the *New York Times*. Reporter Bob Ourlian, an eleven-year veteran at the *News*, was fired three times by the paper for alleged picket line misconduct; he left to go to work for the *Los Angeles Times*. His colleague Allan Lengel, also at the *News* for eleven years, was fired four times and later hired by the *Washington Post*.[65]

Many other experienced workers found work elsewhere or retired and never went back; by one estimate, only about one-third of the strikers had returned by the time the contracts were finally settled at the end of 2000.[66] In May 1998, the Sixth Circuit Court of Appeals upheld O'Meara's ruling and agreed that relief would not "be likely to have much effect on strikers who had already found better jobs or who had retired or relocated permanently, whether in this world or the next."[67] Notwithstanding the court's mordant wit, more than a few strikers did in fact die without ever getting their jobs back. Printer Suzanne Wozniak worked for more than twenty years in the *Free Press* composing room; she was sixty-four when she died. Art Janisch was a thirty-eight-year member of the press operators Local 13N; he died of a heart attack at age fifty-nine. Printers union local vice president Arthur Robbins also died of heart failure; he was sixty-two.[68] At the Action! Motown '97 rally in June 1997, MCNU head Al Derey held up a list of more than a dozen strikers who had died from various causes during the strike. "Not one of them crossed the line," he said.[69] For those and others like them, perhaps, their rights were truly scattered to the winds.

MOBILIZING HOPE: CIVIL SOCIETY AND THE ELUSIVE PUBLIC SPHERE

With the denial of the 10(j) injunction, the unions lost their last legal leverage to force the employers to respond before the appeals in the unfair labor practices case took their course. Meanwhile, the campaign of mobilization continued, including protest actions, the boycotts, and the publication of the *Sunday Journal*. As Teamster organizer Mike Zielinski recalled:

Throughout that period in '97 and '98, there was a group of activist strikers—I keep calling them "strikers" even though at that point the strike was officially over—but newspaper activists, really, rank-and-filers, who wanted to carry on actions regardless of whether the local leadership approved or not. And so quite a few actions in 1997 and 1998 were carried out and organized by this group of activists, rank-and-filers.[70]

In March 1998, ACOSS members launched a month-long "Spring Offensive" tour of cities in Canada and the United States to publicize the continuing dispute and promote the boycott of USA Today. Guild member Kate DeSmet and printer John Martin spoke at rallies in Windsor, St. Catharines, and Toronto, Ontario; Teamster Dennis Nazelli addressed the provincial convention of the Canadian Union of Public Employees in Alberta as part of a twelve-day swing through western Canada; and Local 18 member Barb Ingalls spent ten days in California and the Pacific Northwest, with stops at the San Francisco Central Labor Council and the King County Labor Council in Seattle. Altogether, the trips raised $4,800. "Everywhere I went," said Ingalls, "I was met by people who were aware of the Detroit Newspaper strike-lockout and were completely supportive."[71]

In September 1998, the Teamsters International union supported the creation of the Workers Justice Committee (WJC), led by Zielinski, to employ around fifty locked-out and fired newspaper workers as full-time activists. "They were sort of a full-time force," Zielinski recalled, "sort of a flying squad that could be mobilized on short notice for any kind of action opportunity, as well as to have more consistent pressure day in and day out on the scab papers."[72] In October, the group knocked on doors and gave out leaflets and lawn signs in suburban neighborhoods in Harper Woods, Roseville, Eastpointe, Dearborn, and Sterling Heights. "In the last three weeks, we have put out 15,000 fliers," said WJC member Randy Karpinen. "We normally do 5,000 houses a week when we turn to this door-to-door campaign." Over the next month, protesters also disrupted sale promotions of the News at area Big Boy restaurants, Starbucks Coffee shops, and Total gas stations.[73]

For their part, local community leaders again took the initiative to try to bring the parties toward a settlement. In March 1998, the Religious Leaders for Justice at the Detroit Newspapers began to ask local city councils to support a summit meeting where religious and political leaders could discuss ways to resolve the long-standing dispute.[74] "We needed something to boost the morale of workers who were just trying to survive, and to gather the support that we knew was out there in the community, to basically have a revival of community support for people who were locked out of their jobs," said lead organizer Rev. Ed Rowe of Detroit's Central

United Methodist Church.[75] By late April, more than a dozen local governments, including Clinton Township, Dearborn Heights, Madison Heights, Roseville, Taylor, and Westland, had passed resolutions pledging to take part in the meeting, scheduled for May 18 at the Sacred Heart Major Seminary in Detroit.[76] Macomb County commissioner Mickey Switalski said the effort showed "the community reaching out to the newspapers and saying 'come on, sit down with these workers and resolve this thing.'" He added, "I think the community has to stand up and say, 'This is not right. This has to stop.' Now's the time. This has gone on more than 1,000 days. How can we let this go on in our community?"[77]

On the day of the summit, representatives from twenty-four area city councils and the Macomb, Oakland, and Wayne County commissions were in attendance, along with religious leaders, union officials, and a crowd of around three hundred. Almost all of the political leaders spoke of the difficulty of conducting public business without access to the local dailies. "The communities are not aware of what's going on in government. People of principle are not talking to or reading [the *News* and *Free Press*]," said Oakland County commissioner Jeff Kingzett. Wayne County commissioner Kay Beard agreed, saying, "I think having the religious leaders call the summit must be of concern to these two conglomerates." Noticeably absent, however, were any executives from the newspapers, who in a May 14 letter declined the invitation to participate but expressed a willingness to meet afterward with organizers to hear the results of the discussion. Mayor Aldo Vagnozzi of Farmington Hills agreed to write to the companies about a follow-up session, and Reverend Rowe promised further actions. Rev. Bill Wylie-Kellerman observed that two things emerged from the summit: "One, this thing is not over, and, two, it needs to be."[78]

The mobilization was not over, but as time went on the unions faced an uphill battle. As former strikers left town or slowly returned to work at the newspapers, they became less available to engage in organizing or collective action, and without direct contact or visible demonstrations, public awareness was much harder to sustain. Telemarketers for the DNA repeatedly and inaccurately told prospective customers that the dispute was ended, and after 1997 the *News* and *Free Press* essentially stopped covering union protests, leading the weekly *Metro Times* to declare the strike-lockout the "most ignored local story" in Detroit news media for 1998.[79] Armand Nevers was a discharged printer and among those who did door-to-door outreach. He said, "People tell us, 'We thought the strike was over, we thought you were back to work.'"[80]

There were other breaks in the public narrative of the dispute. *News* editor and publisher Bob Giles announced his retirement in May 1997, three months after the unions' offer to return. The sixty-three-year-old Giles was replaced by Mark Silverman, a bland and colorless manager brought up from Gannett's *Louisville Courier-Journal*, where he had been executive editor for little more than a year. Silverman continued to carry out Gannett's policies at the *News* but was far less controversial as a spokesperson than Giles had been.[81] In July 1998, the *Free Press* transferred its editorial departments out of its iconic seventy-three-year-old building on Lafayette and into the back of the *News* building on Fort Street. The move was a long-planned consolidation of resources, but *Free Press* journalists remained apprehensive. Reporter and returned striker Bill McGraw said, "What bothers me is the widely held perception among the public that the *Free Press* and the *News* are one paper," with little difference in their editorial content or labor practices.[82]

Further changes came from within the unions. In December 1998, after nearly two years of internal conflict and government intervention, James P. Hoffa, son of the legendary James R. Hoffa, won a reconducted election to become president of the Teamsters International union. Hoffa took office determined to clean house of supporters of his predecessor, Ron Carey, and to bring the Detroit struggle to an end. Among the casualties of the shake-up was Mike Zielinski of the Workers Justice Committee, who was fired in April 1999.[83] Finally, in November 1999, the *Detroit Sunday Journal* announced that it would cease publication after November 21, the fourth anniversary of the paper's launch. Since the unconditional offer to return, the weekly tabloid had continually lost staff as former strikers were called back or moved on to other jobs elsewhere, and its "quality had diminished and our ability to circulate it had diminished," said publisher and former striker Tom Schram. In its first year, the *Sunday Journal* reached a peak circulation of 300,000 and averaged forty-eight pages; at the end, its circulation had faded to a reported 37,000.[84]

THE STATE AGAINST ITSELF: THE NLRB VERSUS THE APPEALS COURT

Without a strike, and with dwindling mobilization capacity, the unions nonetheless retained the leverage of the newspapers' potential back pay liability for failing to immediately rehire all of the former strikers. By February 1998, one year after the unconditional offer to return, the employers claimed that 890 union members were still on the recall list. The unions, however, said that the figure was much higher and that it should include workers the companies had excluded, such as those who had been fired, those who turned down offers that were not substantially equivalent to their prestrike positions, and those who elected to wait until all union members were reinstated. Company documents showed that by the end of October 1998, 222 strikers had been fired, 216 had declined what the companies called substantially equivalent offers, and 364 had declined nonsubstantially equivalent offers. At the DNA, only 53 of 297 striking mailers (18 percent) and 191 of 960 striking members of Teamsters Local 372 (20 percent) had actually returned to work.[85] Union attorneys estimated that the potential back pay award might be one of the largest in U.S. history, but warned that the process could take several more years. "I will start looking at back pay when we have a final judgment that cannot be appealed," said NLRB regional director Schaub, "or when the parties come to me and say they're ready to settle."[86]

On November 7, 1997, NLRB judge William Kocol found the employers guilty of the charge of failing to reinstate the strikers immediately upon the unconditional offer to return (O'Meara's "Complaint II"). Kocol's order, however, merely joined the queue awaiting the full adjudication of the earlier consolidated charges against the newspapers ("Complaint I").[87] As the process moved to the full NLRB in Washington, DC, the political stakes surrounding the case intensified. For three years the Republican majority in Congress had been pressuring the Board, limiting its budget, holding up nominations of its members, and criticizing its practices in legislative subcommittee hearings.[88] In March 1997, four Republican senators had signed a letter to Board chair Gould expressing concern over the request for a 10(j) injunction in the Detroit case. The DNA filed a motion to recuse Gould from participating in the appeal decision based on his public statements and opinion in support of the 10(j) petition, but as chair he denied the motion. Finally, on August 27, 1998, the very last day of Gould's term in office, the Board issued its decision finding the newspapers guilty of unfair labor practices that had caused the strike.[89]

Like the Wilks decision, the Board's ruling was not an undivided victory for the unions. It upheld the judge's dismissal of the charge on the printers' jurisdiction, although not for the same reasons. It agreed that the DNA's proposal was a lawfully mandatory subject, but disagreed on the printers' memorandum of agreement: the MOA was not an open-ended contract and would expire when the last lifetime job-holder ceased to work for the DNA. However, the Board decided that the language of the MOA did not conclusively define the union's jurisdiction and so did not preclude the DNA's insistence on its proposal. In addition, the Board overturned the judge's ruling on the DNA's withdrawal from joint bargaining. The majority held that there was no evidence of an "unequivocal agreement" by both sides to be bound by the joint arrangement, so that the legal rules governing such agreements did not apply. The DNA was not pre-

vented from negotiating the joint bargaining issues with each union individually, and its departure from the joint agreement was an attempt "to
accelerate, not delay, the bargaining process and to achieve, not frustrate,
the completion of collective-bargaining agreements."[90] Finally, over
Gould's strong dissent, the Board also severed the charge on the employers' unilateral setting of terms and conditions for the replacements and
reserved a decision on it for a future date. Several months later, well after
Gould's term had expired, the Board voted three-to-two to dismiss the
charge.[91]

The Board's decision thus removed two of the three principal issues in
the unfair labor practice case, leaving only the Guild's charges of bad-faith
bargaining against the *News*. There, however, the Board agreed with Judge
Wilks on the refusal by the *News* to provide information on the overtime
exemption and its unlawful declaration of impasse on the merit pay plan.
Further, the Board applied the recent 1997 appeals court decision in a case
involving the McClatchy newspaper chain ("McClatchy II") to find that
"the unilateral implementation of this proposal, without definable objective procedures and criteria, was inherently destructive of the statutory
collective-bargaining process" and therefore violated the law. As a result,
the Board agreed that the strike was caused by the employers' unfair labor
practices, in a unanimous decision supported by the three Democratic
members, Gould, Sarah Fox, and Wilma Liebman, and the two recently
appointed Republicans, Peter Hurtgen and J. Robert Brame, both of whom
were thought to be hard-line management advocates.[92] The Board ordered
the papers to reinstate the strikers to their former jobs and to pay back
wages, now estimated by the unions to be around $80 million, for any
strikers not reinstated from the date of the offer to return.[93]

As expected, the newspapers immediately announced that they would
appeal the decision. Union leaders expressed hope that the order would
spur the negotiations, but the two sides remained far apart. In a 1998 progress report to employees, DNA chief Vega wrote, "We will continue to
meet with the unions to discuss our differences. But in reality, because of
the lack of desire on the part of union leadership to reach a settlement,
many of the disagreements we have with the unions will likely be settled
in the courts over the next several years."[94] In the interim, some movement
did occur, but within the companies' pattern of seeking to eliminate the
striking workforce. In March 1998, Local 372 members approved an agreement with management to solve a problem of overfunding in a jointly
administered pension plan. The settlement provided enhanced benefits
and allowed early retirement for around 110 members with twenty-five to
twenty-nine years' seniority, or about 10 percent of the local's member-

ship. At that point, however, the union had not engaged in bargaining for a new contract with the DNA in more than a year, since the company declared impasse and imposed conditions in March 1997.[95]

In March 1998, the printers union voted forty-nine to thirty-four to reject a buyout offer from the DNA, which would have been available to eighty-five unit members but excluded those who had been fired during the strike or who were over sixty-five and whom the company would not take back. "It was a very emotional meeting," former Local 18 president David Gray said of the vote. "The people have been out there for 2½ years. A lot would just like to leave. . . . But the local has been united for 2½ years. To let the newspapers divide us, we just can't let that happen."[96] A year later, the printers ratified a partial contract agreement with the DNA that provided for buyouts that included those who had been previously excluded. Within a few months, sixty-two members accepted the offers and retired, leaving only thirty-four full-time printers at the company. The printers' contract also mandated an open shop and provided an annual pay increase of 2 percent with a me-too provision if the DNA agreed to a higher increase in joint bargaining with the other unions. Finally, in April 1999, the small, twenty-member engravers local reached a deal for similar terms, with buyouts offered to eight members with lifetime job guarantees.[97]

MCNU head Al Derey said that the companies were flexible with the printers because their goal was to "get the lifetime job guarantees out of the system."[98] They had no such goal for larger units like the Teamsters and the Guild, however, and hundreds of former strikers remained locked out. On December 17, 1999, NLRB administrative law judge Richard Scully issued a decision ordering the reinstatement of some fifty unlawfully discharged strikers, including eighteen of the participants in the nonviolent sit-in at the *News* on Labor Day weekend in 1996.[99] The companies appealed many of the reinstatement orders, however, and more than six months after Scully's decision, none of the illegally fired workers had yet been returned to their jobs.[100] In August 1999, the DNA and the *News* also asked the Board to dismiss a consolidated complaint involving an additional fifty-nine discharged employees and even filed a complaint in federal district court seeking to enjoin the prosecution of the unfair labor practices in that case.[101] The DNA pursued the litigation up to 2006, when the U.S. Supreme Court declined to review an appellate court ruling affirming the reinstatement orders in the Scully decision.[102]

Nevertheless, as the newspapers continued to appeal the Board's ruling on the Wilks decision, and as the back pay clock continued to run, there were rumors that an agreement might finally be worked out. At one point, Guild attorney Ice later recalled, the newspapers made an informal offer of more than $30 million to settle the case. "But strikers would not be re-turned to work," he said.

> They would continue to be treated as economic strikers who would return if there were vacancies. So the $30 million would in effect be severance pay, retraining expense. And the strikers would walk away. They'd then be given a lot of money to walk away. . . . And by the way, every dischargee would remain discharged, no matter how petty the offense. No amnesty, no return to work. But a lot of money.[103]

The deal never came close to realization. As Ice observed, "The princi-ple was, are we going to bargain a contract, and who gets the jobs? There's no way to compromise that. And the unions were not going to take money to just walk away and abandon the strikers."

Whose Discretion? The Court of Appeals Ruling

In the end, the decision would be made by the D.C. Circuit Court of Ap-peals. The unions were encouraged by the court's opinions in a pair of decisions in the *McClatchy* case that were cited by the Board and seemed a close parallel to the Guild's complaint at the *News*. In contract negotiations at its papers in Sacramento and Modesto, California, the McClatchy com-pany had proposed a merit pay plan giving management full discretion over wage increases. For each merit evaluation, the union could make nonbinding comments and participate in an appeal process at the employ-ee's request, but the decisions were excluded from the contractual griev-ance and arbitration procedure. After negotiations on the plan failed to reach agreement, McClatchy declared impasse and began granting merit raises without consulting the union. In 1992 the D.C. Circuit Court re-jected the NLRB's decision in favor of the union, but it remanded the case to the Board for further consideration ("*McClatchy I*"). The Board eventu-ally concluded that the company's implementation of the plan "bypasse[d] the Guild in its role as employee bargaining representative" and as such was "antithetical to our statutory system of collective bargaining meant to promote industrial stability." In 1997 the appellate court upheld the Board's revised ruling ("*McClatchy II*").[104]

In the Detroit case, the appeal also went to the D.C. Circuit, and oral arguments were scheduled for May 4, 2000, before a three-judge panel of Laurence Silberman, James Buckley, and David Sentelle. All three judges were Republicans appointed by President Ronald Reagan, but Silberman stood out because he had actually authored the court's majority opinion in *McClatchy II*. The D.C. Circuit was considered to be a conservative bench, particularly with regard to labor matters, but overall the U.S. Court of Appeals upheld the NLRB more than 85 percent of the time, according to union attorneys. "I hope these judges will apply established NLRB and federal law to this case," said the unions' Sam McKnight, "because, if they do that, we will prevail."[105]

They did not prevail. The court issued its decision on July 7, and on the crucial charges against the *News* it ruled that the *McClatchy II* precedent did not apply and that the *News* did not engage in bad-faith bargaining with the Guild. In an opinion written by Judge Silberman, the court recognized that the Board could legitimately proceed to develop the legal doctrine established by *McClatchy II*, but it rejected the Board's "blithe extension" of it to this case as "unreasoned and unreasonable." The *News*'s proposal did not compare with the one in *McClatchy*, the court said, because it gave a general outline of the size of the merit pool, based increases on performance evaluations, and allowed employees to grieve the results.

While the court rejected the application of *McClatchy II* to the Detroit case, the Board had also ruled that the *News*'s bad-faith conduct in negotiations had contributed to causing the strike. The court acknowledged that "the Board's finding of bad faith negotiation is, like any question of fact (really a mixed question), entitled to a good deal of deference." However, it then proceeded to engage in a point-by-point rebuttal of the judgment of the ALJ and the Board, based on its own extensive rewriting of the narrative account of the facts in the case.

The court accepted the employer's argument that the Guild refused to bargain on key issues and concluded that the union's repeated questions on the details of the *News*'s proposals were simply stalling. "With the exception of a proposal for an across-the-board pay increase made on May 3 the Guild does not appear to have done anything at these negotiation sessions but ask questions," Judge Silberman wrote. "There was no evidence that the Guild was prepared to engage in real negotiations on the employer's proposals." The Board had found that the *News* "repeatedly obfuscated and withheld details about its merit pay proposal, which details were relevant and necessary to the Guild's understanding of the proposal and to the formulation of a bargaining response." But the court said that the company did not have to give any information beyond the bare details it had already disclosed. The essence of discretion, the court said, "implies that the employer will not be pinned down ex ante as to precisely how its discretion will be exercised."

> The union's questions as to these criteria and procedures were obviously designed to narrow the zone of discretion the employer wished to preserve. That answers satisfactory to the union or the Board were not forthcoming is simply another way to say that the proposal carried insufficient details to

pass the McClatchy test, and we have already rejected the Board's reasoning in that respect.

In at least half a dozen other instances, the court disregarded evidence of the *News*'s bad-faith conduct as "wholly insignificant" or "simply wrong" and substituted its own interpretation. The court concluded by saying that the Board's ruling that the *News* committed unfair labor practices was "legally erroneous and unsupported by substantial evidence" and so reversed the order holding the strikers to be unfair labor practice strikers.[106]

The decision came as a shock to many in the labor community. "This is a very snarling, hostile opinion," said former Board chair Gould. "We [the NLRB] put together an opinion that was nearly unanimous on all the issues, with the two Republicans supporting the three Democrats."[107] To critics, the differences the court held with the case in *McClatchy II* seemed trivial, and the "objective procedures" it found in the *News*'s proposal flimsy. "It was good enough [for Silberman] that Gannett told us there is a pot of money, but we will decide who gets it and how much. To him, that was good faith bargaining," said the Guild's Lou Mleczko.[108] It was hard to see what criteria really bound the *News*'s authority; the court acknowledged that under the proposal raises were not even necessarily tied to evaluations, but said that was permissible within management's discretion. The court noted that employees "would also be permitted to contest the size of their raises using grievance procedures," but without a right to arbitration the employer could easily make that process an empty gesture. Silberman here seemed to backtrack on his earlier *McClatchy II* ruling, radically limiting its scope and leaving employers with broad discretion that effectively individualized bargaining over wages.

In *McClatchy II*, Silberman wrote, "we think the appropriate course, keeping in mind the Board's 'primary responsibility for developing and applying national labor policy,' is to defer to the Board's interpretation of the Act."[109] In this case, former *News* reporter Bob Ourlian observed, "the judges simply chose not to agree." The court was not required to rubber-stamp the Board's decisions, but as Board attorney Pring noted, it was not supposed to "substitute [its] judgment for the Board's 'with respect to issues that Congress intended the Board should resolve,' such as alleged violations of the duty to bargain in good faith."[110] Former Board chair Gould remained indignant: "The Court of Appeals was ingenious in looking for some sort of argument or fact that could disturb our findings and conclusions," he said. "What the court did was extraordinary and inexplicable on any grounds other than political philosophy."[111]

Although disappointed by the court's decision, attorneys for the Board and the unions decided not to appeal the ruling to the Supreme Court or to the full Court of Appeals en banc; such a move would probably have been a long shot anyway. In August, however, they filed petitions asking the D.C. Circuit to remand the case to the Board to allow it to clarify its position, as it had done in the *McClatchy I* case. "The proper course in case by case development of the *McClatchy* doctrine would be for the Board to address the factual differences—identified as relevant by this Court—between the merit pay proposal in this case and the merit pay proposals in *McClatchy*," said the unions. The three-judge panel of Silberman, Buckley, and Sentelle swiftly denied the request.[112]

"If there were a remand, and each party felt vulnerable in its legal position, I think there would've been increased odds of a settlement," Duane Ice later speculated. "We would have gotten some clarification on these issues; there would've been another opportunity for each party to try to resolve it. But that ended it in favor of the employers." The newspapers, meanwhile, wasted no time in reacting to the court's July 7 decision. On July 11, four days after the order overturning the NLRB, the DNA rescinded every one of the proposals it had made in bargaining with the unions in the previous fourteen months.[113]

CONCLUSION: THE DEINSTITUTIONALIZATION OF LABOR

The long, drawn-out litigation over the unfair labor practice charges in the Detroit newspaper strike vividly illustrates the process of institutional grating and displacement between opposing legal orders. The gradual elimination of the charges against the employers—from Judge Wilks's dismissal of the printers' complaint to the NLRB's rejection of the joint bargaining charge, to the appellate court's decision overturning the Board on the *News* proposal—demonstrates the steady shift in the law from its New Deal origins to the ascendant anti-union regime. The results signaled the historic decline in the National Labor Relations Board's traditional role and the return of judicial repression in American labor relations.

That conflict was played out inside the state in the relationship between the NLRB and the courts. The unions twice won their case within the administrative law process of the NLRB, but twice were turned back by federal judges in U.S. district court and the appellate court. The long delays in the appeals process favored the newspapers for two reasons. First, the dominant institutional logic and norms governing the case shifted, as the employers had always trusted would happen, when it moved from one venue to another. Second, the unions' primary leverage, their capacity for mobilization, became harder to sustain as the appeals dragged on. *After the unions' unconditional offer to return to work, the litigation on the un-*

fair labor practice charges went on for more than twice as long as the actual strike itself lasted.

The question was not simply one of individual judges' ideology, but of the institutional place of unionism under the law. The National Labor Relations Act emphasizes the societal value of workers' self-organization, the public's interest in the defense of collective bargaining as an institution, and the Board's role as an expert agency in remediating the process of negotiation.[114] Both the district court and the court of appeals, however, appeared to discount the distinctive nature of the Act's goals, opting instead to focus on the narrow procedural rights of the employers and to decollectivize the relationship between the employer and employees. Their decisions reflected the deinstitutionalization of unions under the current labor law regime. The substantive displacement of labor was visibly embodied in this case in the dual workforces created by the companies' use of permanent replacements and their refusal to reinstate the strikers after the offer to return to work. The majority of the strikers were treated as second-class citizens, left out on the street (or in an empty "decomposing room"), and forced to give up their rights or risk the disintegration of their status as a collective body—as a union.

If the unions suffered from deinstitutionalization, however, the norms of labor solidarity were preserved not only in their formal organizations but also in civil society at large. Time and again, mobilization exceeded routine channels. The Action! Motown '97 rally invoked the cultural values of solidarity and community and defied the papers' framing of the return to work as an act of "surrender," while the 1998 community summit reasserted the public's independent interest in the settlement of the dispute. But if mobilization was not reducible to proper channels, neither was it completely free of institutional context, and civic actors searched for adequate mechanisms to get the newspapers to respond. As Rev. Ed Rowe said later, "I think that in many of the issues, had we, had the collective bargaining process, been allowed to have its way, that community support would have made a difference. It would have brought people back to the table."[115] At least some form of "table" was necessary, but in this case that was part of the problem.

When negotiations resumed after the court's decision, the newspapers reverted to form, repudiating past relationships and bargaining from a take-it-or-leave-it position. In August 2000, the DNA began meeting again with the press operators and Local 372, but refused to engage in joint bargaining with all the unions.[116] On August 30, Jaske wrote a letter addressed to Jack Howe as the representative of the MCNU. "We have given each union a complete contract proposal for a 3-year agreement including wage increases of 2 percent each year," the letter said, although the contracts offered no amnesty or review for fired strikers and included the demand for an open shop. "Negotiations have deadlocked over union demands to re-litigate discharges for strike-related misconduct and to force workers to join a union against their will," Jaske wrote. "We will have *no* further proposals on these two subjects." Jaske delivered the letter to the unions on August 30 and then left town without further discussion.[117]

Howe replied on September 1. "The unions have not declared deadlock and are not deadlocked on any issues," he said. "We can only assume that you are declaring 'deadlock' for your own purposes." The unions had proposed an expedited arbitration process, not amnesty or relitigation, for discharged strikers. The 1999 Scully decision covered less than half of the more than two hundred fired workers, and the papers were fighting to appeal reinstatement orders on dozens of them, including those fired for nonviolent civil disobedience at the Labor Day 1996 rally at the *News*.[118] The majority of the fired strikers had never had any review of their cases; the companies terminated the arbitration process when they canceled the contracts with the unions in July 1995. In addition, Howe wrote, the unions were not proposing to force employees to join against their will; such closed shop provisions were prohibited by law, as Jaske well knew. The unions proposed an "agency shop," an arrangement whereby employees represented by a union pay a part of the cost of collective bargaining. The companies already had such an agreement with the five small craft unions that did not participate in the strike.[119]

The parties met a few more times, but not much really changed. By November, the press operators and the Guild had joined the printers and the engravers in ratifying agreements, and on December 17 the Teamsters Locals 372 and 2040 voted to accept the contracts. The settlements included open shop clauses, a wage reduction for the mailers of $5 per hour from before the strike, and merit pay instead of scheduled increases for nearly all Guild members at the *News*. For the roughly 150 remaining fired strikers, management offered an internal review of each case but retained final discretion.[120] "The ratifications make sure there is still a union at the paper," said MCNU spokesperson Shawn Ellis. "Are these contracts as good as they were prior to 1995? No. But it's better than no contract at all." The two sides agreed to drop the unions' civil rights lawsuit and the companies' RICO charges, and Teamsters International president James P. Hoffa announced the end of the circulation and advertising boycotts.[121] After five and a half years, the Detroit newspaper strike was over.

PART IV | Governing the Workplace: American Labor Today

Chapter 12 | Conclusion:
A Signal Juncture

CONVENTIONAL NEWS ACCOUNTS of labor issues, media scholar Christopher Martin writes, commonly tell a story organized by certain value assumptions, or "frames." Among these frames are, first, the idea that the "consumer is king," meaning that readers are addressed in terms of the values of individual private consumption. Second, the experience of consumption is divorced from the process of production. Except for the occasional scandal affecting consumer safety, *how* goods and services arrive in the market is generally invisible and not a matter of public concern. Since production is mostly offstage, the principal actors in the economy appear instead to be the top business executives and financial entrepreneurs, like the "heroic" Wall Street traders and corporate CEOs who dominate the daily business news. For everyone else, it is presumed, the labor market is meritocratic and mobility is the result of individual choice—workers who do not like their job can and should simply get another. By contrast, collective economic action, by definition, is bad and upsets the "natural" equilibrium of the free market.[1]

As Martin argues, these assumptions inform the ways in which the news media typically cover labor disputes, especially strikes. For example, underlying conflicts of interest between business and labor are often left unexamined in favor of the clash of personalities among management and union leaders. As a result, strikes often appear to be unnecessary or ego-driven conflicts that might be resolved if only the union "bosses" would return to the table. Reports of negotiations highlight the employers' market-driven "offers," while union "demands" seem like unreasonable claims for special privilege. The government, meanwhile, stands apart and is mainly responsible for minimizing public (that is, consumer) inconvenience and the threat of disorder, even if this means forcing strikers to return to work.

259

Not all journalists are constrained by such stereotypes, but frames like these could be found in much of the news coverage and the popular perception of the Detroit strike. If only a different set of union leaders had been in charge, for instance, they would not have blundered their way into a strike. If only the *Free Press* or Knight-Ridder management had stood up for journalistic values, they might have restrained Gannett. If only Coleman Young had still been in office as mayor of Detroit, he would have been able to knock heads and make everyone come to their senses. These kinds of narratives are familiar, but they also reduce the struggles of entire industries and communities to the personalities and egos of a few (usually) men. In addition, hidden within them are traditional social science and legal concepts that continue to shape our understanding of strikes. Collective bargaining is a private contest with a stable set of participants and rules, like a regular Friday night poker game among friends. The two sides play their hands according to their best information, and strikes are just another tactic that union leaders use to win more at the table. Strikers "gamble" on the success of the strike, in the words of Supreme Court justice Sandra Day O'Connor, and bear the full risks of a losing bet.[2] The state is a neutral umpire, and members of the public have no stake in the outcome, except as it might interfere with their own private consumption.

As the experience in Detroit shows, we need a different approach. The newspaper strike was an exceptional case, but as such it allows us to reconsider these issues in a new light. In this book, I have used a critical engagement with strike theory in order to challenge the conventional wisdom about strikes and labor relations in the United States. In this conclusion, I begin by revisiting the theoretical debate in order to generate new propositions for the current era.

AN EXCEPTIONAL CASE: EXPLAINING THE NEWSPAPER STRIKE

Conventional economic theories of strikes focus on communication or information failures in bargaining, but these were not the central problems in Detroit. The six unions had existed at the newspapers for decades, they had bargained both individually and jointly with management, and they had engaged in more than sixty negotiating sessions in the several months before the strike. The differences between the two sides were hardly a mystery; union leaders had foreseen a confrontation as early as 1989, with the formation of the two papers' joint operating agency. Rather, the two sides were simply operating under different sets of rules.

For the unions, the key issues igniting the 1995 strike were not wages but complaints of employer unfair labor practices. Two of the complaints involved unilateral changes limiting the unions' ability to bargain over compensation and working conditions, and the third was in defense of the joint bargaining procedure that had led successfully to a contract in 1992. "This strike has never really been about money, or even about the number of workers to be bought out or laid off," declared the editors of the *Detroit Sunday Journal* in its inaugural issue. "Management has demanded or implemented policies that would virtually wipe unions off the playing field by denying representation to hundreds of employees or denying unions the ability to negotiate wages and other substantive issues."[3]

In short, the strike was fundamentally not about the traditional dollars and cents, but about the control of the workplace and the future of the bargaining relationship. In the 1995 contract negotiations, the newspapers followed neither standard economic concession schedules nor the customary rituals of give-and-take at the table. With an aggressive agenda for restructuring, the Detroit Newspaper Agency had begun preparing to break any potential strike immediately upon signing the 1992 contract. Over the next two and a half years, DNA managers traveled to and consulted with other papers across the country and developed a detailed strike operations strategy embodied in two thick three-ring binders. In November 1994, they went to San Francisco to observe the *Chronicle* and *Examiner* strike, and by January 1995 they had begun outreach to the Sterling Heights police, well before the negotiations with the unions even started.

Never before (or since) had the papers made such efforts in anticipation of a strike. As Alan Lenhoff, the newspapers' director of planning and development, recalled, "It started really long before the contract talks started, and a commitment was made to do a very complete planning job in any event. So there was never a point that the negotiating team came back from the table and said, 'Things aren't looking good, you have to start planning hard.' We were doing it regardless."[4] Once the strike began, the companies only increased their demands, publicly taunting the unions and making a negotiated settlement even less likely. None of the top executives interviewed for this book could recall any conversations in which they seriously considered compromising with the unions' position in order to end the strike quickly or minimize its economic and social costs.

If the strike did not follow a standard economic logic, neither did it display the patterns of stable institutional incorporation predicted by traditional political-organizational theory. The process of the 1995 negotiations already indicated basic changes in the relationship between management and labor. The unions were especially alarmed by the employers' declaration of impasse and imposition of conditions, a dramatic departure

from previous contract talks at the newspapers. "After decades of bargaining, nobody could recall any instance when these employers, the *News*
and *Free Press*, or any other newspaper in Detroit, had bargained to impasse and used the ultimate leverage under the NLRA, basically declaring
an end to collective bargaining," said Duane Ice, attorney for the local
Newspaper Guild. "It meant the unions had no role in the outcome. Basically an employer would go through the motions, bargain impasse, and
say, 'Well, here are the terms and conditions. We're done.'"[5]

Far from assuming institutional stability, the unions believed that their
organizational survival was at stake. Hence, their commitment persisted
despite obvious weaknesses. As a work stoppage, the strike never fully
succeeded in halting the production and distribution of the newspapers.
Union leaders tacitly acknowledged their inability to stop production, relying instead on the circulation and advertising boycotts and on the legal
case. Yet, despite such odds, the unions were able to mobilize considerable
resources against the newspapers. Solidarity reached beyond traditional
boundaries, bringing together the diverse blue-collar, white-collar, and
skilled craft workers in the Metropolitan Council of Newspaper Unions,
winning support from local consumers, residents, and civic and political
leaders, and enlisting the participation of regional and national labor
organizations.

Once the battle entered into the larger community, the normal rules and
channels were again called into question. The unions pressed the boundaries of public space to find ways to challenge the employers, and the
employers pushed back to try to limit that space; meanwhile, other, non-
union actors arose to claim a role as stakeholders in the dispute. Mobilization continued even after the return to work in February 1997 in civic displays like the Action! Motown '97 demonstration and the 1998 community
summit. As the years went on and the struggle shifted to the legal case, the
central issue became how to interpret and apply the rules themselves. The
conflict between competing institutional norms was reproduced within
the state in the opposition between the NLRB and the federal courts.

Events like these reveal important shifts not grasped by conventional
strike theories. In this book, I adopt a three-dimensional framework of
economy, state, and civil society to trace the causes and meaning of strike
mobilization across different time periods. This approach historicizes the
debate between the traditional economic and political theories of strikes:
thus, the economic analysis shifts from the micro-dynamics of behavior in
negotiations to the larger responses of actors to market pressures on the
employment relationship. Politically, the assumption of mature union incorporation or co-optation gives way to historical variability and the con-

sequences of deinstitutionalization. Finally, bringing civil society back in illustrates how the meaning of strike action has changed in the post-accord era. In the United States, the strike has been transformed from a strategic bargaining mechanism and protected legal right into a more basic struggle, across the economy, state, and civil society, to reconstitute the spaces governing labor relations and workers' rights.

THE SIGNAL JUNCTURE: WHY AND HOW
THE STRIKE HAPPENED

As an episode of labor strife, the Detroit newspaper strike exhibits features of what I call a "signal juncture," or a moment when competing institutional paths "collide" in a particular setting or locale. In Detroit, the intersection of economic, political, and cultural forces led to an intense confrontation between the newspaper corporations and the unions of their employees. The resulting conflict embodied the clash of opposing models of workplace governance: the norms and rules of the postwar labor accord, on the one hand, and the rising post-1980 anti-union regime, on the other.

The Collision of Paths in Detroit

In the last decades of the twentieth century, the local newspaper business was transformed by the shift to publicly traded stock ownership, by repeated waves of mergers and acquisitions, and by exposure to market pressures on a corresponding scale. During this time, the most profitable chains enjoyed operating margins of 20 percent or better, while demands for immediate high returns fueled an aggressive cost-cutting and downsizing of the workplace. Gannett, the largest newspaper group in the nation, operated about 80 percent non-union, typifying the new corporate model.[6] Its entry into Detroit was the "trigger" that brought the union avoidance path directly into the area's newspaper market. The creation of the DNA in November 1989 set up a new monopoly agency and an inevitable confrontation with the unions at the bargaining table.

As carriers of the anti-union model, Gannett managers dominated the negotiations and saw the existing contracts as an infringement on their unilateral authority. No other actors from Knight-Ridder or the *Free Press* were prepared to moderate this stance, nor were any other business leaders in Detroit's civic ecology willing or able to intervene. The region was home to the Big Three American automakers, some of the largest corporations in the world. Yet the Big Three looked far beyond the world of Detroit, which lacked the kind of tight-knit, locally oriented business elite that might have acted to mediate the conflict or broker a settlement. Even the Detroit Chamber of Commerce initially took a hands-off position toward the dispute, much to the displeasure of the DNA.[7]

As in other major strikes of the 1980s and early 1990s, the newspaper strike was driven by the restructuring demands of a profitable major national corporation. Unlike many of those conflicts, however, the Detroit strike occurred in a large metropolitan area that was still very much a union town. From Detroit to Ann Arbor and Flint, southeastern Michigan had one of the highest densities of union membership in the nation. The area was crisscrossed with an active network of local affiliates of the UAW and other unions, and the share of labor households provided a sizable foundation of popular support. The unions' historic concentration at the newspapers, an urban service sector deeply embedded in the daily life of the community, further ensured the dispute's high profile in the local public sphere.

As much as anywhere else in the nation, in 1995 the framework of postwar industrial labor relations held strong in Detroit. The leaders in the MCNU were experienced negotiators within that framework and had access to advisers who were veterans of some of the landmark struggles of the era. As the talks began to break down, the unions filed unfair labor practice charges to try to preserve their rights under the law. Only after the companies refused to extend the old contracts and the *News* unilaterally imposed its merit pay plan did the unions set a strike deadline. Refusing to concede, local leaders placed their faith in the ULP charges and the boycott. Thus, the economic power of two large national corporations collided with the institutions of unionism and the culture of labor solidarity in the region. The competing postwar paths of collective bargaining and union avoidance clashed directly with each other, and the conflict poured out into the courts and the streets.

SIGNALING CHANGE: STRIKE MOBILIZATION AND OUTCOMES

This sequence of events explains *why* the strike happened at the particular juncture that it did. Its signal character is illustrated in *how* the events of the strike played out across the arenas of economy, state, and civil society. The Detroit strike was a milestone in post-accord American labor relations, and a measure of the rising dominance of the anti-union path. From its forms of collective action to the mechanisms that led to its defeat, the strike revealed the extent to which the terrain of labor conflict had changed.

The renewed importance of local community, for example, can be seen in the process of mobilization in the strike. The embedded culture of labor in the region contributed to the high level of solidarity among striking workers from different unions. Support was maintained across blue-collar, skilled craft, and professional occupational divides, perhaps most notably in the case of the Newspaper Guild. While just under half of the striking Guild members eventually crossed picket lines, far more stayed out than the employers anticipated, even after the threat of losing their jobs to permanent replacements.

The strike also gained strength from the organizational base and influence of the labor movement in Detroit. Especially in the first months, picket lines and rallies drew hundreds and at times thousands of supporters from other unions, while strategic and material aid was coordinated through local and regional offices of the AFL-CIO, the UAW, and other union organizations. Leading Democratic politicians in the state refused to give interviews to nonstriking reporters, and municipal and county governments voted to pull their legal notices from the papers. More than two hundred local civic and political figures were arrested for civil disobedience in support of the strike, including religious leaders, officers of the National Organization for Women, U.S. congresspersons, and state, county, and city elected representatives.

Finally, grassroots support was essential to the unions' strategic focus on the circulation and advertising boycotts. Strikers canvassed neighborhoods and did one-on-one outreach to home subscribers, protested at retail outlets distributing the papers, and leafleted customers at businesses that kept advertising in them. To a remarkable degree, these efforts worked—the companies admitted to losing nearly $100 million in the first six months and were unable to provide circulation data to the national Audit Bureau of Circulation through the first year.[8]

These actions revealed the depth of the local culture of labor solidarity. If civil society gave room for mobilization, however, it also imposed limits. Incidents of property damage and confrontations on the picket line (highly publicized by the newspapers) alienated some observers and undermined the unions' moral appeal. As the years dragged on, protest fatigue set in and public interest and awareness became harder to sustain. More broadly, the community campaign faced the tasks of organizing on the social terrain of Detroit, with its postwar legacies of suburban metropolitan fragmentation and racial division. Before the strike, the employees at the papers were disproportionately white, relative to the central-city population. During the strike, the unions won support from traditional civil rights and liberal leaders, but many ordinary black Detroiters felt distant from both sides and did not see the struggle as their own.[9]

Civil society was not the only battlefront in the strike. Although they engaged in their own campaign of public relations, the employers recognized the unions' influence in Detroit and relied on their advantages in other arenas. Corporate executives ignored most local civic and political leaders and expressed public disdain for the NLRB.[10] Instead, the companies sought allies in other levels of the state, colluding with suburban police departments to protect access to their facilities and maintain production and distribution; using court injunctions, the RICO suit, and other legal means to restrict picketing and public protest; and aggressively firing strikers, including five of the six local union presidents, for alleged picket line infractions.

Fearful of jeopardizing their members' jobs, union leaders were unwilling to force a political crisis, escalate protest into nonviolent mass civil disobedience, or otherwise openly defy the law. Their dependence on the adjudication of the ULP case, however, contributed to the more than five years' duration of the dispute. Finally, despite inflicting enormous losses on the newspapers, the strike failed to disrupt the employers' economic mechanisms for maintaining their position. The newspapers recruited professional and skilled craft replacements from across the country, downsized workforce levels in production and distribution, and hired unskilled replacement workers at lower wages from the depressed central-city labor market. As the two largest newspaper chains in the nation, Gannett and Knight-Ridder had the resources to absorb the losses in Detroit and await the decision of the federal court. Their actions were fully supported by investors and analysts on Wall Street: throughout the strike, the stock prices of the publicly traded companies were never seriously affected.[11]

Despite its extraordinary features, the Detroit strike was deeply emblematic of historic trends in American labor relations. In the postwar era, American unions gained an institutional footing in the core sectors of the economy under the NLRA, while a historical layer of anti-unionism grew alongside and apart from the New Deal system. The balance of power between the two paths shifted in the early 1980s, after the critical junctures of the PATCO and Phelps Dodge strikes. By the mid-1990s, the Detroit strike signaled the consolidation of the anti-union regime.

UNDERSTANDING STRIKES TODAY: SOME CONDITIONAL PROPOSITIONS

The analysis of the Detroit case allows us to revisit our general understanding of strikes in light of current conditions. The New Deal system established a relationship between collective actors, centralizing wage determination for multiple groups of workers through negotiations between unions and management. With the rise of the anti-union regime, however, such terms are no longer institutionally secure. In the absence of effective deterrence, companies in the United States may instead choose to decentralize wage-setting, restoring the imbalance identified in the Wagner Act between corporately organized employers and individual employees. Without incentives grounded on union density, credible threats of disruption, or adequate state enforcement of workers' rights, employers will seek not just concessions but the *elimination* of the collective bargaining relationship.

This is not a failure of information. Rather, it reflects a structural tendency of one party to try to exit the relationship. Regardless of efficiency, in a neoliberal environment employers are motivated to reduce unionized labor to a non-union standard. This asymmetry between labor and management was noted by the D.C. Circuit Court of Appeals in its *McClatchy II* decision. In a comment on the Supreme Court's *Insurance Agents* case, the court wrote that "a union's tactics, no matter how troubling or even independently unlawful, are always designed to reach a collective bargaining agreement. An employer, on the other hand, may well wish to break the union."[12] Under the current regime, in other words, one side comes to the table looking to make a deal. The other side comes looking to get rid of the table.

A similar logic can be seen in contemporary controversies involving public-sector unions in the United States. In 2011, Republican legislatures and governors in Wisconsin, Ohio, and Idaho passed laws eliminating or drastically reducing public employees' bargaining rights, while Indiana governor Mitch Daniels accomplished the same goal by executive order in 2005.[13] Wisconsin restricts bargaining to wages only and requires employees to vote each year on whether to keep the union.[14] In a statewide referendum voters overwhelmingly repealed Ohio's law, which allowed city councils and school boards to unilaterally impose their final contract offers if management and unions failed to reach an agreement. As journalist Bob Herbert notes, these new laws aim "not just to extract concessions from public employee unions to help balance state budgets, but to actually crush those unions, to deprive them once and for all of the crucial and fundamental right to bargain collectively."[15]

Deliberately negotiating to impasse, unilaterally imposing conditions, and breaking strikes—all of these actions destroy the function of collective bargaining, whether or not the union is actually decertified. Workers therefore may at times be compelled to strike not just for specific economic gains but to defend the ongoing relationship between the employer and their union. Section 8(b)(7) of the NLRA limits the right to picket to force an employer to recognize and bargain with a union that is not the legally certified representative of the employees. When the law fails to protect the status of even certified unions, however, every strike is de facto a recognition strike in which the practical continuity of the relationship hangs in the balance.

The New Deal order both channeled labor conflict and established a framework of democratic rights in the workplace. Under the postwar accord, collective bargaining was concentrated in the firm and substantially limited to bread-and-butter economic issues. Disputes were insulated from the local community and depoliticized by means of NLRB procedural regulation. The integrative prevention of conflict, however, proved historically temporary, and without protection for the right to strike a key mechanism sustaining the New Deal system has been lost. In the post-accord period, the state has largely reverted to a policy of judicial repression in the form of the administrative weakness of the NLRB and the ideological antagonism of the federal courts. The resulting legal regime might therefore be described as aimed at the preventive *destruction*, rather than integration, of workers' collective action in the employment system.

The decline of union density in the economy and the return of judicial repression in the state show the extent of labor's deinstitutionalization under the current regime. With deinstitutionalization, the frequency and impact of strikes can be expected to decline, as they have since the early 1980s.[16] At the same time, workplace struggles that do occur are more likely to spread out into civil society, in contrast to the earlier period. Does that mean that unions that ally with community actors are more likely to win strikes? Not necessarily—civil society is a competitive field no less than the economy and the state. In Detroit, the newspapers deployed tremendous resources to override the power of the NLRB and pressure from an alliance of unions, local civic leaders, and members of the reading public. The outcomes for future strikes will depend on the conjuncture of forces in the economy and the state as well as in civil society.

In this book, I make no attempt to provide a strategic manual drawn from the Detroit case to apply in other labor-management disputes. In hindsight, one can easily second-guess the unions' obvious blunders and weaknesses, from the lack of a comprehensive plan adequate to the scale of the opponents they faced to Derey's missteps in the eleventh-hour bargaining between Local 372 and the DNA, the problems of timing and coordination when the strike began in July 1995, the dilemmas presented by the decision to return to work, and the dependence on the unfair labor practices case. Yet the outcomes in the newspaper strike were not entirely predetermined and were not even finally decided until the 2000 court of appeals ruling. Even then, observers at the time might reasonably have expected the court to follow its *McClatchy II* precedent and decide in favor of the unions. For the public, the Detroit strike offers a window onto the contours of the present system and the problem of democratic workplace governance. For labor movement advocates, the core lesson is the change in the meaning of contemporary strikes: the future of the relationship between organized workers and their employers is now what is fundamentally at stake.

As labor scholars have shown, union growth or revitalization in American history has frequently occurred in episodic bursts or "upsurges."[17] Strike mobilization is a key driver of these upsurges, especially in a liberal market economy with decentralized labor market institutions (like the United States).[18] Such periods often coincide with the growth of new forms of organization or outreach to previously unorganized groups of workers. In the 1890s, native-born and northern European immigrant skilled workers built the craft unions that came together in the American Federation of Labor (AFL). During the 1930s, southern and eastern European ethnic factory workers joined the new wave of industrial unionism in the Congress of Industrial Organizations (CIO).[19] Similarly, African American workers organized into public-sector unions in conjunction with the civil rights movement of the 1960s, and immigrant Hispanic and Asian workers form the base for union growth in low-wage service sectors today.[20]

The newspaper strike was fought on a social terrain of postwar suburbanization, urban industrial decline, and metropolitan class and racial segregation epitomized by Detroit. As cities change, however, unions may find new or different configurations in the local civic ecology. In areas where labor and other structural inequalities coincide, where new immigrant or minority working-class communities combine with local cultures of union militancy, or where organizational and framing strategies redefine previously divided group identities, there may be greater possibilities for collective action.[21] Moreover, the boundaries of mobilization are no longer strictly local. As corporations become larger and more globally integrated, unions have learned to use new leverage, from the strategic location of jobs in worldwide commodity chains, from regulations under national and international law, and from access to global media and civil society.[22] Such changes may prefigure a new layer of opposition to the now-dominant anti-union regime.

THE DECADE OF THE 1990S: BETWEEN CONTINUITY AND CHANGE

"When the history of the labor movement of the '90s is written, the crucial stage of that history is going to be this Detroit strike," said Key Martin, a representative of the New York local Newspaper Guild at the Action! Motown '97 demonstration. "It has the significance for the '90s that PATCO had for the '80s."[23] While the strike did not end as Martin and others might have hoped, many believed at the time that the decade might see a turning point in favor of American labor movement revival. Symbolic of the change was the October 1995 election of Service Employees International Union president John Sweeney as president of the AFL-CIO. Sweeney brought a new leadership team to the national union federation, put new resources into organizing and political mobilization, began initiatives to revitalize local central labor councils and attract young activists into the labor movement, established a Working Women's Department, and moved to transform labor's position on immigration and American foreign policy.[24] Despite these efforts, the struggles that emerged in the 1990s did not widen into a more transformative critical juncture.

On this score, we might briefly compare the newspaper strike with the much larger, partly concurrent, and victorious 1997 strike of the International Brotherhood of Teamsters (IBT) at United Parcel Service, Inc. (UPS). In July 1997, negotiations between the union and management at UPS became deadlocked over the central issues of employment and pay for the company's more than 100,000 part-time workers and the company's participation in a multi-employer pension plan for its employees.[25] On August 4, more than 180,000 Teamster members struck for fifteen days. The two sides reached a settlement on August 19, when the company withdrew its demand to pull out of the pension plan and agreed to union proposals to convert 10,000 part-time jobs to full-time status and raise part-time workers' pay for the first time since 1982. IBT president Ron Carey hailed the agreement as marking a "new era" and a "historic turning point for working people in this country." AFL-CIO president Sweeney agreed. "You could make a million house calls and run a thousand television commercials and stage a hundred strawberry rallies," he said, "and still not come close to doing what the UPS strike did for organizing."[26]

The immediate results of the UPS strike differed sharply from the experience in Detroit. First, the Teamster leaders at UPS responded effectively to the conditions of the post-accord regime in a way that the MCNU leaders did not. Prestrike internal organization and strategic preparation were far superior than in Detroit; comprehensive planning for a contract campaign began at least a year before the strike and included greater mobilization of members and greater coordination with the international union.[27] From the outset, the strike was framed as a public campaign, and the union's demands on behalf of part-time workers resonated clearly and powerfully with an American public that was increasingly anxious about its own job security. A Gallup poll taken during the UPS strike showed that 55 percent of respondents supported the strikers compared to 27 percent for the company.[28] By contrast, the unfair labor practice charges in Detroit centered on technical matters of law that, although crucial, were hardly transparent even for many union members.

On the company's side, UPS relied mainly on managers as substitutes and chose not to hire permanent replacements for the strikers. Without permanent replacements, there were not the same levels of forceful confrontation or militarization of security as in Detroit, and UPS did not try to demonize the strikers or prevent them from returning to work after the strike.[29] Neither could the company use technology to perform the labor of tens of thousands of delivery workers. As a result, UPS lost more than 90 percent of its normal volume of 12 million parcels a day, and executives feared losing permanent market share to their competitors.[30] Unlike the Detroit strike, the union also struck the entire firm nationwide; there was no parent corporation with deep pockets able to absorb a localized loss. The company was not traded on the stock market; its shareholders were primarily its own managers, employees, and retirees; and it did not have the same Wall Street pressures to push down costs and raise operating margins as did many publicly traded firms.[31]

Finally, the state played a different role in the UPS strike than in Detroit. UPS chair James Kelly called on President Clinton to define the strike as a threat to the nation's economy and security under the Taft-Hartley Act and to use his authority to seek an injunction ordering the strikers back to work. The president declined, and his refusal to act made it harder for the news media to portray the strike as a serious inconvenience to consumers, thereby reinforcing the union's public focus on the contract issues of part-time employment and pay.[32] In Detroit, it was the unions that were forced to seek state intervention to protect the strikers' rights, leading to the endless litigation around the unfair labor practice charges and the ultimate decision by the federal courts.

The role of the state, however, also suggests why the UPS strike did not spark a more widespread resurgence of union organization. Four days after the UPS settlement, a federal overseer invalidated IBT president Carey's 1996 election based on allegations of illegal fund-raising by his campaign.[33] Carey himself was eventually cleared of all criminal charges, but he was barred from running for reelection, and a court-appointed review board later expelled him from the union for life. In a rescheduled vote in December 1998, Carey's 1996 opponent, James P. Hoffa, won election as the Teamsters' president.[34] The turmoil within the union sharply diminished the momentum gained from the victory at UPS.

Beyond the internal politics of the Teamsters union, the UPS strike alone did not reverse the wider pattern of institutional change. The dominance of the anti-union regime is now itself a central barrier to any broad revival of American labor. Current law reduces the cost to employers of resisting unionization and allows them to avoid collective bargaining without fear of sanctions from unions or their own workers. "Without an effective right to strike," labor law scholar Julius Getman observes, "collective bargaining becomes ineffectual, and the desire of employees to join unions is inevitably reduced."[35] The failures to protect both collective bargaining and the right to strike are not economically determined but raise problems of law and public policy.

THE PROBLEM OF REFORM: VISIONS OF WORKPLACE GOVERNANCE

Since the 1990s, unions, scholars, and other advocates have put forward many well-considered proposals for labor law reform.[36] As inspired and relevant as many of them are, their specific policy recommendations are constrained by the conflict of opposing institutional orders. At this juncture, the political conflict calls for more than a set of technical fixes; what is needed is an articulation of the underlying institutional values or vision of what good workplace governance should be. The questions are reminiscent of the kinds of issues raised by the Readers United group in the newspaper strike. What does an enterprise exist for, and to whom is it accountable? Who are the proper stakeholders, and how should their interests be represented?

The competing regimes of New Deal collective bargaining and corporate anti-unionism offer strongly contrasting views of the rights and duties of actors in the workplace and in society. Section 1 of the NLRA stresses the imbalance of power between individual employees and employers, which were already allowed to become collective actors under corporate law. Through the law, society endowed corporations with benefits like limited liability, rights of property, and the legal status of fictional persons, while workers enjoyed no similar freedom of association. Rather, workers who acted collectively were often punished as criminal conspirators under the regime of judicial repression.

The imbalance was apparent from the rise of the corporate form in the late 1800s. In its 1898 annual report, the Ohio State Board of Arbitration wrote:

> Stockholders unite their accumulation of capital and knowledge in a particular line of business and create a simple agency called a corporation. The agency secures the best skill and ability money will command to conduct its affairs. Thus, supplied with a sagacious and powerful representative, they stand back and say to their laborers through this representative: "No representative from you will be heard. You must each speak and act for yourself."[37]

The inequality in the employment relationship meant that individual workers could not exercise "actual liberty of contract" in the labor market.[38] Contrary to the tenets of neoclassical economics, labor is not perfectly mobile. Employees become socially embedded in their families, workplaces, and communities, raising the emotional, practical, and economic costs of moving to another job or geographic area. Workers see their labor as a central source of identity and livelihood, perhaps even a calling, and presume continuity in their relationship with the employer. Over time they develop strong interests in keeping their jobs, accruing nontransferable seniority and benefits, acquiring and advancing firm-specific skills and social capital, and contributing their loyalty to the company.[39]

As a result, employees assume a normative ownership of their jobs as legitimate stakeholders in the enterprise.[40] The NLRA embodied this principle in law, while the postwar accord established it at least partially in practice. As Getman writes, "The widespread use of seniority as a result of collective bargaining, and the almost automatic limitation on the employer's right of discharge, established the principle that employees, through their work, develop a legally enforceable claim to their jobs, and that most management decisions affecting significant employee interests must be based on legitimate, objective standards."[41] The moral interest or stake that workers possess further supports the claim that they are entitled to a say in the operation of the employer's business.[42]

Finally, the NLRA expressed a vision of the relationship between the workplace and a democratic society. "Democracy cannot work unless it is honored in the factory as well as the polling booth," Sen. Robert Wagner said on introducing the bill that became the National Labor Relations Act. "[Workers] cannot be truly free in body and spirit unless their freedom extends into the places where they earn their daily bread."[43] On the job, economist Bruce Kaufman notes, unions "checked the arbitrary exercise of management power, introduced bilateral methods of dispute resolution, and gave workers a voice in the determination of the workplace rules they worked under."[44] In the community, unions were schools for citizenship, fostering workers' civic participation, organizational skills, and political awareness. Intrinsically, the basic workplace rights of free association, due process, and collective action were essential for human dignity and a just society.[45]

This ideal differs sharply from the vision of workplace authority in the anti-union regime. The current legal order represents a return to the pre-NLRA era and a reassertion of the philosophy of "at-will" employment. The at-will principle derives from a conception of employment as a master-servant relationship rather than one of mutual rights and obligations. Classically stated by the Tennessee Supreme Court in 1884, the doctrine allows employers the right "to discharge or retain employees at will for good cause or for no cause, or even for bad cause without thereby being guilty of an unlawful act per se."[46] As legal scholar Clyde Summers writes:

The employer, as owner of the enterprise, is viewed as owning the job with a property right to control the job and the worker who fills it. That property right gives the employer the right to impose any requirement on the employee, give any order and insist on obedience, change any term of employment, and discard the employee at any time. The employer is sovereign over his employees.[47]

The assumption is that the employee is only a "hired hand" who has no legal interest or stake in the enterprise beyond the right to be paid for the labor performed. In this interpretation, the NLRA and collective bargaining contracts were no more than specific, limited exceptions to the prior and superior property rights of the employer, who otherwise reserved all rights to unencumbered decision-making and authority.[48]

Although it developed into the common law, the at-will principle was not ancient tradition but only emerged in judicial constructions in the 1870s, and it did not become fully established until the early twentieth century.[49] Nevertheless, after the passage of the NLRA, the courts quickly began to reapply it to the new law. One of the earliest examples was the Supreme Court's 1938 *Mackay* decision permitting the permanent replacement of strikers. *Mackay* directly contradicted the plain language in the statute protecting the right to strike and defended the employer's right "to protect and continue his business," a right not stated or implied in the NLRA. Coming only one year after the Supreme Court had upheld the NLRA itself, the decision helped set the pattern of interpreting the Act to interfere as little as possible with employers' property rights.[50]

Similarly, by the early 1940s the Board and the courts had affirmed the doctrine that allowed employers to impose contract terms upon reaching impasse in negotiations. In the 1980s, the Board under President Ronald Reagan issued a series of decisions making it easier for employers to reach impasse and thus implement their final offers.[51] The combined rules of permanent replacement of strikers and implementation on impasse cast a long shadow back into the collective bargaining process. Labor law scholars Ellen Dannin and Terry Wagar explain:

Demanding deep concessions and demanding unilateral control over working conditions not only get you to an impasse, but once there, the employer is in a position to impose the very terms it wants. . . . All through bargaining, an employer can use the threat of replacement to force the union to agree to its terms, because the union does not dare strike. The employer can threaten this or remind the union of the law, but it does not even need to mention it; the union will know it is in a very weak position.[52]

These actions destroy the NLRA's express purpose to promote collective bargaining, reinforcing the presumption of unilateral employer control and the lack of any employee stake in the enterprise. The employer can make proposals that are predictably unacceptable to the union and then simply decline to move from its position, a process that was painfully evident in the Detroit strike. As NLRB member (and later chair) Wilma Liebman wrote in her dissent against the dismissal of the joint bargaining charge in the case, collective bargaining "is a process to identify issues, facilitate the resolution of joint problems, achieve the terms of an agreement, and maintain or restructure attitudes of the parties toward each other. It is 'a process that look[s] to the ordering of the parties' industrial relationship.'. . . [The] DNA's negotiators' unilateral approach, far from achieving the desired flexibility, was more likely to defeat the bargaining process."[53]

With the consolidation of the anti-union regime, the judicial bias favoring employers has become ever more pronounced. The at-will doctrine gained new legitimacy in the 1980s under the influence of the conservative "law and economics" school of legal theory. Courts now often implicitly assume that whatever the employer wants is rational and good and that the union is wrong for not agreeing.[54] Industrial relations scholar John Budd notes that "common law and free markets—and property rights within them—are rhetorically viewed as apolitical, which serves to elevate the power of property rights in legal and public policy discourse."[55] Yet, as Summers remarks, "so long as these arguments have currency in the courts and the legislatures, the bridge will not be to the twenty-first century but to the nineteenth century."[56]

Institutional Mechanisms: Labor Law and Workers' Rights

"Trade unionism requires a compelling set of ideas and institutions, both self-made and governmental, to give labor's cause power and legitimacy," historian Nelson Lichtenstein writes.[57] The renewal of American labor does not require the restoration of all the elements of the New Deal order, even if that were possible. It does, however, imply a challenge to the logic and legal mechanisms that reproduce the anti-union regime, including the practices of impasse and implementation, the *Mackay* doctrine, and other limits on collective action.

Removing the at-will assumptions in the law, for example, would dissolve much of the justification for the employers' right to impose terms upon impasse. That would make labor law more consistent with most contract law, where it would be inconceivable that one party is allowed to impose its own terms. It is arguably more consistent with the NLRA to say that when negotiations deadlock, the employer's operations should cease.[58] Alternatively, the parties could return to the status quo, where they would be free to use the economic weapons of the strike or lockout or find new means of reaching agreement—through mediation or interest arbitration, for example. Either way, forcing the two sides to negotiate seriously to work through their differences would end the current charade of simply trying to speed up or avoid impasse.[59]

The integrity of the bargaining process rests, ultimately, on a genuine right to strike. A fair exchange assumes that both parties are free to walk away if they do not like the terms being offered. With implementation on impasse, employers have the power to leave the table if they cannot reach agreement with the union. The union enjoys no similar freedom; under the threat of permanent replacement, the union is denied the last resort of the strike. In Detroit, the Rev. Ed Rowe observed, the newspaper strike was "a small piece of a much larger issue about whether there is going to be a right to collective bargaining or whether corporate America has carte blanche. This is not just about Detroit; the civil right of collective bargaining is on the line. I mean, do workers have a *real* right to strike or not?"[60]

Permanent replacement of strikers destroys the lives of individuals and communities and provides employers with a powerful argument against unionization; for most workers there is no practical difference between being fired and being permanently replaced. The *Mackay* doctrine denies that employees are legitimate stakeholders in the firm with strong incentives of their own to reach agreement and end their strike. It punishes workers for exercising their rights under the law and ignores the employers' incentives to reach impasse quickly and "gamble" on daring the union to strike. For the union a strike is no mere gamble but a defense of the workers' collective relationship with the employer.[61]

Changing the law to acknowledge these conditions will be no easy task. Critics object that political forces in the United States make even modest labor law reform nearly impossible, and the record of union efforts to pass legislation in Congress is not encouraging.[62] Even if laws are passed, they face hostile interpretation from the federal courts. Others have suggested alternative litigation strategies for achieving reform. Getman argues that statutory limits on union boycotts and other mutual aid can be challenged on the basis of the First Amendment. In its 1988 *DeBartolo* decision, the Supreme Court found that union handbills that "pressed the benefits of unionism to the community and the dangers of inadequate wages to the economy and the standard of living of the populace" were constitutionally protected speech. Extending this logic, secondary boycotts and picketing that are peaceful and that appeal in broad societal terms can be legal, as they already are for civil rights groups and other non–labor union organizations.[63]

Dannin proposes an approach modeled on the NAACP Legal Defense Fund's struggle for racial equality. Most federal judges are trained in common law and now have little familiarity with the distinctive features of the NLRA, the role of unions, and collective bargaining in general. Trying labor cases therefore requires educating judges in the goals and policies of the Act and freeing their decisions from the legacy of the at-will doctrine. For unions, unfair labor practice cases can be targeted to produce incremental victories, setting precedents for future decisions. As in the NAACP strategy, social science research can play an important role in making visible the real impacts of prior judicial rulings, the importance of the process of collective bargaining, and its value to society as a whole.[64]

Widening the scope of collective action can also enlarge the spaces for public engagement and civic mediation among employers, unions, and community actors. Among other ideas, Paul Osterman, Thomas Kochan, Richard Locke, and Michael Piore have recommended eliminating the distinction between mandatory and permissive subjects of bargaining. That could encourage more flexibility, communication, and innovation in negotiations between management and unions.[65] It could also allow for the development of broader partnerships in support of the firm, its workers, and the local area, as in the recent growth of voluntary community benefits agreements.[66] There is no a priori reason to credit company managers with exclusive wisdom to control the enterprise on behalf of all stakeholders. In the newspaper strike, Gannett pursued a scorched-earth policy toward the strikers in a community that placed a high value on unionism. The newspapers lost one-third of their circulation and at least $130 million and forced the dispute to go through years of litigation. It is not obvious that these actions benefited the workplace, the community, or even the shareholders in the long run.

THE ROLE OF THE PUBLIC SPHERE: THE NEWSPAPER INDUSTRY

As the historic institutions of industrial relations have declined, labor disputes have expanded beyond traditional channels into new arenas in the state and civil society. The result puts an even greater weight on the civic function of news media as enterprises in the local community and as information sources in the urban public sphere. In Detroit, the newspapers never recovered their former audience, notwithstanding the introduction of new technology. Before the strike, the *Free Press* and the *News* had combined daily sales of 888,719, and Sunday sales of 1,113,773, for the six months ending March 31, 1995. By March 2000, combined daily sales were 603,362, and for Sunday 761,384, a loss of 32 percent.[67] In January 2003, the DNA began groundbreaking for a $177 million project to modernize the Sterling Heights plant, including the installation of a high-bay automated storage and retrieval system and six state-of-the-art MAN Roland GEO-MAN 75 presses imported from Germany. The new machines began production in 2005, with each press capable of printing 75,000 newspaper copies per hour.[68]

Just three years later, however, in December 2009, the *Free Press* and the *News* announced that they were ending the daily home delivery of papers except for Thursdays, Fridays, and Sundays. Readers were given the options of subscribing to the electronic editions, receiving copies by mail, or purchasing their own single copies at news outlets. The move eliminated an average of 195,700 home-delivered editions of the *Free Press* and 94,800 copies of the *News* and produced an estimated 190 job cuts and cost savings of around $50 million to $60 million.[69] By 2011, combined average daily circulation (print and online) for the two papers was 387,837, and the Sunday average was 614,226—a loss of around half a million readers from March 1995.[70]

Nationally, the newspaper industry has staggered under the burden of overleveraged debt, competition from Internet media, and the 2008 financial crash and recession. Advertising revenue fell by nearly half between 2006 and 2010, with a 26 percent drop in 2009 alone, and from 2007 to 2009, 11,000 full-time newsroom jobs were lost.[71] The giant Tribune Company, owner of the *Chicago Tribune* and the *Los Angeles Times*, declared bankruptcy in December 2008, and over the next two years a stream of major newspaper companies filed for protection, including the *Minneapolis Star-Tribune*, the *Philadelphia Inquirer* and the *Philadelphia Daily News*, the *Chicago Sun-Times* group, the *Journal-Register* chain, and MediaNews Group, Inc., the owner of the *Detroit News*.[72]

After decades as the darling of Wall Street, newspaper stocks abruptly collapsed; by 2010, most were trading at between one-half and one-tenth of their value just five years earlier. With the wave of bankruptcies, private equity funds took over a substantial portion of the industry. "The days of 25 percent margins, which critics back then often called obscene and a sign of industry harvesting profit rather than investing in the future, are gone forever," said a report by the Pew Research Center's Project for Excellence in Journalism. "The era of newspapers being dominated by expanding publicly traded corporations is now winding down."[73]

Gannett, the pioneer of super-profits in the industry, saw its stock fall from a high of $91 in the second quarter of 2004 to a low of $1.95 in the first quarter of 2009 as its profit margins slipped into single digits.[74] The company slashed its workforce from 52,600 in 2005 to 32,600 in 2010 and imposed mandatory furloughs on the remaining employees. As the company cut jobs, it also reduced severance pay; at the *Arizona Republic*, laid-off workers were told to file for state unemployment insurance first and Gannett would supplement their benefits, allowing it to shift part of the cost onto the state.[75]

At the *Journal News* in Westchester County, New York, all 288 news and advertising employees were laid off in 2009 and told that they could reapply for a smaller pool of 218 redefined jobs. The Gannett management's aggressive cost controls helped restore a degree of profitability and the stock price recovered to the midteens by early 2010. For their accomplishments, Gannett chief executive Craig Debow and chief operating officer Gracia Martore received 2010 cash bonuses of $1.75 million and $1.25 million, respectively, along with stock, options, and deferred compensation that could bring their combined packages up to $17.6 million.[76]

In the newspaper industry, American law gives private firms expansive privileges, and government policy recognizes the special role of the press in the life of a democratic public. These privileges presuppose certain benefits and service to society, resting practically on the labor of newspaper workers and their embedded relations with the community. The past few decades, however, have seen a profound reduction in the social accountability of private enterprise, not only in the news business but across the economy. Whether through collective bargaining with employees, the ethical norms of professions like journalism, or even the informal practices of corporate paternalism, the forms of institutional and cultural regulation have been sacrificed for the sake of unfettered market power.

CODA: THE INTERSECTION OF BIOGRAPHY AND HISTORY

John Jaske was a complicated man. Smart, ambitious, and intensely competitive as a business executive, he was also the father of two daughters, a self-declared "devout liberal," and a member of the Virginia League of Conservation Voters.[77] In his capacity as an officer for Gannett, he played the game as the rules allowed him to do, and he did well for himself, retiring from Gannett in January 2006. In the fourteen months before his departure, SEC filings show that he exercised stock options and sold nearly 47,000 shares of Gannett stock, for net proceeds estimated at around $1.25 million.[78]

Frank Vega made out all right too. In 2005 he was hired as publisher of the *San Francisco Chronicle*, and he took with him his chief financial officer, Gary Anderson, and security consultant John Anthony. Vega felt that it was a good time to leave the struggling market in Detroit. "It became a job in which there wasn't a lot of opportunity for new growth. And I'm a Florida boy. I got tired of shoveling snow," he said from his office in downtown San Francisco. "Across the street from my office in Detroit was a hotel that was for sale the whole fourteen years I was there—an abandoned building. Come on, it wasn't a tough decision."[79]

Robert Battista moved on with his career. In 2002 he was appointed by President George W. Bush to a five-year term as chair of the NLRB. After his confirmation by the U.S. Senate, Battista said that one of his key goals for the Board was to "emphasize collegiality among the members, and try to keep partisanship to a minimum."[80] When his term came to an end in December 2007, more than fifty prominent labor law professors across the country signed a letter stating that, "since it was constituted in late 2002, the current Labor Board has mounted an aggressive campaign to curtail worker rights under the statute. In periodic waves of closely divided, highly partisan decisions, the current Board majority has effectively removed whole categories of workers from the Act's coverage; stripped away protections promised by the Act; and further diluted the strength of already inadequate remedies."[81]

Back in Michigan, Susan Watson was inducted into the Michigan Journalism Hall of Fame in April 2000. She had already won the respect and admiration of her fellow strikers. "The Teamsters like to say, 'I'm going to be out so long I'm going to hold the door for Susan Watson,'" wrote striking *Free Press* features writer Susan Hall-Balduf in November 1995.[82] But Watson never returned to her job at the *Free Press*. An NLRB judge ruled that she was unlawfully fired for taking part in the nonviolent sit-down protest at the *News* building on Labor Day weekend 1996, but the newspaper appealed her reinstatement along with that of others involved in the protest. The company then offered a severance package to a group of striking Guild members, including Watson, but only on condition that all of them jointly waive their rights to return. Watson accepted the settlement, ending her twenty-five-year career as a reporter, editor, and columnist for the *Free Press*. She became editor of *The Detroit Teacher*, a publication of the Detroit Federation of Teachers, and continued to be a strong community and labor advocate in the city.[83]

Other former strikers and supporters went on to pursue their vision of justice in various ways. Printers union member Barb Ingalls had never been very involved in her union before the strike; neither was *News* editorial assistant Alesia Cooper-Cunningham. After the strike, Ingalls became a leading activist in the antiwar and labor-religious solidarity networks in

Detroit, while Cooper-Cunningham was elected secretary of the local Newspaper Guild. Teamster Local 372 member Shawn Ellis used the skills he gained during the strike to become head of community services and communications for the Metro Detroit AFL-CIO. Mailer Jim St. Louis went to work for the southeastern Michigan chapter of the American Red Cross, serving as liaison to area labor unions. Striking copy editor Emily Everett was fired by the *Free Press* for her participation in the 1996 Labor Day sit-down; she later joined the staff of the UAW's *Solidarity* magazine. And in 2010 former UAW Region 1A director Bob King was elected president of the United Auto Workers international union.

The clashes on the picket line also produced a number of individual civil rights suits against the newspapers and local police. Among them was the case of David Zieminski, a UAW member who was beaten by Sterling Heights police on September 16, 1995.[84] As part of the discovery process in the case, Zieminski's attorneys, William Goodman and Julie Hurwitz, obtained records documenting the pattern of collusion between the newspapers and the Sterling Heights Police Department. Top company and municipal officials gave depositions under oath, including John Jaske, Frank Vega, Tim Kelleher, Alan Lenhoff, and John Anthony from the newspapers and police chief Thomas Derocha, Lt. Frank Mowinski, and city manager Steve Duchane from Sterling Heights. Some witnesses were deposed several times as part of this and other litigation surrounding the strike.

Most of the civil rights cases were eventually settled out of court or dismissed, but at least one of them went all the way to trial and a verdict. In December 2000, striker Ben Solomon finally had his day in court. Over the course of twelve wintry days in Judge Nancy Edmunds's courtroom in downtown Detroit, a federal jury heard attorney Kevin Ernst examine witnesses, introduce exhibits, and argue in support of Solomon's case. On December 21, four days after the last contracts were ratified at the newspapers, the jury returned its verdict. The City of Sterling Heights, its police officials Derocha and Mowinski, and the Detroit Newspaper Agency were found guilty of conspiring to deprive Solomon of his constitutional rights and were ordered to pay $2.5 million in compensatory and punitive damages. As Solomon's wife Debbie said afterward, "To actually have a federal jury who has heard all of the issues uphold your side of it, to me that went a long way."[85]

The vindication of Solomon's individual rights did not alter the outcome of the strike, but it did signal the persistence of popular norms of justice opposed to the anti-union regime. The newspaper strike represented the exceptional struggle of one community during the decade of the 1990s, but every generation must decide which rules will govern its collective economic, political, and social relationships. We need not dismiss cases like Detroit as mere outliers or historical failures; such moments, when all involved do their worst and best, can teach us something about crucial institutional conflicts and paths of change. "We did not make history," one former newspaper striker said several years after the strike. Perhaps not, but their actions helped disclose some of the forces that did.

Notes |

INTRODUCTION

1. This account was taken from the following sources: U.S. District Court, *Benjamin L. Solomon v. The City of Sterling Heights et al.*, 98-CV-73900 (E.D. Mich. 2000), trial transcript and Mowinski deposition, August 3, 1999; *Detroit Nightbeat*, WDIV-TV, September 4, 1995; interview with Ben Solomon, Armada, Mich., May 3, 2005.
2. U.S. District Court, *Solomon v. City of Sterling Heights et al.*, trial transcript; interview with Frank Vega, Detroit, October 27, 2004. For brief summaries of the strike, see Gonyea and Hoyt, "Fallout from Detroit" (1997); *Metro Times*, "The Year in Review" (July 3, 1996); Sacharow, "Walking the Line in Detroit" (July 22, 1996); Schlagheck, "Living in the Wake of a Newspaper Strike" (2001).
3. NLRB, *Detroit Newspaper Agency*, 326 NLRB 64 (1998).
4. NLRB, *Detroit Newspaper Agency*, 342 NLRB 24 (2004).
5. Lengel, "Legal Recourse" (July 7, 1996); Craig, "Chamber Blasts Tactics in Paper Strike" (November 21, 1996).
6. U.S. District Court, *Solomon v. City of Sterling Heights et al.*, trial transcript.
7. Leduff and Greenhouse, "Tentative Deal Is Reached in Grocery Labor Dispute" (February 27, 2004); Raine, "Hotel Workers' Lockout Off for Now" (November 21, 2004).
8. Barringer, "The Strike That Ate Circulation" (July 17, 2000).
9. Greenberg (1995, 25–27).
10. Rosenblum (1988/1995); Getman (1998); Franklin (2001).
11. Juravich and Bronfenbrenner (1999).
12. Hirsch and Macpherson (1995).
13. Lambert (2005), 2; U.S. Bureau of Labor Statistics (2011).
14. Voss and Sherman (2000); Bronfenbrenner and Juravich (1998); Milkman and Voss (2004).

15. Moorhead (2003); Kramer et al. (2010).
16. Martin (2004, 8); see also Kumar (2007).
17. Farber and Western (2001); Flanagan (2007); Troy (2004).
18. Flyvbjerg (2006); Seawright and Gerring (2006).
19. Bennett and Elman (2006); Paige (1999).
20. Rosenfeld (2006, 2008).
21. Nicholson (2004), 321.
22. Rosenfeld (2006).
23. Wallace, Rubin, and Smith (1988); Franzosi (1989).
24. Kaufman (1992); McConnell (1989); Tsebelis and Lange (1995).
25. Picard and Lacy (1997); interview with Ben Burns, Detroit, October 20, 2004.
26. Reder and Neumann (1980); Ashenfelter and Johnson (1969).
27. Franzosi (1989); Kaufman (1992).
28. Cohn and Eaton (1989); Shorter and Tilly (1974); Snyder (1975).
29. Rubin (1986); Snyder (1975).
30. Bluestone and Bluestone (1992); Bowles, Gordon, and Weisskopf (1983).
31. McCammon (1993).
32. Kaufman (1992, 119).
33. Griffin, McCammon, and Botsko (1990).
34. Western (1997).
35. Cohen and Arato (1994); Habermas (1996, 299).
36. Estlund (2003); Warren (2001).
37. Ragin (1987); Katznelson (1997).
38. Evans (2007); see also Clawson (2003); Milkman and Voss (2004); Turner and Cornfield (2007).
39. A notable exception is Martin and Dixon (2010), although these authors remain grounded in the social movement theory tradition described earlier.
40. Sewell (1996, 263).
41. Isaac and Christiansen (2002); Isaac, McDonald, and Lukasik (2006); Roscigno and Danaher (2004).
42. Dubofsky (1994); Gutman (1976); Montgomery (1987).
43. Bronfenbrenner and Juravich (1998); Fantasia and Voss (2004); Lopez (2004).
44. Fine (2006); Jarley and Maranto (1990); Turner, Katz, and Hurd (2001).
45. Warner and Low (1947, 1); see also Hartman and Squires (2006); Klinenberg (2002); U.S. Kerner Commission (1968).
46. Orren and Skowrenek (1997).
47. On the concept of "layering"—an active process of amendment, addition, or revision through which new institutional logics emerge on the edges of an established system—see Streeck and Thelen (2005).
48. Gross (1995); Kochan, Katz, and McKersie (1994); McCartin (2006).
49. Rhomberg (2010).
50. Collier and Collier (1991); Mahoney (2000); Pierson (2000).

51. This view was expressed succinctly by Milton Friedman in a 1970 article entitled, "The Social Responsibility of Business Is to Increase Its Profits" (*New York Times Magazine*, September 13, 1970).
52. Jacobs and Skocpol (2005); Macedo (2005); Estlund (2003).
53. Freeman (2007); Greenhouse (2008).
54. Massey (2007, 5); Western and Rosenfeld (2011).
55. Massey (2007, 49).
56. The United States has not ratified the ILO conventions (C87 and C98) on freedom of association and the right to collective bargaining; see Gross (2011, 80–81); International Labor Organization (n.d.).
57. Wallerstein and Western (2000); Soskice (1999).
58. Western and Rosenfeld (2011); Hacker and Pierson (2010, 194–200).

CHAPTER 1

1. Schudson (1995, 37).
2. Baker (2002, 300).
3. Starr (2004, 65–110).
4. Copeland (2003, 113).
5. Ryan (1997, 13).
6. Angelo (1981).
7. Schudson (2003, 76–77); Starr (2004, 131–36).
8. Starr (2004, 252); Kaplan (2002, 114–28); Solomon (1995, 115–16).
9. Starr (2004, 254); Schudson (2003, 81).
10. Schudson (2003, 42).
11. Starr (2004, 258); Kaplan (2002, 107–12).
12. Lutz (1973, 10); Kaplan (2002, 114).
13. Schudson (2003, 79); Angelo (1981, 60); McKercher (2002, 8).
14. Meyer (2004, 5); Copeland (2003, 113).
15. Kaplan (2002, 126–27); Solomon (1995, 113, 131n2).
16. Solomon (1995), 116; Bagdikian (2000), 122–24; Baker (2002), 182, 344n61; McKercher (2002), 18.
17. Gruley (1993, 85–86); Bagdikian (2000, 178–80); Brandt (1993).
18. Kaplan (2002, 190–91).
19. Merritt (2005, 122); McKercher (2002, 35n25).
20. Bogart (1991, 9); Solomon (1995, 133).
21. Merritt (2005, 37–43); Gruley (1993, 112).
22. Gruley (1993, 114); Bogart (1991, 2).
23. Kalleberg et al. (1987, 50–51); Cranberg, Bezanson, and Soloski (2001, 19).
24. Stanger (2002, 184); Bogart (1991, 49); Cranberg, Bezanson, and Soloski (2001, 63).
25. Walton (2001, 20); Cranberg, Bezanson, and Soloski (2001, 2, 27–32).

26. Meyer (2004, 181); Gruley (1993, 88–91).
27. Meyer (2004, 180); McKercher (2002, 24); Bagdikian (2004, 190–97); Weiss, "Invasion of the Gannettoids" (February 2, 1987).
28. Gruley (1993, 161).
29. Merritt (2005, 14, 36, 105); Hoyt (n.d.).
30. Gruley (1993, 117–18); Merritt (2005, 22, 29–35).
31. Merritt (2005, 58).
32. Gruley (1993, 117, 119); Merritt (2005, 21, 37, 118–20).
33. Gruley (1993, 120); Meyer (2004, 174–75).
34. Gruley (1993, 122); Merritt (2005, 95–96).
35. Meyer (2004, 6).
36. Roberts, Kunkel, and Layton (2001, 14); Cranberg, Bezanson, and Soloski (2001), 112.
37. Walton (2001), 21; McKercher (2002), 29.
38. Brubaker (1982).
39. Barnett (1991); Gruley (1993, 169–76).
40. Picard and Brody (1997); Claussen (1999).
41. Bogart (1991, 52–53); Meyer (2004, 36); Cranberg, Bezanson, and Soloski (2001, 24); Picard (2002).
42. Roberts and Kunkel (2002); Cranberg, Bezanson, and Soloski (2001, 25, 93); Bass (2001).
43. Merritt (2005, 217); Cranberg, Bezanson, and Soloski (2001, 35); Overholser (2001, 164).
44. Gleick, "Read All About It" (October 21, 1996).
45. Gruley (1993, 30, 143–44).
46. Gruley (1993, 29–30, 99–100, 122).
47. Gruley (1993, 32–78, 104).
48. Downie and Kaiser (2002, 85–92).
49. Gruley (1993, 103–6, 146–47).
50. Gruley (1993, 157, 167).
51. Gruley (1993, 168, 181).
52. Gruley (1993, 177–78, 228).
53. Mayor Young was also recognized as a representative of the public, but his legal representatives did not take a leading role in the case; see Gruley (1993, 202–10).
54. Gruley (1993, 235–40).
55. Gruley (1993, 247–48, 258–69, 288–92).
56. Gruley (1993, 268).
57. Interview with Lou Mleczko, Detroit, April 18, 2005.
58. Gruley (1993, 347, 376).
59. Shaw and McKenzie (2003, 140); Bagdikian (2000, 115); Merritt (2005, 28, 217); Picard (2002).

60. Meyer (2004, 10).
61. Layton (2006).
62. Seelye and Sorkin, "Newspaper Chain Agrees to a Sale for $4.5 Billion" (March 12, 2006); Seelye, "What-Ifs of a Media Eclipse" (August 27, 2006); Levingston and O'Hara, "McClatchy's Paper Chase: Family-Owned Chain to Buy Knight, Plans to Sell Off 12 Dailies" (March 14, 2006).
63. Rieder (2006).
64. Morton (2006).

CHAPTER 2

1. Farley, Danziger, and Holzer (2000, 1–12, 63–66); Gavrilovich and McGraw (2000, 289).
2. Darden et al. (1987, 28); Farley, Danziger, and Holzer (2000, 2, 64).
3. Orr (2007, 3).
4. Farley, Danziger, and Holzer (2000, 21); Thomas (1989, 149); Barrow (2004); Sugrue (1996, 21–22).
5. Gavrilovich and McGraw (2000, 289).
6. Zunz (1982, 348–93); Boyle (2004, 15); Farley, Danziger, and Holzer (2000, 27).
7. Zunz (1982, 311); Boyle (2004, 102–4); Conot (1986, 197–98, 215).
8. Boyle (2004, 8); Lutz (1973, 93–109).
9. Sugrue (1996, 2). Racial conflict reached a peak in the case of Dr. Ossian Sweet, a black physician whose East Side house was attacked by a mob in 1925, leading to the death of a white neighbor. Sweet was charged with murder but ultimately acquitted in a nationally celebrated trial featuring a defense team organized by the National Association for the Advancement of Colored People (NAACP) and led by attorney Clarence Darrow; see Boyle (2004); Conot (1986, 232–34).
10. Kaplan (2002, 127).
11. Gruley (1993, xii, 3); Angelo (1981, 120–25); McGraw, "*Free Press* to End Era with Change of Address" (July 22, 1998).
12. Lutz (1973, 33–48); Conot (1986, 198).
13. Boyle (2004, 139, 183).
14. Angelo (1981, 93–113, 127–47); Boyle (2004, 251–63).
15. Farley, Danziger, and Holzer (2000, 31); Conot (1986, 283).
16. Widick (1989, 116).
17. Lichtenstein (1995, 48, 85–86); Lutz (1973, 69–72); Babson (1986, 92–94).
18. Babson (1986); Lichtenstein (1995, 99–102).
19. Greenstone (1969, 116–17).
20. Farley, Danziger, and Holzer (2000, 53); Meier and Rudwick (1979).
21. Lichtenstein (1995, 88–89); Angelo (1981, 147–52).

22. Angelo (1981, 148–56).
23. Babson (1986, 133).
24. Greenstone (1969, 113–14); Babson (1986, 136).
25. Widick (1989, 89).
26. Farley, Danziger, and Holzer (2000, 35–36, 150–51); Sugrue (1996, 73); Darden et al. (1987, 68, 116–18); Greenstone (1969, 121).
27. Smith (1999); Dillard (2007, 219).
28. Thomas (1989); Sugrue (1996, 128).
29. Sugrue (1996, 132–37).
30. Darden et al. (1987, 26).
31. Sugrue (1996, 47–50); Darden et al. (1987, 158–66).
32. Freund (2007).
33. Darden et al. (1987, 97); U.S. Bureau of the Census (1995).
34. Darden et al. (1987, 137–38); Farley, Danziger, and Holzer (2000, 160).
35. Greenstone and Peterson (1973); Pratt (2004).
36. Mast (1994, 167); Dillard (2007, 109).
37. Babson (1986, 165–66); Dillard (2007, 211–17).
38. Sugrue (1996, 143–44); Farley, Danziger, and Holzer (2000, 75–76); U.S. Kerner Commission (1968, 89–90).
39. Thompson (2001, 37–45); Darden et al. (1987, 72).
40. Darden et al. (1987, 72–73); Farley, Danziger, and Holzer (2000, 43–44); Gavrilovich and McGraw (2000, 519–21).
41. Mast (1994, 192, emphasis in original).
42. Boyle (1995, 229–31); Lichtenstein (1995, 379, 412–13).
43. Babson (1986, 173–74); Thompson (2001).
44. Angelo (1981, 19).
45. Darden et al. (1987, 165–67); Gavrilovich and McGraw (2000, 110).
46. Lutz (1973, 146–53); Mast (1994, 199); Turrini (1999, 12).
47. Lutz (1973, 94); Angelo (1981, 222).
48. Angelo (1981, 207–16); Gruley (1993, 132); Darden et al. (1987, 69).
49. Angelo (1981, 199–200, 226).
50. Swickard, "A Champion of Fairness, Children, and Detroit" (April 4, 2007); Gruley (1993, 265); Angelo (1981, 242–45).
51. Darden et al. (1987, 216); Neill (2004, 124); Young and Wheeler (1994, 225–26, 243–50).
52. Thomas (1989, 148–50); Darden et al. (1987, 46–54).
53. Thomas (1989, 150–54).
54. Farley, Danziger, and Holzer (2000, 67, 210).
55. U.S. Bureau of the Census (1983, 4, 99).
56. Chafets (1991); Clemens (2005).
57. Cooper, "Kids Killing Kids" (December 1, 1987). Although based on Barry Michael Cooper's article about Detroit, the film version of *New Jack City* moved the setting to New York City.

58. Eisinger (2003); Young and Wheeler (1994, 265); Widick (1989, 234); Orr and Stoker (1994).
59. Darden et al. (1987, 259–60); Young and Wheeler (1994, 203–4, 281).
60. Wacker (2006); Neill (2004).
61. Neill (2004, 143); Farley, Danziger, and Holzer (2000, 169).
62. Thomas (1989, 142).
63. Greenstone and Peterson (1973, 35).
64. Interview with Neal Shine, St. Clair Shores, Mich., April 28, 2005.
65. Fasenfest and Jacobs (2003); Babson (1986).
66. Cooney and Yacobucci (2006); Swoboda, "UAW Thinks It Has Put Outsourcing in Reverse" (October 19, 1996).
67. Bradsher, "Car Makers Predict Strong Sales This Year" (January 4, 1999); Fasenfest and Jacobs (2003); Vlasic, "Can the UAW Put a Brake on Outsourcing?" (June 17, 1996); Muller, "The UAW's New Deal with Ford Could Hardly Be Sweeter" (October 14, 1999).
68. Mast (1994, 197, emphasis in original).
69. Interview with Jocelyn Faniel-Heard, Detroit, July 19, 2006.
70. Interview with Alesia Cooper-Cunningham, Detroit, July 18, 2006.
71. Interview with Alesia Cooper-Cunningham, Detroit, July 18, 2006.
72. Gruley (1993, xii–xiv).
73. Interview with Gary Graff, Beverly Hills, Mich., May 16, 2005.
74. Interview with Joe Swickard, Detroit, May 10, 2005.

CHAPTER 3

1. Interview with Leo Jenkins, Detroit, July 23, 2005.
2. Sleigh (1998, 19).
3. Kalleberg et al. (1987).
4. Interview with Alan Forsyth, Detroit, April 6, 2005; McKercher (2002, 40).
5. McKercher (2002, 39).
6. Kalleberg et al. (1987, 59).
7. McKercher (2002, 43–46).
8. Marjoribanks (2000, 167).
9. Sleigh (1998, 19–22).
10. Kalleberg et al. (1987, 59–60); McKercher (2002, 50); Stanger (2002, 181, 207).
11. Kalleberg et al. (1987, 57); Stanger (2002, 196).
12. McKercher (2002, 53); Cranberg, Bezanson, and Soloski (2001, 49–55).
13. Overholser (2001, 162).
14. Interview with Richard E. Burr, Detroit, March 21, 2005.
15. American Arbitration Association, *DTU 18/CWA 14503 v. Detroit Newspaper Agency*, 54-30-00498-93, hearing transcript (November 8, 1994; award May 22, 1995).
16. McKercher (2002, 9, 70); Sleigh (1998, 26, 51, 79).

17. Sleigh (1998, 49, 93); McKercher (2002, 71).

18. Marjoribanks (2000, 80–81).

19. Interview with Nancy Dunn, Dearborn, Mich., May 11, 2005.

20. Interview with Alan Forsyth, Detroit, April 6, 2005; Angelo (1981, 255).

21. American Arbitration Association, *DTU 18/CWA 14503 v. Detroit Newspaper Agency,* 54-30-00498-93, hearing transcript (November 8, 1994; award May 22, 1995).

22. Interview with Bill Brabenec, Attica, Mich., April 21, 2005.

23. Interview with Barbara Ingalls, Royal Oak, Mich., October 24, 2004.

24. Babson (1986, 190); McGraw, "*Free Press* to End Era with Change of Address" (July 22, 1998).

25. Angelo (1981, 250–51).

26. Lutz (1973, 197); interview with James Case, Romeo Plank, Mich., May 16, 2005; interview with Sam Maci, Detroit, May 17, 2005.

27. Interview with Jack Howe, Detroit, April 12, 2005.

28. Montgomery (1991).

29. Interview with Ben Solomon, Armada, Mich., May 3, 2005.

30. Interview with James St. Louis, Detroit, May 6, 2005.

31. Interview with Alex Young, Detroit, April 27, 2005; NLRB, *Detroit Newspaper Agency,* 342 NLRB 125 (2004).

32. Interview with James St. Louis, Detroit, May 6, 2005.

33. Interview with Ben Solomon, Armada, Mich., May 3, 2005.

34. Interview with Thomas Breyer, Grosse Pointe Farms, Mich., April 13, 2005; NLRB, *Detroit Newspaper Agency,* 342 NLRB 125 (2004), "Transportation—Job Description: Jumper" (attachment to letter from John Taylor to Al Derey), June 15, 1995.

35. Interview with Michael Fahoome, St. Claire Shores, Mich., July 18, 2005.

36. Interview with Paul Kulka, Detroit, May 2, 2005; interview with Dennis Nazelli, Detroit, March 31, 2005; interview with Randy Karpinen, Clinton, Mich., March 30, 2005.

37. Interview with Neil Shine, St. Clair Shores, Mich., April 28, 2005.

38. Interview with Tom Walsh, Detroit, October 22, 2004.

39. Burns (1999); Gruley (1993, 401).

40. Interview with Michael McBride, Detroit, March 28, 2005.

41. Interview with Ben Burns, Detroit, October 20, 2004.

CHAPTER 4

1. Fink (1983); Voss (1994); Ness and Eimer (2001).

2. Lipsitz (1981); Rhomberg (2004).

3. Putnam (2000).

4. Bluestone and Bluestone (1992); Bowles, Gordon, and Weisskopf (1983).

5. Dubofksy (1994); Hattam (1992).
6. Brecher (1977); Nicholson (2004).
7. Dannin (2004).
8. NLRB, National Labor Relations Act, 29 U.S.C. §§ 151–69 (1982).
9. Brody (2005); Lichtenstein and Harris (1996).
10. Kochan, Katz, and McKersie (1994).
11. On the concept of "layering," see Streeck and Thelen (2005).
12. Fantasia (1988).
13. Gordon, Edwards, and Reich (1982).
14. Katznelson (2005).
15. Honey (1993); Horowitz (1997); Needleman (2003).
16. Farley, Danziger, and Holzer (2000); Sugrue (1996).
17. McCammon (1990).
18. Lichtenstein (1995, 280).
19. Bluestone and Bluestone (1992); Harris (1982).
20. Sugrue (1996); Cowie (1999).
21. Getman (2010, 185–90).
22. Soskice (1999).
23. Logan (2006).
24. Dubofsky (1994, 101); Pope (2002).
25. U.S. Supreme Court, *Labor Board v. Insurance Agents' International Union*, 361 U.S. 477 (1960).
26. Reder and Neumann (1980).
27. Interview with William B. Gould IV, Palo Alto, Calif., December 30, 2004.
28. Stone (2005).
29. Serrin (1973); McCammon (1993).
30. Gross (1995); Kochan, Katz, and McKersie (1994); McCartin (2006).
31. Rosenblum (1988/1995); Perry, Kramer, and Schneider (1982).
32. Gruley (1993, 185, 208).
33. Rosenblum (1988/1995, 122–23, 195–98).
34. Getman (1998); Green (1990).
35. Bandzak (1992); Harris (2002).
36. Dannin (2004).
37. Sleigh (1998, 115).
38. Vigilante (1994, 30).
39. Vigilante (1994, 128, 173); Sleigh (1998, 129).
40. Vigilante (1994, 102–7); Sleigh (1998, 137–67).
41. Sleigh (1998, 138).
42. Sleigh (1998, 145–47); Vigilante (1994, 136).
43. Sleigh (1998, 138–41).
44. Sleigh (1998, 122, 154–58); Vigilante (1994, 257–58).
45. Dannin (1997).

46. Simmons (1994); Lendler (1997).
47. Gordon (1999); Johnston (1994); Turner and Cornfield (2007).
48. Milkman (2006).
49. Brisbin (2002); Franklin (2001); Juravich and Bronfenbrenner (1999).
50. Lopez (2004); Milkman (2006).
51. Cranberg, Bezanson, and Soloski (2001); Gruley (1993).
52. Gruley (1993, 98).
53. Simurda (1993).
54. Interview with Jack Howe, Detroit, April 12, 2005; Stanger (2002).
55. Hirsch and Macpherson (1995); interview with David Hecker, Detroit, October 25, 2004; interview with Michele Martin, Detroit, May 23, 2005.
56. Gruley (1993, 208); Sleigh (1998, 145–47); interview with Linda Rabin Hammell, Detroit, July 17, 2006.

CHAPTER 5

1. Newman (1988); Harrison (1994).
2. Gruley (1993, 98); McCord (1996, 140–46); Weiss, "Invasion of the Gannettoids" (February 2, 1987).
3. Gruley (1993, 156–57).
4. Gruley (1993, 183–89); interview with Lou Mleczko, Detroit, April 18, 2005.
5. Gruley (1993, 272, 280–82); NLRB, *Detroit Newspaper Agency*, 326 NLRB 64 (1998, 741); interview with Alfred Derey, Lapeer, Mich., May 12, 2005.
6. Gruley (1993, 270–84, 298–304); interview with Lou Mleczko, Detroit, April 18, 2005.
7. Gruley (1993, 400, 417).
8. Craggs, "Darth Vega to the Rescue" (May 4, 2005); Meyers and Meyers (2000, 1–19); NLRB, *Detroit Newspaper Agency*, 326 NLRB 64 (1998), hearing transcript, 2105.
9. Gruley (1993, 183); NLRB, *Detroit Newspaper Agency*, 326 NLRB 64 (1998), hearing transcript, 752.
10. Interview with John Jaske, McLean, Va., November 4, 2005; NLRB, *Detroit Newspaper Agency*, 326 NLRB 64 (1998), hearing transcript, 2384.
11. Interview with Carole Leigh Hutton, Detroit, April 11, 2005.
12. Konrad, "A Year Later, Solution to Detroit Newspaper Strike Is Elusive" (July 13, 1996); NLRB, *Detroit Newspaper Agency*, 326 NLRB 64 (1998), hearing transcript, 960–65, 1689–90, 2246.
13. Interview with Jack Howe, Detroit, April 12, 2005.
14. Interview with Alfred Derey, Lapeer, Mich., May 12, 2005.
15. Gruley (1993, 185); Sleigh (1998, 145–46).
16. Interview with Alfred Derey, Lapeer, Mich., May 12, 2005.
17. Phone interview with Tom McGrath, October 4, 2006.

18. NLRB, *The Baltimore News American and Baltimore Typographical Union*, 230 NLRB 29 (1977); see also NLRB, *A. S. Abell Company and Baltimore Typographical Union*, 230 NLRB 5 (1977).
19. Interview with John Jaske, McLean, Va., November 4, 2005.
20. Jaske (1982).
21. U.S. Court of Appeals, *Newspaper Printing Corp. v. NLRB*, 692 F.2nd 615 (6th Cir. 1982).
22. U.S. Court of Appeals, *Newspaper Printing Corp. v. NLRB*, 692 F.2nd 615 (6th Cir. 1982).
23. NLRB, *Antelope Valley Press*, 311 NLRB 50 (1993).
24. NLRB, *Detroit Newspaper Agency*, 326 NLRB 64 (1998), general counsel exhibit 167: letter from John Jaske to William Boarman, October 15, 1987.
25. American Arbitration Association, *DTU 18/CWA 14503 v. Detroit Newspaper Agency*, 54-30-00498-93 (May 22, 1995).
26. Michael Rybicki, letter to Tim Kelleher, April 11, 1988.
27. Michael Rybicki, letter to Tim Kelleher, April 11, 1988.
28. NLRB, *Cincinnati Enquirer, et al.*, 298 NLRB 41 (1990).
29. Stanger (2002, 197).
30. Telephone interview with Tom McGrath, October 4, 2006.
31. Interview with Jack Howe, Detroit, April 12, 2005.
32. Kalleberg et al. (1987, 65); American Arbitration Association, *DTU 18/CWA 14503 v. Detroit Newspaper Agency* (May 22, 1995).
33. Agreement between Detroit Newspaper Agency and International Brotherhood of Teamsters, Local 2040, May 1, 1992, Detroit; NLRB, *Detroit Newspaper Agency*, 326 NLRB 64 (1998, 732); *The Alliance*, "Pressmen, Engravers Seek Fair Contracts" (August 11, 1995); NLRB, *Detroit Newspaper Agency*, 326 NLRB 64 (1998), general counsel exhibit 9: agreement between Detroit Newspaper Agency and Detroit Graphic Communications Union Local 13N, May 1, 1992.
34. Sleigh (1998, 81); telephone interview with Tom McGrath, October 4, 2006.
35. Interview with Lou Mleczko, Detroit, April 18, 2005; interview with Jack Howe, Detroit, April 12, 2005.
36. NLRB, *Detroit Newspaper Agency*, 326 NLRB 64 (1998), hearing transcript, 578, 2393.
37. Telephone interview with Tom McGrath, October 4, 2006.
38. Interview with Alfred Derey, Lapeer, Mich., May 12, 2005.
39. Interview with Alan Lenhoff, Detroit, November 4, 2004; interview with Lou Mleczko, Detroit, April 18, 2005; Konrad, "A Year Later, Solution to Detroit Newspaper Strike Is Elusive" (July 13, 1996); Gruley (1993, 417); Schultz, "Showdown on Lafayette" (April 22–28, 1992).
40. NLRB, *Detroit Newspaper Agency*, 326 NLRB 64 (1998), respondent exhibit 3: minutes of "Non-Economic Scale Negotiations Meeting," March 19, 1992.

41. NLRB, *Detroit Newspaper Agency*, 326 NLRB 64 (1998), general counsel exhibit 5: letter from Alfred Derey to Frank Vega, March 19, 1992.
42. Interview with Alfred Derey, Lapeer, Mich., May 12, 2005.
43. NLRB, *Detroit Newspaper Agency*, 326 NLRB 64 (1998), hearing transcript, 516–19.
44. Interview with Alfred Derey, Lapeer, Mich., May 12, 2005.
45. Telephone interview with Tom McGrath, October 4, 2006.
46. Interview with Lou Mleczko, Detroit, April 18, 2005; interview with Jack Howe, Detroit, April 12, 2005.
47. NLRB, *Detroit Newspaper Agency*, 326 NLRB 64 (1998), general counsel exhibit 9; hearing transcript, 2409.
48. Agreement between Detroit Newspaper Agency and International Brotherhood of Teamsters, Local 2040; NLRB, *Detroit Newspaper Agency*, 326 NLRB 64 (1998), hearing transcript, 1529, 2413–15; interview with Alex Young, Detroit, April 27, 2005.
49. Interview with Lou Mleczko, Detroit, April 18, 2005; Gruley (1993), 413; NLRB, *Detroit Newspaper Agency*, 326 NLRB 64 (1998), hearing transcript, 825.
50. Gruley (1993), 193.
51. Telephone interview with Tom McGrath, October 4, 2006.
52. Interview with James St. Louis, Detroit, May 6, 2005.

CHAPTER 6

1. *New York Times*, "Newspaper Unions End Strike" (November 15, 1994); U.S. District Court, *David P. Zieminski v. The City of Sterling Heights et al.*, 96-CV-75820 (E.D. Mich. 2000), Kelleher deposition, January 29, 2001, 20.
2. Interview with Alan Lenhoff, Detroit, November 4, 2004; U.S. District Court, *Zieminski v. City of Sterling Heights et al.*, Lenhoff deposition, November 1, 2000, 7–8.
3. U.S. District Court, *Benjamin L. Solomon v. The City of Sterling Heights et al.*, 98-CV-73900 (E.D. Mich. 2000), trial transcript, vol. 4, p. 78ff.; interview with Alan Lenhoff, Detroit, November 4, 2004; U.S. District Court, *Zieminski v. City of Sterling Heights et al.*, Anthony deposition, November 3, 2000, 16.
4. U.S. District Court, *Zieminski v. City of Sterling Heights et al.*, Anthony and Lenhoff depositions.
5. U.S. District Court, *Mahaffey et al. v. Detroit Newspaper Agency*, 95-CV-75724 (E.D. Mich. 1997); interview with Alan Lenhoff, Detroit, November 4, 2004; Taylor (2008, 167).
6. Taylor (2008, 169); Androshick (1996); Konrad, "Newspaper Foes Pay Dearly for Year-Long Strike" (July 13, 1996).
7. U.S. District Court, *Zieminski v. City of Sterling Heights et al.*, Kelleher deposition, 12; Taylor (2008, 168); Franklin (2001, 96, 100–101).

8. Interview with Alan Lenhoff, Detroit, March 23, 2005.

9. Taylor (2008, 169).

10. U.S. District Court, *Teamsters Local 372 et al. v. Detroit Newspapers*, 95-CV-40474 (E.D. Mich. 1999), Walworth deposition, July 1, 1999; interview with John Anthony, Canton, Mich., April 28, 2005; U.S. District Court, *Solomon v. City of Sterling Heights et al.*, trial transcript, vol. 4, pp. 82–83, 95.

11. U.S. District Court, *Solomon v. City of Sterling Heights et al.*, trial transcript, vol. 4, p. 114.

12. U.S. District Court, *Solomon v. City of Sterling Heights et al.*, trial transcript, vol. 3, pp. 18–22, 119.

13. U.S. District Court, *Teamsters Local 372 et al. v. Detroit Newspapers*, Owens deposition, March 4, 1999, 20–23; U.S. District Court, *Solomon v. City of Sterling Heights et al.*, trial transcript, vol. 4, pp. 86–88; U.S. District Court, *Zieminski v. City of Sterling Heights et al.*, Kelleher deposition, pp. 86–87.

14. Gargaro, "Old Ways Gone, Impasse Persists" (July 8, 1996).

15. Raphael, "SEC Scandal Could Haunt Vega in Talks" (December 19, 1994).

16. McMorris, "Ex-Gannett Aide Admits to Charge of Insider Trading" (March 8, 1996); Norris, "SEC Cites Two Officers of Gannett" (December 9, 1994); Raphael, "SEC Scandal Could Haunt Vega in Talks" (December 19, 1994); Shellum, "Grand Jury Probes Insider Trading Involving DN Chief" (October 2, 1995).

17. NLRB, *Detroit Newspaper Agency*, 326 NLRB 64 (1998), hearing transcript, 220–21.

18. NLRB, *Detroit Newspaper Agency*, 326 NLRB 64 (1998), general counsel exhibit 157: memorandum from Larry Ross to John Taylor, "Things We Will Want in the Near Future," January 8, 1995 (emphasis in original).

19. NLRB, *Detroit Newspaper Agency*, 326 NLRB 64 (1998), general counsel exhibit 157: memorandum from Larry Ross to John Taylor, "Things We Will Want in the Near Future," January 8, 1995 (emphasis in original).

20. NLRB, *Detroit Newspaper Agency*, 326 NLRB 64 (1998), charging party exhibit 5: memorandum from John Jaske to Doug McCorkindale, "Detroit," March 6, 1995.

21. NLRB, *Detroit Newspaper Agency*, 326 NLRB 64 (1998), general counsel exhibit 22: "Detroit News Proposal to Guild #22," February 20, 1995.

22. NLRB, *Detroit Newspaper Agency*, 326 NLRB 64 (1998), 758.

23. Franklin (1995).

24. Henderson, "Pulp Friction" (March 1996).

25. NLRB, *Detroit Newspaper Agency*, 326 NLRB 64 (1998), charging party exhibit 5: memorandum from Jaske to McCorkindale.

26. NLRB, *Detroit Newspaper Agency*, 326 NLRB 64 (1998), charging party exhibit 5: memorandum from Jaske to McCorkindale.

27. Interview with Jack Howe, Detroit, April 12, 2005; NLRB, *Detroit Newspaper*

Agency, 326 NLRB 64 (1998), memorandum from John Jaske to Frank Vega et al., "Mailer Negotiations," May 1, 1995.

28. Interview with James St. Louis, Detroit, May 6, 2005; interview with Alex Young, Detroit, April 27, 2005; NLRB, *Detroit Newspaper Agency*, 326 NLRB 64 (1998), letter from John Jaske to Al Young, "1994 Mailroom Wages," May 4, 1995.
29. Interview with Alex Young, Detroit, April 27, 2005.
30. Interview with James St. Louis, Detroit, May 6, 2005.
31. NLRB, *Detroit Newspaper Agency*, 326 NLRB 64 (1998), charging party exhibit 5: memorandum from Jaske to McCorkindale.
32. NLRB, *Detroit Newspaper Agency*, 326 NLRB 64 (1998), charging party exhibit 5: memorandum from Jaske to McCorkindale.
33. NLRB, *Detroit Newspaper Agency*, 326 NLRB 64 (1998), letter from Jaske to Young, "1994 Mailroom Wages."
34. Interview with James St. Louis, Detroit, May 6, 2005.
35. Interview with James St. Louis, Detroit, May 6, 2005; NLRB, *Detroit Newspaper Agency*, 326 NLRB 64 (1998), memorandum from Jaske to Vega et al., "Mailer Negotiations."
36. NLRB, *Detroit Newspaper Agency*, 326 NLRB 64 (1998), charging party exhibit 5: memorandum from Jaske to McCorkindale.
37. NLRB, *Detroit Newspaper Agency*, 326 NLRB 64 (1998), memorandum from Tommie McLeod to Robert Althaus, "SAP Priorities," February 8, 1995.
38. Christian, "Deadline Pressure: Detroit Newspapers Face an Ugly Standoff with Striking Unions" (August 9, 1995); Lippert and Craig, "Newspaper Carriers at Center of Talks" (July 11, 1995).
39. Lippert and Craig, "Newspaper Deadline for Strike Is Delayed" (July 13, 1995); *Detroit Journal*, "Statement from the Unions" (August 3, 1995).
40. Gruley (1993, 281); International Brotherhood of Teamsters, Local 372, agreement between Detroit Newspaper Agency and Newspaper Drivers and Handlers' Local Union 372, May 1, 1992, Detroit.
41. NLRB, *Detroit Newspaper Agency*, 326 NLRB 64 (1998), charging party exhibit 5: memorandum from Jaske to McCorkindale.
42. NLRB, *Detroit Newspaper Agency*, 326 NLRB 64 (1998), memorandum from John Jaske to Doug McCorkindale, "January-February Monthly Report," February 15, 1995.
43. NLRB, *Detroit Newspaper Agency*, 326 NLRB 64 (1998), general counsel exhibit 101: letter from Tim Kelleher to Sam Attard, February 20, 1995.
44. NLRB, *Detroit Newspaper Agency*, 326 NLRB 64 (1998), general counsel exhibit 13: "Meeting Schedules" (n.d.), and general counsel exhibit 124: "Local 2040 Mailers Meetings March 10, 1995 to July 13, 1995."
45. NLRB, *Detroit Newspaper Agency*, 326 NLRB 64 (1998), general counsel exhibit

100: "DTU #18/Detroit Newspapers Bargaining Meetings"; NLRB, *Detroit Newspaper Agency*, 326 NLRB 64 (1998), 758; U.S. District Court, *Solomon v. City of Sterling Heights et al.*, plaintiff exhibit 1: memorandum from James Owens to Schmidt et al., "Staff Meeting Regarding Possible Detroit Newspaper Strike," March 20, 1995.

46. *Huffmaster Mgmt., Inc., et al. v. The Detroit Newspapers et al.*, 96-1946CK (Michigan Circuit Court, Macomb County, March 15, 1996).

47. U.S. District Court, *Solomon v. City of Sterling Heights et al.*, trial transcript, vol. 4, pp. 89, 93; U.S. District Court, *Teamsters Local 372 et al. v. Detroit Newspapers et al.*, Owens deposition, 23–30.

48. U.S. District Court, *Teamsters Local 372 et al. v. Detroit Newspapers et al.*, Derocha deposition, March 1, 1999, 46.

49. U.S. District Court, *Teamsters Local 372 et al. v. Detroit Newspapers et al.*, Owens deposition, 37.

50. U.S. District Court, *Zieminski v. City of Sterling Heights et al.*, John Anthony depositions, November 3, 2000, 28–29, and January 21, 2000, 53; U.S. District Court, *Solomon v. City of Sterling Heights et al.*, trial transcript, vol. 3, pp. 34–39.

51. U.S. District Court, *Solomon v. City of Sterling Heights et al.*, trial transcript, vol. 2, p. 62; and plaintiff exhibit 2: memorandum from Frank Mowinski to James Owens, "Impending Strike at the Detroit News Plant," May 1, 1995.

52. U.S. District Court, *Solomon v. City of Sterling Heights et al.*, trial transcript, vol. 2, p. 62; and plaintiff exhibit 2: memorandum from Mowinski to Owens.

53. U.S. District Court, *Solomon v. City of Sterling Heights et al.*, trial transcript, vol. 2, pp. 40–42; and plaintiff exhibit 3: memorandum from Frank Mowinski to James Owens, "Contingency Plan for Impending DNA Strike," May 6, 1995; and plaintiff exhibit 3: memorandum from James Owens to all operations division personnel, "Action Plan for Impending Possible Strike at the Detroit News Plant: 16 Mile and Mound," May 8, 1995; U.S. District Court, *Zieminski v. City of Sterling Heights et al.*, Mowinski deposition, June 26, 1997, 76–78.

54. U.S. District Court, *Solomon v. City of Sterling Heights et al.*, trial transcript, vol. 2, pp. 65–66; U.S. District Court, *Teamsters Local 372 et al. v. Detroit Newspapers*, Frank Mowinski deposition, March 3, 1999, 87.

55. U.S. District Court, *Solomon v. City of Sterling Heights et al.*, plaintiff exhibit 4: confidential memo from Thomas Derocha to city manager concerning draft "Action Plan for Impending Possible Strike at the Detroit News Plant: 16 Mile and Mound"; and trial transcript, vol. 2, pp. 38–40, and vol. 3, p. 55.

56. U.S. District Court, *Solomon v. City of Sterling Heights et al.*, plaintiff exhibit 3: memorandum from Owens to all operations division personnel, "Action Plan for Impending Possible Strike at the Detroit News Plant: 16 Mile and Mound."

57. U.S. District Court, *Solomon v. City of Sterling Heights et al.*, trial transcript, vol. 4, p. 64.

58. U.S. District Court, *Solomon v. City of Sterling Heights et al.*, plaintiff exhibit 2: memorandum from Mowinski to Owens, "Impending Strike at the Detroit News Plant."
59. U.S. District Court, *Solomon v. City of Sterling Heights et al.*, plaintiff exhibit 3: memorandum from Owens to all operations division personnel, "Action Plan for Impending Possible Strike at the Detroit News Plant: 16 Mile and Mound."
60. U.S. District Court, *Solomon v. City of Sterling Heights et al.*, trial transcript, vol. 2, pp. 59–60, and vol. 3, pp. 40–42; plaintiff exhibit 72A-E: memorandum from Frank Mowinski to N. Nowak, "Equipment for the Impending Strike," May 11, 1995.
61. U.S. District Court, *Teamsters Local 372 et al. v. Detroit Newspapers*, Mowinski deposition, March 3, 1999, 95–100; U.S. District Court, *Solomon v. City of Sterling Heights et al.*, trial transcript, vol. 4, p. 13; Driskell, "Sterling Police Train for Crowd Control Duties" (June 1, 1995).
62. Craggs, "Darth Vega to the Rescue" (May 4, 2005).

CHAPTER 7

1. Interview with Jack Howe, Detroit, April 12, 2005.
2. NLRB, *Detroit Newspaper Agency*, 326 NLRB 64 (1998), "Negotiations Update," March 10, 1995.
3. Driskell, "Portion of *Detroit News* Plant in Sterling Heights May Close" (April 13, 1995).
4. NLRB, *Detroit Newspaper Agency*, 326 NLRB 64 (1998), Detroit Newspaper Agency, "Mailer Negotiations, March 29, 1995, Conference Room A, 6:55 PM."
5. NLRB, *Detroit Newspaper Agency*, 326 NLRB 64 (1998), Detroit Newspaper Agency, "Mailer Negotiations, March 29, 1995, Conference Room A, 6:55 PM."
6. Interview with Alex Young, Detroit, April 27, 2005.
7. Bohy, "Newspaper Unions Have a Better Idea: Boycotts" (May 24–30, 1995); Howes, "Detroit Newspapers Cancels Threat to Close Macomb Plant" (June 7, 1995).
8. Interview with Alex Young, Detroit, April 27, 2005; *The Alliance*, "Unions Unite for Contract Talks" (January 15, 1995); interview with David Hecker, Detroit, October 25, 2004; *The Alliance*, "Unions Shifting into High Gear" (February 15, 1995).
9. Interview with Lou Mleczko, Detroit, April 18, 2005.
10. *The Alliance*, "Strike Plans Surge Forward" (May 16, 1995).
11. Bohy, "Progress Aside, Newspaper Talks Still Drag On" (June 14–20, 1995).
12. Interview with David Hecker, Detroit, October 25, 2004.

13. NLRB, *Detroit Newspaper Agency*, 326 NLRB 64 (1998), 701, 732; and hearing transcript, 2105.
14. NLRB, *Detroit Newspaper Agency*, 326 NLRB 64 (1998), hearing transcript, 567, 2106; and general counsel exhibit 8c: letter from Alfred Derey to Frank Vega, May 9, 1995.
15. NLRB, *Detroit Newspaper Agency*, 326 NLRB 64 (1998), 733–34.
16. NLRB, *Detroit Newspaper Agency*, 326 NLRB 64 (1998), hearing transcript, 541.
17. NLRB, *Detroit Newspaper Agency*, 326 NLRB 64 (1998), 743–50.
18. NLRB, *Detroit Newspaper Agency*, 326 NLRB 64 (1998), 750.
19. NLRB, *Detroit Newspaper Agency*, 326 NLRB 64 (1998), 751–55.
20. NLRB, *Detroit Newspaper Agency*, 326 NLRB 64 (1998), hearing transcript, 1200.
21. NLRB, *Detroit Newspaper Agency*, 326 NLRB 64 (1998), 729.
22. NLRB, *Detroit Newspaper Agency*, 326 NLRB 64 (1998), 757–59.
23. NLRB, *Detroit Newspaper Agency*, 326 NLRB 64 (1998), 759–60.
24. NLRB, *Detroit Newspaper Agency*, 326 NLRB 64 (1998), 761.
25. NLRB, *Detroit Newspaper Agency*, 326 NLRB 64 (1998).
26. NLRB, *Detroit Newspaper Agency*, 326 NLRB 64 (1998), hearing transcript, 745.
27. NLRB, *Detroit Newspaper Agency*, 326 NLRB 64 (1998), 761–62.
28. Interview with Lou Mleczko, Detroit, April 18, 2005.
29. NLRB, *Detroit Newspaper Agency*, 326 NLRB 64 (1998), 762.
30. NLRB, *Detroit Newspaper Agency*, 326 NLRB 64 (1998), general counsel exhibit 45: memorandum from Robert Giles to staff, June 28, 1995; and NLRB, *Detroit Newspaper Agency*, 326 NLRB 64 (1998), 762.
31. NLRB, *Detroit Newspaper Agency*, 326 NLRB 64 (1998), 763.
32. NLRB, *Detroit Newspaper Agency*, 326 NLRB 64 (1998), 761.
33. NLRB, *Detroit Newspaper Agency*, 326 NLRB 64 (1998), 737.
34. NLRB, *Detroit Newspaper Agency*, 326 NLRB 64 (1998), 734.
35. NLRB, *Detroit Newspaper Agency*, 326 NLRB 64 (1998), hearing transcript, 544.
36. NLRB, *Detroit Newspaper Agency*, 326 NLRB 64 (1998), 736.
37. NLRB, *Detroit Newspaper Agency*, 326 NLRB 64 (1998), hearing transcript, 1206.
38. NLRB, *Detroit Newspaper Agency*, 326 NLRB 64 (1998), 773, 741.
39. Interview with Alfred Derey, Lapeer, Mich., May 12, 2005.
40. NLRB, *Detroit Newspaper Agency*, 326 NLRB 64 (1998), 729, 738–39.
41. *The Alliance*, "Health Insurance Answers" (May 16, 1995), and "Detroit Backs Newspaper Unions" (June 21, 1995).
42. Interview with James St. Louis, Detroit, May 6, 2005.
43. Bohy, "Newspaper Unions Have a Better Idea" (May 24–30, 1995).
44. Interview with Alan Lenhoff, Detroit, March 23, 2005; Detroit Newspapers, Inc. (1995).

45. *Huffmaster Mgmt., Inc., et al. v. The Detroit Newspapers et al.*, 96-1946CK (Michigan Circuit Court, Macomb County, March 15, 1996); U.S. District Court, *Benjamin L. Solomon v. The City of Sterling Heights et al.*, 98-CV-73900 (E.D. Mich. 2000), trial transcript, vol. 4, p. 33; interview with John Anthony, Canton, Mich., April 28, 2005.

46. U.S. District Court, *Solomon v. City of Sterling Heights et al.*, trial transcript, vol. 4, pp. 17, 94.

47. U.S. District Court, *David P. Zieminski v. The City of Sterling Heights et al.*, 98-CV-75820 (E.D. Mich. 2000), memorandum from Frank Mowinski to all operations division personnel, May 30, 1995.

48. U.S. District Court, *David P. Zieminski v. The City of Sterling Heights et al.*, 98-CV-75820 (E.D. Mich. 2000), memorandum from Frank Mowinski to all operations division personnel, June 23, 1995.

49. U.S. District Court, *David P. Zieminski v. The City of Sterling Heights et al.*, 98-CV-75820 (E.D. Mich. 2000), memorandum from James Owens to operations division command officers, June 27, 1995.

50. U.S. District Court, *Solomon v. City of Sterling Heights et al.*, memorandum from Frank Mowinski to all operations division personnel, June 27, 1995.

51. Jackson, "Newspaper Contracts Run Out, Talks Go On" (July 3, 2005).

52. Craig, "Agency Extends Newspaper Union Contracts" (July 1, 1995); Fogel, "The *News* Imposes Its Final Wage Offer" (July 6, 1995).

53. NLRB, *Detroit Newspaper Agency*, 326 NLRB 64 (1998), general counsel exhibit 60–62: "Merit Pay Letters."

54. NLRB, *Detroit Newspaper Agency*, 326 NLRB 64 (1998), 729, 763.

55. Craig, "Unions Set a Strike Deadline for Newspapers" (July 7, 1995); NLRB, *Detroit Newspaper Agency*, 326 NLRB 64 (1998), 773; and general counsel exhibit 113: joint strike resolution.

56. NLRB, *Detroit Newspaper Agency*, 326 NLRB 64 (1998), 738–39.

57. NLRB, *Detroit Newspaper Agency*, 326 NLRB 64 (1998), 739; interview with Alex Young, Detroit, April 27, 2005; Lippert, "Paper, Six Unions Bargain" (July 10, 1995).

58. NLRB, *Detroit Newspaper Agency*, 326 NLRB 64 (1998), 738–39.

59. Telephone interview with Tom McGrath, October 4, 2006.

60. Lippert and Craig, "Newspaper Carriers at Center of Talks" (July 11, 1995); Markiewicz, "Newspapers Contract Talks Suspended" (July 12, 1995).

61. NLRB, *Detroit Newspaper Agency*, 326 NLRB 64 (1998), 739; Lippert and Craig, "Newspaper Deadline for Strike Is Delayed" (July 13, 1995); Markiewicz, "Newspapers, Unions to Meet with Archer" (July 13, 1995).

62. Interview with Alfred Derey, Lapeer, Mich., May 12, 2005.

63. Telephone interview with Tom McGrath, October 4, 2006. McGrath is describing the negotiations using the language of a poker game, as in "I see your bet."

64. Telephone interview with Tom McGrath, October 4, 2006.
65. NLRB, *Detroit Newspaper Agency*, 326 NLRB 64 (1998), 738.
66. Interview with Jack Howe, Detroit, April 12, 2005.
67. Interview with Alex Young, Detroit, April 27, 2005.
68. NLRB, *Detroit Newspaper Agency*, 326 NLRB 64 (1998), 765.
69. Interview with Robert Ourlian, Washington, D.C., March 17, 2006.
70. Lippert and Craig, "Newspaper Deadline for Strike Is Delayed" (July 13, 1995); NLRB, *Detroit Newspaper Agency*, 326 NLRB 64 (1998), respondent exhibit 49: "Compilation News Clips," 35.
71. Interview with Jocelyn Faniel-Heard, Detroit, July 19, 2006.
72. Interview with Nancy Dunn, Dearborn, Mich., May 11, 2005.
73. NLRB, *Detroit Newspaper Agency*, 326 NLRB 64 (1998), 772.
74. Markiewicz, "Newspapers, Unions to Meet with Archer" (July 13, 1995).
75. Finley, "Newspaper Workers Strike" (July 14, 1995).
76. NLRB, *Detroit Newspaper Agency*, 326 NLRB 64 (1998), respondent exhibit 49: "Compilation News Clips," 18.
77. Interview with Alfred Derey, Lapeer, Mich., May 12, 2005.
78. Interview with Lou Mleczko, Detroit, April 18, 2005.
79. NLRB, *Detroit Newspaper Agency*, 326 NLRB 64 (1998), respondent exhibit 49: "Compilation News Clips," 40.
80. Craig, "Unions Set a Strike Deadline for Newspapers" (July 7, 1995).
81. Interview with John Anthony, Canton, Mich., April 28, 2005.
82. Lippert and Craig, "Newspaper Deadline for Strike Is Delayed" (July 13, 1995).

CHAPTER 8

1. Interview with Bill McGraw, Detroit, March 16, 2006.
2. Interview with Michael Betzold, Ann Arbor, Mich., March 18, 2005.
3. Interview with Kate DeSmet, Detroit, April 1, 2005.
4. Interview with Robert Ourlian, Washington, D.C., March 17, 2006.
5. Interview with Rebecca Cook, Detroit, October 21, 2004.
6. Interview with Nancy Dunn, Dearborn, Mich., May 11, 2005.
7. *The Alliance*, "News Brief: From the Battlefront" (July 17, 1995), "Union Teachers on Our Side" (July 23, 1995), "UAW Gives Strikers a $300,000 Boost" (November 11, 1995); Wenner (2001).
8. Interview with Michele Martin, Detroit, May 23, 2005; *The Alliance*, "UAW Adds Muscle to Advertising Campaign" (August 24, 1995); Smith, "Pushier Pickets" (June 5–11, 1996).
9. *The Alliance*, "Latest Union Donations" (August 28, 1995), "UAW, AFL-CIO Pledge Aid for Unions" (October 12, 1995), "Notes from the Battlefront" (September 21, 1995), and "Notes from the Battlefront" (October 25, 1995); Funke, "Building and Restaurant Workers Lend Support" (1995).

10. *The Alliance*, "Hams Available at Food Bank" (September 29, 1995); Grow, "Paper Strike in Detroit May Prove Fight for Union Life" (September 26, 1995); International Brotherhood of Teamsters, press release, "PA Teamsters Deliver 40 Tons of Food for Newspaper Strikers" (September 28, 1995).
11. *The Alliance*, "UAW, AFL-CIO Pledge Aid for Unions" (October 12, 1995), and "AFL-CIO Calls for National Drive" (August 16, 1995).
12. *The Alliance*, "Members Celebrate Solidarity at Rally" (July 26, 1995), "Notes from the Battlefront" (August 13, 1995), and "Notes from the Battlefront" (September 26, 1995).
13. *The Alliance*, "United Way's Decision, Charity Skips Scab Ads" (September 12, 1996); Fitzgerald, "Pick a Side" (November 4, 1995); *The Alliance*, "Detroit Teachers Reject Freep" (November 28, 1995).
14. *The Alliance*, "Notes from the Battlefront" (July 21, 1995), and "Vegas Markets Ready to Help Strikers with Discounts" (August 13, 1995).
15. Christian, "Deadline Pressure" (August 9, 1995); *The Alliance*, "Elsewhere on the Goon Front . . ." (July 26, 1995); Slaughter, "Picketing Continues at Local Center, Newspaper Delivery Sporadic in Area" (July 27, 1995).
16. Slaughter, "Strike Affects Local Readers" (July 20, 1995).
17. Bohy, "Odds and Ends from the Picket Line" (December 13, 1995); Christian, "Deadline Pressure" (August 9, 1995); Stevens, "Strike Support" (Summer 1996).
18. Interview with A. J. Hartley, Detroit, May 4, 2005.
19. *The Alliance*, "Notes from the Battlefront" (December 16, 1995); interview with David Bonior, Detroit, April 7, 2005.
20. *The Alliance*, "Coleman Calls DN 'Illegal, Immoral'" (August 13, 1995).
21. *The Alliance*, "Reno Asked to Rescind JOA" (August 19, 1995), "Shores Latest to Ask for JOA Probe" (August 28, 1995), and "DN Hit with Anti-Trust Lawsuit" (November 28, 1995); Walsh and Walton, "Class Action Lawsuit Filed over Newspapers' Strike Publication" (November 22, 1995).
22. *The Alliance*, "Front Line News" (August 6, 1995), "Notes from the Battlefront" (January 30, 1996), and "Notes from the Battlefront" (April 13, 1996).
23. Moran, "Council Denies DNA Request to Sell Sunday Papers" (October 18, 1995).
24. *Oakland Press*, "Wayne County Bans Ads in Striking Papers" (December 23, 1995); Lippert, "Money, Contracts Slip from *Press, News*" (January 7, 1996); *The Alliance*, "Notes from the Battlefront" (December 16, 1995).
25. Lippert, "The Detroit Newspaper Strike" (n.d.).
26. Interview with Sam Maci, Detroit, May 17, 2005.
27. International Brotherhood of Teamsters, memorandum from Ron Carey, "Dear Brothers and Sisters" (September 14, 1995); interview with Alfred Derey, Lapeer, Mich., May 12, 2005; Craig, "Papers, Unions Vow to Behave in Sterling Heights Picketing" (September 9, 1995).

28. Interview with Kate DeSmet, Detroit, April 1, 2005; interview with Lou Mleczko, Detroit, April 18, 2005.

29. *CWA News*, "CWA and TNG Launch Adopt-A-Family Program to Aid Detroit Newspaper Strikers" (January 1996), and "Adopt-A-Family 'Honor Roll'" (March 1996).

30. Parks, "After Year, Detroit Spirit Strong" (July 1996); interview with Randy Karpinen, Clinton, Mich., March 30, 2005; *The Alliance*, "Strikers Get Financial Aid" (October 14, 1995).

31. Interview with Leo Jenkins, Detroit, July 23, 2005.

32. Interview with Thomas Breyer, Grosse Pointe Farms, Mich., April 13, 2005; interview with Alesia Cooper-Cunningham, Detroit, July 18, 2006.

33. Mather, "When There Are Promises to Keep, We Soon Learn Whom We Can Trust" (1995); interview with Renee Murawski, New York, N.Y., December 12, 2008; Schlagheck, "On Strike in Detroit" (February 1996).

34. Fitzgerald, "Face-off in Detroit" (July 22, 1995); Slaughter, "Strike Affects Local Readers" (July 20, 1995).

35. Hotts, "Strike Papers Not Reaching Macomb, DNA Leaders Say" (July 17, 1995).

36. Ahrens, "Bad News" (July 30, 1995); Christian, "Deadline Pressure" (August 9, 1995).

37. Fitzgerald, "A War of Attrition" (March 16, 1996); Parks, "After Year, Detroit Spirit Strong" (July 1996).

38. Raphael, "Circulation Audit on Hold" (September 25–October 1, 1995).

39. Burroughs, "Strike Rattles Ad Market" (January 1996); Gardner, "Advertising Losses Heavy in Detroit, Knight-Ridder Says" (August 27, 1995).

40. Konrad, "Meijer Ads Return to Detroit Papers" (December 8, 1996); *The Observer*, "Ad Volume to Delay *Observer* Delivery" (August 10, 1995); Fitzgerald, "Tug of War in Detroit" (August 12, 1995); *The Alliance*, "Ad Honor Roll Hits 222" (July 26, 1995); Raphael, "Newspapers Slash Rates" (July 24–30, 1995).

41. Lippert, "Strike's Duration, Cost Surprise Papers, Ridder Admits" (February 4, 1996); interview with Tim Kelleher, Royal Oak, Mich., November 3, 2004; Reed and Barciela, "Strike Dominates Knight-Ridder Annual Meeting" (April 24, 1996).

42. Bureau of National Affairs, "Special Report" (July 8, 1996); Bohy, "Still Smoldering" (July 3, 1996); Bullard, "An Ex-Marine Keeps Chow Coming for *News* Workers" (July 21, 1995).

43. Musial, "Unions, Papers Head Back to the Bargaining Table" (August 18, 1995); interview with Alan Lenhoff, Detroit, March 23, 2005; Bennet, "Detroit: Paper Is Ready to Replace Strikers" (August 9, 1995); Bureau of National Affairs, "Special Report" (July 8, 1996).

44. Konrad, "Newspaper Foes Pay Dearly for Year-Long Strike" (July 13, 1996).

45. *Detroit Free Press,* "Q&A: No Plans to Close One Newspaper Despite the Strike and Delivery Problems" (July 22, 1995); interview with Alan Lenhoff, Detroit, March 23, 2005.

46. Christian, "Deadline Pressure" (August 9, 1995); Ramirez, *"News, Free Press* Racks Are Taking a Pounding" (October 26, 1995); Ahrens, "Bad News" (July 30, 1995).

47. Fitzgerald, "Face-off in Detroit" (July 22, 1995); *Detroit Free Press,* "Strike Simmers at Detroit Papers" (July 15, 1995).

48. Hotts, "Detroit *News, Free Press* Workers Walk Off the Job" (July 14, 1995); Kosdrosky, "Sterling Leaders Argue about Police Conduct in Newspaper Strike" (July 16, 1995); U.S. District Court, *Benjamin L. Solomon v. The City of Sterling Heights et al.,* 98-CV-73900 (E.D. Mich. 2000), trial transcript, vol. 3, p. 38.

49. NLRB, *Detroit Newspaper Agency,* 342 NLRB 24 (2004), 223–315.

50. Christian, "Deadline Pressure" (August 9, 1995).

51. U.S. District Court, *Solomon v. City of Sterling Heights et al.,* plaintiff's exhibit 43: memo from Frank Mowinski to Thomas Derocha, "Violations of Agreements Between DNA and SHPD," July 17, 1995.

52. *Huffmaster Mgmt., Inc., et al. v. The Detroit Newspapers et al.,* 96-1946CK (Michigan Circuit Court, Macomb County, March 15, 1996).

53. Kosdrosky, "Sterling Leaders Argue About Police Conduct in Newspaper Strike" (July 16, 1995); Smith, "Two Teamsters Charged with Stealing Newspapers" (July 25, 1995); Fitzgerald, "Progression of Violence" (March 16, 1996).

54. Interview with Randy Karpinen, Clinton, Mich., March 30, 2005.

55. Fornoff, "Printing Plant Violence Blamed on Outsiders" (August 21, 1995), and "Strikers, Sterling Heights Cops Declare Truce" (August 28, 1995).

56. NLRB, *Detroit Newspaper Agency,* 326 NLRB 64 (1998), 703.

57. Bennet, "Newspaper Strike Divides Labor's Capital, Detroit" (September 2, 1995); Musial, "Unions, Papers Head Back to the Bargaining Table" (August 18, 1995).

58. Interview with Alan Lenhoff, Detroit, November 4, 2004.

59. Gruley, "We're Getting Job Done, Papers Say" (July 20, 1995).

60. NLRB, *Detroit Newspaper Agency,* 326 NLRB 64 (1998), John Jaske memorandum to Jack Howe, "Negotiations," July 26, 1995; Jaske memorandum to Al Young, "Negotiations," July 26, 1995; Jaske memorandum to Frank Kortsch, "Teamster Negotiations," July 26, 1995; Walsh, "Three Free Press Journalists Return as Divisions Surface within Union" (July 29, 1995).

61. Interview with Nolan Finley, Detroit, October 26, 2004.

62. Debenport, "Hard Pressed" (September 2, 1995).

63. *Macomb Daily, "Free Press* Ultimatum: Return or Be Replaced" (August 9, 1995).

64. Interview with Robert Ourlian, Washington, D.C., March 17, 2006.

65. Christian, "Deadline Pressure" (August 9, 1995); Ahrens, "Bad News" (July 30, 1995).

66. Christian, "Deadline Pressure" (August 9, 1995).

67. Interview with Bill McGraw, Detroit, March 16, 2005.

68. Interview with Bill McGraw, Detroit, March 16, 2005.

69. Interview with Tony Ridder, San Jose, Calif., June 14, 2005.

70. *Detroit News*, "*Free Press* Tells Staffers to Return or Risk Job Loss" (August 9, 1995).

71. *Detroit Free Press*, "Striking Workers" (June 24, 1994).

72. *The Alliance*, "News Brief: From the Battlefront" (July 17, 1995); Albom, "I Return Because Readers Are What Matter the Most" (September 5, 1995). Albom did not respond to several requests for an interview for this book.

73. Gonyea and Hoyt (1997).

74. Interview with Carole Leigh Hutton, Detroit, April 11, 2005.

75. Interview with Neil Shine, St. Clair Shores, Mich., April 28, 2005.

76. Walsh, "*Free Press* Owner Seeks Pact, Preservation of 2 Newspapers" (July 22, 1995).

77. Interview with Tony Ridder, San Jose, Calif., June 14, 2005.

78. Giles, "Why Keeping Two Daily Newspapers in Detroit Is Simply Good Business" (July 16, 1995); Raphael, "Consensus: Two Newspapers Better Than One" (July 24–30, 1995).

79. Burns (1999).

80. Fitzgerald, "Face-off in Detroit" (July 22, 1995); Walsh, "Letter Urges Union to Talk with Newspaper" (July 29, 1995); interview with Carole Leigh Hutton, Detroit, April 11, 2005.

81. Shine, "'Shove It' Can't Be Part of the Dialogue" (July 17, 1995).

82. *Macomb Daily*, "*Free Press* Ultimatum" (August 9, 1995).

83. Interview with Gary Graff, Beverly Hills, Mich., May 16, 2005.

84. Fitzgerald, "Tug of War in Detroit" (August 12, 1995).

85. Interview with Patricia Montemurri, Detroit, June 3, 2005.

86. Interview with Nancy Dunn, Dearborn, Mich., May 11, 2005.

87. Interview with Michael Betzold, Ann Arbor, Mich., March 18, 2005.

88. Musial, "*Free Press* Proposal Tries to Win Back Guild" (August 31, 1995), and "NLRB Issues Complaint Against Newspaper Agency" (September 1, 1995); Walsh, "*Free Press* Sweetens Proposal to Union" (August 31, 1995).

89. Walsh, "No Progress Seen in Newspaper Talks" (September 2, 1995).

90. Giles (1997); Grimm (1996); interview with Tom Walsh, Detroit, October 22, 2004.

91. Interview with Ron French, Detroit, May 25, 2005.

92. *Detroit Journal*, "Notes from Our Readers" (August 14, 1995); Bureau of National Affairs, "Special Report" (July 8, 1996).

93. Walsh, "Replacements to Be a Top Issue in Newspaper Talks" (August 12, 1995), and "Teamsters Get Tough with Newspaper Picket Line Crossers" (August 26, 1995).

94. DeSmet, "Religious Leaders Condemn the Hiring of Replacement Workers" (1998).

95. *The Alliance*, "Reno Asked to Rescind JOA" (August 19, 1995); McGrath, "Newspapers Strike Out with Replacements" (March 22, 1996); *The Alliance*, "Cardinal Maida Condemns DN" (August 16, 1995).

96. McGraw, "Neal Shine—A Bond Broken and a Trust Betrayed" (1995).

97. Grow, "Paper Strike in Detroit May Prove Fight for Union Life" (September 26, 1995); *The Alliance*, "News from the Battlefront," (September 15, 1995).

98. Interview with Paul Kulka, Detroit, May 2, 2005.

99. U.S. District Court, *David P. Zieminski v. The City of Sterling Heights et al.*, 98-CV-75820 (E.D. Mich. 2000), memo from Frank Mowinski to Thomas Derocha, "Intelligence Obtained Regarding the DNA Strike," August 28, 1995.

100. Fornoff and Martin, "Mass Rally Blocks Delivery of Newspapers" (September 3, 1995); Walsh and Migoya, "3,000 Strong, Strikers Delay Sunday Paper, Newspapers Decry Violence by Mob" (September 4, 1995).

101. Interview with John Jaske, McLean, Va., November 4, 2005.

102. *Macomb Daily*, "Newspaper Truck Sparks Legal Probe" (September 29, 1995); NLRB, *Detroit Newspaper Agency*, 342 NLRB 24 (2004), 310.

103. U.S. District Court, *Zieminski v. City of Sterling Heights et al.*, Jaske deposition, December 4, 2000, 139; interview with John Jaske, McLean, Va., November 4, 2005.

104. Gardner, "Thousands March in Labor Day Parade Led by Strikers" (September 5, 1995); Johnson, "Blockade Stalls, but Doesn't Stop Newspaper Deliveries" (September 4, 1995); U.S. District Court, *Zieminski v. City of Sterling Heights et al.*, Jaske deposition, 119–20; Walsh and Migoya, "3,000 Strong" (September 4, 1995).

105. *CWA Sector News*, "Detroit Strike in Third Month, No Quick Settlement in Sight" (October 1995); Gardner, "Thousands March in Labor Day Parade Led by Strikers" (September 5, 1995); Walsh, "Hoffa's Son Opens Bid to Head the Teamsters Labor Day Parade" (September 5, 1995).

106. Fornoff, Martindale, and Musial, "Newspaper Talks Resume After Violent Weekend" (September 6, 1995).

107. Fornoff, Martindale, and Musial, "Newspaper Talks Resume After Violent Weekend" (September 6, 1995); U.S. District Court, *Solomon v. City of Sterling Heights et al.*, trial transcript, vol. 3, p. 87; Sader, "Charges Dropped Against Detroit Photographer Arrested During Newspaper Strikers' Rally" (June 1996).

108. *Detroit Free Press*, "Prosecutor Says Guards May Have Set Truck Fire" (March 13, 1996); U.S. District Court, *Zieminski v. City of Sterling Heights et al.*, Jaske deposition, 134.

109. Interview with Alan Lenhoff, Detroit, March 23, 2005.
110. Craig, "Papers, Unions Vow to Behave in Sterling Heights Picketing" (September 9, 1995).
111. Fornoff, Heron, and Rapai, "Papers Use Helicopters After Picketers Block Plant" (September 11, 1995); Driskell, "Police, Strikers Share Frustration at Printing Plant" (September 12, 1995).
112. Interview with Alan Lenhoff, Detroit, March 23, 2005.
113. U.S. District Court, *Zieminski v. City of Sterling Heights et al.*, Jaske deposition, 127–30.
114. U.S. District Court, *Zieminski v. City of Sterling Heights et al.*, Derocha deposition, June 27, 1997, 120–23.
115. U.S. District Court, *Zieminski v. City of Sterling Heights et al.*, 124, 132–33; Driskell, "Police, Strikers Share Frustration at Printing Plant" (September 12, 1995).
116. U.S. District Court, *Zieminski v. City of Sterling Heights et al.*, Derocha deposition, 125–32.
117. Driskell, "Police, Strikers Share Frustration at Printing Plant" (September 12, 1995); U.S. District Court, *Zieminski v. City of Sterling Heights et al.*, Jaske deposition, 128.
118. Bennet, "Helicopters Carry Papers in Detroit Strike" (September 11, 1995); Fornoff, Heron, and Rapai, "Papers Use Helicopters After Picketers Block Plant" (September 11, 1995); U.S. District Court, *Zieminski v. City of Sterling Heights et al.*, Derocha deposition, 129.
119. Interview with Kate DeSmet, Detroit, April 1, 2005.
120. Shellum, Holly, and Graff, "Curb On Picketing Expected" (September 13, 1995); Walsh and McKay, "Pickets Restricted, Newspaper Strikers at Plant Gate Limited to 10" (September 14, 1995).
121. Interview with Alfred Derey, Lapeer, Mich., May 12, 2005; interview with Alex Young, Detroit, April 27, 2005.
122. *Macomb Daily*, "Newspaper Truck Sparks Legal Probe" (September 29, 1995).
123. Interview with Paul Kulka, Detroit, May 2, 2005.
124. Hindes, "Returning Newspaper Strikers Are Told to Get in Line" (October 29, 1995); Bott, "Reaction to Strike Radically Different at *News, Free Press*" (December 3, 1995).
125. Interview with Robert Musial, Grosse Pointe Woods, Mich., April 1, 2005; Craggs, "Darth Vega to the Rescue" (May 4, 2005).
126. Detroit Newspaper Agency, "Detroit Strike Operations Report" (September 9–11, 1995).
127. Perry, Kramer, and Schneider (1982); Taylor (2008).
128. Interview with Tim Kelleher, Royal Oak, Mich., November 3, 2004.
129. Walsh, "Newspapers Resume Separate Weekday Publication; Protests Outpace Negotiation" (September 18, 1995).

CHAPTER 9

1. Schnell and Gramm (1994).
2. Cramton and Tracy (1998).
3. Harris (2002).
4. Gold (1998); Taylor (2008).
5. Harris (2002).
6. Bennet, "Newspaper Strike Divides Labor's Capital, Detroit" (September 2, 1995).
7. Walsh, "Strike Cuts Profits, Papers' Parents Lose $46 Million" (October 4, 1996).
8. Gold (1998); National Labor Relations Board (1997).
9. Getman (2004); Gould (1993).
10. Grow, "Paper Strike in Detroit May Prove Fight for Union Life" (September 26, 1995).
11. Interview with Carole Leigh Hutton, Detroit, April 11, 2005.
12. Taylor (2008).
13. Musial, "NLRB Issues Complaint Against Newspaper Agency" (September 1, 1995); *The Alliance*, "NLRB Ruling Protects Jobs" (September 2, 1995); Fitzgerald, "Return to the Table in Detroit" (September 2, 1995).
14. Telephone interview with Tom McGrath, October 4, 2006; interview with Samuel McKnight, Southfield, Mich., June 4, 2005.
15. *Toledo Blade*, "Newspaper Unions Postpone Contract Talks" (October 5, 1995); Konrad, "The Newspaper Strike Enters a New Arena" (March 22, 1996).
16. Interview with Alex Young, Detroit, April 27, 2005.
17. Metropolitan Council of Newspaper Unions, press release, "Unions Present Principles for Settlement" (October 5, 1995).
18. Shellum and Holly, "Newspaper Unions Offer Job Cuts to End Strike" (October 6, 1995).
19. John Jaske and Tim Kelleher, letter to Alfred P. Derey (October 27, 1995).
20. John Jaske, letter to Jack Howe, "Negotiations" (July 26, 1995); John Jaske, letter to Al Young, "Negotiations" (July 26, 1995); John Jaske, letter to Frank Kortsch, "Teamster Negotiations" (July 26, 1995).
21. NLRB, *Detroit Newspaper Agency*, 326 NLRB 64 (1998), Mailers/DNA negotiating meeting (typewritten notes), August 18, 1995.
22. Henderson, "A Labor of Law" (March 1996, emphasis in original).
23. John Jaske and Tim Kelleher, letter to Alfred P. Derey (October 27, 1995).
24. Walsh and McKay, "Pickets Restricted, Newspaper Strikers at Plant Gate Limited to 10" (September 14, 1995).
25. Interview with Alex Young, Detroit, April 27, 2005; U.S. District Court, *Benjamin L. Solomon v. The City of Sterling Heights et al.*, 98-CV-73900 (E.D. Mich. 2000), plaintiff's exhibit 43: memorandum from Frank Mowinski to Chief

Thomas Derocha, Sterling Heights Police Department, "Violations of Agreements Between DNA and SHPD," July 17, 1995.

26. U.S. District Court, *Solomon v. City of Sterling Heights et al.*, trial transcript, vol. 5, p. 68.

27. U.S. District Court, *Solomon v. City of Sterling Heights et al.*, trial transcript, vol. 5, p. 37.

28. U.S. District Court, *Solomon v. City of Sterling Heights et al.*, trial transcript, vol. 5, p. 69.

29. Anthony testified in a deposition that Duchane presented a letter to Anderson at the July 17 meeting; U.S. District Court, *Solomon v. City of Sterling Heights et al.*, trial transcript, vol. 5, p. 104.

30. U.S. District Court, *Solomon v. City of Sterling Heights et al.*, trial transcript, vol. 5, pp. 41–42.

31. U.S. District Court, *Solomon v. City of Sterling Heights et al.*, trial transcript, vol. 5, p. 84.

32. U.S. District Court, *Solomon v. City of Sterling Heights et al.*, trial transcript, vol. 5, p. 106.

33. U.S. District Court, *Solomon v. City of Sterling Heights et al.*, trial transcript, vol. 5, pp. 43–47, 85; and plaintiff's exhibits 13–26: letters and payments between DNA and SHPD.

34. U.S. District Court, *Solomon v. City of Sterling Heights et al.*, trial transcript, vol. 5, pp. 73–78, 83–87, 103; U.S. District Court, *David P. Zieminski v. The City of Sterling Heights et al.*, 96-CV-75820 (E.D. Mich. 2000), Tim Kelleher deposition, January 29, 2001, 94.

35. U.S. District Court, *Zieminski v. City of Sterling Heights et al.*, Vega deposition, October 27, 2000, 14; and Kelleher deposition, January 29, 2001, 8, 99.

36. U.S. District Court, *Solomon v. City of Sterling Heights et al.*, Anderson deposition, October 20, 1999, 126–30; U.S. District Court, *Zieminski v. City of Sterling Heights et al.*, Anthony deposition, January 21, 2000, 22–28.

37. *The Alliance*, "Sterling Cops Go to Highest Bidder?" (August 24, 1995); Sweeney, "Sterling Heights Restricts Residential Pickets" (September 22, 1996); *The Alliance*, " 'Treasure Island North' for Sterling Cops," (September 15, 1995).

38. U.S. District Court, *Solomon v. City of Sterling Heights et al.*, trial transcript, vol. 3, pp. 71–74, and vol. 4, pp. 99–100.

39. U.S. District Court, *Solomon v. City of Sterling Heights et al.*, plaintiff exhibit 3: memorandum from Frank Mowinski to James Owens, "Contingency Plan for Impending DNA Strike," May 6, 1995; and trial transcript, vol. 3, p. 133.

40. U.S. District Court, *Solomon v. City of Sterling Heights et al.*, trial transcript, vol. 5, pp. 128–29; vol. 3, p. 134; and vol. 2, p. 181.

41. U.S. District Court, *Solomon v. City of Sterling Heights et al.*, plaintiff's exhibit 8: letter from John Anthony to Capt. James Owens, August 24, 1995.

42. U.S. District Court, *Solomon v. City of Sterling Heights et al.*, plaintiff's exhibit 64: "Strike Activity: Applicable Ordinances and Statues," and plaintiff's exhibit 65: "Index to Selected Michigan Statutes of Possible Application in Strike and Picketing Situations."
43. U.S. District Court, *Solomon v. City of Sterling Heights et al.*, trial transcript, vol. 3, pp. 87–88, and vol. 2, pp. 112–15.
44. U.S. District Court, *Solomon v. City of Sterling Heights et al.*, trial transcript, vol. 2, pp. 121–22, 138.
45. U.S. District Court, *Solomon v. City of Sterling Heights et al.*, plaintiff's exhibit 10: letter from Carl Marlinga to Thomas Derocha, September 8, 1995.
46. U.S. District Court, *Solomon v. City of Sterling Heights et al.*, pp. 127, 131.
47. Interview with John Jaske, McLean, Va., November 4, 2005.
48. U.S. District Court, *Solomon v. City of Sterling Heights et al.*, trial transcript, vol. 2, p. 140; and vol. 3, p. 100.
49. Walsh, "Picketing, Politics, and Prayer Mark Strike's 22nd Day" (August 5, 1995); Fitzgerald, "Groping for Labor Peace in Detroit" (October 3, 1998).
50. Judge's citations of case precedents are omitted from quote. NLRB, *Detroit Newspaper Agency*, 342 NLRB 24 (2004), 228–29.
51. Taylor (2008, 177).
52. Interview with Ann Musial, Grosse Pointe Woods, Mich., April 1, 2005; interview with John A. Taylor, Farmington Hills, Mich., May 17, 2005; NLRB, *Detroit Newspaper Agency*, 342 NLRB 24 (2004), 229.
53. NLRB, *Detroit Newspaper Agency*, 342 NLRB 24 (2004), 277, 281.
54. NLRB, *Detroit Newspaper Agency*, 342 NLRB 24 (2004), 239–40, 245.
55. NLRB, *Detroit Newspaper Agency*, 342 NLRB 24 (2004), 270, 274, 282, 299–301.
56. Lippert, "Teamsters Get Long-Awaited Raise in Strike Pay" (February 11, 1996); Forsyth, "Jury Rules That DN Libeled Part-time Mailer" (February 28, 1999).
57. NLRB, *Detroit Newspaper Agency*, 342 NLRB 24 (2004), 223, 227; Fitzgerald, "Detroit Union Leaders: Five Strikes—You're Out" (December 26, 1998).
58. Heron, Schabath, and Graff, "Strike's Action Shifts from Plants to Distribution Centers" (September 25, 1995).
59. Anderson, "17 Strikers Arrested at Newspaper Facilities" (October 4, 1995); *Detroit Free Press*, "Q&A: No Plans to Close One Newspaper Despite the Strike and Delivery Problems" (July 22, 1995); Lori Matthews, "Six Injured in Clashes at Papers' Centers, at Least Fifteen Arrested as Violence Surges" (October 2, 1995); Holly, "A Top Cop Criticizes Guards' Actions at Picket Site" (October 4, 1995).
60. *The Alliance*, "Two Injured Mailers Sue DN" (December 7, 1995); *Oakland Press*, "Two Strikers Sue Detroit Newspapers over Injuries" (December 5, 1995); Holly, "A Top Cop Criticizes Guards' Actions at Picket Site" (October 4, 1995).
61. Lippert, "Newspaper War Is More Than Words for Two Men" (January 21,

1996); *Detroit Free Press*, "Newspaper Striker Injured When Van Runs over Him" (October 4, 1995); NLRB, *Detroit Newspaper Agency*, 342 NLRB 24 (2004), 302–3.

62. *Detroit Free Press*, "Newspapers Report Smooth Delivery, Quieter Pickets" (October 16, 1995).

63. *Detroit Free Press*, "Violence Ebbs, Papers' Spokesman Says" (October 23, 1995); Szczesny, "Strikers End 'Peaceful' Siege" (October 16, 1995) and "120 Officers, 300 Strikers Face Off at Papers' Center" (October 23, 1995); Varcie, "Early Morning Ruckus at Newspaper Distribution Site" (November 16, 1995).

64. Driskell, "Crossbow Found in Replacement Worker's Car" (October 10, 1995).

65. Szczesny, "Six Strikers Face Vandalism Charges" (October 30, 1995).

66. *Detroit Free Press*, "Pipe Bombs Placed in Shelby Township Newspaper Boxes" (November 2, 1995).

67. Sweeney, "Paper Carriers to Stand Trial in Bombing of Striker's Home" (February 18, 1996).

68. Musial and Elmer, "Unions File Suit Against Newspapers and Sterling Heights" (October 3, 1995); Fitzgerald, "Hard-Line Tactics" (October 28, 1995).

69. Bott, "Racketeering Suit Filed Against Strikers" (November 16, 1995); Walsh and Taylor, "Detroit Newspapers Sues Unions, Company Wants Violence Stopped" (November 16, 1995).

70. *Detroit Free Press*, "Union Chief: Hurt the Bottom Line, Plans Focus on Advertisers" November 16, 1995, p. 1B.

71. NLRB, *Detroit Newspaper Agency*, 326 NLRB 64 (1998), memorandum from John Jaske to Douglas McCorkindale, December 27, 1995.

72. Interview with William Hanson, Detroit, March 24, 2005.

73. Szczesny, "Strikers Unveil New Campaign" (November 24, 1995).

74. *Detroit Free Press*, "Violence Ebbs" (October 23, 1995).

75. By 1999 the UAW international union had donated nearly $1.5 million to the striking newspaper workers. Mleczko, "UAW's Big Shoulders" (March 28, 1999).

76. *The Alliance*, "UAW Issues Gift Checks" (December 16, 1995); Creager and Johnson, "Journalists Strike Out in New Directions" (October 27, 1995); Devine, "'The Spiritual Godfather' of the Newspaper Bows Out" (December 7, 1995).

77. Konrad and Walsh, "Strikers, Papers Returning to Table" (December 20, 1995).

78. Konrad, "No Progress in Strike, Despite Archer's Effort, Unions Flatly Reject Newspaper Proposals" (December 21, 1995); Lippert and Gallagher, "Strikers' JOA Sacrifices Deserve Respect, Mayor Says" (December 24, 1995); *The Alliance*, "DN Says Bah Humbug" (December 22, 1995).

79. Walsh, "Newspapers to Unions: Job Openings Shrink" (October 31, 1995).

80. *Louis Abate et al. v. Detroit Newspapers et al.*, MUL96 51200, Department of Consumer and Industry Services, Michigan Unemployment Agency, Office of Appeals, October 27, 1997.

81. *The Alliance*, "DN Says Bah Humbug" (December 22, 1995); Konrad, "No Progress in Strike" (December 21, 1995).

82. Lippert and Gallagher, "Strikers' JOA Sacrifices Deserve Respect" (December 24, 1995).

83. NLRB, *Detroit Newspaper Agency*, 326 NLRB 64 (1998), memorandum from John Jaske to John Curley, Douglas McCorkindale, and Gary Watson, December 21, 1995.

CHAPTER 10

1. Interview with Joe Swickard, Detroit, May 10, 2005.

2. Interview with Gary Graff, Beverly Hills, Mich., May 16, 2005; interview with Lou Mleczko, Detroit, April 18, 2005.

3. Musial, "'Scrappy Tabloid' Begins Its Second Year" (November 17, 1996); Tyson, "Paper-and-Ink Insurgency Hits Detroit" (January 12, 1996); Battagello, "Stuck in a Stalemate" (July 6, 1996).

4. Schlagheck, "Living in the Wake of a Newspaper Strike" (March 2001).

5. Watson, "Journalists Speak Out for Those Who Cannot" (November 26, 1995).

6. Elmer, "Union Launches Boycott of *USA Today*" (February 25, 1996); Reed, "Unions Launch *Herald* Boycott" (March 28, 1996); Hudis and Sacharow, "*USA Today* on Toast" (January 22, 1996).

7. Watson, "Strikers Confront Ridder with the Truth" (April 28, 1996); Reed and Barciela, "Strike Dominates Knight-Ridder Annual Meeting" (April 24, 1996); Lippert, "Ridder Seems Confused Over Strike Facts" (April 28, 1996).

8. *The Alliance*, "400 Descend on Annual Meeting, Gannett Stockholders Get an Earful" (May 8, 1996); Lippert, "Gannett Boss Trades Verbal Jabs with Strikers" (May 12, 1996).

9. Hissom, "Detroit's Bottom Line . . . News Strike!" (February 22, 1996); Wilmsen, "Strikers Picket Knight-Ridder" (March 15–17, 1996); *Detroit Sunday Journal*, "Georgia Workers Support Newspaper Strike" (June 30, 1996).

10. Interview with Mike Zielinski, Washington, D.C., March 16, 2006.

11. *The Alliance*, "Leaflet Pressure Convinces Nine Dealers" (January 20, 1996), "Four Auto Dealers Junk DN for Unions" (February 8, 1996), and "'Avoid Scab Advertisers' UAW Asks" (February 13, 1996).

12. Samuel McKnight, letter to law enforcement agencies, "Dear Chief" (January 4, 1996, emphasis in original).

13. *Oakland Press*, "Strikers Inform Police of Plan to Follow Carriers" (January 20, 1996); Shine and Robles, "Pickets Can Follow Newspaper Carriers" (January 24, 1996); Fitzgerald, "Progression of Violence" (March 16, 1996).

14. Interview with Mike Zielinski, Washington, D.C., March 16, 2006; *The Alliance*, "Unions Launch Spring Offensive" (May 16, 1996).
15. Lippert, "Strikers Redeployed" (May 19, 1996); *The Alliance*, "UAW Staff 'Magnificent,' Strikers Get Direct Action Training" (May 30, 1996).
16. Lippert, "New Union Tactics Are 'Message to Detroit'" (May 26, 1996), and "Top Union Leaders Gather in Washington" (June 2, 1996).
17. *The Alliance*, "Strikers Sink Scab Street Sales" (May 23, 1996); Watson, "Pickets Preach the Word and Win Converts" (June 23, 1996).
18. *The Alliance*, "Bishop Gumbleton Says at Rally: King Would Support Strikers" (January 17, 1996).
19. Religious Leaders for Justice at the Detroit Newspapers, "An Appeal by Metro Detroit Area Religious Leaders" (1996).
20. *The Alliance*, "'Papers Have Sinned,' Clergy Takes a Stand" (February 17, 1996).
21. *The Alliance*, "Notes from the Battlefront" (March 2, 1996); Religious Leaders for Justice at the Detroit Newspapers, press release (April 19, 1996).
22. Readers United, leaflet, "Readers Before Profits" (1995); Wylie-Kellerman, "Anatomy of a Strike" (September 1996).
23. Readers United, leaflet, "Readers Before Profits" (1995); Jeanie Wylie-Kellerman, letter to Linda Foley (October 20, 1995); interview with Bill Wylie-Kellerman, Detroit, May 11, 2005.
24. Readers United, letter to newspaper strikers and supporters (February 27, 1996); *The Alliance*, "24 Community Leaders Arrested at Rally" (March 7, 1996).
25. Readers United, press release, "44 Women Arrested during Protest at Detroit News" (March 14, 1996); *Detroit News*, "List of Protesters Who Were Arrested" (March 15, 1996).
26. *Detroit News*, "Former UAW Chief, 21 Others Arrested at Rally at *News* Building" (March 22, 1996); *The Alliance*, "UAW, AFL-CIO Leaders Confront DN" (April 2, 1996).
27. *The Alliance*, "Ravitz, Other Pols Show Support in Rally" (April 13, 1996); Wylie-Kellerman, "Anatomy of a Strike" (September 1996).
28. Readers United, "Readers Before Profits" (1995).
29. Interview with Bill Wylie-Kellerman, Detroit, May 11, 2005.
30. Wylie-Kellerman, "Dailies Fall Far Short of Noble Statements" (August 25, 1996).
31. Angeles, "Mahaffey's Dealing with Police Helps Delay Newspapers" (October 9, 1995); Samulski, "Protesters, University Professor, Arrested in Newspaper Strike Incident" (March 22, 1996).
32. Jones, "Labor's Painful Crossroads: Detroit's Newspaper Dispute Drags On, with Mounting Losses, No End in Sight" (February 11, 1996).
33. Jurkowitz, "Nieman a Battleground of Detroit Newspaper War" (July 6, 2000).

34. Robert Giles, letter to Rev. Joseph Summers (August 23, 1995).
35. Marian Krzaklewski, letter to the editor, *Detroit News* (August 30, 1995).
36. Giles, "Who Strikes Best Example for Civil Disobedience?" (March 10, 1996).
37. Guest, "King Brings Hope to Newspaper Strikers" (March 31, 1996); *Detroit News*, "King's Son Tells Strikers to Persevere" (March 31, 1996); Owens, "King Joins Strikers" (March 31, 1996).
38. Ahrens, "Bad News" (July 30, 1995).
39. Cooper (1996).
40. Bott, "Reaction to Strike Radically Different at *News, Free Press*" (December 3, 1995).
41. Ourlian and Martelle, "Starved for News" (July 7, 1996).
42. Fitzgerald, "Strike Coverage" (March 16, 1996).
43. Gewolb, "Contender for Nieman Post Under Scrutiny" (July 7, 2000).
44. Fitzgerald, "Strike Coverage" (March 16, 1996).
45. Fitzgerald, "Strike Coverage" (March 16, 1996); Bohy, "Strike Coverage Spin Control" (September 20–26, 1995).
46. Schabath, "Truck Fire Points to Detroit Newspapers" (March 10, 1996).
47. Interview with Duane Ice, Royal Oak, Mich., April 30, 2005; interview with Bill Wylie-Kellerman, Detroit, May 11, 2005.
48. *Detroit News*, "Newspaper Strikers Urged to Bring Kids to Picket Lines" (May 5, 1996); Lessenberry, "Papers Not Fit for Your Cat Box" (May 15–21, 1996).
49. *Detroit News*, "Strike: A Failure of Leadership" (July 11, 1996); Christian, "Teamsters Drop Some Demands in Strike at Detroit Papers in Bid for Resolution" (April 11, 1996).
50. Walsh, "Vega: No End in Sight, Newspaper CEO Sets New Goals as Strike Grinds On" (November 10, 1995); Bernick, "Integrity, Credibility Lost Meaning with DN" (July 28, 1996); NLRB, *Detroit Newspaper Agency*, 326 NLRB 64 (1998), 732, and hearing transcript, 2105.
51. Detroit Newspapers, "An Open Letter to Our Community" (July 19–25, 1995).
52. Interview with Thomas Breyer, Grosse Pointe Farms, Mich., April 13, 2005.
53. Detroit Newspapers, "An Open Letter to Our Community" (July 19–25, 1995).
54. *The Alliance*, "Notes from the Battlefront" (October 28, 1995); Forsyth, "Kelleher's Son Nabbed" (December 21, 1997).
55. Hofsess and Teegardin, "Shining On" (December 3, 1995).
56. Walsh, "Newspapers Are Cool to Unions' Truce Offer" (October 6, 1995).
57. Walsh, "Vega: No End in Sight" (November 10, 1995).
58. Althaus, letter, "Dear Pastor or Rector" (August 2, 1995).
59. Interview with Alan Lenhoff, Detroit, March 23, 2005.
60. Fitzgerald, "A War of Attrition" (March 16, 1996).
61. Watson, "The *Free Press* Has Changed, and So Have I" (March 24, 1996).
62. Gonyea and Hoyt (1997).
63. NLRB, *Detroit Newspaper Agency*, 326 NLRB 64 (1998), general counsel exhibit

158: Detroit Newspaper Agency, 1996 replacement employee data, June 20, 1996; and hearing transcript, 1868–83.

64. NLRB, *Detroit Newspaper Agency*, 326 NLRB 64 (1998), general counsel exhibit 158: Detroit Newspaper Agency, 1996 replacement employee data, June 20, 1996; and hearing transcript, 1868–83.

65. Siegel and Robertson, "Public Seems Divided on Strike Blame" (July 9, 1996).

66. Interview with Crawford Webb, Detroit, July 25, 2006.

67. Walsh, "Vega: No End in Sight" (November 10, 1995).

68. *Oakland Press*, "Newspaper Strikers Swear Off Violence" (January 13, 1996); Fitzgerald, "Progression of Violence" (March 16, 1996); Yung and Ramirez, "Auto Dealers Angry over Union Boycott Campaign" (January 26, 1996).

69. Konrad, "NLRB Threatens Injunction to Stop Violence by Detroit Newspaper Unions" (July 11, 1996).

70. Bohy, "Commandments or Compromise?" (July 17, 1996).

71. NLRB, case 7-CC-1647(1), "Charge Against Labor Organization or Its Agents" (October 4, 1995); *Detroit Free Press*, "Picketers Must Leave Art Van, NLRB Rules Against Newspaper Unions" (October 14, 1995).

72. Lippert, "Teamsters Get Long-Awaited Raise in Strike Pay" (February 11, 1996); Jachman, "Labor Complaint Is Settled Out of Court" (July 4, 1996).

73. David Radtke, letter to Chief Lawrence Carey (June 11, 1996), letter to Susan Lancaster, Esq. (June 24, 1996), and letter to Charles R. Towner, Esq. (September 18, 1996).

74. Michalak, "You Can Picket Your Friends—Well, Maybe Not in Troy" (August 4, 1996); Justin, "Newspaper Picketers Aren't Backing Down" (August 8, 1996).

75. Gamache, "City Strikes Back at Picketing" (September 22, 1996); Hotts, "Testing the Rules" (October 7, 1996).

76. *The Alliance*, "Pickets 1; New Sterling Hts. Law 0" (October 10, 1996); Ourlian, "Strikers Make Some Visits" (October 27, 1996); Craig, "Chamber Blasts Tactics in Paper Strike" (November 21, 1996); Ourlian, "Media's Influence Warrants Labor's Attention" (December 15, 1996), and "Boycott Gets Clearance from the NLRB" (December 22, 1996).

77. Matthews, "DN Sues UAW in Strike Violence" (June 4, 1996); *Oakland Press*, "UAW Added to Newspapers' Countersuit" (June 5, 1996).

78. Bohy, "Civil Display or Union Tactic?" (April 3, 1996).

79. Grant, "Council President, Bishops Arrested at Rally" (March 7, 1996).

80. Samuel McKnight, letter to Mark Rubin, Esq. (March 19, 1996).

81. Readers United, press release (March 26, 1996), and "Statement of Readers United Following a Meeting with Mr. Mark Rubin, Attorney for the NLRB" (March 26, 1996).

82. NLRB, *Detroit Newspaper Agency*, 326 NLRB 64 (1998), hearing transcript, 20; *The Alliance*, "NLRB Trial Opens on Nine ULP Complaints" (April 17, 1996).

83. NLRB, *Detroit Newspaper Agency*, 326 NLRB 64 (1998), 729.

84. Konrad, "The Newspaper Strike Enters a New Arena" (March 22, 1996); interview with Linda Rabin Hammell, Detroit, July 17, 2006.

85. Interview with Amy Bachelder, Huntington Woods, Mich., March 17, 2005; interview with Linda Rabin Hammell, Detroit, July 17, 2006. Robert Battista did not respond to requests for an interview.

86. NLRB, *Detroit Newspaper Agency*, 326 NLRB 64 (1998), hearing transcript, 82–88, 99–105, 113–21.

87. Konrad, "Dispute over Documents Slows Strike Hearing" (April 18, 1996); NLRB, *Detroit Newspaper Agency*, 326 NLRB 64 (1998), hearing transcript, 150–54.

88. NLRB, *Detroit Newspaper Agency*, 326 NLRB 64 (1998), 751n25.

89. NLRB, *Detroit Newspaper Agency*, 326 NLRB 64 (1998), hearing transcript, 50–60.

90. NLRB, *Detroit Newspaper Agency*, 326 NLRB 64 (1998), hearing transcript, 62–64.

91. Interview with Linda Rabin Hammell, Detroit, July 17, 2006.

92. NLRB, *Detroit Newspaper Agency*, 326 NLRB 64 (1998), hearing transcript, 74.

93. NLRB, *Detroit Newspaper Agency*, 326 NLRB 64 (1998), hearing transcript, 75–79.

94. NLRB, *Detroit Newspaper Agency*, 326 NLRB 64 (1998), hearing transcript, 1903–10.

95. NLRB, *Detroit Newspaper Agency*, 326 NLRB 64 (1998), hearing transcript, general counsel exhibit 18: letter from John Jaske to Jack Howe, March 4, 1996; and general counsel exhibit 19: letter from Jack Howe to John Jaske, March 13, 1996.

96. NLRB, *Antelope Valley Press* 311 NLRB 459 (1993); NLRB, *Detroit Newspaper Agency*, 326 NLRB 64 (1998), hearing transcript, 1900–02, 2497.

97. NLRB, *Detroit Newspaper Agency*, 326 NLRB 64 (1998), hearing transcript, 1892–98.

98. Interview with Linda Rabin Hammell, Detroit, July 17, 2006.

99. NLRB, *Detroit Newspaper Agency*, 326 NLRB 64 (1998), hearing transcript, 938–52, 1190–91, 1237–42.

100. NLRB, *Detroit Newspaper Agency*, 326 NLRB 64 (1998), hearing transcript, 751n25.

101. NLRB, *Detroit Newspaper Agency*, 326 NLRB 64 (1998), hearing transcript, 2969.

102. Interview with Linda Rabin Hammell, Detroit, July 17, 2006; Ourlian, "NLRB Case Could Drag into 1997" (August 4, 1996).

103. Ourlian, "Hearings Conclude; Mediation Fizzles" (October 6, 1996).

104. Fitzgerald, "A War of Attrition" (March 16, 1996).

105. Freedman, "Picketers Protest as CEO Vega Defends Newspapers" (April 14,

1996); Lippert, "Gannett Boss Trades Verbal Jabs With Strikers" (May 12, 1996).

106. Konrad, "Audit of Papers Released" (September 7, 1996); Fitzgerald, "Feeling the Effects of the Strike" (September 28, 1996); Driskell, "Audit Shows Sharp Drop in *Detroit News, Free Press* Circulation in Macomb County" (October 1, 1996).

107. Gargaro, "Old Ways Gone, Impasse Persists" (July 8, 1996); Lippert, "Top Union Leaders Gather in Washington" (June 2, 1996).

108. Brodesser, "Strike Hangover" (May 26, 1997); Lippert, "War Wounds in Detroit" (May-June 1998).

109. *Washington Post*, "Gannett Profit Falls 9 Percent in 3rd Quarter" (October 10, 1995); *Oakland Press*, "Fourth-Quarter Earnings Rise 4 Percent at Gannett" (February 7, 1996).

110. Jones, "For Newspapers, a Bundle of Woes" (October 29, 1995); *Oakland Press*, "Strike Cuts into Knight-Ridder Profit" (April 23, 1996).

111. *Oakland Press*, "Fourth-Quarter Earnings Rise 4 Percent at Gannett" (February 7, 1996).

112. Merzer, "Tony Ridder: At the Center of a Maelstrom" (March 31, 1996); Lippert, "Overruled! Papers' Stories Become Evidence" (June 30, 1996).

113. Danese, "1,000 March to Mark Newspapers' Year on Strike" (July 15, 1996).

114. Ourlian, "Archer Renews Offer to Mediate Talks" (July 28 1996); *The Alliance*, "Mayor Resurfaces, Archer Tries to Jumpstart Talks" (August 8, 1996).

115. Ourlian, "Archer, Unions Push for Meaningful Talks" (August 18, 1996); NLRB general counsel, brief in support of petition for injunction under section 10(j) of the National Labor Relations Act, as amended, *Schaub v. Detroit Newspaper Agency*, CV-97-1920 (6th Cir. 1998).

116. *The Alliance*, "Management Slaps Archer in Face" (October 3, 1996); Konrad and Walsh, "Striking Newspaper Unions Say Detroit Dailies Reject Mediation" (October 3, 1996).

117. Ourlian, "'You're Going to Win'" (September 1, 1996); Konrad, "Police Arrest 21 at Latest Protest in Paper Strike" (August 31, 1996); NLRB, *Detroit Newspaper Agency*, 342 NLRB 24 (2004), 291–93.

118. Fitzgerald, "Firing Greet Detroit Strikers" (November 9, 1996); Ourlian, "Key Areas Shunning Scab Papers" (October 13, 1996).

119. Smith, "Unconditional Offer Meets with Skepticism" (December 4–10, 1996); interview with Alfred Derey, Lapeer, Mich., May 12, 2005; Konrad and Craig, "Newspaper Unions Discuss an End to Strike" (February 14, 1997).

120. Interview with Lou Mleczko, Detroit, April 18, 2005.

121. *The Alliance*, "Strike Enters Return-to-Work Phase" (February 15, 1997); Ourlian, "Strike On! Unions Launch New Offensive with Offer" (February 16, 1997).

122. Konrad and Craig, "Unions Seek Return, But Won't End War on Papers" (February 15, 1997).

CHAPTER 11

1. McCammon (1993).
2. Konrad and Craig, "Unions Seek Return, but Won't End War on Papers" (February 15, 1997).
3. Peterson, "Detroit Papers Refuse to Re-Hire Ex-Strikers Immediately" (February 20, 1997).
4. Craig and Oguntoyinbo, "Newspapers' Unions Seek Immediate Return" (February 22, 1997); Craig, "Newspaper Agency Declares an Impasse" (March 22, 1997).
5. Craig and Oguntoyinbo, "Newspapers' Unions Seek Immediate Return" (February 22, 1997); Watson, "Her Place Is Back in the Kitchen" (March 9, 1997).
6. *The Alliance*, "It's 'Re-Union' Time at Detroit Newspapers" (March 24, 1997); interview with Gary Graff, Beverly Hills, Mich., May 16, 2005.
7. Wilson, "Bragg Boasts of Bold Strikers" (September 21, 1997); Guyette, "A House Divided" (July 7–13, 1999).
8. Ourlian, "Papers 'Stonewall' Unions Over Returns" (April 27, 1997); *The Alliance*, "It's 'Re-Union' Time at Detroit Newspapers" (March 24, 1997); *CWA News*, "Returning Detroit Members Confront Idleness, Isolation" (May 1997).
9. Ourlian, "Back to 'Work'" (May 25, 1997); *The Alliance*, "Notes from the Battlefront" (May 1, 1997).
10. *Detroit Sunday Journal*, "Newspaper Spin Doctors Twirl Themselves Silly" (July 6, 1997).
11. Forsyth, "Getting to Work" (June 8, 1997), and "DN Closes Its 'Decomposing Room'" (February 1, 1998).
12. Craig, "Newspaper Strike to Get Day in Court" (July 30, 1997); Forsyth, "Two at the News" (September 7, 1997).
13. Ourlian, "Papers Finally Recall 28 Mailers, Slash Pay" (August 10, 1997); Forsyth, "Local 2040 Says DN Takes Steps to Keep Mailers Out" (December 7, 1997).
14. Forsyth, "More of the Same" (December 14, 1997).
15. Konrad, "Papers' Slow Staff Return Called Unfair" (April 15, 1997).
16. Ourlian, "Sweeney Sees Light at End of the Tunnel" (July 21, 1996); *Detroit Sunday Journal*, "Talks with Teamsters Uneventful" (August 25, 1996).
17. DeSmet, "Newspaper Strikers Renew Call for National March in Detroit" (January 1997); Ourlian, "National March Backed" (January 12, 1997); *Detroit Sunday Journal*, "National March Update" (February 2, 1997).
18. Interview with Paul Kulka, Detroit, May 2, 2005; interview with Armand

Nevers, Detroit, April 29, 2005; *Detroit Sunday Journal,* "Rally Puts Labor's Focus on Detroit" (June 15, 1997).

19. *The Alliance,* "Action! Motown '97 Needs *Your* Help, Too!" (May 1, 1997); interview with Mike Zielinski, Washington, D.C., March 16, 2006; *The Alliance,* "Thousands of Labor Supporters to Join Action! Motown '97," June 12, 1997, p. 2.

20. Robert Ourlian, "Unions Mobilize for June Demonstrations" (April 27, 1997).

21. *The Alliance,* "'Wow!' Over 100,000 Jam Hart Plaza for Action! Motown 97" (June 25, 1997).

22. Interview with Robert Ourlian, Washington, D.C., March 17, 2006.

23. Interview with Mike Zielinski, Washington, D.C., March 16, 2006.

24. *The Alliance,* "Action! Motown '97 is Friday and Saturday: Be There!" (June 19, 1997); *Detroit Sunday Journal,* "A Family Reunion: Brothers and Sisters Gather for an International Show of Solidarity" (June 29, 1997).

25. *Detroit Sunday Journal,* "A Family Reunion" (June 29, 1997); *The Alliance,* "'Wow!' Over 100,000 Jam Hart Plaza for Action! Motown 97" (June 25, 1997); Forsyth, "Supporters Coming in on Wheels of All Kinds" (June 22, 1997).

26. Interview with Randy Karpinen, Clinton, Mich., March 30, 2005.

27. Lichtenstein (1995, 263); *The Alliance,* "'Wow!' Over 100,000 Jam Hart Plaza for Action! Motown 97" (June 25, 1997).

28. *Detroit Sunday Journal,* "A Family Reunion" (June 29, 1997); *The Alliance,* "'Wow!' Over 100,000 Jam Hart Plaza for Action! Motown 97" (June 25, 1997).

29. Interview with Jocelyn Faniel-Heard, Detroit, July 19, 2006.

30. Mullen, "Solidarity Delayed" (June 18–24, 1997); *The Alliance,* "'Wow!' Over 100,000 Jam Hart Plaza for Action! Motown 97" (June 25, 1997).

31. *Detroit Sunday Journal,* "A Family Reunion" (June 29, 1997).

32. Lynch and Garrett, "Unions Stage Anti Newspaper Rally" (June 22, 1997).

33. Cooper (1997).

34. NLRB, *Detroit Newspaper Agency,* 326 NLRB 64 (1998), 756.

35. NLRB, *Detroit Newspaper Agency,* 326 NLRB 64 (1998), 757.

36. NLRB, *Detroit Newspaper Agency,* 326 NLRB 64 (1998), 780–81.

37. NLRB, *Detroit Newspaper Agency,* 326 NLRB 64 (1998), 781.

38. *The Alliance,* "'Wow!' Over 100,000 Jam Hart Plaza for Action! Motown 97" (June 25, 1997).

39. Pring (2001, 282–83).

40. NLRB, *Detroit Newspaper Agency,* 326 NLRB 64 (1998), 714n7.

41. Gould (2000), 65–68; Forsyth, "'Another Step Toward Justice'" (July 6, 1997).

42. *Detroit Sunday Journal,* "Q&A" (July 6, 1997).

43. NLRB, *Detroit Newspaper Agency,* 326 NLRB 64 (1998), 713–17.

44. Craig and Konrad, "Judge Asked to Reinstate Strikers" (July 8, 1997); Ourlian, "O'Meara Has History with Papers" (August 24, 1997).

45. Interview with Duane Ice, Royal Oak, Mich., April 30, 2005.

46. Ramirez, "Hearing on Ruling Set for July 31" (July 9, 1997).
47. Ourlian, "Papers 'Stonewall' Unions Over Returns" (April 27, 1997); Craig and Konrad, "Judge Asked to Reinstate Strikers" (July 8, 1997); Perry, Kramer, and Schneider (1982).
48. Interview with Linda Rabin Hammell, Detroit, July 17, 2006.
49. Pring (2001, 289–94); Ourlian, "Judge to Weigh Ramifications of Injunction" (July 27, 1997).
50. Pring (2001, 279, 285, 289); Ourlian, "Judge to Weigh Ramifications of Injunction" (July 27, 1997).
51. Ourlian, "10(j) Decision Could Be 10 Days Away, Judge Says" (August 3, 1997); Craig, "Ruling on Ex-Strikers Due Soon" (August 2, 1997).
52. Ourlian, "10(j) Decision Could Be 10 Days Away, Judge Says" (August 3, 1997); Craig, "Ruling on Ex-Strikers Due Soon" (August 2, 1997).
53. *The Alliance*, "Judge's Decision on 10J Could Come Soon" (August 7, 1997); Ourlian, "10(j) Decision Could Be 10 Days Away, Judge Says" (August 3, 1997).
54. U.S. District Court, *Schaub v. Detroit Newspaper Agency*, 984 F. Supp. 1048 (E.D. Mich. 1997), *aff'd*, 154 F.3rd 276 (6th Circ 1998).
55. U.S. District Court, *Schaub v. Detroit Newspaper Agency*, 1057.
56. Ourlian, "NLRB Will Seek Reversal of Injunction Denial" (August 17, 1997); interview with Linda Rabin Hammell, Detroit, July 17, 2006.
57. NLRB, *Detroit Newspaper Agency*, 326 NLRB 64 (1998), 718.
58. Pring (2001, 299–300).
59. Craig, "Newspaper Strike to Get Day in Court" (July 30, 1997).
60. Pring (2001, 302).
61. General Counsel, National Labor Relations Board, brief in support of petition for injunction under section 10(j) of the National Labor Relations Act, as amended, *Schaub v. Detroit Newspaper Agency*, CV-97-1920 (6th Cir. 1998).
62. Metropolitan Council of Newspaper Unions, brief on behalf of the unions, *Schaub v. Detroit Newspaper Agency*, CV-97-1920 (6th Cir. 1998).
63. Pring (2001, 301).
64. Ourlian, "NLRB Will Seek Reversal of Injunction Denial" (August 17, 1997).
65. Interview with Renee Murawski, New York, N.Y., December 12, 2008; interview with Robert Ourlian, Washington, D.C., March 17, 2006; interview with Allan Lengel, Washington, D.C., March 17, 2006.
66. Dulzo, "Striking Out: The Dailies and Their Unions Were Wounded" (January 24–30, 2001).
67. U.S. District Court, *Schaub v. Detroit Newspaper Agency*, 984 F. Supp. 1048 (E.D. Mich. 1997), *aff'd*, 154 F.3rd 276 (6th Cir. 1998).
68. *Detroit Sunday Journal*, "Longtime Printer Dies at 64" (June 9, 1996); *The Alliance*, "Memorial Set for Pressman Janisch" (October 31, 1996); *Detroit Sunday Journal*, "Funeral Set for Striking Printer" (December 22, 1996).

69. *The Alliance*, "'Wow!' Over 100,000 Jam Hart Plaza for Action! Motown 97" (June 25, 1997).

70. Interview with Mike Zielinski, Washington, D.C., March 16, 2006.

71. Forsyth, "Printers Turn Down DN's Buyout Offer" (March 8, 1998); *Detroit Sunday Journal*, "ACOSS Takes Story of Lockout Far and Wide" (April 12, 1998); Forsyth, "Locked-Out Workers Rattle Tony Ridder" (June 7, 1998).

72. Interview with Mike Zielinski, Washington, D.C., March 16, 2006.

73. Forsyth, "Streets Are Alive with Sound of Unions" (October 4, 1998), and "Another Detroit News Promotion Is Totaled" (November 8, 1998).

74. Forsyth, "Westland Company Ordered to Turn Back the Clock" (March 22, 1998).

75. Interview with Edwin A. Rowe, Detroit, May 26, 2005.

76. Forsyth, "Six More City Councils Sign on for Lockout Summit" (April 19, 1998), and "Summit Numbers Grow" (April 26, 1998).

77. Forsyth, "Enough Already! Community Works for End to Newspaper Dispute" (May 17, 1998).

78. Forsyth, "Summit's Clear Message: We Want Action" (May 24, 1998).

79. Forsyth, "Is It Over? Telemarketers Say So" (January 11, 1998); Slaughter, "Strike (Year) Four" (March 17, 1999).

80. Forsyth, "Scab Convicted for Driving into Pickets" (October 12, 1997).

81. Craig, "Publisher Giles Leaving Detroit News" (May 13, 1998); *Detroit Sunday Journal*, "Did Giles Jump or Was He Pushed?" (May 18, 1997).

82. Rohan, "*Free Press* Editorial Moves into *News* Building" (July 30, 1998).

83. Schram, "Lockout 'One of My Top Priorities'" (December 13, 1998); interview with Mike Zielinski, Washington, D.C., March 16, 2006.

84. *Detroit Sunday Journal*, "It's Not Over! *Journal* Closing Doesn't Signal Settlement with Dailies" (November 14, 1999); Robertson and Guensburg (2000).

85. Forsyth, "A Year Later, Workers Trickle In" (February 15, 1998); Kristen Strait, email message to Heath Meriwether, "Strike/Recall Numbers" (October 26, 1998).

86. *Detroit Sunday Journal*, "Back Pay Will Take Time" (July 25, 1999).

87. *The Alliance*, "DN Guilty (Again) of Ignoring Federal Labor Laws" (November 13, 1997).

88. Bernstein, "How Business Is Winning Its War with the NLRB" (October 27, 1997); Pring (2001, 283–84).

89. Forsyth, "Gould: NLRB Board Is Too Slow" (August 30, 1998); Gould (2000).

90. NLRB, *Detroit Newspaper Agency*, 326 NLRB 64 (1998), 702–4, 705–6.

91. NLRB, *Detroit Newspaper Agency*, 327 NLRB 164 (1999).

92. NLRB, *Detroit Newspaper Agency*, 326 NLRB 64 (1998), 706–7; Bernstein, "How Business Is Winning Its War with the NLRB" (October 27, 1997).

93. Greenhouse, "Detroit Papers Ordered to Rehire Strikers and Pay Back Wages" (September 2, 1998).

94. *Detroit Sunday Journal*, "Vega Sees No Settlement" (February 7, 1999).

95. Ramirez, "Teamsters Approve Newspapers' Offer" (March 9, 1998); Forsyth, "Papers' Circulation Going Down Again" (March 15, 1998).
96. Forsyth, "Printers Turn Down DN's Buyout Offer" (March 8, 1998).
97. Forsyth, "DTU Deal a Sign of Hope?" (February 21, 1999), and "Engravers Reach Tentative Agreement" (April 4, 1999).
98. Forsyth, "DTU Deal a Sign of Hope?" (February 21, 1999).
99. NLRB, *Detroit Newspaper Agency*, 342 NLRB 24 (2004).
100. Gallagher, "Newspapers Are Not at Fault" (July 8, 2000).
101. NLRB, *Detroit Newspaper Agency et al.*, 330 NLRB 81 (2000); U.S. Court of Appeals, *Detroit Newspaper Agency et al. v. NLRB*, 286 F.3rd 391 (2006); *The Alliance*, "U.S. Judge Shoots Down Firings Case" (August 17, 2000).
102. Gallagher, "High Court Won't Hear Newspaper Strike Case" (October 3, 2006).
103. Interview with Duane Ice, Royal Oak, Mich., April 30, 2005.
104. U.S. Court of Appeals, *McClatchy Newspapers, Inc., v. NLRB*, 131 F.3rd 1026 (D.C. Cir. 1997).
105. McBride, "Appeals Court Sets May 4 Hearing Date" (October 31, 1999); Fix, "Detroit Dailies, Unions Get Hearing" (May 5, 2000).
106. U.S. Court of Appeals, *Detroit Typographical Union 18 v. NLRB*, 216 F.3rd 109, 122 (D.C. Cir. 2000).
107. Pring (2001); Price, "Judges Rule Against Detroit Newspaper Workers" (July-August 2000).
108. Zachem, "Court Blow to Detroit Newspaper Workers Sounds 'Wake-Up' Call" (August-September 2000).
109. U.S. Court of Appeals, *McClatchy Newspapers, Inc., v. NLRB*, 131 F.3rd 1026 (D.C. Cir. 1997).
110. Ourlian, "Judges Ignored Evidence" (July 16–30, 2000); Pring (2001, 302).
111. Dulzo, "Striking Out" (January 24–30, 2001).
112. *The Alliance*, "Let NLRB Explain Ruling? The DC-3 Say No" (September 7, 2000); Angel, "Vote Could Bring Newspaper Peace" (September 1, 2000).
113. Interview with Duane Ice, Royal Oak, Mich., April 30, 2005; Barringer, "The Strike That Ate Circulation" (July 17, 2000); *The Alliance*, "Bargaining? Wait Till September; Raises? Maybe After Bargaining" (August 3, 2000).
114. Pring (2001); Dannin (2006).
115. Interview with Edwin A. Rowe, Detroit, May 26, 2005.
116. *The Alliance*, "Gannett Resumes Bargaining with Newspaper Unions" (August 24, 2000).
117. John Jaske, letter to Jack Howe (August 30, 2000, emphasis in original); *The Alliance*, "Metropolitan Council of Newspaper Unions' Sept. 1 Statement" (September 14, 2000).
118. NLRB, *Detroit Newspaper Agency*, 342 NLRB 24 (2004); *The Alliance*, "Fairness for Fired Strikers" (September 21, 2000).

119. Jack Howe, letter to John Jaske, September 1, 2000.

120. *Editor and Publisher*, "Newspaper Labor Pains" (December 4, 2000); *The Alliance*, "Teamsters to Vote on DN Proposals" (December 14, 2000).

121. Greenhouse, "After 5½ Years, a Labor War Ends at 2 Detroit Papers" (December 19, 2000); Fitzgerald, "Detroit Disputes Settling Down?" (January 1, 2001).

CHAPTER 12

1. Martin (2004, 8); see also Kumar (2007).

2. Quoted in Gould (1993, 187); see also Lambert (2005), 165.

3. *Detroit Sunday Journal*, "Notice Is Served" (November 19, 1995).

4. Interview with Alan Lenhoff, Detroit, November 4, 2004.

5. Interview with Duane Ice, Royal Oak, Mich., April 30, 2005.

6. Cranberg, Bezanson, and Soloski (2001); Gruley (1993).

7. Fitzgerald, "Pick a Side: Detroit Newspapers' Chief Challenges Chamber of Commerce and United Way to Choose a Side in the Ongoing Newspaper Strike" (November 4, 1995); Thomas (1989, 142–60).

8. Sacharow, "Walking the Line in Detroit" (July 22, 1996); Wenner (2001).

9. Telephone interview with Hiawatha Bray, February 16, 2005; interview with Crawford Webb, Detroit, July 25, 2006.

10. Freedman, "Picketers Protest as CEO Vega Defends Newspapers" (April 14, 1996).

11. Ivar Peterson, "After the Detroit Strike, Unions Switch Tactics" (March 11, 1997).

12. U.S. Court of Appeals, *McClatchy Newspapers, Inc., v. NLRB*, 131 F.3rd 1026 (D.C. Cir. 1997).

13. Greenhouse, "In Indiana, Clues to Future of Wisconsin Labor" (February 26, 2011); Williams, "The Battle over Union Rights, State by State" (March 10, 2011).

14. Greenhouse, "Ohio's Anti-Union Law Is Tougher Than Wisconsin's" (March 31, 2011); Provance, "Kasich accepts Defeat of Issue 2," (November 8, 2011).

15. Herbert, "Unintended, but Sound Advice" (March 1, 2011).

16. Rosenfeld, "Strike Predictors in the Modern United States" (August 14, 2006).

17. Freeman (1998); Clawson (2003).

18. Wallerstein and Western (2000); Franzosi (1995, 344).

19. Montgomery (1987); Zieger (1994).

20. Honey (2007); Milkman (2000).

21. Milkman (2006); Ness (2005); Jung (2006).

22. Lund and Wright (2003); Bonacich and Wilson (2007); Ross (2004); Seidman (2007).

23. *The Alliance*, "'Wow!' Over 100,000 Jam Hart Plaza for Action! Motown 97" (June 25, 1997).

24. Fletcher and Gapasin (2008); Ness and Eimer (2001).
25. Kumar (2001, 91); Greenhouse, "For the Teamsters' Leader, UPS Is an Ancient Enemy" (August 7, 1997).
26. Rothstein (1997); Clawson (2003, 198).
27. IBT president Carey came out of a UPS local in Queens, New York, and the UPS membership formed his political base within the union. Carey was not as close to the locals in Detroit, the home of his rival for the union presidency, James P. Hoffa. Greenhouse, "For the Teamsters' Leader, UPS Is an Ancient Enemy" (August 7, 1997).
28. Rothstein (1997); Nagourney, "In Strike Battle, Teamsters Borrow a Page from Politics" (August 16, 1997).
29. Kumar (2001, 147).
30. Greenhouse, "Labor Unions Plan a Teamsters Loan to Sustain Strike" (August 13, 2007), and "Yearlong Effort Key to Success for Teamsters" (August 25, 2007).
31. Greenhouse, "A Victory for Labor, but How Far Will It Go?" (August 20, 1997).
32. Kumar (2001, 149).
33. Greenhouse, "Teamster Voting That Chose Carey Declared Invalid" (August 23, 1997).
34. Greenhouse, "An Overseer Bars Teamster Leader from Reelection" (November 18, 1997), "Board Expels Ron Carey from Teamsters for Life" (July 28, 1998), and "Hoffa Will Lead Teamsters After Chief Rival Concedes" (December 6, 1998).
35. Getman (2003).
36. Gould (1993); Getman (2010); Osterman et al. (2001); Human Rights Watch (2009).
37. Quoted in Budd (2004, 87).
38. See National Labor Relations Act, 29 U.S.C. § 151. The 1932 Norris-LaGuardia Act similarly declared: "Whereas under prevailing economic conditions, developed with the aid of governmental authority for owners of property to organize in the corporate and other forms of ownership association, the individual unorganized worker is commonly helpless to exercise actual liberty of contract and to protect his freedom of labor, and thereby to obtain acceptable terms and conditions of employment" (29 U.S.C. § 102).
39. Dannin (2006, 67); Kuttner (1997, 68).
40. A study by Pauline Kim (1997) found that employees commonly believe that discharge must be based on cause, even in the absence of any union or contractual protections.
41. Getman (2003, 134).
42. Budd (2004, 95).
43. Quoted in Block et al. (2006, 1).

44. Kaufman (1997, 34).
45. Macedo (2005); Gross (2003).
46. *Payne v. Western and Atlantic Railroad*, Supreme Court of Tennessee, 81 Tenn. 507 (1884).
47. Summers (2000, 78).
48. Summers (2000, 80–88).
49. Summers (2000, 66–68).
50. Dannin (2004, 249); Getman (2003, 128).
51. Dannin (1997).
52. Dannin and Wagar (2000).
53. NLRB, *Detroit Newspaper Agency*, 326 NLRB 64 (1988), 725–27 (citing *NLRB v. Insurance Agents*, 361 U.S. 477, 485 [1960]).
54. Dannin (2006, 93).
55. Budd (2004, 41).
56. Summers (2000, 86).
57. Lichtenstein (2002, 43).
58. Dannin (2006, 91); Summers (2000, 80–81).
59. Dannin (1997, 39).
60. Interview with Edwin A. Rowe, Detroit, May 26, 2005.
61. Lambert (2005, 165).
62. Kochan (2004, 47–70); Farber and Western (2001).
63. Getman (2003, 140–43).
64. Dannin (2006, 39–40).
65. Osterman et al. (2001, 174).
66. Parks and Warren (2009, 88–106).
67. Accola, "Motown JOA Had a Rough Start" (July 11, 2000).
68. *Detroit Free Press*, "Building a Better Newspaper" (October 17, 2005); Rosenberg, Fitzgerald, and Crow, "Saluting Seven Top Managers" (September 2007).
69. Saba, "Downshift in Motor City" (January 2009), and "What's the Frequency?" (February 2009).
70. Audit Bureau of Circulation (2011).
71. Edmonds, Guskin, and Rosensteil (2011).
72. Langeveld (2011).
73. Edmonds, Guskin, and Rosensteil (2011).
74. U.S. Securities and Exchange Commission, Gannett Co., Inc., Form 10-K 2010 Annual Report (2010, 27).
75. Perez-Pena, "Gannett to Furlough Workers for Week" (January 15, 2009), and "As It Cuts Jobs, Gannett Also Cuts Severance Pay" (July 27, 2009).
76. Carr, "You're Gone, but Hey, You Can Reapply" (August 31, 2009), and "Furloughs, but Paydays for the Brass" (April 11, 2011).
77. Interview with John Jaske, McLean, Va., November 4, 2005.

78. Gannett Co., Inc., press release, "Van Lare to Head Gannett Labor Relations" (January 12, 2006); Yahoo Finance, "Insider and Form 144 Filings—Jaske, John B."
79. Craggs, "Darth Vega to the Rescue" (May 4, 2005).
80. Gallagher, "Battista to Chair Labor Board" (November 16, 2002).
81. Johansson (2007).
82. Hall-Balduf, "End of Your Rope? Ask for Help" (November 22, 1995).
83. Michigan Journalism Hall of Fame (2000); NLRB, *Detroit Newspaper Agency*, 342 NLRB 24 (2004); interview with Rebecca Cook, Detroit, October 21, 2004; interview with Emily Everett, Detroit, April 26, 2005.
84. Mullen, "A Million-Dollar Question" (April 19–25, 2000).
85. *The Alliance*, "Jury Says DN, Sterling Heights Conspired" (January 11, 2001).

References

NEWSPAPERS AND PERIODICALS

Accola, John. 2000. "Motown JOA Had a Rough Start." *Rocky Mountain News* (Denver), July 11, p. 1G.

Ahrens, Frank. 1995. "Bad News." *Washington Post*, July 30, p. F-01.

Albom, Mitch. 1995. "I Return Because Readers Are What Matter the Most." *Detroit Free Press*, September 5, p. 1D.

The Alliance. 1995. "Unions Unite for Contract Talks." January 15.

———. 1995. "Unions Shifting into High Gear." February 15.

———. 1995. "Strike Plans Surge Forward." May 16.

———. 1995. "Health Insurance Answers." May 16.

———. 1995. "Detroit Backs Newspaper Unions." June 21.

———. 1995. "News Brief: From the Battlefront." July 17.

———. 1995. "Notes from the Battlefront." July 21.

———. 1995. "Union Teachers on Our Side." July 23.

———. 1995. "Members Celebrate Solidarity at Rally." July 26.

———. 1995. "Elsewhere on the Goon Front. . . ." July 26.

———. 1995. "Ad Honor Roll Hits 222; Builders Square Joins List." July 26.

———. 1995. "Front Line News." August 6.

———. 1995. "Pressmen, Engravers Seek Fair Contracts." August 11.

———. 1995. "Notes from the Battlefront." August 13.

———. 1995. "Vegas Markets Ready to Help Strikers with Discounts." August 13.

———. 1995. "Coleman Calls DN 'Illegal, Immoral.'" August 13.

———. 1995. "AFL-CIO Calls for National Drive." August 16.

———. 1995. "Cardinal Maida Condemns DN." August 16.

———. 1995. "Reno Asked to Rescind JOA." August 19.

———. 1995. "UAW Adds Muscle to Advertising Campaign." August 24.

———. 1995. "Sterling Cops Go to Highest Bidder?" August 24.

———. 1995. "Shores Latest to Ask for JOA Probe." August 28.

———. 1995. "Latest Union Donations." August 28.

———. 1995. "NLRB Ruling Protects Jobs." September 2.

———. 1995. "'Treasure Island North' for Sterling Cops." September 15.

———. 1995. "News from the Battlefront." September 15.

———. 1995. "Notes from the Battlefront." September 21.

———. 1995. "Notes from the Battlefront." September 26.

———. 1995. "Hams Available at Food Bank." September 29.

———. 1995. "UAW, AFL-CIO Pledge Aid for Unions." October 12.

———. 1995. "Strikers Get Financial Aid." October 14.

———. 1995. "Notes from the Battlefront." October 25.

———. 1995. "Notes from the Battlefront." October 28.

———. 1995. "UAW Gives Strikers a $300,000 Boost." November 11.

———. 1995. "Detroit Teachers Reject Freep." November 28.

———. 1995. "DN Hit with Anti-Trust Lawsuit." November 28.

———. 1995. "Two Injured Mailers Sue DN." December 7.

———. 1995. "UAW Issues Gift Checks." December 16.

———. 1995. "Notes from the Battlefront." December 16.

———. 1995. "DN Says 'Bah Humbug.'" December 22.

———. 1996. "Bishop Gumbleton Says at Rally: King Would Support Strikers." January 17.

———. 1996. "Leaflet Pressure Convinces Nine Dealers." January 20.

———. 1996. "Notes from the Battlefront." January 30.

———. 1996. "Four Auto Dealers Junk DN for Unions." February 8.

———. 1996. "'Avoid Scab Advertisers' UAW Asks." February 13.

———. 1996. "'Papers Have Sinned,' Clergy Takes a Stand." February 17.

———. 1996. "Notes from the Battlefront." March 2.

———. 1996. "24 Community Leaders Arrested at Rally." March 7.

———. 1996. "UAW, AFL-CIO Leaders Confront DN." April 2.

———. 1996. "Ravitz, Other Pols Show Support in Rally." April 13.

———. 1996. "Notes from the Battlefront." April 13.

———. 1996. "NLRB Trial Opens on Nine ULP Complaints." April 17.

———. 1996. "400 Descend on Annual Meeting, Gannett Stockholders Get an Earful." May 8.

———. 1996. "Unions Launch Spring Offensive." May 16.

———. 1996. "Strikers Sink Scab Street Sales." May 23.

———. 1996. "UAW Staff 'Magnificent,' Strikers Get Direct Action Training." May 30.

———. 1996. "Mayor Resurfaces, Archer Tries to Jumpstart Talks." August 8.

———. 1996. "United Way's Decision, Charity Skips Scab Ads." September 12.

———. 1996. "Management Slaps Archer in Face." October 3.

———. 1996. "Pickets 1; New Sterling Hts. Law 0." October 10.

———. 1996. "Memorial Set for Pressman Janisch." October 31.

———. 1997. "Strike Enters Return-to-Work Phase." February 15.

———. 1997. "It's 'Re-Union' Time at Detroit Newspapers." March 24.

———. 1997. "Action! Motown '97 Needs *Your* Help, Too!" May 1.

———. 1997. "Notes from the Battlefront." May 1.

———. 1997. "Thousands of Labor Supporters to Join Action! Motown '97." June 12, p. 2.

———. 1997. "Action! Motown '97 Is Friday and Saturday: Be There!" June 19.

———. 1997. "'Wow!' Over 100,000 Jam Hart Plaza for Action! Motown 97." June 25, pp. 1–2.

———. 1997. "Judge's Decision on 10J Could Come Soon." August 7.

———. 1997. "DN Guilty (Again) of Ignoring Federal Labor Laws." November 13, p. 1.

———. 2000. "Bargaining? Wait Till September. Raises? Maybe After Bargaining." August 3, p. 1.

———. 2000. "U.S. Judge Shoots Down Firings Case." August 17, p. 1.

———. 2000. "Gannett Resumes Bargaining with Newspaper Unions." August 24, p. 1.

———. 2000. "Let NLRB Explain Ruling? The DC-3 Say No." September 7, p. 2.

———. 2000. "Metropolitan Council of Newspaper Unions' Sept. 1 Statement." September 14, p. 1.

———. 2000. "Fairness for Fired Strikers." September 21, p. 1.

———. 2000. "Teamsters to Vote on DN Proposals." December 14, p. 1.

———. 2001. "Jury Says DN, Sterling Heights Conspired." January 11, pp. 1–2.

Anderson, Kelly. 1995. "17 Strikers Arrested at Newspaper Facilities." *Macomb Daily*, October 4, p. 1A.

Androshick, Julie. 1996. "Kaboom!" *Forbes* 158(2): 18–19.

Angel, Cecil. 2000. "Vote Could Bring Newspaper Peace; Unions Will Submit Contract to Members." *Detroit Free Press*, September 1, p. 1E.

Angeles, Mark. 1995. "Mahaffey's Dealing with Police Helps Delay Newspapers." *Detroit News*, October 9, p. 1A.

Barringer, Felicity. 2000. "The Strike That Ate Circulation: In Detroit, Profits Are Up but Readers Have Left." *New York Times*, July 17.

Battagello, Mark. 1996. "Stuck in a Stalemate." *Windsor Star*, July 6, p. E1.

Bennet, James. 1995. "Detroit: Paper Is Ready to Replace Strikers." *New York Times*, August 9, p. D7.

———. 1995. "Newspaper Strike Divides Labor's Capital, Detroit." *New York Times*, September 2, p. A5.

———. 1995. "Helicopters Carry Papers in Detroit Strike." *New York Times*, September 11, p. A13.

Bernick, Thomas. 1996. "Integrity, Credibility Lost Meaning with DN." *Detroit Sunday Journal*, July 28, p. 15.

Bernstein, Aaron. 1997. "How Business Is Winning Its War with the NLRB." *Business Week*, October 27.

Bohy, Ric. 1995. "Newspaper Unions Have a Better Idea: Boycotts." *Metro Times* (Detroit), May 24–30.

———. 1995. "Progress Aside, Newspaper Talks Still Drag On." *Metro Times* (Detroit), June 14–20, p. 6.

———. 1995. "Odds and Ends from the Picket Line." *Metro Times* (Detroit), December 13, p. 6.

———. 1995. "Strike Coverage Spin Control." *Metro Times* (Detroit), September 20–26, p. 6.

———. 1996. "Civil Display or Union Tactic?" *Metro Times* (Detroit), April 3, p. 7.

———. 1996. "Still Smoldering: The Detroit Newspaper Strike Heads into Year Two." *Metro Times* (Detroit), July 3, pp. 10–16.

———. 1996. "Commandments or Compromise?" *Metro Times* (Detroit), July 17, p. 6.

Bott, Jennifer. 1995. "Racketeering Suit Filed Against Strikers." *Oakland Press*, November 16.

———. 1995. "Reaction to Strike Radically Different at *News, Free Press*." *Oakland Press*, December 3.

Bradsher, Keith. 1999. "Car Makers Predict Strong Sales This Year." *New York Times*, January 4, p. C6.

Brodesser, Claude. 1997. "Strike Hangover; DNA May Not Regain Old Life." *MediaWeek* 7(1): 14.

Bullard, George. 1995. "An Ex-Marine Keeps Chow Coming for *News* Workers." *Detroit News*, July 21, p. 10A.

Bureau of National Affairs. 1996. "Special Report: Detroit Newspapers Official Describes Operating Plan Adopted to Counter Strike." *Employee Relations Weekly* 14(July 8): 754.

Burroughs, Elise. 1996. "Strike Rattles Ad Market." *Presstime* (January): 14–15.

Carr, David. 2009. "You're Gone, but Hey, You Can Reapply." *New York Times*, August 31, p. B1.

———. 2011. "Furloughs, but Paydays for the Brass." *New York Times*, April 11, p. B1.

Christian, Nichole M. 1995. "Deadline Pressure: Detroit Newspapers Face an Ugly Standoff with Striking Unions." *Wall Street Journal*, August 9, p. 1.

———. 1996. "Teamsters Drop Some Demands in Strike at Detroit Papers in Bid for Resolution." *Wall Street Journal*, April 11, p. B8.

Cooper, Barry Michael. 1987. "Kids Killing Kids: New Jack City Eats Its Young." *Village Voice*, December 1, pp. 23–30.

Craggs, Tommy. 2005. "Darth Vega to the Rescue." *SF Weekly*, May 4. Available at: http://www.sfweekly.com/2005-05-04/news/darth-vega-to-the-rescue/ (accessed April 23, 2010).

Craig, Charlotte. 1995. "Papers, Unions Vow to Behave in Sterling Heights Picketing." *Detroit Free Press*, September 9, p. 10B.

———. 1995. "Agency Extends Newspaper Union Contracts." *Detroit Free Press*, July 1, pp. 8A, 10A.

———. 1995. "Unions Set a Strike Deadline for Newspapers." *Detroit Free Press*, July 7, p. 1E.

———. 1996. "Chamber Blasts Tactics in Paper Strike." *Detroit Free Press*, November 21, p. 1E.

———. 1997. "Newspaper Agency Declares an Impasse." *Detroit Free Press*, March 22, p. 9B.

———. 1997. "Publisher Giles Leaving Detroit News." *Detroit Free Press*, May 13, p. 2E.

———. 1997. "Newspaper Strike to Get Day in Court." *Detroit Free Press*, July 30, p. 1E.

———. 1997. "Ruling on Ex-Strikers Due Soon; Return to Newspaper Jobs at Issue." *Detroit Free Press*, August 2, p. 9B.

Craig, Charlotte, and Rachel Konrad. 1997. "Judge Asked to Reinstate Strikers." *Detroit Free Press*, July 8, p. 1A.

Craig, Charlotte, and Lekan Oguntoyinbo. 1997. "Newspapers' Unions Seek Immediate Return; *Free Press* Begins a Few Callbacks." *Detroit Free Press*, February 22, p. 9B.

Creager, Ellen, and Reed Johnson. 1995. "Journalists Strike Out in New Directions." *Detroit Journal*, October 27.

CWA Sector News. 1995. "Detroit Strike in Third Month, No Quick Settlement in Sight." Vol. 10(9): 6A.

CWA News. 1996. "CWA and TNG Launch Adopt-A-Family Program to Aid Detroit Newspaper Strikers." January, p. 5.

———. 1996. "Adopt-A-Family 'Honor Roll.'" March, p. 11.

———. 1997. "Returning Detroit Members Confront Idleness, Isolation." May, p. 8B.

Danese, Roseann. 1996. "1,000 March to Mark Newspapers' Year on Strike." *Windsor Star*, July 15, p. A4.

Debenport, Ellen. 1995. "Hard Pressed: Detroit Papers' Strike Hurts Both Sides, and Even Those Caught in the Middle." *Cleveland Plain Dealer*, September 2, p. 1C.

DeSmet, Kate. 1995. "Religious Leaders Condemn the Hiring of Replacement Workers." *Detroit Union* 1(1): 3.

———. 1997. "Newspaper Strikers Renew Call for National March in Detroit." *Labor Notes* 214(January): 3–4.

Detroit Free Press. 1994. "Striking Workers: Protection Bill Deserves the Senate's Active Support." June 24, p. 10A.

———. 1995. "Strike Simmers at Detroit Papers; 'It Seems There's a Better Way'; Free Press Publisher Says No Bargaining in Sight." July 15, p. 1A.

———. 1995. "Q&A: No Plans to Close One Newspaper Despite the Strike and Delivery Problems." July 22, p. 1A.

———. 1995. "Newspaper Striker Injured When Van Runs over Him." October 4, p. 1B.

———. 1995. "Picketers Must Leave Art Van, NLRB Rules Against Newspaper Unions." October 14, p. 10B.

———. 1995. "Newspapers Report Smooth Delivery, Quieter Pickets." October 16, p. 1B.

———. 1995. "Building a Better Newspaper." October 17, 2005, p. F15.

———. 1995. "Violence Ebbs, Papers' Spokesman Says." October 23, p. 2B.

———. 1995. "Pipe Bombs Placed in Shelby Township Newspaper Boxes." November 2, p. 1B.

———. 1995. "Union Chief: Hurt the Bottom Line, Plans Focus on Advertisers." November 16, p. 1B.

———. 1996. "Prosecutor Says Guards May Have Set Truck Fire." March 13.

Detroit Journal. 1995. "Statement from the Unions: Why We Are on Strike." August 3.

———. 1995. "Notes from Our Readers." August 14.

Detroit News. 1995. "*Free Press* Tells Staffers to Return or Risk Job Loss." August 9, pp. 1A, 9A.

———. 1996. "List of Protestors Who Were Arrested." March 15, p. C-4.

———. 1996. "Former UAW Chief, 21 Others Arrested at Rally at *News* Building." March 22.

———. 1996. "King's Son Tells Strikers to Persevere." March 31, p. B-4.

———. 1996. "Newspaper Strikers Urged to Bring Kids to Picket Lines." May 5, p. 1-C.

———. 1996. "Strike: A Failure of Leadership." July 11, p. 10A.

Detroit Newspapers. 1995. "An Open Letter to Our Community." *Michigan Chronicle*, July 19–25, p. 8-D.

Detroit Sunday Journal. 1995. "Notice Is Served." November 19, p. 16.

———. 1996. "Longtime Printer Dies at 64." June 9, p. 2.

———. 1996. "Georgia Workers Support Newspaper Strike." June 30, p. 8.

———. 1996. "Talks with Teamsters Uneventful." August 25, p. 9.

———. 1996. "Funeral Set for Striking Printer." December 22, p. 2.

———. 1997. "National March Update." February 2, p. 8.

———. 1997. "Did Giles Jump or Was He Pushed?" May 18, p. 9.

———. 1997. "Rally Puts Labor's Focus on Detroit." June 15, p. 9.

———. 1997. "A Family Reunion: Brothers and Sisters Gather for an International Show of Solidarity." June 29, pp. 1A–8A.

———. 1997. "Q&A." July 6, p. 14.

———. 1997. "Newspaper Spin Doctors Twirl Themselves Silly." July 6, p. 16.

———. 1998. "ACOSS Takes Story of Lockout Far and Wide." April 12, p. 4.

———. 1999. "Vega Sees No Settlement." February 7, p. 6.

———. 1999. "Back Pay Will Take Time." July 25, p. 8.

———. 1999. "It's Not Over! *Journal* Closing Doesn't Signal Settlement with Dailies." November 14, p. 1.

Devine, Lawrence. 1995. "'The Spiritual Godfather' of the Newspaper Bows Out." *Detroit Free Press*, December 7, p. 1A.

Driskell, Bill. 1995. "Portion of *Detroit News* Plant in Sterling Heights May Close." *Macomb Daily*, April 13, p. 4A.

———. 1995. "Sterling Police Train for Crowd Control Duties." *Macomb Daily*, June 1.

———. 1995. "Police, Strikers Share Frustration at Printing Plant." *Macomb Daily*, September 12, p. 3A.

———. 1995. "Crossbow Found in Replacement Worker's Car." *Macomb Daily*, October 10, p. 4A.

———. 1996. "Audit Shows Sharp Drop in Detroit *News, Free Press* Circulation in Macomb County." *Macomb Daily*, October 1.

Dulzo, Jim. 2001. "Striking Out: The Dailies and Their Unions Were Wounded. Are There Lessons Here?" *Metro Times* (Detroit), January 24–30, p. 16.

Editor & Publisher. 2000. "Newspaper Labor Pains." December 4, p. 24.

Elmer, Vickie. 1996. "Union Launches Boycott of *USA Today*." *Detroit Sunday Journal*, February 25, p. 9.

Finley, Nolan. 1995. "Newspaper Workers Strike." *Detroit News*, July 14, p. 1A.

Fitzgerald, Mark. 1995. "Face-off in Detroit: Newspapers, Unions Settle in for What Looks Like a Long Strike." *Editor & Publisher*, July 22, pp. 11–13.

———. 1995. "Tug of War in Detroit." *Editor & Publisher*, August 12, pp. 20–21.

———. 1995. "Return to the Table in Detroit: Striking Unions and Management Restart Talks Under Federal Mediation." *Editor & Publisher*, September 2, pp. 10–11.

———. 1995. "Hard-Line Tactics." *Editor & Publisher*, October, p. 13.

———. 1995. "Pick a Side: Detroit Newspapers' Chief Challenges Chamber of Commerce and United Way to Choose a Side in the Ongoing Newspaper Strike." *Editor & Publisher*, November 4, p. 26.

———. 1996. "A War of Attrition." *Editor & Publisher*, March 16, p. 8.

———. 1996. "Progression of Violence." *Editor & Publisher*, March 16, pp. 10–11.

———. 1996. "Strike Coverage." *Editor & Publisher*, March 16, p. 15.

———. 1996. "Feeling the Effects of the Strike." *Editor & Publisher*, September 28, p. 11.

———. 1996. "Firing Greet Detroit Strikers." *Editor & Publisher*, November 9, p. 12.

———. 1998. "Groping for Labor Peace in Detroit." *Editor & Publisher* 131(40): 16.

———. 1998. "Detroit Union Leaders: Five Strikes—You're Out." *Editor & Publisher* 131(52): 6.

———. 2001. "Detroit Disputes Settling Down?" *Editor & Publisher*, January 1, p. 8.

Fix, Janet. 2000. "Detroit Dailies, Unions Get Hearing; Appeals Court to Decide Newspaper Strike Cause." *Detroit Free Press*, May 5, p. 1E.

Fogel, Helen. 1995. "The *News* Imposes Its Final Wage Offer." *Detroit News*, July 6, p. 1B.

Fornoff, Robin. 1995. "Printing Plant Violence Blamed on Outsiders." *Detroit Journal*, August 21.

———. 1995. "Strikers, Sterling Heights Cops Declare Truce." *Detroit Journal*, August 28.

Fornoff, Robin, Kim Heron, and Bill Rapai. 1995. "Papers Use Helicopters After Picketers Block Plant." *Detroit Journal*, September 11.

Fornoff, Robin, and Antoinette Martin. 1995. "Mass Rally Blocks Delivery of Newspapers." *Detroit Journal*, September 3.

Fornoff, Robin, Mike Martindale, and Robert Musial. 1995. "Newspaper Talks Resume After Violent Weekend." *Detroit Journal*, September 6.

Forsyth, Alan. 1997. "Getting to Work." *Detroit Sunday Journal*, June 8, p. 12.

———. 1997. "Supporters Coming in on Wheels of All Kinds." *Detroit Sunday Journal*, June 22, p. 12.

———. 1997. "'Another Step Toward Justice.'" *Detroit Sunday Journal*, July 6, p. 1.

———. 1997. "Two at the News." *Detroit Sunday Journal*, September 7, p. 11.

———. 1997. "Scab Convicted for Driving into Pickets." *Detroit Sunday Journal*, October 12, p. 7.

———. 1997. "Local 2040 Says DN Takes Steps to Keep Mailers Out." *Detroit Sunday Journal*, December 7, p. 4.

———. 1997. "More of the Same." *Detroit Sunday Journal*, December 14, p. 4.

———. 1997. "Kelleher's Son Nabbed." *Detroit Sunday Journal*, December 21, pp. 4–5.

———. 1998. "Is It Over? Telemarketers Say So." *Detroit Sunday Journal*, January 11, p. 4.

———. 1998. "DN Closes Its 'Decomposing Room.'" *Detroit Sunday Journal*, February 1, p. 4.

———. 1998. "A Year Later, Workers Trickle In." *Detroit Sunday Journal*, February 15, p. 4.

———. 1998. "Printers Turn Down DN's Buyout Offer." *Detroit Sunday Journal*, March 8, pp. 3, 5.

———. 1998. "Papers' Circulation Going Down Again." *Detroit Sunday Journal*, March 15, p. 4.

———. 1998. "Westland Company Ordered to Turn Back the Clock." *Detroit Sunday Journal*, March 22, p. 4.

———. 1998. "Six More City Councils Sign On for Lockout Summit." *Detroit Sunday Journal*, April 19, p. 4.

———. 1998. "Summit Numbers Grow." *Detroit Sunday Journal*, April 26, p. 4.

———. 1998. "Enough Already! Community Works for End to Newspaper Dispute." *Detroit Sunday Journal*, May 17, p. 1.

———. 1998. "Summit's Clear Message: We Want Action." *Detroit Sunday Journal*, May 24, p. 4.

———. 1998. "Locked-Out Workers Rattle Tony Ridder." *Detroit Sunday Journal*, June 7, p. 4.

———. 1998. "Gould: NLRB Board Is Too Slow." *Detroit Sunday Journal*, August 30, p. 4.

———. 1998. "Streets Are Alive with Sound of Unions." *Detroit Sunday Journal*, October 4, p. 4.

———. 1998. "Another Detroit News Promotion Is Totaled." *Detroit Sunday Journal*, November 8, p. 3.

———. 1999. "DTU Deal a Sign of Hope?" *Detroit Sunday Journal*, February 21, p. 1.

———. 1999. "Jury Rules That DN Libeled Part-time Mailer." *Detroit Sunday Journal*, February 28, p. 4.

———. 1999. "Engravers Reach Tentative Agreements." *Detroit Sunday Journal*, April 4, p. 4.

Freedman, Eric. 1996. "Picketers Protest as CEO Vega Defends Newspapers." *Detroit Sunday Journal*, April 14, p. 10.

Funke, Michael. 1995. "Building and Restaurant Workers Lend Support." *Detroit Union* 1(3): 7.

Gallagher, John. 2000. "Newspapers Are Not at Fault." *Detroit Free Press*, July 8, p. 1A.

———. 2000. "High Court Won't Hear Newspaper Strike Case." *Detroit Free Press*, October 3, p. F6.

———. 2000. "Battista to Chair Labor Board; Detroit Lawyer Hopes to Bring Civility to Panel." *Detroit Free Press*, November 16, 2002, p. A13.

Gamache, Gabrielle. 1996. "City Strikes Back at Picketing." *The Source* (Sterling Heights, Mich.), September 22, p. A1.

Gardner, Greg. 1995. "Advertising Losses Heavy in Detroit, Knight-Ridder Says." *Detroit Journal*, August 27.

———. 1995. "Thousands March in Labor Day Parade Led by Strikers." *Detroit Journal*, September 5.

Gargaro, Paul. 1996. "Old Ways Gone, Impasse Persists." *Crain's Detroit Business*, July 8, p. 1.

Gewolb, Joshua. 2000. "Contender for Nieman Post Under Scrutiny." *Harvard Crimson Online*, July 7. Available at: http://www.thecrimson.harvard.edu/article/2000/7/7/contender-for-nieman-post-under-scrutiny/ (accessed July 7, 2010).

Giles, Robert. 1995. "Why Keeping Two Daily Newspapers in Detroit Is Simply Good Business." *Detroit News*, July 16, p. 1A.

———. 1996. "Who Strikes Best Example for Civil Disobedience?" *Detroit News*, March 10, p. C-5.

Gleick, Elizabeth. 1996. "Read All About It." *Time*, October 21, pp. 66–69.

Grant, David. 1996. "Council President, Bishops Arrested at Rally." *Detroit News*, March 7, p. 1A.

Greenhouse, Steven. 1997. "For the Teamsters' Leader, UPS Is an Ancient Enemy." *New York Times*, August 7, p. B8.

———. 1997. "Labor Unions Plan a Teamsters Loan to Sustain Strike." *New York Times*, August 13, p. A20.

———. 1997. "A Victory for Labor, but How Far Will It Go?" *New York Times*, August 20, p. D18.

———. 1997. "Teamster Voting That Chose Carey Declared Invalid." *New York Times*, August 23, p. A1.

———. 1997. "Yearlong Effort Key to Success for Teamsters." *New York Times*, August 25, p. A15.

———. 1997. "An Overseer Bars Teamster Leader from Reelection." *New York Times*, November 18.

———. 1998. "Board Expels Ron Carey from Teamsters for Life." *New York Times*, July 28.

———. 1998. "Detroit Papers Ordered to Rehire Strikers and Pay Back Wages." *New York Times*, September 2, p. A25.

———. 1998. "Hoffa Will Lead Teamsters After Chief Rival Concedes." *New York Times*, December 6, p. A1.

———. 2000. "After 5½ Years, a Labor War Ends at 2 Detroit Papers." *New York Times*, December 19, p. A20.

———. 2011. "In Indiana, Clues to Future of Wisconsin Labor." *New York Times*, February 26.

———. 2011. "Ohio's Anti-Union Law Is Tougher Than Wisconsin's." *New York Times*, March 31.

Grimm, Joe. 1996. "Orientation: The First Important Thing You Do." *American Editor* (April-May): 12–14.

Grow, Doug. 1995. "Paper Strike in Detroit May Prove Fight for Union Life." *Minneapolis Star Tribune*, September 26, p. 3B.

Gruley, Bryan. 1995. "We're Getting Job Done, Papers Say." *Detroit News*, July 20, p. 4-A.

Guest, Greta. 1996. "King Brings Hope to Newspaper Strikers." *Oakland Press*, March 31, p. A-21.

Guyette, Curt. 1999. "A House Divided: Four Years Later the Labor Dispute Lingers, While Scabs and Returnees Work Side by Side." *Metro Times* (Detroit), July 7–13, p. 12.

Hall-Balduf, Susan. 1995. "End of Your Rope? Ask for Help." *Detroit Journal*, November 22.

Henderson, Tom. 1996. "Pulp Friction." *Corporate Detroit* 14(3): 9–17.

———. 1996. "A Labor of Law." *Corporate Detroit* 14(3): 16.

Herbert, Bob. 2011. "Unintended, but Sound Advice." *New York Times*, March 1, p. A-27.

Heron, W. Kim, Gene Schabath, and Gary Graff. 1995. "Strike's Action Shifts from Plants to Distribution Centers." *Detroit Journal*, September 25.

Hindes, Martha. 1995. "Returning Newspaper Strikers Are Told to Get in Line." *Detroit Journal*, October 29.

Hissom, Doug. 1996. "Detroit's Bottom Line . . . News Strike!" *Milwaukee Shepherd-Express*, February 22, p. 5.

Hofsess, Diane, and Carol Teegardin. 1995. "Shining On." *Detroit Sunday Journal*, December 3, p. 35.

Holly, Dan. 1995. "A Top Cop Criticizes Guards' Actions at Picket Site." *Detroit Journal*, October 4.

Hotts, Mitch. 1995. "Detroit *News*, *Free Press* Workers Walk off the Job." *Macomb Daily*, July 14, p. 3A.

———. 1995. "Strike Papers Not Reaching Macomb, DNA Leaders Say." *Macomb Daily*, July 17, p. 1A.

———. 1996. "Testing the Rules." *Macomb Daily*, October 7, p. 1A.

Howes, Daniel. 1995. "Detroit Newspapers Cancels Threat to Close Macomb Plant." *Detroit News*, June 7.

Hudis, Mark, and Anya Sacharow. 1996. "*USA Today* on Toast." *MediaWeek* 6(4): 40.

Jachman, Matt. 1996. "Labor Complaint Is Settled Out of Court." *Livonia Observer*, July 4, p. 1.

Jackson, Irvin. 2005. "Newspaper Contracts Run Out, Talks Go On." *Detroit News*, July 3, p. 9A.

Johansson, Erin. 2007. "Law Professors to Congress: Do Something Already!" *American Rights at Work*, December 19. Available at: www.americanrightsat work.org/eye-on-the-nlrb/blog/law-professors-to-congress-do-something -already-20071219-490-388-388.html (accessed August 28, 2010).

Johnson, Reed. 1995. "Blockade Stalls, but Doesn't Stop Newspaper Deliveries." *Detroit Journal*, September 4.

Jones, Tim. 1995. "For Newspapers, a Bundle of Woes." *Chicago Tribune*, October 29, p. E-1.

———. 1996. "Labor's Painful Crossroads: Detroit's Newspaper Dispute Drags On, with Mounting Losses, No End in Sight." *Chicago Tribune*, February 11, p. B-1.

Jurkowitz, Mark. 2000. "Nieman a Battleground of Detroit Newspaper War." *Boston Globe*, July 6, p. E1.

Justin, Kristina. 1996. "Newspaper Picketers Aren't Backing Down." *Daily Tribune* (Royal Oak, Mich.), August 8.

Konrad, Rachel. 1995. "Meijer Ads Return to Detroit Papers." *Detroit Free Press*, December 8, p. 1E.

———. 1995. "No Progress in Strike Despite Archer's Effort, Unions Flatly Reject Newspaper Proposals." *Detroit Free Press*, December 21, p. 1A.

———. 1996. "The Newspaper Strike Enters a New Arena." *Detroit Free Press*, March 22, p. 1E.

———. 1996. "Dispute over Documents Slows Strike Hearing." *Detroit Free Press*, April 18, p. 7E.

———. 1996. "NLRB Threatens Injunction to Stop Violence by Detroit Newspaper Unions." *Knight-Ridder/Tribune Business News*, July 11.

———. 1996. "Newspaper Foes Pay Dearly for Year-Long Strike." *Detroit Free Press*, July 13, p. 1A.

———. 1996. "A Year Later, Solution to Detroit Newspaper Strike Is Elusive." *Knight Ridder/Tribune Business News*, July 13.

———. 1996. "Police Arrest 21 at Latest Protest in Paper Strike." *Detroit Free Press*, August 31, p. 3A.

———. 1996. "Audit of Papers Released." *Detroit Free Press*, September 7, p. 7A.

———. 1997. "Papers' Slow Staff Return Called Unfair." *Detroit Free Press*, April 15, p. 6E.

Konrad, Rachel, and Charlotte Craig. 1997. "Newspaper Unions Discuss an End to Strike." *Detroit Free Press*, February 14, p. 1E.

———. 1997. "Unions Seek Return, but Won't End War on Papers." *Detroit Free Press*, February 15, p. 1A.

Konrad, Rachel, and Tom Walsh. 1995. "Strikers, Papers Returning to Table: Archer, Maida Push Accord, Today's Talks." *Detroit Free Press*, December 20, p. 1E.

———. 1996. "Striking Newspaper Unions Say Detroit Dailies Reject Mediation." *Detroit Free Press*, October 3, p. 2E.

Kosdrosky, Terry. 1995. "Sterling Leaders Argue About Police Conduct in Newspaper Strike." *Macomb Daily*, July 16, p. 1A.

Leduff, Charlie, and Steven Greenhouse. 2004. "Tentative Deal Is Reached in Grocery Labor Dispute." *New York Times*, February 27, p. A16.

Lengel, Allan. 1996. "Legal Recourse: Strike Spawns Lawsuits with Charges from Sabotage to Brutality." *Detroit Sunday Journal*, July 7, p. S7.

Lessenberry, Jack. 1996. "Papers Not Fit for Your Cat Box." *Metro Times* (Detroit), May 15–21.

Levingston, Steven, and Terence O'Hara. 2006. "McClatchy's Paper Chase: Family-Owned Chain to Buy Knight, Plans to Sell Off 12 Dailies." *Washington Post*, March 14, p. D-01.

Lippert, John. 1995. "Paper, Six Unions Bargain." *Detroit Free Press* July 10, p. 4B.

———. 1996. "Money, Contracts Slip from *Press, News*." *Detroit Sunday Journal*, January 7, p. 8.

———. 1996. "Newspaper War Is More Than Words for Two Men." *Detroit Sunday Journal*, January 14, p. 5.

———. 1996. "Strike's Duration, Cost Surprise Papers, Ridder Admits." *Detroit Sunday Journal*, February 4, p. 9.

———. 1996. "Teamsters Get Long-Awaited Raise in Strike Pay." *Detroit Sunday Journal*, February 11, p. 11.

———. 1996. "Ridder Seems Confused over Strike Facts." *Detroit Sunday Journal*, April 28, p. 9.

———. 1996. "Gannett Boss Trades Verbal Jabs with Strikers." *Detroit Sunday Journal*, May 12, p. 6.

———. 1996. "Strikers Redeployed; Talk of a Deal Overheard." *Detroit Sunday Journal*, May 19, p. 8.

———. 1996. "New Union Tactics Are 'Message to Detroit.'" *Detroit Sunday Journal*, May 26, p. 11.

———. 1996. "Top Union Leaders Gather in Washington." *Detroit Sunday Journal*, June 2, p. 9.

———. 1996. "Overruled! Papers' Stories Become Evidence." *Detroit Sunday Journal*, June 30, p. 8.

———. 1998. "War Wounds in Detroit." *Columbia Journalism Review* (May-June).

Lippert, John, and Charlotte Craig. 1995. "Newspaper Carriers at Center of Talks." *Detroit Free Press*, July 11, p. 1E.

———. 1995. "Newspaper Deadline for Strike Is Delayed; Archer to Assist Slow-Moving Talks." *Detroit Free Press*, July 13, metro edition, p. 1E.

Lippert, John, and John Gallagher. 1995. "Strikers' JOA Sacrifices Deserve Respect, Mayor Says." *Detroit Sunday Journal*, December 24, p. 9.

Lynch, Kevin, and Craig Garrett. 1997. "Unions Stage Anti Newspaper Rally; Some Throw Rocks, Trash *News* Racks in Downtown Detroit." *Detroit News*, June 22, p. 2B.

Macomb Daily. 1995. "*Free Press* Ultimatum: Return or Be Replaced." August 9, p. 1A.

———. 1995. "Newspaper Truck Sparks Legal Probe." September 29, p. 1A.

Markiewicz, David. 1995. "Newspapers Contract Talks Suspended." *Detroit News*, July 12, p. 1-B.

———. 1995. "Newspapers, Unions to Meet with Archer." *Detroit News*, July 13, p. 1-A.

Mather, Robin. 1995. "When There Are Promises to Keep, We Soon Learn Whom We Can Trust." *Detroit Union* 1(1): 3.

Matthews, Lori. 1995. "Six Injured in Clashes at Papers' Centers, at Least Fifteen Arrested as Violence Surges." *Detroit Free Press*, October 2, p. 1B.

———. 1996. "DN Sues UAW in Strike Violence." *Detroit Free Press*, June 4, p. 5B.

McBride, Michael. 1999. "Appeals Court Sets May 4 Hearing Date." *Detroit Sunday Journal*, October 31, p. 3.

McGrath, Ned. 1996. "Newspapers Strike Out with Replacements." *Michigan Catholic*, March 22.

McGraw, Bill. 1995. "Neal Shine—A Bond Broken and a Trust Betrayed." *Detroit Union* 1(1): 4.

———. 1998. "*Free Press* to End Era with Change of Address." *Detroit Free Press*, July 22, p. 1A.

McMorris, Frances A. 1996. "Ex-Gannett Aide Admits to Charge of Insider Trading." *Wall Street Journal*, March 8.

Merzer, Martin. 1996. "Tony Ridder: At the Center of a Maelstrom." *Miami Herald*, March 31, p. 21A.

Metro Times. 1996. "The Year in Review." July 3, pp. 10–11.

Michalak, John. 1996. "You Can Picket Your Friends—Well, Maybe Not in Troy." *Daily Tribune* (Royal Oak, Mich.), August 4.

Mleczko, Lou. 1999. "UAW's Big Shoulders: Newspaper Workers Get By with the Help of Our Friends." *Detroit Sunday Journal*, March 28, p. 4.

Moran, Michelle. 1995. "Council Denies DNA Request to Sell Sunday Papers." *Grosse Pointe Times*, October 18.

Mullen, Ann. 1997. "Solidarity Delayed: Newspaper Activists Wonder Why Approval for Mass Action Took So Long." *Metro Times* (Detroit), June 18–24, pp. 14–15.

———. 2000. "A Million-Dollar Question." *Metro Times* (Detroit), April 19–25, pp. 12–13.

Muller, Joann. 1999. "The UAW's New Deal with Ford Could Hardly Be Sweeter." *BusinessWeek*, October 14.

Musial, Robert. 1995. "Unions, Papers Head Back to the Bargaining Table." *Detroit Journal*, August 18.

———. 1995. "*Free Press* Proposal Tries to Win Back Guild." *Detroit Journal*, August 31.

———. 1995. "NLRB Issues Complaint Against Newspaper Agency." *Detroit Journal*, September 1.

———. 1996. "'Scrappy Tabloid' Begins Its Second Year." *Detroit Sunday Journal*, November 17, p. 14.

Musial, Robert, and Vickie Elmer. 1995. "Unions File Suit Against Newspapers and Sterling Heights." *Detroit Journal*, October 3.

Nagourney, Adam. 1997. "In Strike Battle, Teamsters Borrow a Page from Politics." *New York Times*, August 16, p. A9.

New York Times. 1994. "Newspaper Unions End Strike." November 15. Available at: http://www.nytimes.com/1994/11/15/newspaper-unions-end-strike.html (accessed April 4, 2010).

Norris, Floyd. 1994. "SEC Cites Two Officers of Gannett." *New York Times*, December 9, p. D4.

Oakland Press. 1995. "Two Strikers Sue Detroit Newspapers over Injuries." December 5, p. B12.

———. 1995. "Wayne County Bans Ads in Striking Papers." December 23, p. B10.

———. 1996. "Newspaper Strikers Swear off Violence." January 13, p. B-8.

———. 1996. "Strikers Inform Police of Plan to Follow Carriers." January 20, p. A-8.

———. 1996. "Fourth-Quarter Earnings Rise 4 Percent at Gannett." February 7, p. B-7.

———. 1996. "Strike Cuts into Knight-Ridder Profit." April 23, p. B-7.

———. 1996. "UAW Added to Newspapers' Countersuit." June 5, p. B-8.

The Observer. 1995. "Ad Volume to Delay *Observer* Delivery." August 10, p. 5A.

Ourlian, Robert. 1996. "Sweeney Sees Light at End of the Tunnel." *Detroit Sunday Journal*, July 21, p. 10.

———. 1996. "Archer Renews Offer to Mediate Talks." *Detroit Sunday Journal*, July 28, p. 12.

———. 1996. "NLRB Case Could Drag into 1997." *Detroit Sunday Journal*, August 4, p. 9.

———. 1996. "Archer, Unions Push for Meaningful Talks." *Detroit Sunday Journal*, August 18, pp. 8, 9.

———. 1996. "'You're Going to Win': Labor Chief's Arrest Fires Up Strike, Holiday Weekend." *Detroit Sunday Journal*, September 1, p. 1.

———. 1996. "Hearings Conclude; Mediation Fizzles." *Detroit Sunday Journal*, October 6, p. 10.

———. 1996. "Key Areas Shunning Scab Papers." *Detroit Sunday Journal*, October 13, pp. 10–11.

———. 1996. "Strikers Make Some Visits." *Detroit Sunday Journal*, October 27, p. 12.

———. 1996. "Media's Influence Warrants Labor's Attention." *Detroit Sunday Journal*, December 15, p. 8.

———. 1996. "Boycott Gets Clearance from the NLRB." *Detroit Sunday Journal*, December 22, p. 7.

———. 1997. "National March Backed." *Detroit Sunday Journal*, January 12, p. 5.

———. 1997. "Strike On! Unions Launch New Offensive with Offer." *Detroit Sunday Journal*, February 16, p. 1.

———. 1997. "Papers 'Stonewall' Unions over Returns." *Detroit Sunday Journal*, April 27, p. 10.

———. 1997. "Unions Mobilize for June Demonstrations." *Detroit Sunday Journal*, April 27, p. 11.

———. 1997. "Back to 'Work.'" *Detroit Sunday Journal*, May 25, p. 8.

———. 1997. "Judge to Weigh Ramifications of Injunction." *Detroit Sunday Journal*, July 27, p. 32.

———. 1997. "10(j) Decision Could Be 10 Days Away, Judge Says." *Detroit Sunday Journal*, August 3, p. 1.

———. 1997. "Papers Finally Recall 28 Mailers, Slash Pay." *Detroit Sunday Journal*, August 10, p. 7.

———. 1997. "NLRB Will Seek Reversal of Injunction Denial." *Detroit Sunday Journal*, August 17, p. 1.

———. 1997. "O'Meara Has History with Papers." *Detroit Sunday Journal*, August 24, pp. 8–9.

———. 2000. "Judges Ignored Evidence." *Metro Detroit Labor News*, July 16–30, p. 1.

Ourlian, Robert, and Scott Martelle. 1996. "Starved for News." *Detroit Sunday Journal*, July 7, pp. 10S–11S.

Owens, Keith. 1996. "King Joins Strikers; Son of Civil Rights Legend Slams Exec, Papers." *Detroit Sunday Journal*, March 31, p. 1.

Parks, James. 1996. "After Year, Detroit Spirit Strong." *AFL-CIO News* (July).

Perez-Pena, Richard. 2009. "Gannett to Furlough Workers for Week." *New York Times*, January 15, p. B12.

———. 2009. "As It Cuts Jobs, Gannett Also Cuts Severance Pay." *New York Times*, July 27, p. B5.

Peterson, Ivar. 1997. "Detroit Papers Refuse to Re-hire Ex-strikers Immediately." *New York Times*, February 20, p. A14.

———. 1997. "After the Detroit Strike, Unions Switch Tactics." *New York Times*, March 11, p. A19.

Price, Tom. 2000. "Judges Rule Against Detroit Newspaper Workers." *The Dispatcher*, July-August, p. 8.

Provance, Jim. 2011. "Kasich Accepts Defeat of Issue 2." *ToledoBlade.com*, November 8, 2011. Available at: http://www.toledoblade.com/Politics/2011/11/08/Issue-2.html (accessed November 25, 2011).

Raine, George. 2004. "Hotel Workers' Lockout Off for Now; Employers, Union OK 60 Day Cooling-Off Period; Neighbors and Merchants Sure to Welcome Quiet During Holiday Season." *San Francisco Chronicle*, November 21, p. A-1.

Ramirez, Charles. 1995. "*News, Free Press* Racks Are Taking a Pounding." *Detroit News*, October 26, p. 1-B.

———. 1997. "Hearing on Ruling Set for July 31." *Detroit News*, July 9, p. 3B.

———. 1998. "Teamsters Approve Newspapers' Offer." *Detroit News*, March 9, p. 1D.

Raphael, Steve. 1994. "SEC Scandal Could Haunt Vega in Talks." *Crain's Detroit Business*, December 19, p. 3.

———. 1995. "Newspapers Slash Rates." *Crain's Detroit Business*, July 24–30, p. 1.

———. 1995. "Consensus: Two Newspapers Better Than One." *Crain's Detroit Business*, July 24–30, p. 26.

———. 1995. "Circulation Audit on Hold." *Crain's Detroit Business*, September 25–October 1, p. 1.

Reed, Ted. 1996. "Unions Launch *Herald* Boycott." *Miami Herald*, March 28, p. C-1.

Reed, Ted, and Susana Barciela. 1996. "Strike Dominates Knight-Ridder Annual Meeting." *Miami Herald*, April 24, p. 7B.

Rohan, Barry. 1998. "*Free Press* Editorial Moves into *News* Building." *The Alliance*, July 30.

Rosenberg, Jim, Mark Fitzgerald, and Sabrina Crow. 2009. "Saluting Seven Top Managers." *Editor & Publisher*, September, p. 22.

Saba, Jennifer. 2009. "Downshift in Motor City." *Editor & Publisher*, January, p. 6.

———. 2009. "What's the Frequency?" *Editor & Publisher*, February, p. 28.

Sacharow, Anya. 1996. "Walking the Line in Detroit." *Brandweek*, July 22.

Sader, Jennifer. 1996. "Charges Dropped Against Detroit Photographer Arrested During Newspaper Strikers' Rally." *News Photographer* 51(6): 24.

Samulski, Stephanie. 1996. "Protesters, University Professor, Arrested in Newspaper Strike Incident." *The South End*, March 22, p. 1.

Schabath, Gene. 1996. "Truck Fire Points to Detroit Newspapers." *Detroit Sunday Journal*, March 10, p. 6.

Schlagheck, Carol. 1996. "On Strike in Detroit." *News Photographer* 51(2): 20.

———. 2001. "Living in the Wake of a Newspaper Strike." *Quill* 89(2): 19.

Schram, Tom. 1998. "Lockout 'One of My Top Priorities.'" *Detroit Sunday Journal*, December 13, p. 7.

Schultz, John. 1992. "Showdown on Lafayette." *Metro Times* (Detroit), April 22–28, pp. 6–8.

Seelye, Katherine. 2006. "What-Ifs of a Media Eclipse." *New York Times*, August 27, p. D1.

Seelye, Katherine, and Andrew Ross Sorkin. 2006. "Newspaper Chain Agrees to a Sale for $4.5 Billion." *New York Times*, March 12, p. 1A.

Shellum, Bernie. 1995. "Grand Jury Probes Insider Trading Involving DN Chief." *Detroit Journal*, October 2.

Shellum, Bernie, and Dan Holly. 1995. "Newspaper Unions Offer Job Cuts to End Strike." *Detroit Journal*, October 6.

Shellum, Bernie, Dan Holly, and Gary Graff. 1995. "Curb on Picketing Expected; Talks Are on Hold." *Detroit Journal*, September 13.

Shine, Dan, and Jennifer Juarez Robles. 1996. "Pickets Can Follow Newspaper Carriers." *Detroit Free Press*, January 24, p. 2B.

Shine, Neal. 1995. "'Shove It' Can't Be Part of the Dialogue." *Detroit Free Press*, July 17, p. 1A.

Siegel, Suzanne, and Blair Anthony Robertson. 1996. "Public Seems Divided on Strike Blame." *Detroit Free Press*, July 9, p. 1B.

Slaughter, Jane. 1999. "Strike (Year) Four." *Metro Times* (Detroit), March 17, p. 99.

Slaughter, Sally. 1995. "Strike Affects Local Readers; Picketing at Distribution Site." *Dearborn Press & Guide*, July 20, p. 3A.

———. 1995. "Picketing Continues at Local Center, Newspaper Delivery Sporadic in Area." *Dearborn Press & Guide*, July 27, p. 14.

Smith, Dena. 1996. "Pushier Pickets; New Union Organizers Say They're Going to Vault the Newspaper Strike Back into the Public Eye." *Metro Times* (Detroit), June 5–11, p. 16.

———. 1996. "Unconditional Offer Meets with Skepticism." *Metro Times* (Detroit), December 4–10, p. 8.

Smith, Jeanette. 1995. "Two Teamsters Charged with Stealing Newspapers." *Macomb Daily*, July 25.

Stevens, Liz. 1996. "Strike Support: Union Members Nationwide Help Detroit Strikers." *Union Plus* (summer): 10–11.

Sweeney, Ann. 1996. "Paper Carriers to Stand Trial in Bombing of Striker's Home." *Detroit Sunday Journal*, February 18, p. 6.

———. 1996. "Sterling Heights Restricts Residential Pickets." *Detroit Sunday Journal*, September 22, p. 9.

Swickard, Joe. 2007. "A Champion of Fairness, Children, and Detroit." *Detroit Free Press*, April 4.

Swoboda, Frank. 1996. "UAW Thinks It Has Put Outsourcing in Reverse." *Washington Post*, October 19, p. H-1.

Szczesny, Joseph. 1995. "Strikers End 'Peaceful' Siege." *Oakland Press*, October 16, p. A6.

———. 1995. "120 Officers, 300 Strikers Face Off at Papers' Center." *Oakland Press*, October 23, p. A6.

———. 1995. "Six Strikers Face Vandalism Charges." *Oakland Press*, October 30, p. A6.

———. 1995. "Strikers Unveil New Campaign." *Oakland Press*, November 24, p. A8.

Toledo Blade. 1995. "Newspaper Unions Postpone Contract Talks." October 5, p. 14.

Tyson, James L. 1996. "Paper-and-Ink Insurgency Hits Detroit." *Christian Science Monitor*, January 12, p. 1.

Varcie, Tom. 1995. "Early Morning Ruckus at Newspaper Distribution Site." *Dearborn Press and Guide*, November 16, p. 1-A.

Vlasic, Bill. 1996. "Can the UAW Put a Brake on Outsourcing?" *Bloomberg BusinessWeek*, June 17. Available at: http://www.businessweek.com/archives/1996/b3480109.arc.htm#B3480109 (accessed June 26, 2011).

Walsh, Tom. 1995. "*Free Press* Owner Seeks Pact, Preservation of Two Newspapers." *Detroit Free Press*, July 22, p. 2A.

———. 1995. "Letter Urges Union to Talk with Newspaper." *Detroit Free Press*, July 29, p. 1A.

———. 1995. "Three Free Press Journalists Return as Divisions Surface Within Union." *Detroit Free Press*, July 29, p. 1A.

———. 1995. "Picketing, Politics, and Prayer Mark Strike's 22nd Day." *Detroit Free Press*, August 5, p. 7A.

———. 1995. "Replacements to Be a Top Issue in Newspaper Talks." *Detroit Free Press*, August 12, p. 8B.

———. 1995. "Teamsters Get Tough with Newspaper Picket Line Crossers." *Detroit Free Press*, August 26, p. 7B.

———. 1995. "*Free Press* Sweetens Proposal to Union." *Detroit Free Press*, August 31, p. 1C.

———. 1995. "No Progress Seen in Newspaper Talks." *Detroit Free Press*, September 2, p. 8B.

———. 1995. "Hoffa's Son Opens Bid to Head the Teamsters Labor Day Parade: Rally Focus on Newspapers Strike." *Detroit Free Press*, September 5, p. 1A.

———. 1995. "Newspapers Resume Separate Weekday Publication; Protests Outpace Negotiation." *Detroit Free Press*, September 18, p. 1B.

———. 1995. "Newspapers Are Cool to Unions' Truce Offer." *Detroit Free Press*, October 6, p. 1A.

———. 1995. "Newspapers to Unions: Job Openings Shrink." *Detroit Free Press*, October 31, p. 1B.

———. 1995. "Vega: No End in Sight, Newspaper CEO Sets New Goals as Strike Grinds On." *Detroit Free Press*, November 10, p. 1C.

———. 1996. "Strike Cuts Profits, Papers' Parents Lose $46 Million." *Detroit Free Press*, October 4.

Walsh, Tom, and David McKay. 1995. "Pickets Restricted, Newspaper Strikers at Plant Gate Limited to 10." *Detroit Free Press*, September 14, p. 1C.

Walsh, Tom, and David Migoya. 1995. "3,000 Strong, Strikers Delay Sunday Paper, Newspapers Decry Violence by Mob." *Detroit Free Press*, September 4, p. 1A.

Walsh, Tom, and Louise Taylor. 1995. "Detroit Newspapers Sues Unions, Company Wants Violence Stopped." *Detroit Free Press*, November 16, p. 1B.

Walsh, Tom, and Chris Walton. 1995. "Class Action Lawsuit Filed over Newspapers' Strike Publication." *Detroit Free Press*, November 22, p. 1E.

Washington Post. 1995. "Gannett Profit Falls 9 Percent in Third Quarter." October 10, p. D02.

Watson, Susan. 1995. "Journalists Speak Out for Those Who Cannot." *Detroit Sunday Journal*, November 26, p. 3.

———. 1996. "The *Free Press* Has Changed, and So Have I." *Detroit Sunday Journal*, March 24, p. 3.

———. 1996. "Strikers Confront Ridder with the Truth." *Detroit Sunday Journal*, April 28, p. 3.

———. 1996. "Pickets Preach the Word and Win Converts." *Detroit Sunday Journal*, June 23, p. 3.

———. 1997. "Her Place Is Back in the Kitchen." *Detroit Sunday Journal*, March 9, p. 3.

Weiss, Philip. 1987. "Invasion of the Gannettoids." *The New Republic*, February 2, pp. 18–22.

Williams, Timothy. 2011. "The Battle over Union Rights, State by State." *New York Times*, March 10.

Wilmsen, Erik. 1996. "Strikers Picket Knight-Ridder." *Colorado Daily*, March 15–17, p. 1.

Wilson, Shirley. 1997. "Bragg Boasts of Bold Strikers." *Detroit Sunday Journal*, September 21, p. 29.

Wylie-Kellerman, Bill. 1996. "Dailies Fall Far Short of Noble Statements." *Detroit Sunday Journal*, August 25, p. 15.

Wylie-Kellerman, Jeanie. 1996. "Anatomy of a Strike." *The Witness* 79(9): 10–15.

Yahoo Finance. "Insider and Form 144 Filings—Jaske, John B." Accessed November 26, 2005 at: http://biz.yahoo.com/t/84/578.html (defunct).

Yung, Katherine, and Charles Ramirez. 1996. "Auto Dealers Angry over Union Boycott Campaign." *Detroit News*, January 26.

Zachem, Susan. 2000. "Court Blow to Detroit Newspaper Workers Sounds 'Wake-Up Call.'" *Graphic Communicator*, August-September, p. 1.

BOOKS, ARTICLES, AND OTHER PUBLISHED SOURCES

Angelo, Frank. 1981. *On Guard: A History of the* Detroit Free Press. Detroit: Detroit Free Press.

Ashenfelter, Orley, and George E. Johnson. 1969. "Bargaining Theory, Trade Unions, and Industrial Strike Activity." *American Economic Review* 59(1): 35–49.

Audit Bureau of Circulation. 2011. "U.S. Newspaper Circulation Averages for the Six Months Ended March 31, 2011." Available at: http://abcas3.accessabc.com/ecirc/newstitlesearchus.asp (accessed June 25, 2011).

Babson, Steve. 1986. *Working Detroit*. Detroit: Wayne State University Press.

Bagdikian, Ben. 2000. *The Media Monopoly*, 6th ed. Boston: Beacon Press.

———. 2004. *The New Media Monopoly*. Boston: Beacon Press.

Baker, C. Edwin. 2002. *Media, Markets, and Democracy*. Cambridge: Cambridge University Press.

Bandzak, Ruth A. 1992. "The Strike as a Management Strategy." *Journal of Economic Issues* 26(2): 645–59.

Barnett, Stephen R. 1991. "The JOA Scam." *Columbia Journalism Review* (November-December): 47–48.

Barrow, Heather B. 2004. "'The American Disease of Growth': Henry Ford and the Metropolitanization of Detroit, 1920–1940." In *Manufacturing Suburbs: Building Work and Home on the Metropolitan Fringe*, edited by Robert Lewis. Philadelphia: Temple University Press.

Bass, Jack. 2001. "Newspaper Monopoly." In *Leaving Readers Behind: The Age of Corporate Newspapering*, edited by Gene Roberts, Thomas Kunkel, and Charles Layton. Fayetteville: University of Arkansas Press.

Bennett, Andrew, and Colin Elman. 2006. "Qualitative Research: Recent Developments in Case Study Methods." *Annual Review of Political Science* 9: 455–76.

Block, Richard, Sheldon Friedman, Michelle Kaminski, and Andy Levin, eds. 2006. *Justice on the Job: Perspectives on the Erosion of Collective Bargaining in the United States*. Kalamazoo, Mich.: W. E. Upjohn Institute for Employment Research.

Bluestone, Barry, and Irving Bluestone. 1992. *Negotiating the Future: A Labor Perspective on American Business*. New York: Basic Books.

Bogart, Leo. 1991. *Preserving the Press*. New York: Columbia University Press.

Bonacich, Edna, and Jake B. Wilson. 2007. *Getting the Goods: Ports, Labor, and the Logistics Revolution*. Ithaca, N.Y.: Cornell University Press.

Bowles, Samuel, David M. Gordon, and Thomas E. Weisskopf. 1983. *Beyond the Waste Land: A Democratic Alternative to Economic Decline*. Garden City, N.Y.: Anchor Press/Doubleday.

Boyle, Kevin. 1995. *The UAW and the Heyday of American Liberalism, 1945–1968.* Ithaca, N.Y.: Cornell University Press.

———. 2004. *Arc of Justice: A Saga of Race, Civil Rights, and Murder in the Jazz Age.* New York: Holt.

Brandt, J. Donald. 1993. *A History of Gannett, 1906–1993.* Arlington, Va.: Gannett Co.

Brecher, Jeremy. 1977. *Strike!* Cambridge, Mass.: South End Press.

Brisbin, Richard, Jr. 2002. *A Strike Like No Other Strike: Law and Resistance During the Pittston Coal Strike of 1989–1990.* Baltimore: Johns Hopkins University Press.

Brody, David. 2005. *Labor Embattled: History, Power, Rights.* Champaign: University of Illinois Press.

Bronfenbrenner, Kate, and Tom Juravich. 1998. "It Takes More Than House Calls: Organizing to Win with a Comprehensive Union-Building Strategy." In *Organizing to Win: New Research on Union Strategies,* edited by Kate Bronfenbrenner, Sheldon Friedman, Richard W. Hurd, Rudolph A. Oswald, and Ronald L. Seeber. Ithaca, N.Y.: Cornell/ILR Press.

Brubaker, Randy. 1982. "The Newspaper Preservation Act: How It Affects Diversity in the Newspaper Industry." *Journal of Communication Inquiry* 7(2): 91–104.

Budd, John. 2004. *Employment with a Human Face: Balancing Efficiency, Equity, and Voice.* Ithaca, N.Y.: Cornell University Press.

Chafets, Ze'ev. 1991. *Devil's Night: And Other True Tales of Detroit.* New York: Vintage Books.

Clawson, Dan. 2003. *The Next Upsurge: Labor and the New Social Movements.* Ithaca, N.Y.: Cornell University Press.

Clemens, Paul. 2005. *Made in Detroit: A South of 8 Mile Memoir.* New York: Doubleday.

Cohen, Jean L., and Andrew Arato. 1994. *Civil Society and Political Theory.* Cambridge, Mass.: MIT Press.

Cohn, Samuel, and Adrienne Eaton. 1989. "Historical Limits on Neoclassical Strike Theories: Evidence from French Coal Mining, 1890–1935." *Industrial and Labor Relations Review* 42(4): 649–62.

Collier, Ruth, and David Collier. 1991. *Shaping the Political Arena: Critical Junctures, the Labor Movement, and Regime Dynamics in Latin America.* Princeton, N.J.: Princeton University Press.

Conot, Robert. 1986. *American Odyssey.* Detroit: Wayne State University Press.

Cooney, Stephen, and Brent Yacobucci. 2006. *U.S. Automotive Industry: Policy Overview and Recent History.* New York: Nova Science Publishers.

Cooper, Gloria. 1996. "Darts and Laurels." *Columbia Journalism Review* 35(4): 26.

———. 1997. "Darts and Laurels." *Columbia Journalism Review* 36(3): 27–28.

Copeland, David. 2003. "Newspapers in the Americas." In *The Function of Newspapers in Society: A Global Perspective,* edited by Shannon Martin and David Copeland. Westport, Conn.: Praeger.

Cowie, Jefferson. 1999. *Capital Moves: RCA's Seventy-Year Quest for Cheap Labor.* Ithaca, N.Y.: Cornell University Press.

Cramton, Peter, and Joseph Tracy. 1998. "The Use of Replacement Workers in Union Contract Negotiations: The U.S. Experience, 1980–1989." *Journal of Labor Economics* 16(4): 667–701.

Cranberg, Gilbert, Randall Bezanson, and John Soloski. 2001. *Taking Stock: Journalism and the Publicly Traded Newspaper Company.* Ames: Iowa State University Press.

Dannin, Ellen. 1997. "Legislative Intent and Impasse Resolution Under the National Labor Relations Act: Does Law Matter?" *Hofstra Labor and Employment Law Journal* 15(fall): 11–43.

———. 2004. "From Dictator Game to Ultimatum Game . . . and Back Again: The Judicial Impasse Amendments." *University of Pennsylvania Journal of Labor and Employment Law* 6(2): 241–94.

———. 2006. *Taking Back the Workers' Law: How to Fight the Assault on Labor Rights.* Ithaca, N.Y.: Cornell/ILR Press.

Dannin, Ellen, and Terry Wagar. 2000. "Lawless Law? The Subversion of the National Labor Relations Act." *Loyola of Los Angeles Law Review* 34: 197–232.

Darden, Joe, Richard C. Hill, June Thomas, and Richard Thomas. 1987. *Detroit: Race and Uneven Development.* Philadelphia: Temple University Press.

Detroit Newspapers, Inc. 1995. "The Detroit Newspaper Strike: July 13, 1995" (videotape). Detroit Newspapers, Market Development Division.

Dillard, Angela. 2007. *Faith in the City: Preaching Radical Social Change in Detroit.* Ann Arbor: University of Michigan Press.

Downie, Leonard, and Robert Kaiser. 2002. *The News About the News.* New York: Knopf.

Dubofsky, Melvyn. 1994. *The State and Labor in Modern America.* Chapel Hill: University of North Carolina Press.

Edmonds, Rick, Emily Guskin, and Tom Rosensteil. 2011. "Newspapers: Missed the 2010 Media Rally." In *The State of the News Media 2011*, Pew Research Center's Project for Excellence in Journalism. Available at: http://stateofthemedia .org/2011/newspapers-essay/ (accessed June 1, 2011).

Eisinger, Peter. 2003. "Reimagining Detroit." *City and Community* 2(2): 85–99.

Estlund, Cynthia. 2003. *Working Together: How Workplace Bonds Strengthen a Diverse Democracy.* Oxford: Oxford University Press.

Evans, Peter. 2007. "Foreword." In *Labor in the New Urban Battlegrounds: Local Solidarity in a Global Economy*, edited by Lowell Turner and Daniel Cornfield. Ithaca, N.Y.: Cornell/ILR Press.

Fantasia, Rick. 1988. *Cultures of Solidarity: Consciousness, Action, and Contemporary American Workers.* Berkeley: University of California Press.

Fantasia, Rick, and Kim Voss. 2004. *Hard Work: Remaking the American Labor Movement.* Berkeley: University of California Press.

Farber, Henry, and Bruce Western. 2001. "Accounting for the Decline of Unions in the Private Sector, 1973–1998." *Journal of Labor Research* 22(3): 459–85.

Farley, Reynolds, Sheldon Danziger, and Harry Holzer. 2000. *Detroit Divided.* New York: Russell Sage Foundation.

Fasenfest, David, and James Jacobs. 2003. "An Anatomy of Change and Transition: The Automobile Industry of Southeast Michigan." *Small Business Economics* 21(2): 153–72.

Fine, Janice. 2006. *Worker Centers: Organizing Communities at the Edge of the Dream.* Ithaca, N.Y.: Cornell/ILR Press.

Fink, Leon. 1983. *Workingmen's Democracy: The Knights of Labor and American Politics.* Urbana: University of Illinois Press.

Flanagan, Robert. 2007. "Has Management Strangled U.S. Unions?" In *What Do Unions Do? A Twenty-Year Perspective,* edited by James Bennet and Bruce Kaufman. New Brunswick, N.J.: Transaction Publishers.

Fletcher, Bill, Jr., and Fernando Gapasin. 2008. *Solidarity Divided: The Crisis in Organized Labor and a New Path Toward Social Justice.* Berkeley: University of California Press.

Flyvbjerg, Brent. 2006. "Five Misunderstandings About Case-Study Research." *Qualitative Inquiry* 12(2): 219–45.

Franklin, Stephen. 1995. "Detroit: Which Side Are You On?" *Columbia Journalism Review* 34(4): 13–15.

———. 2001. *Three Strikes: Labor's Heartland Losses and What They Mean for Working Americans.* New York: Guilford Press.

Franzosi, Roberto. 1989. "One Hundred Years of Strike Statistics: Methodological and Theoretical Issues in Quantitative Strike Research." *Industrial and Labor Relations Review* 42(3): 348–62.

———. 1995. *The Puzzle of Strikes: Class and State Strategies in Postwar Italy.* Cambridge: Cambridge University Press.

Freeman, Richard. 1998. "Spurts in Union Growth: Defining Moments and Social Processes." In *The Defining Moment: The Great Depression and the American Economy in the Twentieth Century,* edited by Michael Bordo, Claudia Goldin, and Eugene White. Chicago: University of Chicago Press.

———. 2007. *America Works: Critical Thoughts on the Exceptional U.S. Labor Market.* New York: Russell Sage Foundation.

Freund, David M. 2007. *Colored Property: State Policy and White Racial Politics in Suburban America.* Chicago: University of Chicago Press.

Friedman, Milton. 1970. "The Social Responsibility of Business Is to Increase Its Profits." *New York Times Magazine,* September 13, 1970.

Gavrilovich, Peter, and Bill McGraw, eds. 2000. *The Detroit Almanac.* Detroit: Detroit Free Press.

Getman, Julius. 1998. *The Betrayal of Local 14: Paperworkers, Politics, and Permanent Replacements.* Ithaca, N.Y.: Cornell/ILR Press.

———. 2003. "The National Labor Relations Act: What Went Wrong; Can We Fix It?" *Boston College Law Review* 45(1): 125–46.

———. 2004. "Another Look at Labor and the Law." In *The Future of Labor Unions: Organized Labor in the Twentieth Century*, edited by Julius Getman and Ray Marshall. Austin: University of Texas, Lyndon B. Johnson School of Public Affairs.

———. 2010. *Restoring the Power of Unions: It Takes a Movement*. New Haven, Conn.: Yale University Press.

Giles, Robert. 1997. "Rebuttal: Lessons from the Detroit Newspaper Strike." *Newspaper Research Journal* (winter): 28.

Gold, Michael Evan. 1998. *An Introduction to Labor Law*, 2d ed. ILR bulletin 66. Ithaca, N.Y.: Cornell/ILR Press.

Gonyea, Don, and Mike Hoyt. 1997. "Fallout from Detroit: From a Brutal Strike, Bitter Lessons and Lasting Losses." *Columbia Journalism Review* (May-June): 36–41.

Gordon, Colin. 1999. "The Lost City of Solidarity: Metropolitan Unionism in Historical Perspective." *Politics and Society* 27(4): 561–85.

Gordon, David M., Richard Edwards, and Michael Reich. 1982. *Segmented Work, Divided Workers: The Historical Transformation of Labor in the United States*. Cambridge: Cambridge University Press.

Gould, William B., IV. 1993. *Agenda for Reform: The Future of Employment Relationships and the Law*. Cambridge, Mass.: MIT Press.

———. 2000. *Labored Relations: Law, Politics, and the NLRB—A Memoir*. Cambridge, Mass.: MIT Press.

Green, Hardy. 1990. *On Strike at Hormel: The Struggle for a Democratic Labor Movement*. Philadelphia: Temple University Press.

Greenberg, Stanley. 1995. *Middle Class Dreams: The Politics and Power of the New American Majority*. New York: Random House.

Greenhouse, Steven. 2008. *The Big Squeeze: Tough Times for the American Worker*. New York: Knopf.

Greenstone, J. David. 1969. *Labor in American Politics*. Chicago: University of Chicago Press.

Greenstone, J. David, and Paul E. Peterson. 1973. *Race and Authority in Urban Politics: Community Participation and the War on Poverty*. Chicago: University of Chicago Press.

Griffin, Larry J., Holly J. McCammon, and Christopher Botsko. 1990. "The 'Unmaking' of a Movement? The Crisis of U.S. Trade Unions in Comparative Perspective." In *Change in Societal Institutions*, edited by Maureen T. Hallinan, David M. Klein, and Jennifer Glass. New York: Plenum Press.

Gross, James A. 1995. *Broken Promise: The Subversion of U.S. Labor Relations Policy, 1947–1994*. Philadelphia: Temple University Press.

———, ed. 2003. *Workers' Rights as Human Rights*. Ithaca, N.Y.: Cornell University Press.

————. 2011. *A Shameful Business: The Case for Human Rights in the American Workplace.* Ithaca, N.Y.: Cornell/ILR Press.

Gruley, Bryan. 1993. *Paper Losses: A Modern Epic of Greed and Betrayal at America's Two Largest Newspaper Companies.* New York: Grove Press.

Gutman, Herbert. 1976. *Work, Culture, and Society in Industrializing America: Essays in American Working-Class and Social History.* New York: Knopf.

Habermas, Jürgen. 1996. *Between Facts and Norms: Contributions to a Discourse Theory of Law and Democracy.* Cambridge, Mass.: MIT Press.

Hacker, Jacob, and Paul Pierson. 2010. *Off Center: The Republican Revolution and the Erosion of American Democracy.* New Haven, Conn.: Yale University Press.

Harris, Howell John. 1982. *The Right to Manage: Industrial Relations Policies of American Business in the 1940s.* Madison: University of Wisconsin Press.

Harris, Seth. 2002. "Coase's Paradox and the Inefficiency of Permanent Strike Replacements." *Washington University Law Journal* 80: 1185–2002.

Harrison, Bennett. 1994. *Lean and Mean: The Changing Landscape of Corporate Power in the Age of Flexibility.* New York: Basic Books.

Hartman, Chester W., and Gregory D. Squires. 2006. *There Is No Such Thing as a Natural Disaster: Race, Class, and Hurricane Katrina.* New York: Routledge.

Hattam, Victoria. 1992. *Labor Visions and State Power.* Princeton, N.J.: Princeton University Press.

Hirsch, Barry, and David Macpherson. 1995. "Union Membership and Coverage Database from the Current Population Survey." Available at: http://www.unionstats.com (accessed May 18, 2010).

Honey, Michael K. 1993. *Southern Labor and Black Civil Rights: Organizing Memphis Workers.* Urbana: University of Illinois Press.

————. 2007. *Going Down Jericho Road: The Memphis Strike, Martin Luther King's Last Campaign.* New York: W. W. Norton & Co.

Horowitz, Roger. 1997. *Negro and White, Unite and Fight! A Social History of Industrial Unionism in Meatpacking, 1930–1990.* Urbana: University of Illinois Press.

Hoyt, Clark. N.d. "John S. Knight: An Appreciation." John S. Knight Journalism Fellowships, Stanford University. Available at: http://knight.stanford.edu/jsk/index.html (accessed March 25, 2007).

Human Rights Watch. 2009. *The Employee Free Choice Act: A Human Rights Imperative.* January 29. Available at: http://www.hrw.org/en/reports/2009/01/27/united-states-employee-free-choice-act (accessed June 15, 2011).

International Labor Organization. N.d. "Freedom of Association and the Effective Recognition of the Right to Collective Bargaining." Available at: http://www.ilo.org/declaration/principles/freedomofassociation/lang--en/index.htm (accessed January 12, 2011).

Isaac, Larry, and Lars Christiansen. 2002. "How the Civil Rights Movement Revitalized Labor Militancy." *American Sociological Review* 67(5): 722–47.

Isaac, Larry, Steve McDonald, and Greg Lukasik. 2006. "Takin' It from the Streets:

How the Sixties Mass Movement Revitalized Unionization." *American Journal of Sociology* 112(1): 46–97.

Jacobs, Lawrence, and Theda Skocpol, eds. 2005. *Inequality and American Democracy: What We Know and What We Need to Learn*. New York: Russell Sage Foundation.

Jarley, Paul, and Cheryl Maranto. 1990. "Union Corporate Campaigns: An Assessment." *Industrial and Labor Relations Review* 43(5): 505.

Jaske, John B. 1982. "Collective Bargaining Issues in Newspapers." *Hastings Communications and Entertainment Law Journal* 4(4): 595–604.

Johnston, Paul. 1994. *Success While Others Fail: Social Movement Unionism in the Public Workplace*. Ithaca, N.Y.: Cornell/ILR Press.

Jung, Moon-Kie. 2006. *Reworking Race: The Making of Hawaii's Interracial Labor Movement*. New York: Columbia University Press.

Juravich, Tom, and Kate Bronfenbrenner. 1999. *Ravenswood: The Steelworkers Victory and the Revival of American Labor*. Ithaca, N.Y.: Cornell University Press.

Kalleberg, Arne, Michael Wallace, Karyn Loscoco, Kevin Leicht, and Hans-Helmut Ehm. 1987. "The Eclipse of Craft: The Changing Face of the Newspaper Industry." In *Workers, Managers, and Technical Change: Emerging Patterns of Labor Relations*, edited by Daniel Cornfield. New York: Plenum Press.

Kaplan, Richard L. 2002. *Politics and the American Press: The Rise of Objectivity, 1865–1920*. Cambridge: Cambridge University Press.

Katznelson, Ira. 1997. "Structure and Configuration in Comparative Politics." In *Comparative Politics: Rationality, Culture, and Structure*, edited by Mark Irving Lichbach and Alan Zuckerman. Cambridge: Cambridge University Press.

———. 2005. *When Affirmative Action Was White: An Untold History of Racial Inequality in Twentieth-Century America*. New York: Norton.

Kaufman, Bruce E. 1992. "Research on Strike Models and Outcomes in the 1980s: Accomplishments and Shortcomings." In *Research Frontiers in Industrial Relations and Human Resources*, edited by David Lewin, Olivia S. Mitchell, and Peter D. Sherer. Madison, Wisc.: Industrial Relations Research Association.

———. 1997. "Labor Markets and Employment Regulation: The View of the 'Old' Institutionalists." In *Government Regulation of the Employment Relationship*, edited by Bruce Kaufman. Madison, Wisc.: Industrial Relations Research Association.

Kim, Pauline. 1997. "Bargaining with Imperfect Information: A Study of Worker Perceptions of Legal Protection in an At-Will World." *Cornell Law Review* 83(1): 105–60.

Klinenberg, Eric. 2002. *Heat Wave: A Social Autopsy of Disaster in Chicago*. Chicago: University of Chicago Press.

Kochan, Thomas. 2004. "Restoring Workers' Voice: A Call to Action." In *The Future of Labor Unions: Organized Labor in the Twenty-First Century*, edited by Julius Getman and Ray Marshall. Austin: University of Texas, Lyndon B. Johnson School of Public Affairs.

Kochan, Thomas, Harry Katz, and Robert McKersie. 1994. *The Transformation of American Industrial Relations*. Ithaca, N.Y.: Cornell/ILR Press.

Kramer, Andrew, Curt Kirschner, Shondella McClellan, and Scott Medsker. 2010. "Recent Developments in Traditional Labor Law." Employment Law Conference, National Employment Law Institute (November). Available at: http://www.jonesday.com/_lawyers/bio.aspx?attorneyID=91e6b5f2-9e99-47f1-b473-2b65722d1f88&section=Publications (accessed September 13, 2011).

Kumar, Deepa. 2007. *Outside the Box: Corporate Media, Globalization, and the UPS Strike*. Urbana: University of Illinois Press.

Kuttner, Robert. 1997. *Everything for Sale: The Virtues and Limits of Markets*. New York: Alfred A. Knopf.

Lambert, Josiah B. 2005. *"If the Workers Took a Notion": The Right to Strike and American Political Development*. Ithaca, N.Y.: Cornell/ILR Press.

Langeveld, Martin. 2011. "The Shakeup at MediaNews: Why It Could Be the Leadup to a Massive Newspaper Consolidation." Cambridge, Mass.: Harvard University, Nieman Foundation, Nieman Journalism Lab. Available at: http://www.niemanlab.org/2011/01/the-shakeup-at-medianews-why-it-could-be-the-leadup-to-a-massive-newspaper-consolidation/ (accessed June 17, 2011).

Layton, Charles. 2006. "Sherman's March." *American Journalism Review* 28(1): 18–24.

Lendler, Marc. 1997. *Crisis and Political Beliefs: The Case of the Colt Firearms Strike*. New Haven, Conn.: Yale University Press.

Lichtenstein, Nelson. 1995. *The Most Dangerous Man in Detroit: Walter Reuther and the Fate of American Labor*. New York: Basic Books.

———. 2002. *State of the Union: A Century of American Labor*. Princeton, N.J.: Princeton University Press.

Lichtenstein, Nelson, and Howell J. Harris, eds. 1996. *Industrial Democracy in America: The Ambiguous Promise*. Washington, D.C.: Woodrow Wilson Center Press.

Lipsitz, George. 1981. *Class and Culture in Cold War America: A Rainbow at Midnight*. New York: Praeger.

Logan, John. 2006. "The Union Avoidance Industry in the United States." *British Journal of Industrial Relations* 44(4): 651–75.

Lopez, Steven Henry. 2004. *Reorganizing the Rust Belt: An Inside Study of the American Labor Movement*. Berkeley: University of California Press.

Lund, John, and Christopher Wright. 2003. "Integrating the Supply Chain: Industrial Relations Implications in U.S. Grocery Distribution." *New Technology, Work, and Employment* 18(2): 101–14.

Lutz, William W. 1973. *The News of Detroit: How a Newspaper and a City Grew Together*. Boston: Little, Brown.

Macedo, Stephen. 2005. *Democracy at Risk: How Political Choices Undermine Citizen Participation, and What We Can Do About It*. Washington, D.C.: Brookings Institution.

Mahoney, James. 2000. "Path Dependence in Historical Sociology." *Theory and Society* 29(4): 507–48.

Marjoribanks, Timothy. 2000. *News Corporation, Technology, and the Workplace: Global Strategies, Local Change*. Cambridge: Cambridge University Press.

Martin, Andrew, and Marc Dixon. 2010. "Changing to Win? Threat, Resistance, and the Role of Unions in Strikes, 1984–2002." *American Journal of Sociology* 116(1): 93–129.

Martin, Christopher R. 2004. *Framed: Labor and the Corporate Media*. Ithaca, N.Y.: Cornell/ILR Press.

Massey, Douglas. 2007. *Categorically Unequal: The American Stratification System*. New York: Russell Sage Foundation.

Mast, Robert H., ed. 1994. *Detroit Lives*. Philadelphia: Temple University Press.

McCammon, Holly J. 1990. "Legal Limits on Labor Militancy: U.S. Labor Law and the Right to Strike Since the New Deal." *Social Problems* 37(2): 206–29.

———. 1993. "From Repressive Intervention to Integrative Prevention: The U.S. State's Legal Management of Labor Militancy, 1881–1978." *Social Forces* 71(3): 569–602.

McCartin, Joseph. 2006. "A Historian's Perspective on the PATCO Strike, Its Legacy, and Lessons." *Employee Responsibilities and Rights Journal* 18(3): 215–22.

McConnell, Sheena. 1989. "Strikes, Wages, and Private Information." *American Economic Review* 79(4): 801–15.

McCord, Richard. 1996. *The Chain Gang: One Newspaper Versus the Gannett Empire*. Columbia: University of Missouri Press.

McKercher, Catherine. 2002. *Newsworkers Unite: Labor, Convergence, and North American Newspapers*. Lanham, Md: Rowman & Littlefield.

Meier, August, and Elliott Rudwick. 1979. *Black Detroit and the Rise of the UAW*. Oxford: Oxford University Press.

Merritt, Davis. 2005. *Knightfall: Knight Ridder and How the Erosion of Newspaper Journalism Is Putting Democracy at Risk*. New York: AMACOM Books (American Management Association).

Meyer, Philip. 2004. *The Vanishing Newspaper: Saving Journalism in the Information Age*. Columbia: University of Missouri Press.

Meyers, Gerald C., and Susan Meyers. 2000. *Dealers, Healers, Brutes, and Saviors: Eight Winning Styles for Solving Giant Business Crises*. New York: John Wiley and Sons.

Michigan Journalism Hall of Fame. 2000. "Susan Watson." Available at: http://hof.jrn.msu.edu/bios/watson.html (accessed June 25, 2011).

Milkman, Ruth, ed. 2000. *Organizing Immigrants: The Challenge for Unions in Contemporary California*. Ithaca, N.Y.: Cornell/ILR Press.

———. 2006. *LA Story: Immigrant Workers and the Future of the U.S. Labor Movement*. New York: Russell Sage Foundation.

Milkman, Ruth, and Kim Voss. 2004. *Rebuilding Labor: Organizing and Organizers in the New Union Movement*. Ithaca, N.Y.: Cornell University Press.

Montgomery, David. 1987. *The Fall of the House of Labor: The Workplace, the State, and American Labor Activism, 1865–1925*. Cambridge: Cambridge University Press.

Montgomery, James D. 1991. "Social Networks and Labor Market Outcomes: Toward an Economic Analysis." *American Economic Review* 81(5): 1408–18.

Moorhead, Thomas. 2003. "U.S. Labor Law Serves Us Well." In *Workers' Rights as Human Rights*, edited by James Gross. Ithaca, N.Y.: Cornell/ILR Press.

Morton, John. 2006. "The Tragedy of Public Ownership." *American Journalism Review* 28(3): 68.

Needleman, Ruth. 2003. *Black Freedom Fighters in Steel: The Struggle for Democratic Unionism*. Ithaca, N.Y.: Cornell/ILR Press.

Neill, William. 2004. *Urban Planning and Cultural Identity*. New York: Routledge.

Ness, Immanuel. 2005. *Immigrants, Unions, and the New U.S. Labor Market*. Philadelphia: Temple University Press.

Ness, Immanuel, and Stuart Eimer. 2001. *Central Labor Councils and the Revival of American Unionism: Organizing for Justice in Our Communities*. Armonk, N.Y.: M. E. Sharpe.

Newman, Katherine. 1988. *Falling from Grace: Downward Mobility in the Age of Affluence*. New York: Free Press.

Nicholson, Philip Y. 2004. *Labor's Story in the United States*. Philadelphia: Temple University Press.

Orr, Marion, ed. 2007. *Transforming the City: Community Organizing and the Challenge of Political Change*. Lawrence: University Press of Kansas.

Orr, Marion, and Gerry Stoker. 1994. "Urban Regimes and Leadership in Detroit." *Urban Affairs Quarterly* 30(1): 48–73.

Orren, Karen, and Stephen Skowrenek. 1997. "Institutions and Intercurrence: Theory Building in the Fullness of Time." In *Nomos*, vol. 38, edited by Ian Shapiro and Russell Hardin. New York: New York University Press.

Osterman, Paul, Thomas Kochan, Richard Locke, and Michael Piore. 2001. *Working in America: A Blueprint for the New Labor Market*. Cambridge, Mass.: MIT Press.

Overholser, Geneva. 2001. "Editor, Inc." In *Leaving Readers Behind: The Age of Corporate Newspapering*, edited by Gene Roberts, Thomas Kunkel, and Charles Layton. Fayetteville: University of Arkansas Press.

Paige, Jeffery. 1999. "Conjuncture, Comparison, and Conditional Theory in Macrosocial Inquiry." *American Journal of Sociology* 105(3): 781–800.

Parks, Virginia, and Dorian Warren. 2009. "The Politics and Practice of Economic Justice: Community Benefits Agreements as Tactic of the New Accountable Development Movement." *Journal of Community Practice* 17(1–2): 88–106.

Perry, Charles, Andrew Kramer, and Thomas Schneider. 1982. *Operating During Strikes: Company Experience, NLRB Policies, and Governmental Regulations*. Labor Relations and Public Policy Series 23. Philadelphia: University of Pennsylvania, Wharton School, Industrial Research Unit.

Picard, Robert. 2002. "U.S. Newspaper Ad Revenue Shows Consistent Growth." *Newspaper Research Journal* 23(4): 21–33.

Picard, Robert, and Jeffrey Brody. 1997. *The Newspaper Publishing Industry*. Boston: Allyn and Bacon.

Picard, Robert, and Stephen Lacy. 1997. "Commentary: Lessons from the Detroit Newspaper Strike." *Newspaper Research Journal* 18(1–2): 19.

Pierson, Paul. 2000. "Not Just What, but When: Timing and Sequence in Political Processes." *Studies in American Political Development* 14(1): 72–92.

Pope, James Gray. 2002. "The Thirteenth Amendment Versus the Commerce Clause: Labor and the Shaping of American Constitutional Law, 1921–1957." *Columbia Law Review* 102(1): 1–123.

Pratt, Henry. 2004. *Churches and Urban Government in Detroit and New York, 1895–1994*. Detroit: Wayne State University Press.

Pring, Sarah. 2001. "Justice Delayed, Justice Denied: The Detroit Newspaper Strike and the Future of Section 10(j) Injunctions in the Sixth Circuit." *Wayne Law Review* 47: 277–305.

Putnam, Robert. 2000. *Bowling Alone: The Collapse and Revival of American Community*. New York: Simon & Schuster.

Ragin, Charles C. 1987. *The Comparative Method: Moving Beyond Qualitative and Quantitative Strategies*. Berkeley: University of California Press.

Reder, M. W., and G. R. Neumann. 1980. "Conflict and Contract: The Case of Strikes." *Journal of Political Economy* 88(5): 867–86.

Rieder, Rem. 2006. "The Knight Ridder Fade-out." *American Journalism Review* 28(2): 6.

Rhomberg, Chris. 2004. *No There There: Race, Class, and Political Community in Oakland*. Berkeley: University of California Press.

———. 2010. "A Signal Juncture: The Detroit Newspaper Strike and Post-Accord Labor Relations in the United States." *American Journal of Sociology* 115(6): 1853–94.

Roberts, Gene, and Thomas Kunkel, eds. 2002. *Breach of Faith: A Crisis of Coverage in the Age of Corporate Newspapering*. Fayetteville: University of Arkansas Press.

Roberts, Gene, Thomas Kunkel, and Charles Layton, eds. 2001. *Leaving Readers Behind: The Age of Corporate Newspapering*. Fayetteville: University of Arkansas Press.

Robertson, Lori, and Carol Guensburg. 2000. "Bylines: All Good Things. . . ." *American Journalism Review* 22(1): 82.

Roscigno, Vincent J., and William F. Danaher. 2004. *The Voice of Southern Labor: Radio, Music, and Textile Strikes, 1929–1934*. Minneapolis: University of Minnesota Press.

Rosenblum, Jonathan. 1995. *Copper Crucible: How the Arizona Miners' Strike of 1983 Recast Labor-Management Relations in America*. Ithaca, N.Y.: Cornell University Press. (Originally published in 1988.)

Ross, Robert J. S. 2004. *Slaves to Fashion: Poverty and Abuse in the New Sweatshops*. Ann Arbor: University of Michigan Press.

Rothstein, Richard. 1997. "Union Strength in the United States: Lessons from the UPS Strike." *International Labor Review* 136(4): 469–91.

Rubin, Beth A. 1986. "Class Struggle American Style: Unions, Styles, and Wages." *American Sociological Review* 51: 618–33.

Ryan, Mary. 1997. *Civic Wars*. Berkeley: University of California Press.

Schnell, John F., and Cynthia L. Gramm. 1994. "The Empirical Relations Between Employers' Striker Replacement Strategies and Strike Duration." *Industrial and Labor Relations Review* 47(2): 189–206.

Schudson, Michael. 1995. *The Power of News*. Cambridge, Mass.: Harvard University Press.

———. 2003. *The Sociology of News*. New York: Norton.

Seawright, Jason, and John Gerring. 2006. "Case Selection Techniques in Case Study Research: A Menu of Qualitative and Quantitative Options." *Political Research Quarterly* 61(2): 294–308.

Seidman, Gay. 2007. *Beyond the Boycott: Labor Rights, Human Rights, and Transnational Activism*. New York: Russell Sage Foundation.

Serrin, William. 1973. *The Company and the Union: The "Civilized Relationship" of the General Motors Corporation and the United Automobile Workers*. New York: Knopf.

Sewell, William, Jr. 1996. "Three Temporalities: Toward an Eventful Sociology." In *The Historic Turn in the Human Sciences*, edited by Terrance McDonald. Ann Arbor: University of Michigan Press.

Shaw, Donald, and Charles McKenzie, eds. 2003. *American Daily Newspaper Evolution: Past, Present . . . and Future?* Westport, Conn.: Praeger.

Shorter, Edward, and Charles Tilly. 1974. *Strikes in France, 1830–1968*. London: Cambridge University Press.

Simmons, Louise. 1994. *Organizing in Hard Times: Labor and Neighborhoods in Hartford*. Philadelphia: Temple University Press.

Simurda, Stephen J. 1993. "Sticking with the Union?" *Columbia Journalism Review* 31(6): 25–30.

Sleigh, Stephen. 1998. *On Deadline: Labor Relations in Newspaper Publishing*. Bayside, N.Y.: Social Change Press.

Smith, Suzanne. 1999. *Dancing in the Street: Motown and the Cultural Politics of Detroit*. Cambridge, Mass.: Harvard University Press.

Snyder, David. 1975. "Institutional Setting and Industrial Conflict: Comparative Analyses of France, Italy, and the United States." *American Sociological Review* 40(3): 259–78.

Solomon, William. 1995. "The Site of Newsroom Labor: The Division of Editorial Practices." In *Newsworkers: Toward a History of the Rank and File*, edited by Hanno Hardt and Bonnie Brennan. Minneapolis: University of Minneapolis Press.

Soskice, David. 1999. "Divergent Production Regimes: Coordinated and Uncoordinated Market Economies in the 1980s and 1990s." In *Continuity and Change in Contemporary Capitalism*, edited by Herbert Kitschelt, Peter Lange, Gary Marks, and John Stephens. Cambridge: Cambridge University Press.

Stanger, Howard. 2002. "Newspapers: Collective Bargaining Decline Amidst Technological Change." In *Collective Bargaining in the Private Sector*, edited by Paul Clark, John Delaney, and Ann Frost. Champaign: Industrial Relations Research Association, University of Illinois.

Starr, Paul. 2004. *The Creation of the Media: Political Origins of Modern Communications*. New York: Basic Books.

Stone, Katherine. 2005. "The *Steelworkers' Trilogy*: The Evolution of Labor Arbitration." In *Labor Law Stories*, edited by Laura Cooper and Catherine Fisk. New York: Foundation Press.

Streeck, Wolfgang, and Kathleen Thelen. 2005. "Introduction: Institutional Change in Advanced Political Economies." In *Beyond Continuity: Institutional Change in Advanced Political Economies*, edited by Wolfgang Streeck and Kathleen Thelen. Oxford: Oxford University Press.

Sugrue, Thomas J. 1996. *The Origins of the Urban Crisis: Race and Inequality in Postwar Detroit*. Princeton, N.J.: Princeton University Press.

Summers, Clyde. 2000. "Employment at Will in the United States: The Divine Right of Employers." *University of Pennsylvania Journal of Labor and Employment Law* 3(1): 65–86.

Taylor, John. 2008. "The Detroit Newspaper Strike: A Template for Employers on Preparing for and Operating During a Labor Strike." *Labor Law Journal* 59(2): 166–89.

Thomas, June Manning. 1989. "Detroit: The Centrifugal City." In *Unequal Partnerships: The Political Economy of Urban Redevelopment in Postwar America*, edited by Gregory Squires. New Brunswick, N.J.: Rutgers University Press.

Thompson, Heather Ann. 2001. *Whose Detroit? Politics, Labor, and Race in a Modern American City*. Ithaca, N.Y.: Cornell University Press.

Troy, Leo. 2004. *The Twilight of the Old Unionism*. Armonk, N.Y.: M. E. Sharpe.

Tsebelis, George, and Peter Lange. 1995. "Strikes Around the World: A Game Theoretic Approach." In *The Workers of Nations: Industrial Relations in a Global Economy*, edited by Sanford Jacoby. Oxford: Oxford University Press.

Turner, Lowell, and Daniel Cornfield, eds. 2007. *Labor in the New Urban Battlegrounds: Local Solidarity in a Global Economy*. Ithaca, N.Y.: Cornell/ILR Press.

Turner, Lowell, Harry Katz, and Richard Hurd, eds. 2001. *Rekindling the Movement: Labor's Quest for Relevance in the Twenty-First Century*. Ithaca, N.Y.: Cornell/ILR Press.

Turrini, Joseph. 1999. "Phooie on Louie: African American Detroit and the Election of Jerry Cavanagh." *Michigan History* (November-December): 11–17.

U.S. Kerner Commission. 1968. *Report of the National Advisory Commission on Civil Disorders*. New York: Bantam Books.

Vigilante, Richard. 1994. *Strike: The Daily News War and the Future of American Labor*. New York: Simon & Schuster.

Voss, Kim. 1994. *The Making of American Exceptionalism: The Knights of Labor and Class Formation in the Nineteenth Century*. Ithaca, N.Y.: Cornell University Press.

Voss, Kim, and Rachel Sherman. 2000. "Breaking the Iron Law of Oligarchy: Union Revitalization in the American Labor Movement." *American Journal of Sociology* 106(2): 303–49.

Wacker, Fred R. 2006. "Michigan Gambling: The Interactions of Native American, Detroit, and Canadian Casinos." *American Behavioral Scientist* 50(3): 373–81.

Wallace, Michael, Beth A. Rubin, and Brian T. Smith. 1988. "American Labor Law: Its Impact on Working-Class Militancy, 1901–1980." *Social Science History* 12(1): 1–29.

Wallerstein, Michael, and Bruce Western. 2000. "Unions in Decline? What Has Changed and Why." *Annual Review of Political Science* 3: 355–77.

Walton, Mary. 2001. "The Selling of Small-Town America." In *Leaving Readers Behind: The Age of Corporate Newspapering*, edited by Gene Roberts, Thomas Kunkel, and Charles Layton. Fayetteville: University of Arkansas Press.

Warner, W. Lloyd, and Josiah Orne Low. 1947. *The Social System of the Modern Factory: The Strike: A Social Analysis.* New Haven, Conn.: Yale University Press.

Warren, Mark. 2001. *Democracy and Association.* Princeton, N.J.: Princeton University Press.

Wenner, Kathryn. 2001. "Whither the Guild?" *American Journalism Review* 23: 46–49.

Western, Bruce. 1997. *Between Class and Market: Postwar Unionization in the Capitalist Democracies.* Princeton, N.J.: Princeton University Press.

Western, Bruce, and Jake Rosenfeld. 2011. "Unions, Norms, and the Rise in U.S. Wage Inequality." *American Sociological Review* 76(4): 513–37.

Widick, B. J. 1989. *Detroit: City of Race and Class Violence.* Detroit: Wayne State University Press.

Young, Coleman, and Lonnie Wheeler. 1994. *Hard Stuff: The Autobiography of Coleman Young.* New York: Viking.

Zieger, Robert. 1994. *American Workers, American Unions*, 2d ed. Baltimore: Johns Hopkins University Press.

Zunz, Olivier. 1982. *The Changing Face of Inequality: Urbanization, Industrial Development, and Immigrants in Detroit, 1880–1920.* Chicago: University of Chicago Press.

GOVERNMENT DOCUMENTS

U.S. Supreme Court

Labor Board v. Insurance Agents' International Union, 361 U.S. 477 (1960). Available at: http://supreme.justia.com/us/361/477/case.html (accessed May 11, 2010).

U.S. Court of Appeals

Newspaper Printing Corp. v. NLRB, 692 F.2nd 615 (6th Cir. 1982).

McClatchy Newspapers, Inc., v. NLRB, 131 F.3rd 1026 (D.C. Cir. 1997).

Schaub v. Detroit Newspaper Agency, 154 F.3rd 276 (6th Cir. 1998).
  Metropolitan Council of Newspaper Unions. 1997. Brief on behalf of the unions.
  National Labor Relations Board. 1997. Brief for the petitioner-appellant 10.

Detroit Typographical Union 18 v. NLRB, 216 F.3rd 109, 122 (D.C. Cir. 2000).
Detroit Newspaper Agency et al. v. NLRB, 286 F.3rd 391 (6th Cir. 2006).

U.S. District Court

Mahaffey et al. v. Detroit Newspaper Agency, 95-CV-75724 (E.D. Mich. 1997).
Schaub v. Detroit Newspaper Agency, 984 F. Supp. 1048 (E.D. Mich. 1997), *aff'd*, 154 F.3rd 276 (6th Cir. 1998).
  General Counsel, National Labor Relations Board, brief in support of petition for injunction under section 10(j) of the National Labor Relations Act, as amended, *Schaub v. Detroit Newspaper Agency*, CV-97-1920 (6th Cir. 1998).
  Metropolitan Council of Newspaper Unions, brief on behalf of the unions, *Schaub v. Detroit Newspaper Agency*, CV-97-1920 (6th Cir. 1998).

Teamsters Local 372 et al. v. Detroit Newspapers et al., 95-CV-40474 (E.D. Mich. 1999).
  DEPOSITIONS
  Derocha, Thomas. Sterling Heights, Mich., March 1, 1999.
  Mowinski, Frank. Sterling Heights, Mich., March 3, 1999.
  Owens, James. Sterling Heights, Mich., March 4, 1999.
  Walworth, David. Sterling Heights, Mich., July 1, 1999.

Benjamin L. Solomon v. The City of Sterling Heights et al., 98-CV-73900 (E.D. Mich. 2000).
  Trial transcript, vols. 2–5, 8.
  DEPOSITIONS
  Anderson, Gary. Detroit, October 20, 1999.
  Mowinski, Frank. Detroit, August 3, 1999.
  PLAINTIFF EXHIBITS (BY NUMBER)
    1: Memorandum from James Owens to Schmidt et al., "Staff Meeting Regarding Possible Detroit Newspaper Strike," March 20, 1995.
    2: Memorandum from Frank Mowinski to James Owens, "Impending Strike at the Detroit News Plant," May 1, 1995.
    3: Memorandum from James Owens to all operations division personnel, "Action Plan for Impending Possible Strike at the Detroit News Plant: 16 Mile and Mound," May 8, 1995, including memorandum from Frank Mowinski to James Owens, "Contingency Plan for Impending DNA Strike," May 6, 1995.
    4: Confidential memo from Thomas Derocha to city manager concerning

draft "Action Plan for Impending Possible Strike at the Detroit News Plant: 16 Mile and Mound."

8: Letter from John Anthony to James Owens, August 24, 1995.

10: Letter from Carl Marlinga to Thomas Derocha, September 8, 1995.

13–26: Letters and payments between DNA and SHPD.

43: Memorandum from Frank Mowinski to Chief Thomas Derocha, Sterling Heights Police Department, "Violations of Agreements Between DNA and SHPD," July 17, 1995.

64: "Strike Activity: Applicable Ordinances and Statues," n.d.

65: "Index to Selected Michigan Statutes of Possible Application in Strike and Picketing Situations," n.d.

72A-E: Memorandum from Frank Mowinski to N. Nowak, "Equipment for the Impending Strike," May 11, 1995.

OTHER SUBPOENAED DOCUMENTS

Memorandum from Frank Mowinski to all operations division personnel, June 27, 1995.

David P. Zieminski v. The City of Sterling Heights et al., 96-CV-75820 (E.D. Mich. 2000).

DEPOSITIONS

Anthony, John. Detroit, January 21, 2000.

———. Detroit, November 3, 2000.

Derocha, Thomas. Sterling Heights, Mich., June 27, 1997.

Jaske, John. Detroit, December 4, 2000.

Kelleher, Tim. Detroit, January 29, 2001.

Lenhoff, Alan. Detroit, November 1, 2000.

Mowinski, Frank. Detroit, June 26, 1997.

Vega, Frank. Detroit, October 27, 2000.

OTHER SUBPOENAED DOCUMENTS

Memorandum from Frank Mowinski to all operations division personnel, May 30, 1995.

Memorandum from Frank Mowinski to all operations division personnel, June 23, 1995.

Memorandum from James Owens to operations division command officers, June 27, 1995.

Memorandum from Frank Mowinski to Thomas Derocha, "Intelligence Obtained Regarding the DNA Strike," August 28, 1995.

National Labor Relations Board

A. S. Abell Company and Baltimore Typographical Union, 230 NLRB 5 (1977).

The Baltimore News American and Baltimore Typographical Union, 230 NLRB 29 (1977).

Cincinnati Enquirer et al., 298 NLRB 41 (1990).

Antelope Valley Press, 311 NLRB 459 (1993).

Detroit Newspaper Agency, 326 NLRB 64 (1998).

　　Hearing transcript.

　　GENERAL COUNSEL EXHIBITS (BY NUMBER)

　　　　5: Letter from Alfred Derey to Frank Vega, March 19, 1992.

　　　　8c: Letter from Alfred Derey to Frank Vega, May 9, 1995.

　　　　9: Agreement between Detroit Newspaper Agency and Detroit Graphic Communications Union No. 13N, May 1, 1992.

　　　　13: "Meeting Schedules," n.d.

　　　　18: Letter from John Jaske to Jack Howe, March 4, 1996.

　　　　19: Letter from Jack Howe to John Jaske, March 13, 1996.

　　　　22: "Detroit News Proposal to Guild #22," February 20, 1995.

　　　　45: Memorandum from Robert Giles to staff, June 28, 1995.

　　　　60–62: "Merit Pay Letters," n.d.

　　　　100: "DTU #18/Detroit Newspapers Bargaining Meetings."

　　　　101: Letter from Tim Kelleher to Sam Attard, February 20, 1995.

　　　　113: Joint strike resolution, n.d.

　　　　124: "Local 2040 Mailers Meetings, March 10, 1995, to July 13, 1995."

　　　　157: Memorandum from Larry Ross to John Taylor, "Things We Will Want in the Near Future," January 8, 1995.

　　　　158: Detroit Newspaper Agency, 1996 replacement employee data, June 20, 1996.

　　　　167: Letter from John Jaske to William Boarman, October 15, 1987.

　　CHARGING PARTY EXHIBITS (BY NUMBER)

　　　　5: Memorandum from John Jaske to Doug McCorkindale, "Detroit," March 6, 1995.

　　RESPONDENT EXHIBITS (BY NUMBER)

　　　　3: Minutes of "Non-Economic Scale Negotiations Meeting," March 19, 1992.

　　　　49: "Compilation News Clips," n.d.

　　OTHER SUBPOENAED DOCUMENTS

　　　Detroit Newspaper Agency. "Mailer Negotiations, March 29, 1995, Conference Room A, 6:55 PM."

　　　———. Mailers/DNA negotiating meeting (typewritten notes). August 18, 1995.

　　　Jaske, John. Memorandum to Doug McCorkindale, "January-February Monthly Report," February 15, 1995.

　　　———. Memorandum to Frank Vega et al., "Mailer Negotiations," May 1, 1995.

　　　———. Letter to Al Young, "1994 Mailroom Wages," May 4, 1995.

　　　———. Memorandum to Jack Howe, "Negotiations," July 26, 1995.

　　　———. Memorandum to Al Young, "Negotiations," July 26, 1995.

———. Memorandum to Frank Kortsch, "Teamster Negotiations," July 26, 1995.

———. Memorandum to John Curley, Douglas McCorkindale, and Gary Watson, December 21, 1995.

———. Memorandum to Douglas McCorkindale, December 27, 1995.

———. Letter to Jack Howe, August 30, 2000.

McLeod, Tommie. Memorandum to Robert Althaus, "SAP Priorities," February 8, 1995.

"Negotiations Update," March 10, 1995.

Taylor, John. Letter to Al Derey, June 15, 1995, with attachment: "Transportation—Job Description: Jumper."*Detroit Newspaper Agency*, 327 NLRB 164 (1999).

Detroit Newspaper Agency, 326 NLRB 65 (1998).

Detroit Newspaper Agency, 327 NLRB 164 (1999).

Detroit Newspaper Agency, 330 NLRB 81 (2000).

Detroit Newspaper Agency, 342 NLRB 24 (2004).

Detroit Newspaper Agency, 342 NLRB 125 (2004).

American Arbitration Association

DTU 18/CWA 14503 v. Detroit Newspaper Agency, 54-30-00498-93 (November 8, 1994; award May 22, 1995).

Other Federal Documents

National Labor Relations Board (NLRB). U.S. National Labor Relations Act. 29 U.S.C. §§ 151–69. Available at: http://www.nlrb.gov/national-labor-relations -act. (accessed May 22, 2010).

———. 1995. Case 7-CC-1647(1), "Charge Against Labor Organization or Its Agents." October 4, 1995.

———. 1997. *Basic Guide to the National Labor Relations Act*. Washington: U.S. Government Printing Office.

U.S. Bureau of the Census. 1983. "1980 Census of Population and Housing: Census Tracts, Detroit, Michigan." Available at: http://www2.census.gov/prod2/ decennial/documents/1980/tracts-cities/CensusTracts1980-DetroitMIs1of2 .pdf (accessed June 30, 2011).

———. 1995. "Michigan: Population of Counties by Decennial Census: 1900 to 1990." Washington: U.S. Bureau of the Census (March 27). Available at: http:// www.census.gov/population/cencounts/mi190090.txt (accessed April 14, 2010).

U.S. Bureau of Labor Statistics. 2011. "Major Work Stoppages in 2010" (news release). Table 1. February 8. Available at: http://www.bls.gov/news.release/ pdf/wkstp.pdf (accessed September 27, 2011).

U.S. Securities and Exchange Commission. 2010. Gannett Co., Inc., Form 10-K 2010 Annual Report. Commission file 1-6961. Available at: http://www.sec.gov/ Archives/edgar/data/39899/000095012311017139/c11288e10vk.htm (accessed June 15, 2011).

State Government Documents

Huffmaster Mgmt., Inc., et al. v. The Detroit Newspapers et al., 96-1946CK, Michigan Circuit Court, Macomb County, March 15, 1996.

Louis Abate et al. v. Detroit Newspapers et al., MUL96 51200, Department of Consumer and Industry Services, Michigan Unemployment Agency, Office of Appeals, October 27, 1997.

Payne v. Western and Atlantic Railroad, Supreme Court of Tennessee, 81 Tenn. 507 (1884).

UNPUBLISHED SOURCES (DOCUMENTS IN THE POSSESSION OF THE AUTHOR UNLESS OTHERWISE SPECIFIED)

Althaus, Robert. 1995. Letter, "Dear Pastor or Rector." August 2.

Burns, Ben. 1999. "News Media in Metro Detroit." Detroit: Wayne State University, Detroit Orientation Institute.

Claussen, Dan. 1999. "The Myths and Realities of Newspaper Acquisition Costs: Fiduciary Responsibilities, Fungibility of Assets, Winners' Penalties, and Excess Cash 'Problems.'" Paper presented to the Association for Education in Journalism and Media Communications convention. New Orleans, La. (August).

Detroit Newspaper Agency. 1995. "Detroit Strike Operations Report." September 9–11.

Gannett Co., Inc. 2006. Press release, "Van Lare to Head Gannett Labor Relations." January 12. Available at: http://www.gannett.com/apps/pbcs.dll/article ?AID=/99999999/PRESSRELEASES06/100426070/ (accessed June 26, 2011).

Giles, Robert. 1995. Letter to Rev. Joseph Summers. August 23.

Howe, Jack. 2000. Letter to John Jaske. September 1.

International Brotherhood of Teamsters. 1995. Memorandum from Ron Carey, "Dear Brothers and Sisters." September 14.

———. 1995. Press release, "PA Teamsters Deliver 40 Tons of Food for Newspaper Strikers." September 28, Washington, D.C..

———. Local 372. 1992. Agreement between Detroit Newspaper Agency and Newspaper Drivers and Handlers' Local Union 372. May 1, Detroit.

————. Local 2040. 1992. Agreement between Detroit Newspaper Agency and International Brotherhood of Teamsters, Local 2040. May 1, Detroit.

Jaske, John. 1995. Letter to Jack Howe, "Negotiations." July 26.

————. 1995. Letter to Al Young, "Negotiations." July 26.

————. 1995. Letter to Frank Kortsch, "Teamster Negotiations." July 26.

————. 2000. Letter to Jack Howe. August 30.

Jaske, John, and Tim Kelleher. 1995. Letter to Alfred P. Derey, Chair, Metropolitan Council of Newspaper Unions. October 27.

Krzaklewski, Marian. 1995. Letter to the editor, *Detroit News*. August 30.

Lippert, John. N.d. "The Detroit Newspaper Strike."

McKnight, Samuel. 1996. Letter to law enforcement agencies, "Dear Chief." January 4.

————. 1996. Letter to Mark Rubin, Esq. March 19.

Metropolitan Council of Newspaper Unions. 1995. Press release, "Unions Present Principles for Settlement." October 5.

Radtke, David. 1996. Letter to Chief Lawrence Carey. June 11.

————. 1996. Letter to Susan Lancaster, Esq. June 24.

————. 1996. Letter to Charles R. Towner, Esq. September 18.

Readers United. 1995. Leaflet, "Readers Before Profits." N.d.

————. 1996. Letter to newspaper strikers and supporters. February 27.

————. 1996. Press release, "44 Women Arrested During Protest at Detroit News." March 14.

————. 1996. Press release. March 26.

————. 1996. "Statement of Readers United Following a Meeting with Mr. Mark Rubin, Attorney for the NLRB."

Religious Leaders for Justice at the Detroit Newspapers. 1996. "An Appeal by Metro Detroit Area Religious Leaders." N.d.

————. 1996. Press release. April 19.

Rosenfeld, Jake. 2006. "Strike Predictors in the Modern United States." Paper presented to the annual meeting of the American Sociological Association. Montreal (August 14).

————. 2008. Personal communication with the author.

Rybicki, Michael. 1988. Letter to Tim Kelleher. April 11.

Strait, Kristen. 1998. Email message to Heath Meriwether, "Strike/Recall Numbers," with attachments.

Wylie-Kellerman, Jeanie. 1995. Letter to Linda Foley. October 20.

INTERVIEWS WITH THE AUTHOR

Anderson, Gary. 2005. San Francisco, June 16.

Anstett, Patricia. 2005. Detroit, April 27.

Anthony, John. 2005. Canton, Mich., April 28.

Archer, Dennis. 2005. Detroit, April 18.
Ashenfelter, David. 2005. Detroit, May 9.
Bachelder, Amy. 2005. Huntington Woods, Mich., March 17.
Bechard, Larry A. 2005. Rochester Hills, Mich., May 14.
Bernick, Thomas. 2005. Detroit, March 17.
Betzold, Michael. 2005. Ann Arbor, Mich., March 18.
Bonior, David. 2005. Detroit, April 7.
Brabenec, Bill. 2005. Attica, Mich., April 21.
Bray, Hiawatha. 2005. February 16 (telephone).
Breyer, Thomas. 2005. Grosse Pointe Farms, Mich., April 13.
Burns, Ben. 2004. Detroit, October 20.
Burr, Richard. 2005. Detroit, March 21.
Burzynski, Sue. 2005. Detroit, May 10.
Carey, Ron. 2007. New York, N.Y., June 20.
Case, James. 2005. Romeo Plank, Mich., May 16.
Cook, Rebecca. 2004. Detroit, October 21.
Cooper-Cunningham, Alesia. 2006. Detroit, July 18.
Crumm, David. 2005. July 5 (telephone).
DeChane, Frances A. 2005. Detroit, April 19.
Decker, Robert. 2004. Detroit, October 25.
Derey, Alfred. 2005. Lapeer, Mich., May 12.
DeSmet, Kate. 2005. Detroit, April 1.
Dunn, Nancy. 2005. Dearborn, Mich., May 11.
Ellis, Shawn D. 2005. Detroit, March 10.
Elsila, David. 2005. New York, N.Y., January 8.
Everett, Emily. 2005. Detroit, April 26.
Fahoome, Michael. 2006. St. Claire Shores, Mich., July 18.
Faniel-Heard, Jocelyn. 2006. Detroit, July 19.
Finley, Nolan. 2004. Detroit, October 26.
Foley, Linda. 2006. April 5 (telephone).
Forsyth, Alan. 2005. Detroit, April 6.
Freedman, Eric. 2005. East Lansing, Mich., May 15.
French, Ron. 2005. Detroit, May 25.
Gallagher, John. 2006. Detroit, July 28.
Gould, William B., IV. 2004. Palo Alto, Calif., December 30.
Graff, Gary. 2005. Beverly Hills, Mich., May 16.
Gumbleton, Thomas J. 2005. Detroit, May 13.
Hammel, Linda Rabin. 2006. Detroit, July 17.
Hanson, William. 2005. Detroit, March 24.
Hartley, A. J. 2005. Detroit, May 4.
Hecker, David. 2004. Detroit, October 25.
Heron, W. Kim. 2004. Detroit, October 28.

Howe, Jack. 2005. Detroit, April 12.

Hurwitz, Julie H. 2005. Detroit, June 2.

Hutton, Carole Leigh. 2005. Detroit, April 11.

Ice, Duane. 2005. Royal Oak, Mich., April 30.

Ingalls, Barbara. 2004. Royal Oak, Mich., October 24.

Jaske, John. 2005. McLean, Va., November 4.

Jenkins, Leo. 2005. Detroit, July 23.

Josar, David. 2006. Detroit, July 19.

Karpinen, Randy. 2005. Clinton, Mich., March 30.

Kelleher, Tim. 2004. Royal Oak, Mich., November 3.

King, Bob. 2005. Detroit, April 15.

Kiska, Tim. 2005. Detroit, May 4.

Kulka, Paul. 2005. Detroit, May 2.

Lengel, Allan. 2006. Washington, D.C., March 17.

Lenhoff, Alan. 2004. Detroit, November 4.

———. 2005. Detroit, March 23.

Maci, Sam. 2005. Detroit, May 17.

Mahaffey, Maryann. 2005. Detroit, April 11.

Martin, Michele. 2005. Detroit, May 23.

McBride, Michael. 2005. Detroit, March 28.

McGrath, Tom. 2006. October 4 (telephone).

McGraw, Bill. 2005. Detroit, March 16.

McKnight, Samuel. 2005. Southfield, Mich., June 4.

McNatt, Robert. 2005. New York, N.Y., March 1.

Mishra, Raja. 2005. March 1 (telephone).

Mleczko, Lou. 2005. Detroit, April 18.

Montemurri, Patricia. 2005. Detroit, June 3.

Murawski, Renee. 2008. New York, N.Y., December 12.

Musial, Ann. 2005. Grosse Point Woods, Mich., April 1.

Musial, Robert. 2005. Grosse Pointe Woods, Mich., April 1.

Nazelli, Dennis. 2005. Detroit, March 31.

Nevers, Armand. 2005. Detroit, April 29.

Norton, James. 2006. September 26 (telephone).

Ourlian, Robert. 2006. Washington, D.C., March 17.

Pattison, Mark. 2005. January 4 (telephone).

Pearce, Dia. 2005. July 12 (telephone).

Perry, J. J. 2006. Detroit, July 20.

Rabin Hammel, Linda. 2006. Detroit, July 17.

Ridder, Tony. 2005. San Jose, Calif., June 14.

Robinson, David. 2005. Detroit, April 27.

Rowe, Edwin A. 2005. Detroit, May 26.

Schram, Tom. 2004. Detroit, October 25.

Schroeder, Mary. 2005. Detroit, May 22.
Shine, Neil. 2005. St. Clair Shores, Mich., April 28.
Smith, Robert. 2005. Detroit, May 2.
Solomon, Ben. 2005. Armada, Mich., May 3.
St. Louis, James. 2005. Detroit, May 6.
Sweeney, John. 2006. Washington, D.C., March 15.
Swickard, Joe. 2005. Detroit, May 10.
Taylor, John A. 2005. Farmington Hills, Mich., May 17.
Uehlein, Joe. 2006. Washington, D.C., March 16.
Van Moorlehem, Tracy. July 7 (telephone).
Vega, Frank. 2004. Detroit, October 27.
————. 2005. San Francisco. June 15.
Wallace, Walter T. 2005. Detroit, May 2.
Walsh, Tom. 2004. Detroit, October 22.
Watson, Joann. 2006. Detroit, July 28.
Webb, Crawford. 2006. Detroit, July 25.
Whitall, Susan L. 2005. Detroit, May 10.
Wolach, Oscar. 2004. Ferndale, Mich., October 20.
Wylie-Kellerman, Bill. 2005. Detroit, May 11.
Young, Alex. 2005. Detroit, April 27.
Zielinski, Mike. 2006. Washington, D.C., March 16.
Znamer, Ann Marie. 2005. August 8 (telephone).

INDEX |

contract negotiations (1995) (*cont.*)
joint bargaining, 133–34, 138–39;
management-labor relationship
changes, 261–62; Newspaper Guild,
136–38; printers, 134–35; strike preparations during, 108–14, 116, 139–41
Conyers, John, 171, 202–3, 225
Cooper-Cunningham, Alesia, 54, 200,
280–81
Copper Crucible (Rosenblum), 7
copy editors, 58, 60
corporate restructuring, 16, 87, 88, 108
cost-cutting strategies, 33, 38–39
Coughlin, Charles, 45
Court of Appeals ruling, 6, 227, 237–44,
251–54
Cox, John, 232
Cramton, Peter, 177
crime, 49, 51
critical juncture, 15
Crockett, George, 47
Curley, John, 195–96, 200, 222
Curtin, George, 132
CWA (Communication Workers of
America), 135, 225–26

Dale, Charles, 91
Daniels, Mitch, 267
Dannin, Ellen, 75, 274, 277
data sources, 21
DC Circuit Court of Appeals, 6, 227,
237–44, 251–54
Dearborn, 41, 46, 191, 201, 245
Dearborn Heights, 166, 246
DeBartolo decision, 276
Debow, Craig, 279
decertification, union, 80–81
de-democratization of institutional
regulation of labor disputes, 17
deinstitutionalization, 12
Democratic Party, 44, 50, 265

demonstrations and protests: Action!
Motown '97, **127,** 228, 231–35, 244;
DNA's efforts to control, 185–87;
Labor Day weekend, 1–4, 169–76,
224–25; legal battle over, 214–22;
newspaper coverage of, 208–9; by
Readers United, 204; in suburban
neighborhoods, 202; union mobilization, 200–201; violence, 2–4, **122–23,**
170–74, 177, 190–93, 208–9
Derey, Alfred, **120;** 1992 contract negotiations, 99–101; 1995 contract negotiations, 133–34, 135, 138–39, 142–43;
IBT meeting, 225; Labor Day weekend protests (1996), 225; MCNU
leadership, 93; on printer buyout offer, 250; remembrance of dead strikers, 244; on return to work offer, 226;
RU's meeting with, 204
Derocha, Thomas: deposition in striker
civil rights suits, 281; on DNA's financial payments to SHPD, 184; letter from Marlinga explaining unlawful assembly charges, 186; Mound
Road demonstrations, 173; North
Plant access, 173, 183; picketing at
home of, 215; police escorts in and
out of North Plant, 169–70; strike
preparation, 107, 114–16, 117, 118
Desantis, Cathy, **125**
DeSmet, Kate, **126,** 174, 225, 232, 245
Des Moines Register, 35
Detroit: civic ecology legacy, 40–41, 52–
55, 263–64; demographics, 40, 41–42,
51; industry expansion (1900-1945),
41–45; introduction, 18; news culture, 54–55; postwar era (1945-1980),
45–52; racial issues, 45–49; unionization, 43–45, 86, 264
Detroit Chamber of Commerce, 264
Detroit Free Press: audience and edito-